JACOB NEEDLEMAN
THE SWORD
OF GNOSIS

Jacob Needleman is Professor of Philosophy at San Francisco
State University and former director of the Center for the Study of
New Religions at the Graduate Theological Union, Berkeley.
Educated in philosophy at Harvard, Yale and the University of
Freiburg, he had served as research associate at the Rockefeller
Institute for Medical Research and was a research fellow at Union
Theological Seminary. He is the author of *The New Religions*, *A Sense
of the Cosmos*, *Lost Christianity*, *The Heart of Philosophy* and, most
recently, *The Way of the Physician*, and was general editor of the
fifteen-volume Penguin Metaphysical Library. In addition to his
teaching and writing he serves as a consultant in the fields of
psychology, education, medicine, philanthropy and business.

THE SWORD
OF GNOSIS

METAPHYSICS, COSMOLOGY, TRADITION, SYMBOLISM

EDITED BY
JACOB NEEDLEMAN

ARKANA

London, Boston and Henley

First published in 1974
by Penguin Books Inc.
ARKANA edition 1986
ARKANA PAPERBACKS is an imprint of
Routledge & Kegan Paul plc

14 Leicester Square, London WC2H 7PH, England

9 Park Street, Boston, Mass. 02108, USA and

Broadway House, Newtown Road,
Henley on Thames, Oxon RG9 1EN, England

Printed and bound in Great Britain
by The Guernsey Press Co. Ltd,
Guernsey, Channel Islands

Library of Congress Cataloging in Publication Data

Main entry under titles
The Sword of Gnosis
1. Religion—addresses, essays, lectures.
I. Needleman, Jacob.
BL50.S87   1985   200   85–28278
British Library CIP data also available
ISBN 1-85063-048-8

Contents

Preface to the Second Edition

Only eleven years have passed since the first publication of this volume and it is perhaps too soon to assess the impact of these exceptional thinkers upon our threatened world. But the course of events of the past decade warrants our asking again the central question that formed the basis of the introductory essay: *What, precisely, is needed in order to awaken contemporary man?* Or, in other terms, what is needed in our time for gnosis to be effective, for there to exist a salvational knowledge that actually brings about spiritual change in the midst of the material world as we actually find it?

There are two aspects to the idea—or, rather, to the fact of *gnosis*. The first is the effective realization of the fundamental truths about the cosmic and meta-cosmic order, those truths which have so happily been named *principial*. The other aspect is not so readily named. I refer here to the knowledge not of the supernal order, but of the infernal order—not in the sense of an unrestrained and arbitrary amassing of sensory data, together with an attachment to explanatory constructs, all of which contribute to the failings of modern science. I am referring rather to a true and exact understanding of the whole condition of fallen man, without which even the highest knowledge of universal truths must fail in its principial task of leading man out of his darkness and suffering.

Such knowledge is intrinsic to the very idea of spiritual method—the practical means of transmitting the way. But method itself is based on the Great Knowledge which has a twofold object: the supernal order of liberation and the infernal order of bondage; the principial truths and the precise modalities and significant details by which man in this or that culture or era has fallen away from an awareness of these truths.

A true physician must not only know the laws of the healthy body and the principles of pathology; he must also be able to diagnose and treat the illness of the individual who happens to stand before him and moreover, to speak to him in such a way that he accepts the treatment offered. And then, the treatment must actually work!

There is little question that now the patient, modern man, knows he is sick. I say this in the most serious sense possible. There is not much more to be gained by criticism alone, even at the level of a Guénon or Schuon. Modern man knows he is at the end of his tether. He may not know the reasons why he has come to this pass and he may have only the palest idea of what he has lost. He may think, wrongly, that it is only his physical existence that is threatened or he may identify the destruction of the human spirit with elements in his society that are merely distant effects of man's fundamental metaphysical failure. Granted all this, he still knows he is facing the end of the road. But the saving power for man will inevitably have to be as real as the factors that have led him to the brink of destruction. That is to say, they have to work in the material world—the same world in which the discoveries and inventions of science work. A gnosis that does not have an action in the material world may be many things, but it is not a gnosis defined as a salvational or effective knowledge.

This notion of a salvational knowledge that actually works in the material world is reflected in many traditional symbols, from the "scandal" of the Christian Incarnation to the numerous expressions of the alchemical and tantric spiritual mode. Yet, after all is said about the pervasiveness of the symbols of gnosis as materially effective knowledge, the existential question remains: what actually works now and here in the world of today? The discussion of the meaning of symbols, even when conducted at the most profound level, still must face the question: has man been helped, have we been actually tangibly changed by this discussion?

Or, to put the question in another language: what does the incarnation of God look like now? What kind of "flesh" (materiality) will the Truth take upon itself? There is no way to proceed with this question apart from facing the complexity of our own human condition and the precise extent to which modern man needs help. It is, of course, important to draw the distinction between the permanent needs of man and the needs of man in this or that era. And yet, the question returns: Does this distinction help? Is it drawn and formulated in a way that acts beneficently on the hearer? To relegate such criticism to the realm of rhetoric is tragically to miss the point—or, rather, tragically to underestimate what it is of which rhetoric authentically forms a part. With a certain kind of knowledge, it may make little difference how it is communicated—this is so of much of modern knowledge and therefore the term "information" is more applicable to it than the term "knowledge." But a knowledge intended to make a change in the very substance of man must be expressed so that it can be heard or it is not salvational knowledge. For this, the knowledge has to include an exact awareness of all that prevents man from hearing. We cannot demand of man that he listen if he is incapable of listening. The saving powers have to help man listen as well.

If a man is drowning in a raging sea, I cannot shout at him from the shore. He will not hear me. The wind is too loud. He is too frightened and agitated. Perhaps, even, his head is under the water.

What are the factors that prevent modern man, the citizen of today, from hearing the call of Truth? That is the only real basis, in my opinion, upon which to engage now in cultural criticism. The lightning-bolt of Guénon's *Reign of Quantity* has illuminated our situation. But more is needed, far more. Men need this lightning-bolt to strike them unceasingly, always and everywhere, in their own lives. The question, "how can modern man be helped to hear the truth?" goes far deeper than the insight that he no longer listens to the truth, important though that insight is. If I am gravely ill, the question of how to become well is far more important than the repeated exposure of my situation, except insofar as that exposure impels me toward accepting the help I need.

The problem of modern man is not so much the depth of his sleep, but as it were, its width, its extent over so many areas of his existence. This "width" of modern man's sleep gives cause for great alarm, but to mistake the width for depth may be a grave error of diagnosis. To see mankind as deeply asleep, possessed by Satan, willing evil, etc., may provoke us either to give up on man or merely to shout at him again and again, or in any case to focus our efforts so narrowly that no matter how authentic the source of our call to him, it cannot have the proper material action upon him. The call needs to touch all the points where man is deaf because to touch one thing cannot lead to awakening but only to momentary shock. And, in the worst case, to a momentary awakening which is then re-absorbed into man's fallen condition, in which case spiritual truth is placed in the service of the egoistic passions. This is practically a definition of the demonic.

What are the conditions under which the whole width and extent of modern man's sleep can be understood and penetrated? What conditions are needed for us to see the *whole* of our condition and in this seeing to experience in ourselves the "mourning" or energy of remorse, which alone can call forth the higher Self of man as a sacrosanct idea? We are speaking, if we may be permitted, *to* The Reign of Quantity, and of the power of God to sacralize even the Kali Yuga, as Christ and the Buddha entered hell.

Or, perhaps, God is tired. Perhaps there are no more revelations possible and we are simply to wait for the end of our civilization. This cannot be, if by such a thought we mean to say the material world is stronger than truth and goodness. The esoteric, however we twist and turn, remains that which is hidden, inner. No explanation of the esoteric is fully possible simply because of its very nature an explanation is not a living, moving form.

The inner dimension, however, as the writings of Meister Eckhart continually remind us, is always what escapes the rigid, fixed vision. The esoteric always has to be found; it always recedes from my grasp until, in the end, I surrender my effort to grasp it and, in a moment of law-conformable grace, *I am* appears, which means a new energy, a transformed materiality that the powers of matter recognize and obey—even, so it is somewhere written, with joy in their unfrozen hearts.

The truth is *always* "the last revelation," for it is only the "last revelation" that appears in the present moment, in one's own personal "contemporary world."

I need to put my cards on the table: what is required is that the great esoteric principles expounded in *The Sword of Gnosis* be made actually esoteric, actually effective in the material plane. The truth is always new and always very, very old—that is, it always applies just to me now and here and yet emanates from an eternally unchanging source. Therefore, it is equally true that for real religion to exist, there must be perpetual revelation.

Similarly, the idea of the Kali Yuga stands in need of re-interiorization since the awakening force of this idea as Guénon first brought it has by now tended, inevitably, to deteriorate into a quite generally acceptable, if not yet actually respectable, idea.

The Kali Yuga is a movement of energy, not a fixed external period of time. Or rather, it is a metaphysical and cosmic time precisely because it designates a fundamental movement of energy, which in essence appears in the life of every individual—as it was recognized by the term *accidie* among the early Christians, or given the more general name of passion: the attachment to one of the holy forces of the universal order without allowing in the action of the holy spirit, or reconciling force.

He who rules out the action of the holy spirit now and here in the life of men—is he not really the true captive of the Kali Yuga? And this brings us back to our fundamental question.

What can enable modern man to hear and to be open to the higher? What sort of language? What ideas? What vibration? What shocks? What will penetrate into our misunderstanding of technology, our scattered attention, our weakness in the face of money, sex, physical fear, our infatuation with the printed word, the electronic image, the binary mind of the computer— in short, all that is included in the width of contemporary man's sleep? What ideas are *needed*? Not what ideas are true; that is not the only question. Ideas are only one expression of the greast energy of truth. Formulations of truth which do not share that energy perhaps do not deserve even to be called ideas, certainly not *gnosis*.

And which people are needed?—surely, this is the question that surpasses everything in importance. What qualities of the human person can actually bring real force and justified hope to the seeker of today?

Jacob Needleman
San Francisco, 1986

Erratum p.8 1.10
for 'greast' read 'great'.

Foreword

ONE of the most interesting intellectual developments of the 1960's was the publication in England of a periodical called *Studies in Comparative Religion*. When it first came across my desk, it had seemed to me merely another gray scholarly journal —an impression that was only strengthened by its stated purpose of presenting essays concerning "traditional studies." Like many Americans, I was put off by the very word "tradition." But I pressed on because I had heard that this journal contained some of the most serious thinking of the twentieth century.

And in fact I quickly saw that its contributors were not interested in the hypothesizing and the marshaling of piece-meal evidence that characterizes the work of most academicians. On close reading, I felt an extraordinary intellectual force radiating through their intricate prose. These men were out for the kill. For them, the study of spiritual traditions was a sword with which to destroy the illusions of contemporary man.

Even more remarkable was the sense of an invisible thread connecting them together, something both firmer and subtler than the mere sharing of attitudes or points of view. All I could have said definitely was that they seemed to take metaphysical ideas more seriously than one might have thought possible. It was as though for them such ideas were the most real things in the world. They conformed their thought to these ideas in the way the rest of us tend to conform our thought to material things. Perhaps it was this aspect that gave their essays a flavor that was both slightly archaic and astonishingly fresh at the same time. They were clearly men "under authority"—but under what authority, and from where did they receive the energy to speak from an idea without veering off into apologetics and argumentation?

Strangely enough, I did not at that time feel the connection between the appearance of this journal and the sudden sprouting all around me of the "new religions." By this latter term I include more than the groups of young people clustering around an individual guru. I mean the attraction toward all things mystical and experiential: the fascination with the American Indian way of life, for example, and the formation of spiritually oriented communes, and even the new emphasis among certain psychologists on techniques of "self-actualization" and encounter as methods of transcending the meaninglessness of so-called normal life.

It is now obvious to me that I failed to see this connection because I had never really questioned my understanding of the idea of tradition. Like many others, I thought of tradition only as a collection of rituals, customs, and beliefs handed down from generation to generation. To me, the most essential characteristic of tradition was that it was sourced in the past. Therefore, like most everyone else, I could speak of the traditions of Buddhism or Christianity in much the same way as I would speak of the "tradition" of the American novel, for example, or the "traditions" of social etiquette.

It never occurred to me that the so-called revolution of consciousness that was taking place in this country was really the hunger for tradition. Yet if these authors were right, that was exactly what was taking place—and moreover it was happening blindly and disastrously. Of course, the target of their essays was always much larger than the present scene; it embraced the entire history of Western civilization from the end of the Middle Ages to the present day, a history that they understood as an accelerating downward spiral.

I was forced to ask myself: What, then, *is* the proper understanding of tradition? Is there such a thing as the transmission of truth without distortion? How did this transmission take place in the past, and can it take place in the conditions under which mankind now lives? To read the essays in this volume is suddenly to find this question about the nature of tradition at the heart of *every* serious intellectual and spiritual issue.

This will be hard to swallow for many American readers who, like myself, are accustomed to believe that in order to understand anything it is first of all necessary to set aside other people's thoughts and make a direct approach based on one's own experience and logic.

A very strong expression of this subject is found in the works of a remarkable Frenchman, René Guénon, many of whose ideas about the nature of tradition have influenced the writers in this volume. Writing in the 1930's and 1940's, Guénon posited the existence of what he called a Primordial Tradition, a body of the highest universal truths, or Principles, as he called them, that lie at the heart of every authentic religion. The various traditions are each a manifestation of this Primordial Tradition, and each is a path toward the practical realization of these Principles in the life of man.

For Guénon, all civilization worthy of the name serves a spiritual function: to act as a channel for the influence of tradition upon every sphere of human life. The modern division between the sacred and the secular struck him as perverse, one of many examples of the way modern society has made it impossible for man to fulfill his inner destiny. Many of Guénon's books, notably *The Reign of Quantity*,[1] are such potent and detailed metaphysical attacks on the downward drift of Western civilization as to make all other contemporary critiques—be they sociological, psychological, or moralistic—seem half-hearted by comparison. His idea was that traditional civilization is the reflection in the human social order of the entire reach of universal reality. By this standard he saw absolutely every aspect of present-day civilization as "antitraditional." In cutting himself off from Primordial Tradition, modern man cut away the only hope he could ever have to struggle for that individual transformation of being that is both the highest potentiality of human life and the one goal that justifies all the burdens and sufferings of man on earth.

Guénon's mission was twofold: to reveal the metaphysical roots of "the crisis of the modern world" with its inexorable cataclysmic outcome and to explain the ideas behind the authentic esoteric teachings that still remained alive in India and

[1] René Guénon, *The Reign of Quantity and the Signs of the Times* (Baltimore, Md.: Penguin Books Inc, 1972).

the East. The only hope that Guénon offered—and he thought of it as an exceedingly slender possibility—was for traditional Christianity to rediscover the metaphysical basis of its ancient traditions through exposure to the authenticity of Eastern religious ideas.

It is this aspect of Guénon's mission that contains so many question marks for us. It is no exaggeration to say that in this view modern man stands naked and alone in front of the truths expressed in the great traditions. Taken by itself, Guénon's work condemns man collectively to the grinding decay of civilization and to the destruction of human life as we know it. The new birth is not for this era of mankind. Individually—that is, for selected individual human beings—the situation is not so completely dark, yet it is terrifying nevertheless. Guénon himself converted to Islam and spent the last part of his life in Egypt. Both from his writings and from his life he seems to be saying to us: "Search out the few dwindling traces of orthodox spirituality that still exist in the world, cast away your present life, and depart—or else face the life of anxiety, pseudoreligion, superficial knowledge, and the all-pervasive illusory pleasures and commitments that characterize the civilization of the Dark Age." In short, a man must choose to give up everything—especially his ideas, opinions, likes, and dislikes—before he can begin on the Way. The force of Guénon's ideas is to bring man to a state of intellectual penitence, a moment of mental crisis and decision all the more painful because Guénon offers so little hope that there is anything to be done. The profundity of Guénon's thought is thus matched by an austerity that has led one observer to call him "an eye without a heart." Yet it is just this quality of austerity that still protects his ideas against being absorbed by the sort of psychological moralism that he felt brings truth down to the level of pragmatism. What, for example, would be the effect upon the church's present awareness of itself were it to attempt a real answer to Guénon? Certainly no other modern writer has so effectively communicated the absoluteness of truth—a sheer mountain face to which all paths are now blocked or hidden. Guénon's uniqueness lies not only in that he makes men feel the need for a radical acceptance but also in that he makes it impossible to believe that this acceptance will bear any fruit without the help of authentic traditional forms, forms that no longer exist in the conditions of modern life.

Yet the haunting question remains: Is the eternal energy that created the revelations of old incapable of manifesting anew in these conditions? What forms would this new "revelation" take? Is radical acceptance the only stance that it will allow man to take? Or is the fact that we feel ourselves called upon to choose—to choose in the absence of understanding and cut off from that in ourselves that is connected to the force of will—is this fact itself a sign not that we have removed ourselves from tradition, but that on the contrary the established traditions have removed themselves from us and have lost sight of the shifting balance of strength and weakness peculiar to our time and place?

One wonders what Guénon's answer would have been had this question been put to him in a serious manner. He seems never to have considered the possibility of a Way that does not demand the immediate alteration of the conditions of twentieth-century life, but that nevertheless emanates from the same source as the recognized traditions.

At this point we encounter the formidable mind of Frithjof Schuon:

> Nothing is more misleading than to pretend, as is so glibly done in our day, that the religions have compromised themselves hopelessly in the course of the centuries or that they are now played out. If one knows what a religion really consists of, one also knows that the religions cannot compromise themselves and that they are independent of human doings. . . . Tradition speaks to each man the language he can comprehend, provided he wishes to listen. The latter proviso is crucial, for tradition, let it be repeated, cannot "become bankrupt"; rather it is of the bankruptcy of man that one should speak, for it is he that has lost all intuition of the supernatural. It is man who has let

himself be deceived by the discoveries and inventions of a falsely totalitarian science. . . .

Guénon certainly could not have said it more forcefully. But Schuon—although he was an early collaborator with Guénon and shared many of his views—seems to be attempting what Guénon did not believe possible: to make tradition once again an effective force in the mind of Western man. In "The Human Margin," Schuon freely admits that "there is something in religion that no longer works" and that "the individualistic and sentimental argumentation with which traditional piety operates has lost almost all its power to move consciences." The reason "is not merely that modern man is irreligious but also that the usual religious arguments, through not probing sufficiently to the depths of things and moreover not having previously had any need to do so, are psychologically somewhat outworn. . . ." What is needed is a better quality of spiritual thinking, "arguments of a higher order, intellectual rather than sentimental. . . ."

Far more than Guénon, Schuon offers metaphysical ideas as a practical instrument for leading men back to the traditions in their purity:

> All too many people no longer even know what is meant by an idea, what is its value and what its function; they do not so much as suspect that perfect and definite theories have always existed, theories which are therefore on their own level fully adequate and effective, and that there is nothing to add to what has been said by the sages of old except effort on our part to understand it.[2]

"The world is full of people who complain that they have been seeking but have not found: this is because they have not known how to seek. . . ."

Readers of this volume will certainly find in the writings of Schuon and those he has influenced completely new perspec-

[2] Frithjof Schuon, *Understanding Islam* (Baltimore, Md.: Penguin Books Inc, 1972), p. 112.

tives in every aspect of religious thought—on the meaning of symbolism, for example, or the idea of sin, or the warfare between scientism and religion, or the idea of esotericism, and much, much else. Very probably, it will seem to the reader that until now he has ignored an entire dimension in his thinking about tradition.

That these writings bring something that has been entirely lacking in Western religious thought is therefore not open to question. But that is not the court at which their work deserves to be judged, nor would they wish it so. Something much more serious is at stake than merely renewing the comparative study of religion throughout the land.

For the question remains: It *is* true that we do not know how to seek, but can metaphysical ideas teach us? What is it that I need if great ideas are to awaken me not merely to other ideas, but to myself?

The answer, we find, is that ideas alone cannot change anything essential in myself. Is it not our perception of this important fact—enfeebled and garbled as that perception may be—that has led us to so much of what is characteristically "Western" or "modern" or even "American"? And is not the disaster that overtook Western religion due largely to the creeping ignorance by religious officials that a practical bridge is needed to connect men to ideas, however great these ideas may be? Without this bridge, even the ideas of the greatest teachers become ineffectual or destructive. Are the rituals, prayers, and music of modern religion tiny broken fragments of what once was such a bridge? Were the great cathedrals and sacred art meant to serve that function—as a help, a sacred psychological help so that men could stand before metaphysical ideas with more than their emotionally riven intellect?

Without such a bridge, I stand before the ideas of the past as either a believer or a doubter. The assent or denial by my intellect—an intellect cut off from the deeper layers of human feeling and from the forces that move my body—only, therefore, reaffirms my inner fragmentation, my psychological dualism, and I continue through the years with a plurality of lives going on unconsciously inside me unconnected, unassociated, unintegrated. Surely this is the evil of what we call "blind faith." We are speaking now about sacred psychology—the presentation of spiritual truth in a manner that actually helps us to hear it and to take it in a way that already begins to provide the material of a real experience of myself.

What little we can understand about the transmission of the great spiritual traditions of the past shows us that this bridge of sacred psychology—or "method"—is far from easy. Men seem to have experienced it more as a swaying footbridge over a ravine that one crosses with nothing to hold to and with only one's guide going behind. Yet the determination required to move onto and across this bridge is, we may surmise, a human possibility. One senses this in the records left by extraordinary men such as Milarepa or Saint Augustine, which move us so deeply precisely because we feel that their struggle could be ours.

In modern times, for some reason, Western religion allowed this bridge to fall, with nothing to take its place. Ideas were presented merely as dogma, and the fragments of method that survived somehow seemed suddenly to be placed along with these ideas on the far side of the chasm. Men were urged to leap fantastically.

But only the mind can leap fantastically, leaving the body behind with who knows what subtle energies locked inside of it. Men were given no help to search for their natural attraction to reality. Instead they were threatened, bullied, or persuaded. "Hypnotized," perhaps, is not too strong a word.

I think modern science was born as a reaction to this hypnosis. That its pragmatic successes soon led it to construct a sub-human metaphysics ought not to blind us to the sacred impulse that originally fed it: the wish to know reality for oneself. I take all true skepticism to be the search for a quiet center within the mind that can resist the pull of subjective opinion, mechanical logic, and authoritarian belief. Nearer to that center of the mind, it seems that a double certainty appears—the certainty that it is humanly possible to know reality directly and the certainty that there are infinitely higher levels of being to be served beyond and within the human frame. Thus does a form

of faith arise alongside the rejection of belief. By faith I mean
a miraculous quality of certainty.

In Titus Burckhardt's brilliant essay "Cosmology and Modern Science," included in this volume, we find an unremitting
critique of scientism that fully extends the line of thought laid
down by Guénon and Schuon. It is hard to see how supporters
of the scientific world view will rebut this sweeping attack as
they might the various romantic critiques of science that have
lately been fashionable. Yet so intent is Burckhardt on exposing
the arrogance and errors of modern scientism that he does not
acknowledge the spiritual question of which the scientific impulse is an expression. The effect is to force us to choose between a relative truth that we feel and an absolute truth that
we do not really understand, and to leave us ever more in need
of knowledge that includes and makes room for our weak,
vagrant impulses toward greater being.

But if we follow our minds without maturing in our feelings
and without coming in touch with our natural body, from
where will come the energy to be what we know? Must not all
parts of us be moved from the very beginning? Must not ideas
be expressed in a way that to some extent reaches the whole
of us from the outset? Can the old forms of thought, the old
language, the old connections, no matter how profoundly
exposited (and no one exposits them as profoundly as these
writers), ever touch us in this way—so that they can have real
power in our lives, the lives we lead from moment to moment
in the extraordinary chaos of modern life?

One of the most arresting components of Schuon's thought
is his insistence that the appearance of a new and complete
sacred teaching is an *impossibility*.

> It is quite out of the question that a "revelation," in the
> full sense of the word, should arise in our time, one compa-
> rable, that is to say, to the imparting of one of the great
> sutras or any other primary scripture; the day of revela-
> tions is past on this globe and was so already long ago.

Coming from a lesser mind than Schuon, such an assertion

might be dismissed as merely doctrinaire, certainly not an instance of that "argument of a higher order" that he wishes to offer. But there are many places in Schuon's writings where an idea that seems functional only within one particular religious system is stunningly linked to general metaphysical principles that apply not only to all the known traditions but to all of reality as we can conceive it. This particular assertion that no new revelation is possible Schuon links to the more general idea of the cycles of human and earthly existence. The idea of cycles, in turn, is subordinate to the fundamental metaphysical notion of the relationship between principle and its manifestation. Manifestation tends outward and downward until the point of the great Return. It was Guénon who first saw the centrality of this general idea for an understanding of the manner in which the modern age has drifted down and away from traditional truth (see "Oriental Metaphysics" in the present volume and especially *The Reign of Quantity and the Signs of the Times*).

However, all of this hinges on what we understand to be the nature of a revelation. What are we? What do we need in order for new knowledge to begin to affect us in all aspects of our being? Obviously, if it does not—or cannot—do that, then no matter how inspired, "revealed," or metaphysically true, it will not have power in our lives.

If we sincerely ask what stands in the way of our being able to receive a sacred—that is, a complete—teaching, we gradually begin to see the justice of Schuon's assertion, even though he presents his particular idea in scholastic and dogmatic fashion.

If we honestly look at ourselves and at the conditions of life that we accept as inevitable, and even as desirable, we begin to feel the weight of Guénon's accusation of antitraditionalism.

We see that in our society there is nothing to support the psychological realization of the sacred ideas exposited by Guénon, Schuon, and those they have influenced. We see that from the moment we are born everything conspires to block the influences that radiate from the traditions.

How, for example, can any modern man receive deep impressions of his own egoism and its contradictions—that egoism that cuts man off completely from the deeper layer of feeling that forms the psychological bridge between levels of reality in ourselves? Modern psychology has driven us far from this in persuading us to equate violence of emotion with depth and subtlety of feeling. So much so that none of the sacred symbols of past traditions are able in any effective way to stir that subtlety of feeling that is actually a form of higher knowledge.

We may surmise that the external conditions of traditional society contained numerous factors to remind men that what is needed is impressions of their own egoism—so that even in the midst of a man's perversity and brutality, as well as in the midst of his exalted moments of triumph, he was not without the help of the cosmic, universal scale by which to measure his insignificance and need for help. Many thinkers who hold up the violence or injustices of the past as marks of inferiority fail to consider that a higher civilization is not necessarily one in which men behave like angels, but one in which men can experience *both* their divinity and their animality.

Therefore we need to bring a new question to the diagnosis of the modern world that is offered by Guénon and Schuon. Of what use, we must ask, would it be were we suddenly to surround ourselves with sacred symbols once again and even with ancient patterns of community relationship? Without some help to touch the deeper layers of feeling in ourselves that would open our eyes to the egoism that accepts, believes, trusts, and distorts everything—how could a traditional way of life transform our being?

We are surrounded by countless "new religions." At the same time, teachers from the Orient and the Middle East are struggling to preserve their own traditions within the frame of our society where the political conditions, the affluence, and the emotional needs conspire to offer tolerance to any teaching that brings striking ideas about man

How does it help us to be intellectually persuaded in one set of ideas or another? Can a teaching, however authoritative, be true for us if it persuades us to exercise a faculty that we do not possess, a faculty that is itself the product of long spiritual work? How many of these "new religions" urge us to accept one set of ideas, to enter into one or another stream of practice, while rejecting others? What is the meaning of the call for choice to men who have no power of real choice?

What is needed, it seems to me, is a teaching in which *we are known* not only for what we can become but for what we are—a teaching that provides us both with experiences of our possibilities and with impressions of our actuality, our real egoism and our possible freedom. Surely the power to choose can only be born in the center, between these two qualities of experience. And, I feel sure, without our being situated between these two experiences no ideas from whatever sacred source can act as a guide in the struggle for consciousness of self.

I think the central reason that modern psychology undermined the established religions of the West was that through psychology we realized that we had not been known. The ideas of Christianity and Judaism were suddenly revealed to be, for us, mere ideals. With the psychologists we finally felt known.

But, as time has shown, not deeply known. Therein lies the disillusionment with modern psychology. The scale was too small against which we measured our failures as men. So that all the self-acceptance in the world (which was the mercy of modern psychology) could not help us but kept us mired in illusions about ourselves. In attempting to free us from neurotic guilt, psychology only helped us for a time to feel comfortable about ourselves, but never to discover the struggle for greater being. The reason for the method of self-acceptance was too small, too egoistic and introverted.

Yet for all its failures and for all its exaggeration of the importance of certain partial insights about human nature, modern psychology left us with the indelible hope for ideas and methods that can actually work real changes in ourselves. No wonder new religions have now appeared that attempt to blend sacred traditions with the general orientation of modern psychology.

The truth is, we lack the touchstone by which to distinguish authenticity. The real hiddenness and the real corruption of tradition stem from the ignorance of this fact.

But does this mean we ought to abandon the question of how

to recognize great knowledge? On the contrary, I think it would be madness to approach the writings in this volume—not to mention the multitude of teachings now offering themselves to us—without holding onto this question. It *is* our question, and to deny it is to deny our starting point.

But there is another question, equally fundamental, that we rarely ask or rarely ask in a serious way. That question is: "What does it mean to learn?" What is great learning?

The first question—that of recognizing authority—when taken in isolation drives us outward to experience reality for ourselves (thus the origin of modern science). This movement outward is something that dogmatic religion obstructs even though it thinks it is doing good by shaping our thought to conform to great ideas. Perhaps there is a place for dogmatic metaphysics in a culture that provides the shocks of the real experience of death, physical effort, and the wide-ranging struggle for sexual balance. But as cultures and nations now interact with an increasingly accidental and violent quality, the necessary order of a society cannot be maintained on a large scale for the masses of men. The experiences available in any nation tend to become both more uniform and more excessive—overwhelming shocks interspersing the general drift toward ease and self-deception. So the cultivation of real experience remains for the separate few in schools of awakening that may exist without ever being known to the public.

In the absence of the necessary real experiences, metaphysical dogma edges man into the wastelands of mental identity, the closure of thought around great ideas that are never understood by the whole man in body and heart.

The second question, "What does it mean to learn?" has the power to lead us inward to observe for ourselves what is required if the parts of our inner nature are to come together if only for an instant. A man who realizes that he has never observed what happens to himself during real learning is in a better position to question the criterion he sets up for a teacher or a teaching. Without asking this question, without realizing that we do not know what learning is, we abandon ourselves instead to finding a teaching with "credentials" both in the sphere of ordinary education and in the far subtler sphere of spiritual work.

We need to acknowledge that there are two kinds of learning —one given, as is said, by life and the other by books. Even the previous generation maintained this distinction, which has played an important role in American life and which has been one of the factors that has distinguished American life, for all its faults, from that of the more sophisticated European. But the present generation in this country has obliterated even that weakened version of the distinction between what a man learns with the whole of himself and what he learns only with his mind—that is to say, what he takes in as material for the growth of a new consciousness and what he takes in for utilitarian reasons for the sake of comfort, psychological safety, or physical pleasure.

The new generation of Americans who have been captured by drugs, encounter groups, Eastern religion, or the Jesus movement have this one thing in common with the generation that precedes them: We were all raised and educated by a system that tried to consider both emotional and mental factors as part of ordinary learning. Up until rather recent times, modern civilization, for all its antitraditionalism, left the development of the emotional life to the family. The mother's role in this was of overwhelming importance. A person had to find himself somewhere between his mother and the shocks of life. The place of the father was as a representative of aspiration. Mother and father therefore had the task of preparing a man to grow in the midst of life and not to forget God.

The spread of public education, the growth of psychoanalysis and other psychological theories resulted in the mixing of book-learning with emotional training sometimes explicitly carried out by educational theorists and often carried out by schoolteachers who had themselves read and believed in the theories of the psychologists.

Public emotional training placed the emphasis on connecting feelings and performance, assuming that feelings were for the support of the ego rather than a special and irreplaceable access to a higher intelligence. The uniqueness of feeling was drowned out by the noise of general emotional training. In this respect, regarding the subtle uniqueness of feeling that arises in the child and that can be maintained through adolescence only with the support of a family reality containing in some measure the aspiration of man—in this respect, the family was always the first spiritual teacher or in any event the preparer of the psyche for the spiritual teacher.

Into the present milieu many traditional teachers bring ideas, doctrines, and methods of the past, speaking to men and women who have never directly faced life as a learner and who, due to the disintegration of family feeling, do not have access to subtle feeling and do not even trust those more obvious and vivid emotions that are the by-product of the hopeless struggle for mental identity. Teachers who come to America from more traditional surroundings seem unaware of how far this has gone here in the West and are perhaps deceived by the apparent willingness of thousands to listen to them.

As I see it, therefore, it is not the content of our beliefs that makes us an antitraditional society, nor even the forms of our behavior. It is the ease with which we ignore the distinction between two kinds of learning—so much so that the deeper learning, the reception of real experiences for the sake of forging inward connections between the vast scales of reality that are reflected in man, is forgotten. And with it is forgotten the possible evolution of man as a being between two worlds.

Jacob Needleman

Primordial Truth

"No Activity without Truth"

BY FRITHJOF SCHUON

(This paper was originally composed, by request, to be read at a congress convened for the purpose of considering the deeper causes of the crisis through which the world is passing with a view to positive remedial action in the light of religion. The congress was held in Japan in 1961, hence the number of allusions to Japanese Buddhism to be found in the text.)

THE PURPOSE of this congress is of the most extreme importance, since it concerns, directly or indirectly, the destiny of mankind. In the face of the perils of the modern world, we ask ourselves: What must we do? This is an empty question if it be not founded upon antecedent certainties, for action counts for nothing unless it be the expression of a knowing and also of a manner of being. Before it is possible to envisage any kind of remedial activity, it is necessary to see things as they are, even if, as things turn out, it costs us much to do so; one must be conscious of those fundamental truths that reveal to us the values and proportions of things. If one's aim is to save mankind, one must first know what it means to be a man; if one wishes to defend the spirit, one must know what is spirit. "Before doing, one must be," says the proverb; but without knowing, it is impossible to do. "The soul is all that it knows," as Aristotle said.

In our time one has often heard it said that in order to fight against materialism—or materialist pseudoidealism—a new ideology is needed, one capable of standing up to all seductions and assaults. Now, the need for an ideology or the wish to oppose one ideology to another is already an admission of weakness, and anything undertaken on this basis is false and doomed to defeat. What must be done is to oppose truth purely and simply to the false ideologies, that same truth that has always been and that we could never invent for the reason that it exists outside us and above us. The present-day world is obsessed with "dynamism," as if this constituted a "categorical imperative" and a universal remedy and as if dynamism had any meaning or positive efficacy outside truth.

No man in his senses can have the intention of merely substituting one error for another, whether "dynamic" or otherwise; before speaking of force and effectiveness one must therefore speak of truth and nothing else. A truth is powerful in such measure as we assimilate it; if the truth does not confer on us the strength of which we stand in need, this only goes to prove that we have not really grasped it. It is not for truth to be dynamic, but for ourselves to be dynamic in function of a true conviction. That which is lacking in the present world is a profound knowledge of the nature of things; the fundamental truths are always there, but they do not impose themselves in actual practice because they cannot impose themselves on those who are unwilling to accept them.

It is obvious that here we are concerned, not with the quite external data with which experimental science can possibly provide us, but with realities which that science does not and indeed cannot handle and which are transmitted through quite a different channel, that of mythological and metaphysical symbolism. The symbolical language of the great traditions of mankind may indeed seem arduous and baffling to some minds, but it is nevertheless perfectly intelligible in the light of the orthodox commentaries; symbolism—this point must be stressed—is a real and rigorous science, and nothing can be more naïve than to suppose that its apparent naïvety springs from an immature and "prelogical" mentality. This science, which can properly be described as "sacred," quite plainly does not have to adjust itself to the modern experimental approach; the realm of revelation, of symbolism, of pure and direct intellection, stands in fact above both the physical and the psychological realms, and consequently it lies beyond the scope of so-called scientific methods. If we feel we cannot accept the language of traditional symbolism because to us it seems fanciful and arbitrary, this shows we have not yet understood that language, and certainly not that we have advanced beyond it.

Nothing is more misleading than to pretend, as is so glibly done in our day, that the religions have compromised themselves hopelessly in the course of the centuries or that they are now played out. If one knows what a religion really consists of, one also knows that the religions cannot compromise themselves and that they are independent of human doings; in fact, nothing men do is able to affect the traditional doctrines, symbols, or rites. The fact that a man may exploit religion in order to bolster up national or private interests in no wise affects religion as such. In Japan, Shinto, for example, was latterly made to serve political ends, but it was in no wise compromised in itself by this fact, nor could it be. Its symbols, rites, traditions, moral code, and doctrine remain what they always were, from the "Divine Epoch" down to our own times; and as for an exhausting of the religions, one might speak of this if all men had by now become saints or Buddhas. In that case only could it be admitted that the religions were exhausted, at least as regards their forms.

Tradition speaks to each man the language he can comprehend, provided he wishes to listen. The latter proviso is crucial, for tradition, let it be repeated, cannot "become bankrupt"; rather is it of the bankruptcy of man that one should speak, for it is he that has lost all intuition of the supernatural. It is man who has let himself be deceived by the discoveries and inventions of a falsely totalitarian science; that is to say, a science that does not recognize its own proper limits and for that same reason misses whatever lies beyond those limits.

Fascinated alike by scientific phenomena and by the erroneous conclusions he draws from them, man has ended by being submerged by his own creations; he will not realize that a traditional message is situated on quite a different plane or how much more real that plane is, and he allows himself to be dazzled all the more readily since scientism provides him with all the excuses he wants in order to justify his own attachment to the world of appearances and to his ego and his consequent flight from the presence of the Absolute.

People speak of a duty to make oneself useful to society, but they neglect to ask the question whether that society does or does not in itself possess the usefulness that a human society normally should exhibit, for if the individual must be useful to the collectivity, the latter for its part must be useful to the individual, and one must never lose sight of the fact that there exists no higher usefulness than that which envisages the final ends of man. By its divorce from traditional truth—as primarily perceivable in that "flowering forth" that is revelation—society forfeits its own justification, doubtless not in a perfunctorily animal sense, but in the human sense. This human quality implies that the collectivity, as such, cannot be the aim and purpose of the individual but that, on the contrary, it is the individual who, in his "solitary stand" before the Absolute and in the exercise of his supreme function, is the aim and purpose of the collectivity. Man, whether he be conceived in the plural or the singular, or whether his function be direct or indirect, stands like "a fragment of absoluteness" and is made for the Absolute; he has no other choice before him. In any case, one can define the social in terms of truth, but one cannot define truth in terms of the social.

Reference is often made to the "selfishness" of those who busy themselves with salvation, and it is said that instead of saving oneself one ought to save others; but this is an absurd kind of argument, since either it is impossible to save others, or else it is possible to save them but only in virtue of our own salvation or of our own effort toward salvation. No man has ever done a service to anyone else whatsoever by remaining "altruistically" attached to his own defects. He who is capable of being a saint but fails to become such certainly will save no one else; it is sheer hypocrisy to conceal one's own weakness and spiritual lukewarmness behind a screen of good works believed to be indispensable and of absolute value.

Another error, closely related to the one just pointed out, consists in supposing that contemplative spirituality is opposed to action or renders a man incapable of acting, a belief that is belied by all the sacred scriptures and especially by the Bhagavad-gita. In Japan the example of saints such as Shotoku

Taishi, Hojo Tokimune, Shinran Shonin, and Nichiren proves —if proof is needed—that spirituality is neither opposed to action nor dependent upon it, and also that spirituality leads to the most perfect action whenever circumstances require it, just as it can also, if necessary, turn away from the urge to action when no immediate aim imposes the need for it.

To cut off man from the Absolute and reduce him to a collective phenomenon is to deprive him of all right to existence qua man. If man deserves that so many efforts should be spent on his behalf, this cannot be simply because he exists, eats, and sleeps or because he likes what is pleasant and hates what is unpleasant, for the lowest of the animals are in similar case without being considered for this reason our equals and treated accordingly. To the objection that man is distinguished from the animal by his intelligence, we will answer that it is precisely this intellectual superiority that the social egalitarianism of the moderns fails to take into account, so much so that an argument that is not applied consistently to men cannot then be turned against the animals. To the objection that man is distinguished from animals by his "culture" we will answer that the completely profane and worldly "culture" in question is nothing more than a specifically dated pastime of the human animal; that is to say, this culture can be anything you please, while waiting for the human animal to suppress it altogether. The capacity for absoluteness that characterizes human intelligence is the only thing conferring on man a right of primacy; it is only this capacity that gives him the right to harness a horse to a cart. Tradition, by its above-worldly character, manifests the real superiority of man; tradition alone is a "humanism" in the positive sense of the word. Antitraditional culture, by the very fact that it is without the sense of the Absolute and even the sense of truth—for these two things hang together— could never confer on man that unconditional value and those indisputable rights that modern humanitarianism attributes to him a priori and without any logical justification.

The same could also be expressed in another way: When people speak of "culture," they generally think of a host of contingencies, of a thousand ways of uselessly agitating the mind and dispersing one's attention, but they do not think of that principle that alone confers lawfulness on human works; this principle is the transcendent truth, whence springs all genuine culture. It is impossible to defend a culture effectively—such as the traditional culture of Japan, which is one of the most precious in the world—without referring it back to its spiritual principle and without seeking therein the sap that keeps life going. Agreement as between cultures means agreement on spiritual principles; for truth, despite great differences of expression, remains one.

Many people of our time reason along the following lines: The religions—or the differing spiritual perspectives within a given religion—contradict one another, therefore they cannot all be right; consequently none is true. This is exactly as if one said: Every individual claims to be "I," thus they cannot all be right; consequently none is "I." This example shows up the absurdity of the antireligious argument, by recalling the real analogy between the inevitable external limitation of religious language and the no less inevitable limitation of the human ego. To reach this conclusion, as do the rationalists who use the above argument, amounts in practice to denying the diversity of the knowing subjects as also the diversity of aspects in the object to be known. It amounts to pretending that there are neither points of view nor aspects; that is to say, that there is but a single man to see a mountain and that the mountain has but a single side to be seen. The error of the subjectivist and relativist philosophers is a contrary one. According to them, the mountain would alter its nature according to whoever viewed it; at one time it might be a tree and at another a stream. Only traditional metaphysics does justice both to the rigor of objectivity and to the rights of subjectivity; it alone is able to explain the unanimity of the sacred doctrines as well as the meaning of their formal divergencies.

In sound logic, to observe the diversity of religions should give rise to the opposite conclusion, namely: Since at all periods and among all peoples religions are to be found that unanimously affirm one absolute and transcendent reality, as also a beyond that receives us according to our merit or knowledge

—or according to our demerit and ignorance—there is reason
to conclude that every religion is right, and all the more so since
the greatest men that have walked the earth have borne witness
to spiritual truths. It is possible to admit that all the materialists
have been mistaken, but it is not possible to admit that all the
founders of religions, all the saints and sages, have been in error
and have led others into error; for if one had to admit that error
lay with them and not with those who contradicted them, mankind itself would cease to offer any interest, so that a belief in
progress or in the possibility of progress would become doubly
absurd. If the Buddha or Christ or a Plotinus or a Kobo Daishi
were not intelligent, then no one is intelligent, and there is no
such thing as human intelligence.

The diversity of religions, far from proving the falseness of
all the doctrines concerning the supernatural, shows on the
contrary the supraformal character of revelation and the formal character of ordinary human understanding; the essence
of revelation—or enlightenment—is one, but human nature
requires diversity. Dogmas or other symbols may contradict
one another externally, but they concur internally.

Howbeit, it is easy to foresee the following objection: Even
if it be admitted that there is a providential and inescapable
cause underlying the diversity of religions and even their exoteric incompatibility in certain cases, ought we not then to try
to get beyond these differences by creating a single universal
religion? To this it must be answered first that these differences
have at all times been transcended in the various esotericisms
and second that a religion is not something one can create for
the asking. Every attempt of this kind would be an error and
a failure, and this is all the more certain inasmuch as the age
of the great revelations had closed centuries ago. No new religion can see the light of day in our time for the simple reason
that time itself, far from being a sort of uniform abstraction,
on the contrary alters its value according to every phase of its
development. What was still possible a thousand years ago is
so no longer, for we are now living in the age known to Buddhist tradition as "the latter times." However, what we are able
to do and must do is to respect all the religions—but without

any confusing of forms and without asking to be fully understood by every believer—while waiting till heaven itself wills
to unite those things that now are scattered. For we find ourselves on the threshold of great upheavals, and what man himself has neither the power nor the right to realize will be
realized by heaven, when the time for it shall be ripe.

The world is full of people who complain that they have been
seeking but have not found; this is because they have not
known how to seek and have only looked for sentimentalities
of an individualistic kind. One often hears it said that the
priests of such and such a religion are no good or that they have
brought religion itself to naught, as if this were possible or as
if a man who serves his religion badly did not betray himself
exclusively; men quite forget the timeless value of symbols and
of the graces they vehicle. The saints have at all times suffered
from the inadequacy of certain priests; but far from thinking
of rejecting tradition itself for that reason, they have by their
own sanctity compensated for whatever was lacking in the
contemporary priesthood. The only means of "reforming" a
religion is to reform oneself. It is indispensable to grasp the fact
that a rite vehicles a far greater value than a personal virtue.
A personal initiative that takes a religious form amounts to
nothing in the absence of a traditional framework such as alone
can justify that initiative and turn it to advantage, whereas a
rite at least will always keep fresh the sap of the whole tradition
and hence also its principial efficacy—even if men do not know
how to profit thereby.

If things were otherwise or if spiritual values were to be
found outside the sacred traditions, the function of the saints
would have been, not to enliven their religion, but rather to
abolish it, and there would no longer be any religion left on
earth, or else on the contrary there would be religions by the
million, which amounts to the same thing; and these millions
of personal pseudoreligions would themselves be changing at
every minute. The religions and their orthodox developments—such as the various traditional schools of Buddhism
—are inalienable and irreplaceable legacies to which nothing
essential can be added and from which nothing essential can

be subtracted. We are here, not in order to change these things, but in order to understand them and realize them in ourselves.

Today two dangers are threatening religion: from the outside, its destruction—were it only as a result of its general desertion—and from the inside, its falsification. The latter, with its pseudointellectual pretensions and its fallacious professions of "reform," is immeasurably more harmful than all the "superstition" and "corruption" of which, rightly or wrongly, the representatives of the traditional patrimonies have been accused; this heritage is absolutely irreplaceable, and in the face of it men as such are of no account. Tradition is abandoned, not because people are no longer capable of understanding its language, but because they do not wish to understand it, for this language is made to be understood till the end of the world; tradition is falsified by reducing it to flatness on the plea of making it more acceptable to "our time," as if one could—or should—accommodate truth to error. Admittedly, a need to reply to new questions and new forms of ignorance can always arise. One can and must explain the sacred doctrine, but not at the expense of that which gives it its reason for existing, that is to say, not at the expense of its truth and effectiveness. There could be no question, for instance, of adding to the Mahayana or of replacing it by a new vehicle, such as would necessarily be of purely human invention; for the Mahayana—or shall we say Buddhism?—is infinitely sufficient for those who will give themselves the trouble to look higher than their own heads.

One point that has been already mentioned is worth recalling now because of its extreme importance. It is quite out of the question that a "revelation," in the full sense of the word, should arise in our time, one comparable, that is to say, to the imparting of one of the great sutras or any other primary scripture; the day of revelations is past on this globe and was so already long ago. The inspirations of the saints are of another order, but these could in any case never falsify or invalidate tradition or intrinsic orthodoxy by claiming to improve on it or even to replace it, as some people have suggested. "Our own time" possesses no quality that makes it the measure or the criterion of values in regard to that which is timeless. It is the timeless that, by its very nature, is the measure of our time, as indeed of all other times; and if our time has no place for authentic tradition, then it is self-condemned by that very fact. The Buddha's message, like every other form of the one and only truth, offers itself to every period with an imperishable freshness. It is as true and as urgent in our day as it was two thousand years ago; the fact that mankind finds itself in the "latter days," the days of forgetfulness and decline, only makes that urgency more actual than ever. In fact, there is nothing more urgent, more actual, or more real than metaphysical truth and its demands. It alone can of its own right fill the vacuum left in the contemporary mentality—especially where young people are concerned—by social and political disappointments on the one hand and by the bewildering and indigestible discoveries of modern science on the other. At the risk of repetition let the following point be stressed, for to doubt it would be fatal: To search for an "ideology" in the hopes of filling up that vacuum—as if it were simply a matter of plugging a hole—is truly a case of "putting the cart before the horse." It is a case of subordinating truth and salvation to narrowly utilitarian and in any case quite external ends, as if the sufficient cause of truth could be found somewhere below truth. The sufficient cause of man is to know the truth, which exists outside and above him; the truth cannot depend for its meaning and existence on the wishes of man. The very word "ideology" shows that truth is not the principal aim people have in mind; to use that word shows that one is scarcely concerned with the difference between true and false and that what one is primarily seeking is a mental deception that will be comfortable and workable, or utilizable for purposes of one's own choosing, which is tantamount to abolishing both truth and intelligence.

Outside tradition there can assuredly be found some relative truths or views of partial realities, but outside tradition there does not exist a doctrine that catalyzes absolute truth and transmits liberating notions concerning total reality. Modern science is not a wisdom but an accumulation of physical experiments coupled with many unwarrantable conclusions; it can neither add nor subtract anything in respect of the total truth or of mythological or other symbolism or in respect of the principles and experiences of the spiritual life.

One of the most insidious and destructive illusions is the belief that depth psychology (or in other words psychoanalysis) has the slightest connection with spiritual life, which these teachings persistently falsify by confusing inferior elements with superior. We cannot be too wary of all these attempts to reduce the values vehicled by tradition to the level of phenomena supposed to be scientifically controllable. The spirit escapes the hold of profane science in an absolute fashion. It is not the positive results of experimental science that one is out to deny (always assuming that they really are positive in a definite sense) but the absurd claim of science to cover everything possible, the whole of truth, the whole of the real; this quasi-religious claim to totality moreover proves the falseness of the point of departure. If one takes into account the very limited realm within which science moves, the least one can say is that nothing justifies the so-called scientific denials of the beyond and of the Absolute.

If it be essential to distinguish between the realm of religion or traditional wisdom and that of experimental science, it is also essential to distinguish between the intellect, which is intuitive, and reason, which is discursive; reason is a limited faculty, whereas intellect opens out upon the Universal and the Divine. For metaphysical wisdom, reason only possesses a dialectical, not an illuminative, usefulness; reason is not capable of grasping in a concrete way that which lies beyond the world of forms, though reason is able to reach further than imagination. All ratiocination condemns itself to ignorance from the moment it claims to deal with the roots of our existence and of our spirit.

We all know that the need to account for things in terms of causality, as felt by modern man, is apt to remain unsatisfied in the face of the ancient mythologies; but the fact is that attempts to explain the mythological order with the aid of reasonings that are necessarily arbitrary and vitiated by all sorts of prejudices are bound to fail in any case. Symbolisms reveal their true meaning only in the light of the contemplative intellect, which is analogically represented in man by the heart and not by the brain. Pure intellect—or intuition and suprarational intelligence—can flower only in the framework of a traditional orthodoxy, by reason of the complementary and therefore necessary relationship between intellection and revelation.

The fundamental intention of every religion or wisdom is the following: first, discernment between the real and the unreal, and then concentration upon the real. One could also render this intention otherwise: truth and the way, *prajnā* and *upāya*, doctrine and its corresponding method. One must know that the Absolute or the Infinite—whatever may be the names given it by respective traditions—is what gives sense to our existence, just as one must know that the essential content of life is the consciousness of this supreme reality, a fact that explains the part to be played by continual prayer; in a word we live to realize the Absolute. To realize the Absolute is to think of it, under one form or another as indicated by revelation and tradition, by a form such as the Japanese nembutsu or the Tibetan *Om mani padme hum* or the Hindu *japa-yoga*, not forgetting the Christian and Islamic invocations, such as the Jesus Prayer and the dhikr of the dervishes. Here one will find some very different modalities, not only as between one religion and another but also within the fold of each religion, as can be shown, for instance, by the difference between Jodo Shinshu and Zen. However this may be, it is only on the basis of a genuine spiritual life that we can envisage any kind of external action with a view to defending truth and spirituality in the world.

All the traditional doctrines agree in this: From a strictly spiritual point of view, though not necessarily from other much more relative and therefore less important points of view, mankind is becoming more and more corrupted; the ideas of "evolution," of "progress," and of a single "civilization" are in effect the most pernicious pseudodogmas the world has ever produced, for there is no newfound error that does not eagerly attach its own claims to the above beliefs. We say not that evolution is nonexistent, but that it has a partial and most often a quite external applicability; if there be evolution on the one hand, there are degenerations on the other, and it is in any case radically false to suppose that our ancestors were intellectually, spiritually, or morally our inferiors. To suppose this is the most childish of "optical delusions"; human weakness alters its style in the course of history, but not its nature. A question that now arises is as follows: Seeing that humanity is decaying inescapably and seeing that the final crisis with its cosmic consummation as foretold in the sacred books is inevitable, *what then can we do?* Does an external activity still have any meaning?

To this it must be answered that an affirmation of the truth, or any effort on behalf of truth, is never in vain, even if we cannot from beforehand measure the value or the outcome of such an activity. Moreover we have no choice in the matter. Once we know the truth, we must live in it and fight for it; but what we must avoid at any price is to let ourselves bask in illusions. Even if, at this moment, the horizon seems as dark as possible, one must not forget that in a perhaps unavoidably distant future the victory is ours and cannot but be ours. Truth by its very nature conquers all obstacles: *Vincit omnia veritas.*

Therefore, every initiative taken with a view to harmony between the different cultures and for the defense of spiritual values is good, if it has as its basis a recognition of the great principial truths and consequently also a recognition of tradition or of the traditions.

"When the inferior man hears talk about Tao, he only laughs at it; it would not be Tao if he did not laugh at it . . . the self-evidence of Tao is taken for a darkness." These words of Lao-tse were never more timely than now. Errors cannot but be, as long as their quite relative possibility has not reached its term; but for the Absolute errors have never been and never shall be. On their own plane they are what they are, but it is the Changeless that shall have the final say.

Oriental Metaphysics

BY RENÉ GUENON

For the subject of this essay I have taken Oriental metaphysics. Perhaps it would have been better to have said simply metaphysics unqualified, for in truth, pure metaphysics, being essentially above and beyond all form and all contingency, is neither Eastern nor Western but universal. The exterior forms with which it is covered only serve the necessities of exposition, to express whatever is expressible. These forms may be Eastern or Western, but under the appearance of diversity there is always a basis of unity, at least, wherever true metaphysics exists, for the simple reason that truth is one.

If this be so, what need is there to deal specifically with Oriental metaphysics? The reason is that in the present intellectual state of the Western world metaphysics is a thing forgotten, generally ignored and almost entirely lost, whereas in the East it still remains the object of effective knowledge. Thus it is to the East that one must look if one wishes to discover the true meaning of metaphysics; or even if one's wish is to recover some of the metaphysical traditions formerly existing in a West that was in many respects much closer to the East than it is today, it is above all with the help of Oriental doctrines and by comparison with them that one may succeed, since these are the only doctrines in the domain of metaphysics that can still be studied directly. As for these, however, it is quite clear that they must be studied as the Orientals themselves study them, and one must certainly not indulge in more or less hypothetical interpretations, which may sometimes be quite imaginary; it is too often forgotten that Eastern civilizations still exist and still have qualified representatives from whom it is possible to inquire in order to discover the exact truth about the subject in question.

I have said "Eastern metaphysics" and not merely Hindu

metaphysics, for doctrines of this order, with all they imply, are not to be found only in India, as some people believe, who, moreover, barely grasp their true nature. The case of India is by no means exceptional in this respect; it is precisely that of all civilizations that possess what might be termed a traditional basis. On the contrary, what is exceptional and abnormal is civilizations without such a basis, and to tell the truth, the only one known to us is that of the modern West. To take only the principal Eastern civilizations: The equivalent of Hindu metaphysics is found in China (in Taoism) and is also to be found elsewhere in certain esoteric schools of Islam; it should be understood, however, that this Islamic esotericism has nothing in common with the overt philosophy of the Arabs, which is for the most part Greek-inspired. The only difference is that except in India these doctrines are reserved for a relatively restricted and closed elite. This was also the case in the West in the Middle Ages, in an esotericism comparable in many respects to that of Islam and as purely metaphysical as the Islamic one; of this the moderns, for the most part, do not even suspect the existence. In India it is not possible to speak of esotericism in the true sense of the word, because there is no doctrinal dualism of exoteric and esoteric; it can only be a matter of natural esotericism, in the sense that each goes more or less deeply into the doctrine and more or less far according to the measure of his abilities, since there are, for certain individualities, limitations that are inherent in their own nature and that are impossible to overcome.

Naturally, forms differ from one civilization to another, but though more accustomed myself to the Hindu forms, I have no scruple in employing others when necessary if they can contribute to the understanding of certain points; there are no objections to this, since they are only different expressions of the same thing. Once again, truth is one, and it is the same for all those who, by whatever way, have attained to its understanding.

This said, it should be made clear in what sense the word "metaphysics" is used, all the more so since I have frequently had occasion to state that everyone does not understand it in the same way. I think the best course to take with words that can give rise to ambiguity is to reduce them, as far as possible, to their primary and etymological meaning. Now, according to its composition, this word "metaphysics" means literally "beyond physics," taking the word "physics" in the accepted meaning it always had for the ancients, that is, as the science of nature in its widest sense. Physics is the study of all that appertains to the domain of nature; metaphysics, on the other hand, is the study of what lies beyond nature. How, then, can some claim that metaphysical knowledge is natural knowledge, either in respect of its object or with regard to the faculties by which it is obtained? There we have a complete misconception, a contradiction in terms; and what is more amazing, this confusion affects even those who should preserve some idea of the true metaphysics and know how to distinguish it clearly from the pseudometaphysics of modern philosophers.

But, one might say, if this word "metaphysics" gives rise to such confusion, would it not be better to abandon it and substitute something more suitable? Plainly, this would not be advisable, since, by its formation, this word meets the exact requirements; also, it is hardly possible because Western languages have no other word equally adapted to this usage. Simply to use the word "knowledge," as is done in India, because this is indeed knowledge par excellence and that which alone can be dignified by that name, is out of the question, for it would only make things more confusing for Occidentals who habitually associate knowledge with nothing beyond the scientific and rational. Also, is it necessary to concern ourselves with the abuse to which a word is put? If we rejected all such, what would be left? Is it not sufficient to take precautions to avoid misunderstandings and misrepresentations? We are not any more enamored of the word "metaphysics" than of any other, but since a better term cannot be suggested to replace it, we will continue to use it as before.

Unfortunately one comes across people who claim to "judge" that which they do not know and who, because they apply the name "metaphysics" to a purely human and rational knowledge (which for us is only science or philosophy), imagine that

Oriental metaphysics is no more and no other than that; from which they arrive logically at the conclusion that this metaphysics cannot in reality lead to any particular results. They fail to see that it is an effective guide just because it is something quite other than they suppose. What they envisage has really nothing to do with metaphysics, since it is only knowledge of a natural order, an outward and profane scholarship; it is not of this that we wish to speak. Can one then make "metaphysical" synonymous with "supernatural"? We are prepared to accept such an analogy, since if one does not go beyond nature—that is to say, the manifest world in its entirety (and not only the world of the senses, which is only an infinitesimal part of it)—one is still in the realm of the physical. Metaphysics is, as we have already said, that which lies beyond and above nature; hence it can properly be described as "supernatural."

But an objection will undoubtedly be raised here: Is it possible to go beyond nature? We do not hesitate to answer plainly: Not only is it possible, but it is a fact. Again it might be said, is this not merely an assertion; what proofs thereof can be adduced? It is truly strange that proof is demanded concerning the possibility of a kind of knowledge instead of searching for it and verifying it for oneself by undertaking the work necessary for its acquisition. For those who possess this knowledge, what interest can there be in all this discussion? Substituting a "theory of knowledge" for knowledge itself is perhaps the greatest admission of impotence in modern philosophy.

Moreover, all certitude contains something incommunicable. Nobody can truly attain to any knowledge other than by a strictly personal effort; all that one can do for another is to offer him the opportunity and indicate the means by which to attain the same knowledge. That is why it would be vain to attempt to impose any belief in the purely intellectual realm; the best argument in the world could not in this respect replace direct and effective knowledge.

Now, is it possible to define metaphysics as we understand it? No, for to define is always to limit, and that with which we are concerned is, in itself, truly and absolutely unlimited and cannot be confined to any formula or any system. Metaphysics might be partly described, for example, by saying that it is the knowledge of universal principles, but that is not a definition in the proper sense and only conveys a rough idea. Something can be added by saying that the scope of these principles is far greater than was thought by some Occidentals who, although really studying metaphysics, did so in a partial and incomplete way. Thus when Aristotle envisages metaphysics as a knowledge of being qua being, he identifies it with ontology; that is to say, he takes the part for the whole. For Oriental metaphysics, pure being is neither the first nor the most universal principle, for it is already a determination. It is thus necessary to go beyond being, and it is this that is of the greatest significance. That is why in all true metaphysical conceptions it is necessary to take into account the inexpressible: Just as everything that can be expressed is literally nothing in comparison with that which surpasses expression, so the finite, whatever its magnitude, is nothing when faced with the infinite. One can hint at much more than can be expressed, and this is the part played by exterior forms. All forms, whether it is a matter of words or symbols, act only as a support, a fulcrum for rising to possibilities of conception that far outstrip them; we will return to this later.

We speak of metaphysical conceptions for lack of any other term whereby to make ourselves understood, but it is not to be concluded from this that there is here something comparable to scientific or philosophic conceptions; it is not a question of any "abstractions," but of attaining an intuitive and immediate suprarational knowledge. This pure intellectual intuition, without which there is no true metaphysics, has, moreover, no connection with the intuition spoken of by certain contemporary philosophers, which is, on the contrary, infrarational. There is an intellectual intuition and a sensible intuition; one lies beyond reason, but the other is situated on its hither side; the latter can know only the world of changing and becoming, that is to say, nature, or rather, an inferior part of nature. The domain of intuition, on the contrary, is the province of eternal and immutable principles; it is the realm of metaphysics.

To comprehend universal principles directly, the transcendent intellect must itself be of the universal order; it is no longer an individual faculty, and to consider it as such would be contradictory, as it is not within the power of the individual to go beyond his own limits and leave the conditions that limit him qua individual. Reason is a specifically human faculty, but that which lies beyond reason is truly "nonhuman"; it is this that makes metaphysical knowledge possible, and that knowledge, one must again emphasize, is not a human knowledge. In other words, it is not as man that man can attain it, but because this being that is human in one of its aspects is at the same time something other and more than a human being. It is the attainment of effective consciousness of supraindividual states that is the real object of metaphysics, or better still, of metaphysical knowledge itself. We come here to one of the most vital points, and it is necessary to repeat that if the individual were a complete being, if he made up a closed system like the monad of Leibnitz, metaphysics would not be possible; irremediably confined in himself, this being would have no means of knowing anything outside his own mode of existence. But such is not the case; in reality the individuality represents nothing more than a transitory and contingent manifestation of the real being. It is only one particular state among an indefinite multitude of other states of the same being; and this being is, in itself, absolutely independent of all its manifestations, just as, to use an illustration that occurs frequently in Hindu texts, the sun is absolutely independent of the manifold images in which it is reflected. Such is the fundamental distinction between "self" and "I," the personality and the individuality; as the images are connected by the luminous rays with their solar source, without which they would have neither existence nor reality, so the individuality, either of the human individual or of any other similar state of manifestation, is bound by the personality to the principial center of being by this transcendent intellect of which we are speaking. It is impossible, within the limits of this exposition, to develop these lines of thought more completely or to give a more exact idea of the theory of multiple states of being, but I think I have said enough to show the extreme importance of all truly metaphysical doctrine.

I said "theory," but here it is not a question of theory alone; this is a point that needs further explanation. Theoretical knowledge, which is only indirect and in some sense symbolic, is merely a preparation, though indispensable, for true knowledge. It is, moreover, the only knowledge that is communicable, even then only in a partial sense. That is why all statements are no more than a means of approaching knowledge, and this knowledge, which is in the first place only virtual, must later be effectively realized. Here we find another discrepancy in the more limited metaphysics to which we referred earlier, for example that of Aristotle. This remains theoretically inadequate in that it limits itself to being, and its theory seems to be presented as self-sufficient instead of being expressly bound up with a corresponding realization, as is the case in all Oriental doctrines. However, even in this imperfect metaphysics (we might be tempted to say this demi-metaphysics), sometimes statements are encountered that, if properly understood, would lead to totally different conclusions; thus, did not Aristotle specifically state that a being is all that it knows? This affirmation of identification through knowledge is the same in principle as metaphysical realization. But here the principle remains isolated; it has no value other than that of a merely theoretical statement, it carries no weight, and it seems that, having propounded it, one thinks no more about it. How was it that Aristotle himself and his followers failed to see all that here was implied? It is the same in many other cases, where apparently other equally essential things are forgotten, such as the distinction between pure intellect and reason, even after having defined them quite explicitly; these are strange omissions. Should one see in this the effect of certain limitations inherent in the Occidental mind, apart from some rare but always possible exceptions? This might be true in a certain measure; nevertheless, it is not necessary to believe that Western intellectuality has always been as narrowly limited as it is in the present age. But after all, we have been speaking only of outward doctrines, though these are certainly superior to many others since, in spite of all, they comprise a part of the true metaphysics. For our part we are certain that there has been something other than this in the West during the Middle Ages and in olden times; there certainly have existed among an elite purely metaphysical doctrines that could be called complete, including their realization, a thing that for most moderns is barely conceivable. If the West has lost the memory of this completely, it is because it has broken with its proper tradition, which explains why modern civilization is abnormal and deviationist.

If purely theoretical knowledge were an end in itself and if metaphysics went no further, it would still assuredly be worth something, but yet it would be altogether insufficient. In spite of conferring the genuine certainty, even greater than mathematical certainty, that belongs to such knowledge, it would yet remain, though in an incomparably superior order, analogous to that which, at an inferior level, constitutes terrestrial and human, scientific and philosophical, speculation. That is not what metaphysics is meant for; if others choose to interest themselves in a "mental sport" or suchlike, that is their affair; these things leave us cold, and moreover we think that the curiosities of psychology should be completely indifferent to the metaphysician. What he is concerned with is to know what is, and to know it in such fashion as to be oneself, truly and effectively, what one knows.

As for the means of metaphysical realization, we are well aware of such objections as can be made by those who find it necessary to challenge its possibility. These means, indeed, must be within man's reach; they must, in the first stages at least, be adapted to the human state, since it is in this state that the being now exists that subsequently will assume the higher states. Thus it is in these formal means, appropriate to this world as presently manifested, that the being finds a fulcrum for raising itself beyond this world. Words, symbolism, signs, rites, or preparatory methods of any sort have no other reason for existence and no other function; as we have already said, they are supports and nothing else. But some will ask, how is it possible that merely contingent means can produce an effect that immeasurably surpasses them and that is of a totally different order from that to which the instruments themselves belong? We should first point out that these means are, in reality, only fortuitous. The results they help to attain are by no means consequential. They place the being in the position requisite for attainment, and that is all. If the above-mentioned objections were valid in this case, they would be equally so for religious rites, for the sacraments, for example, where the disproportion between the means and the end is no less; some of those who have raised the above objections might have thought of this too. As for us, we do not confuse a simple means with a cause in the true sense of the word, and we do not regard metaphysical realization as an effect, since it is not the production of something that does not yet exist, but the knowing of that which is, in an abiding and immutable manner, beyond all temporal succession, for all states of the being, considered under their primary aspect, abide in perfect simultaneousness in the eternal now.

Thus we see no difficulty in recognizing that there is nothing in common between metaphysical realization and the means leading to it or, if preferred, that prepare us for it. This is why, moreover, no means are strictly or absolutely necessary; or at least there is only one indispensable preparation, and that is theoretical knowledge. This, on the other hand, cannot go far without a means that will play the most important and constant part: This means is concentration. This is something completely foreign to the mental habits of the modern West, where everything tends toward dispersion and incessant change. All other means are only secondary in comparison; they serve above all to promote concentration and to harmonize the diverse elements of human individuality in order to facilitate effective communication between this individuality and the higher states of being.

Moreover, at the start, these means can be varied almost indefinitely, for they have to be adapted to the temperament of each individual and to his particular aptitudes and disposition. Later on the differences diminish, for it is a case of many ways that all lead to the same end; after reaching a certain stage all multiplicity vanishes, but by that time the contingent and individual means will have played their part. This part, which it is unnecessary to enlarge upon, is compared, in certain

Hindu writings, to a horse that helps a man to reach the end of his journey more quickly and easily, but without which he would still have been able to arrive. Rites and various methods point the way to metaphysical realization, but one could nevertheless ignore them and by unswervingly setting the mind and all powers of the being to the aim of this realization could finally attain the supreme goal; but if there are means that make the effort less laborious, why choose to neglect them? Is it confusing the contingent with the absolute to take into account the limitations of our human state, since it is from this state, itself contingent, that we are at present compelled to start in order to attain higher states and finally the supreme and unconditioned state?

After considering the teachings common to all traditional doctrines, we must now turn to the principal stages of metaphysical realization. The first is only preliminary and operates in the human domain and does not go beyond the limits of the individuality. It consists of an indefinite extension of this individuality of which the corporeal modality, which is all that is developed in the ordinary man, represents the smallest portion; it is from this corporeal modality that it is necessary to start by means borrowed from the sensible order, but which, however, must have repercussions in the other modalities of the human being. The phase in question is, in short, the realization or development of all the potentialities that are contained in the human individuality and that, comprising, as they do, manifold extensions, reach out in diverse directions beyond the realm of the corporeal and sensible; and it is by these extensions that it is possible to establish communication with the other states.

This realization of the integral individuality is described by all traditions as the restoration of what is called the primordial state, which is regarded as man's true estate and which moreover escapes some of the limitations characteristic of the ordinary state, notably that of the temporal condition. The person who attains this "primordial state" is still only a human individual and is without effective possession of any supraindividual states; he is nevertheless freed from time, and the apparent succession of things is transformed for him into simultaneity; he consciously possesses a faculty that is unknown to the ordinary man and that one might call the sense of eternity. This is of extreme importance, for he who is unable to leave the viewpoint of temporal succession and see everything in simultaneity is incapable of the least conception of the metaphysical order. The first thing to be done by those who wish to achieve true metaphysical understanding is to take up a position outside time, we say deliberately in "nontime," if such an expression does not seem too peculiar and unusual. This knowledge of the intemporal can, moreover, be achieved in some real measure, if incompletely, before having fully attained this "primordial state" that we are considering.

It might be asked, Why this appellation of "primordial state"? It is because all traditions, including that of the West (for the Bible says nothing different), are in agreement in teaching that this state was originally normal for humanity, whereas the present state is merely the result of a fall, the effect of a progressive materialization that has occurred in the course of the ages and throughout the duration of a particular cycle. We do not believe in "evolution" in the sense that the moderns give the word. The so-called scientific hypotheses just mentioned in no way correspond to reality. It is not possible here to make more than a bare allusion to the theory of cosmic cycles, which is particularly expounded in the Hindu doctrines; this would be going beyond our subject, for cosmology is not metaphysics, even though the two are closely related. It is no more than an application of metaphysics to the physical order, while the true natural laws are only the consequences, in a relative and contingent domain, of universal and necessary principles.

To revert to metaphysical realization: Its second phase corresponds to supraindividual but still conditioned states, though their conditions are quite different from those of the human state. Here, the world of man, previously mentioned, is completely and definitely exceeded. It must also be said that that which is exceeded is the world of forms in its widest meaning, comprising all possible individual states, for form is the common denominator of all these states; it is that which determines individuality as such. The being, which can no longer be called human, has henceforth left the "flow of forms," to use a Far Eastern expression. There are, moreover, further distinctions to be made, for this phase can be subdivided. In reality it includes several stages, from the achievement of states that though informal still appertain to manifested existence, up to that degree of universality that is pure being.

Nevertheless, however exalted these states may be when compared with the human state, however remote they are from it, they are still only relative, and that is just as true of the highest of them, which corresponds to the principle of all manifestation. Their possession is only a transitory result, which should not be confused with the final goal of metaphysical realization; this end remains outside being, and by comparison with it everything else is only a preparatory step. The highest objective is the absolutely unconditioned state, free from all limitation; for this reason it is completely inexpressible, and all that one can say of it must be conveyed in negative terms by divestment of the limits that determine and define all existence in its relativity. The attainment of this state is what the Hindu doctrine calls deliverance when considered in connection with the Supreme Principle.

In this unconditioned state all other states of being find their place, but they are transformed and released from the special conditions that determined them as particular states. What remains is that which has a positive reality, since herein it is that all things have their own principle; the "delivered" being is truly in possession of the fullness of its own potentialities. The only things that have disappeared are the limiting conditions, which are negative, since they represent no more than a "privation" in the Aristotelian sense. Also, far from being a kind of annihilation, as some Westerners believe, this final state is, on the contrary, absolute plenitude, the supreme reality in the face of which all else remains illusion.

Let us add once more that every result, even partial, obtained by the being in the course of metaphysical realization is truly its own. This result constitutes a permanent acquisition for the being, of which nothing can deprive it; the work accomplished in this way, even if interrupted before it is completed, is achieved once and for all, since it is beyond time. This is true even of merely theoretical knowledge, for all knowledge carries its benefit in itself, contrary to action, which is only a momentary modification of a being and is always separated from its various effects. These effects belong to the same domain and order of existence as that which has produced them. Action cannot have the effect of liberating from action, and its consequences cannot reach beyond the limits of individuality considered in its fullest possible extension. Action, whatever it may be, is not opposed to, and cannot banish, ignorance, which is the root of all limitation; only knowledge can dispel ignorance as the light of the sun disperses darkness, and it is thus that the "self," the immutable and eternal principle of all manifest and unmanifest states, appears in its supreme reality.

After this brief and very imperfect outline, which can give only the merest idea of metaphysical realization, it is absolutely essential to stress one point in order to avoid grave errors of interpretation: All with which we are here concerned has no connection whatever with phenomena of any sort, however extraordinary. All phenomena are of the physical order; metaphysics is beyond the phenomenal, even if we use the word in its widest sense. It follows from this, among other inferences, that the states to which we are referring are in no way "psychological"; this must be specifically stated, since strange confusions sometimes arise in this connection. By definition psychology can only be concerned with human states, and further, what it stands for today is only a very limited part of the potentialities of the individual, who includes far more than specialists in this science are able to imagine. The human individual is, at one and the same time, much more and much less than is ordinarily supposed in the West. He is greater by reason of his possibilities of indefinite extension beyond the corporeal modality, in short, of all that refers to what we have been studying; but he is also much less, since, far from constituting a complete and sufficient being in himself, he is only an exterior manifestation, a fleeting appearance clothing the true being, which in no way affects the essence of the latter in its immutability.

It is necessary to insist on this point, that the metaphysical domain lies entirely outside the phenomenal world, for the moderns hardly ever know or investigate anything other than phenomena; it is with these that they are almost exclusively concerned, as is demonstrated by the attention they have given to the experimental sciences. Their metaphysical ineptitude arises from the same tendency. Undoubtedly some phenomena may occur during the work for metaphysical realization, but in a quite accidental manner. They can also have unfortunate consequences, as things of this nature are only an obstacle for those who are tempted to attach importance to them. Those who are halted or turned aside by phenomena, and above all those who indulge in search for extraordinary "powers," have very little chance of pressing on to a realization beyond the point already arrived at before this deviation occurred.

This observation leads naturally to the rectification of some erroneous interpretations on the subject of the term "yoga." Has it not been claimed that what the Hindus mean by this word is the development of certain powers latent in the human being? What we are about to say will suffice to show that such a definition should be rejected. In reality the word "yoga" is the same as that which we have translated as literally as possible by the word "union" and which, correctly defined, thus means the supreme goal of metaphysical realization; the "yogi," in the strictest sense of the term, is solely the man who attains this end. However, it is true that in a wider sense the same terms, in some cases, may be applied to stages preparatory to "union" or even to simple preliminary means, as well as to the being who has reached states corresponding to those stages that these means are employed in order to attain. But how can it be supposed that a word primarily meaning "union" applies correctly and originally to breathing exercises or other things of that sort? These and other exercises, usually based on what we might call the science of rhythm, admittedly figure among the most usual means for the promoting of realization; but one must not mistake for the end that which amounts to no more than contingent and accidental aids, nor must one confuse the original meaning of a word with a secondary acceptation that is more or less distorted.

Referring to the original "yoga," and while declaring that it has always meant essentially the same thing, one must not forget to put a question of which we have as yet made no mention. What is the origin of these traditional metaphysical doctrines from which we have borrowed all our fundamental ideas? The answer is very simple, although it risks raising objections from those who would look at everything from a historical viewpoint: It is that there is no origin, by which we mean no human origin subjected to determination in time. In other words, the origin of tradition, if indeed the word "origin" has any applicability in such a case, is "nonhuman," as is metaphysics itself. Doctrines of this order have not appeared at any particular moment in the history of humanity; the allusion we have made to the "primordial state," and also what we have said of the nontemporal nature of all that is metaphysical, enables one to grasp this point without too much difficulty, on condition that it be admitted, contrary to certain prejudices, that there are some things to which the historical point of view is not applicable. Metaphysical truth is eternal; even so, there have always existed beings who could truly and completely know. All that changes is only exterior forms and contingent means; and the change has nothing to do with what people today call evolution. It is only a simple adaptation of such and such particular circumstances to special conditions of some given race or epoch. From this results the multiplicity of forms; but the basis of the doctrine is no more modified and affected than the essential unity and identity of the being is altered by the multiplicity of its states of manifestation.

Metaphysical knowledge, as well as the realization that will turn it into all that it truly ought to be, is thus possible everywhere and always, at least in principle and when regarded in a quasi-absolute sense; but in fact and in a relative sense, can it be said that this is equally possible in any sphere and without making the least allowance for contingencies? On this score we shall be much less positive, at least as far as realization is concerned; this is explained by the fact that in its beginning such a realization must take its support from the realm of contingencies. Conditions in the modern West are particularly unfavorable, so much so that such a work is almost impossible and can even be dangerous in the absence of any help from the environment and in conditions that can only impede or destroy the efforts of one who undertakes such a task. On the other hand, those civilizations that we call traditional are organized in such a way that one can find effectual aid, though this is not absolutely necessary, any more than anything else of an external kind; nevertheless without such help it is difficult to obtain effective results. Here is something that exceeds the strength of an isolated human individual, even if that individual possesses the requisite qualifications in other respects; also we do not want to encourage anyone, in present conditions, to embark thoughtlessly upon such an enterprise, and this brings us to our conclusion.

For us, the outstanding difference between the East and West (which means in this case the modern West), the only difference that is really essential (for all others are derivative), is on the one side the preservation of tradition, with all that this implies, and on the other side the forgetting and loss of this same tradition; on one side the maintaining of metaphysical knowledge, on the other, complete ignorance of all connected with this realm. Between civilizations that open to their elite the possibilities of which we have caught a glimpse and offer the most appropriate means for their effective realization (thus allowing of their full realization by some at least)—between those traditional civilizations and a civilization that has developed along purely material lines, what common measure can be found? And how, without being blinded by I know not what prejudices, dare one claim that material superiority compensates for intellectual inferiority? When we say intellectual, we mean the true intellectuality, that which is restricted by neither limitations of the human nor the natural order and which makes pure metaphysical knowledge possible in its absolute transcendence. It seems to me that only a moment's reflection on these questions leaves no doubt or hesitation as to the answer that should be given.

The material prosperity of the West is incontrovertible; nobody denies it, but it is hardly a cause for envy. Indeed one can go further; sooner or later this excessive material development threatens to destroy the West if it does not recover itself in time and if it does not consider seriously a "return to the source," using an expression that is employed in certain Islamic esoteric schools. Today one hears from many quarters of the "defense of the West," but unfortunately it does not seem to be understood that it is against itself that the West needs to be defended and that it is its own present tendencies that are the chief and most formidable of all the dangers that really threaten it. It would be as well to meditate deeply on this; one cannot urge this too strongly on all who are still capable of reflection. So it is with this that I will end my account; I have done my best to make it, if not fully comprehensible, at least suggestive of that Oriental intellectuality that no longer has any equivalent in the West. This has been a sketch, even if imperfect, of the true metaphysics, of that knowledge that, according to the sacred works of India, is alone completely true, absolute, infinite, and supreme.

The Catholic Church in Crisis

Thinking around *The Vatican Oracle,* by the Reverend Brocard Sewell

BY MARCO PALLIS

In THIS BOOK is to be found a genuine attempt, on the part of a sincere and sensitive Catholic, to come to grips with the causes that have provoked the present crisis in his church and that might, as he does not shrink from admitting, result in the irretrievable fragmentation of what, not so long ago, seemed like a crackless monolith, all too easily confused by the complacent with that Rock against which the Gates of Hell never could prevail. Now the visible signs are otherwise, and the consequent revulsion from a false sense of security has not rendered their task easier for those, in the church, who wish to arrive at an impartial diagnosis of the disease from which it is suffering, such as must needs precede any consideration of possible remedial action. The present book's chief purpose is to provide material for such a diagnosis, and in this respect one can say from the outset that even those who do not share all the author's views on particular points will still find here much to help them think clearly, and this, in itself, is a useful service to have rendered at the present juncture.

Though the operative factors behind the present crisis can in large measure be defined in terms of their historical antecedents—the book is rich in apposite historical data—it must also be recognized that in a more far-reaching sense, it is an intellectual crisis that Western Christians are now having to face, one affecting the nature of proof in the context of faith and, parallel with this, the nature and scope of the traditional authority both in itself and, more particularly, as vested in the person and function of the Roman Pontiff. In the author's opinion, considerably distorted views of what the "Petrine

primacy" implies have prevailed in the Western church since
relatively early times, though with more oscillations of emphasis than is commonly supposed by the historically uninformed.
Nor does the author consider the attempt of the first Vatican
Council of 1870 to impart a watertight definition to the idea
of *"infallibility"* (itself a not very happily chosen term) to have
resulted in anything but added embarrassment for those for
whom the Pope's specific functions in the church needed to be
presented, not merely as a matter of personal loyalty, but also
as something objectively intelligible within the general framework of Christian tradition: Hankering after a foolproof
criterion that will automatically show the degree of authorita-
tiveness attaching to any particular papal pronouncement at
a given time is not an intelligent attitude to take up in regard
to the providential action of the spirit whereby the church's
teachings are kept in the line of truth and away from error. The
quality of infallibility does indeed pertain to tradition in the
deepest sense, and this quality can also be attributed legiti-
mately to the organs of tradition, but only on condition that
a *mechanical* character be not read into this attribution, as the
Roman juridicism has too often tended to do.

In fact, the view the author takes both of the original promise
given by Jesus Christ to Saint Peter and of its ulterior implications as affecting the Apostle's successors in the see of Rome
approximates very closely to the interpretation the Eastern
Orthodox Church has given to this particular sacred charge.
From this standpoint the enactments of two councils ranked
as "ecumenical" by universal consent, namely those of Constantinople in A.D. 381 and Chalcedon in 451 by which the status
of the various patriarchal sees was canonically defined, do not
need adding to, and this definition applies also to Rome, whose
traditional primacy is not being called in question, but only an
overloaded interpretation of that same primacy.

Throughout his book, Father Brocard Sewell expresses the
view that in most, if not all, of the matters at issue between the
Latin and the Eastern churches it was the latter who took the
sane view of the Roman see's traditional privileges (but also of
their limits) and the Westerners who were the innovators in

straining the Roman primacy into meaning far more than that word actually implies. This does not mean that the author rejects the papal claims in toto, as the Protestant Reformers did subsequently—in his view, the Pope does have a special part to play which the word "primacy" appropriately expresses; he would gladly see Rome relieved of some obsessive historical encumbrances, but not deprived of that which belongs to her traditionally.

Here some may ask: Why is it that Father Sewell, having come round to a position hardly differing from that of the Orthodox East, does not simply adhere to the Orthodox Church, as a number of Catholic priests have done in our time, and carry on from there? Why hang on to the vestiges of an allegiance that, by comparison with the conventional Latin view, has worn very thin? Those who argue thus have misunderstood Father Sewell's own position, and a closer examination of the present book would explain why. For Father Sewell, the *integral* Christian tradition is now, and has never ceased to be, represented by the Latin and the Eastern churches inseparably, and it is there that the ultimate Christian allegiance is due. In a more local sense he remains firmly a Western Christian; to label himself an "Easterner" would amount to a denial of the integral church now as much as a one-sidedly Latin view would have done in the past. In the mind of the author there is never a question of a de jure schism having taken place, but of a series of historical bickerings that have gradually hardened into a de facto state of separation leaving the seamless garment of Christ nevertheless unparted for those "who have eyes to see" beyond the surface of events.

The author is not the first to have pointed out that the mutual excommunications pronounced by the papal legate and the Byzantine Patriarch in 1054 never engaged the totality of the faithful on either side, for whom the quarrels in high places (no new thing in the Christian world) did not affect their own participation in the full sacramental life of an unbroken church. It was the scandalous sack of Constantinople in 1204 by the professed crusaders, cleverly egged on by the Venetians from commercial and expansionist motives, that more than any other single event rendered an East-West reconciliation virtually impossible, thus creating in Christendom that appearance of permanent rift we have all grown up with. Despite appearances the church has remained *one in principle*—Father Brocard Sewell insists on this; one is not justified in speaking of "two churches." From which it follows that, thanks to the canceling out of the 1054 censures by Pope Paul VI and the Ecumenical Patriarch Athenagoras at their meeting in 1967, this principle of unbroken unity takes on, despite past happenings, a renewed and effective importance which, as the author eloquently pleads in his concluding chapter, may well prove to be the key to Christian renewal in the face of a militant materialism that threatens all religions alike in their very existence. It is here that the author would have his fellow Christians place their hopes, banishing from their minds any thought that this means a surrender of West to East or vice versa; to take cognizance of a reality can never be anything but a victory for the spirit and for those who submit to its guidance.

If his reviewer has not misinterpreted his thoughts, the above sums up the author's focal thesis, on which this book ultimately stands or falls.

Besides its several well-documented chapters dealing directly with the question of authority and its exercise in the Roman Church formerly and lately, *The Vatican Oracle* also contains two important sections devoted to the Christian ministry and to monasticism as providing a formal framework for the contemplative life, though without claiming to hold a monopoly of the latter. In two final chapters the author resumes his central theme of the reciprocal need for both East and West to share in any regenerative effort in the church such as might give grounds for genuine hope; it is this twofold contribution, so he argues, that would again after centuries of one-sided development allow one to speak of a "Catholic" consensus in the full and unqualified sense of the word. There are some in the West, and doubtless also in the East, who will jib at such a statement; but even so, I think the objectors would stand to gain by a careful study of Father Sewell's arguments even if this led them to a different opinion as to the best way to deal with the Christian crisis and its consequences. I have even heard a fear expressed by some that a too close rapprochement with the West at the present juncture might only have the result of infecting the East itself with disorders it had escaped hitherto; but can it hope to escape them much longer by merely keeping aloof? The pull of the modern secularist civilization is all in the direction of a diluting of the Christian message, as a prelude to its eventual abolition. On all sides one finds the same antitraditional, antimetaphysical, anticontemplative bias gaining a hold over the minds of men; the Christian East is not without some troubles of its own, as Father Sewell observes with good reason. If these troubles (political pressures apart) are not yet as acute as those of the Western church, this is cause for thankfulness but certainly not for self-complacency, since the same disintegrative tendencies are threatening all alike, and none can say that they will not gather sudden momentum in places that previously had seemed relatively immune. The only effective means of defense is a keen and vigilant sense of intellectual discrimination of a kind not commonly to be found in either East or West; to exercise this virtue consciously at all times is certainly the best preparation for the more testing days that lie ahead.

Here it will not be inopportune to point out that, by comparison with the Roman Catholic Church, Eastern Orthodoxy has remained not less, but far more conservative in respect of its doctrinal and institutional expressions, a fact that goes with less "activist" attitudes generally; it is the juridical and rationalistic bent of the Roman mentality that has given to Western Christianity its rather cut-and-dried authoritarianism on the one hand and, on the other, a certain restlessness that breaks out from time to time in the form of uncalled-for innovations. In Orthodox parlance "innovation" *(neoterismos)* is always a term of reproach; not the least of the accusations leveled at the Latins during the period of mounting East-West tension was their proneness to innovate, whereof the famous *filioque* clause interpolated in the text of the Nicene Creed—the Orientals say the "Symbol" of Nicaea—provides a typical example. Apart from any question of whether or not the added words could be explained in a manner that would be doctrinally acceptable, it was the mere fact of imposing an *innovation* on the prototype of all Christian dogma that most gravely offended the feelings of the Easterners; in their eyes the innovating impulse carried with it a latent inclination in the direction of error which rendered it condemnable. The personal intentions of those who presume to tamper with time-hallowed traditional forms remain secondary to the offense of innovation in itself—in Orthodox countries such is still the popular mood in all such cases.

It must, however, be admitted that in quite recent years certain innovating tendencies have begun to be discernible also in the Orthodox world, notably among the Greeks (less so among the Russians), though few are prepared to admit the fact because the bias of popular feeling still runs so strongly the other way. Nowhere is this feeling more apparent than in the sphere of liturgy where the splendid archaism of the Byzantine liturgical forms is especially valued as a perpetually renewed token of traditional continuity and therefore also as a powerful safeguard for the faith. Changes of the kind that are now playing havoc with the Roman Mass would be unthinkable in an Eastern setting; to suggest such a thing would be to court a popular uprising—which all goes to prove that there is such a thing as a healthy conservatism, one that is perfectly reconcilable with traditional adaptation wherever such is really called for. The ease with which the changes in the Mass have been imposed in the West is not a healthy sign, for it indicates a passivity versus innovation that can only go with a weakening of the traditional instinct at all levels within the church.

It almost passes belief that the shapers of church policy should have chosen this most critical moment in its history in order to scrap what was probably the greatest single asset of coherence in the Catholic world, namely the familiar form and language of the Mass, thus compromising all the feelings and habits that centuries of worship and prayer had built up around its celebration. When one thinks of all the immense advantages inherent in the fact that any Catholic attending any church of the Latin rite in any country throughout the world was immediately made to feel at home without the least need for adjustment, one simply cannot imagine what went on in the minds of those who pushed through these gratuitous innovations—here the Orthodox term applies with literal force. What they seemed intent on ignoring was the fact that a liturgical language, hallowed by tradition, has a stable *resonance* to which the souls of the faithful become attuned; *lex orandi* is something that cannot be disturbed without serious risk that *lex credendi* will also be detrimentally affected, so delicate is the balance of factors making up a life of piety. In his appendix on the liturgy Father Sewell has assembled a number of telling quotations illustrating this point, to which I should like to add an example drawn from recent experience.

Not long ago while wandering in the Alps I happened to talk with a peasant woman who was a member of the choir of her parish church in one of the high-lying villages. I asked her which she preferred, the old Latin or the new French words. She answered without sign of emotion but also without hesitation, "Why, I like the Latin better. You see it has something about it one misses with the French." What this shows is that ordinary people of simple but deep piety keep a sense of the *numinous* which "experts" called in to sit on papal commissions have long since outgrown. The Orthodox, provided they go to church at all, nearly always have this sense, and this is one of the secrets of their steadfastness in worship. But after all, it is not the common Catholic people who asked for these changes, which were wished onto them by sophisticated minds anxious above all to appear "progressive" and "democratic" in the bourgeois sense of these senseless words; their obsessive stressing of the *collective* aspect of things in opposition to the essential *solitude* of life in the spirit well shows whose favor they were out to buy. The most pathetic illusion of these innovators is their belief that by this means they will attract back the young and arrest the flight from religion. What they fail to see is that whatever has the effect of further weakening the traditional instinct can only accelerate that flight. The only way to attract people to any cause, especially young people, is to make great demands of them, thus showing that one values their aspira-

tions at a high price. No one was ever won over by playing
down to his or her weaknesses; to play down to people is always
instinctively sensed by them as a sign of disrespect, and this,
where religion is concerned, can only increase their alienation.

It is worth pausing to scrutinize the kind of arguments put
forth by those who wish to justify their new-fangled arrangements regarding church worship, in which a supposedly collective interest is invoked as the one and only consideration of
importance; this point has already been mentioned once.
Roughly speaking, these arguments amount to this: For centuries the minister officiating at Mass has been a man set apart,
offering (so they say) a solitary sacrifice to which his congregation remained largely passive, and much the same applied to
the parish priest when exercising his other functions. Now this
separative trend has to be reversed; the celebrant must address
himself first and last to his hearers, as cocelebrants. Whatever
might suggest a hierarchical superiority as attaching to his
person must be played down to a minimum. Likewise people
must be got to abstain from various old-established gestures
now considered "outmoded." This applies especially to such
gestures as symbolically imply an attitude of awe: fear of God
is "out"; kneeling to receive the Sacrament betokens an attitude
of servility that may perhaps have suited our rather naïve
forefathers but hardly becomes the "adult" men and women
of the Space Age. A Christianity in process of being "demythologized" cannot stomach these things any longer; it is not
"wonder" we want from our people, but a feeling of brother-
hood toward other men through which alone the Christ-like
ideal may be realized . . . and so on ad nauseam. Most of this
may sound like nonsense, but such is the fashionable thinking
of the moment, and few dare to hold out against it.

The tendentious sentimentality attaching to this way of
thinking is not the end of the matter, however, since the data
that provide its point of departure are themselves highly con-
testable. This indiscriminate attribution of a culpable passivity
to the congregations of the past simply is not true; neither
historically nor psychologically does it agree with the elementary facts of human experience.

To take first a feature of the Mass that is often cited because of its ulterior implications, namely the position of the priest in relation to the people, whether with his back mostly turned, as used to be the case, or else facing, as imposed under the latest arrangements. If the altar, symbolically speaking, is the seat of the Divine, then the priest facing toward the altar was deemed to be speaking and acting on behalf of his people while leading them toward God. Obviously to face toward them is also a possible attitude giving rise to a different symbolism—precedent for this is not in question. What however is totally false is the argument that would make the position facing toward the people one of greater communication than the other; the motives invoked in favor of such a belief are demagogic, not symbolical.

And secondly, concerning the alleged passivity of the congregation under the old arrangements: Does silent prayer or meditation, does simple repose in one's own being while in the presence of God (how few of us accomplish this much!), indicate a passive attitude? Silent prayer is in fact the most active of all acts for the Christian, unless it be silent worship. Though there obviously can be no objection to people joining in certain responses (e.g., those at the start of the Canon of the Mass, which go back to earliest times) or to their singing the Creed (to its plainchant tune) or to any other such acts of sonorous adoration, it must be made clear that those who choose so to join in the service are not participating more closely than those of their neighbors who prefer to witness the Mysteries silently and on their knees in intimate communion. If anything, it is these who will be the more active participants.

But surely, some will object, there must often have been people whose silence was merely a cloak for inattention; they came to church out of convention, because this was the rule, but far from praying, they simply let their minds wander among worldly thoughts. All this is a truism; inattention is an all too common human failing. No one can say, however, that such inattention is commoner at Catholic (or Orthodox) services than at Protestant ones, where the element of vocal participation is at its maximum; the latter factor is irrelevant to the argument. The essential point is: God's grace is ever present, but *we* are absent. Here is the whole religious problem of mankind, and all the expedients, public or private, recommended by the saints or by the church in her ordinary teachings have it as their aim to foster attention and, if possible, to render it unceasing.

The experience of the Orthodox Church can here provide a particularly convincing testimony, and all the more so since the author himself has shown such keen appreciation of Eastern attitudes and practice in many other connections.

In churches of the Eastern rite congregational services of the kind familiar in the West are practically unknown; participation is "passive" as far as joining in responses, hymn-singing, etc., are concerned. Yet no one who has attended an Orthodox liturgy can for a moment remain in doubt as regards the high average of participation on the part of the people. Admittedly occasional inattention and chatter is to be met with in Greek churches at times (never in Russian), but by and large the congregations share in the liturgy with evident delight, and this is true even of quite small children. Since in most Orthodox churches there are no seats, excepting a few for aged or sick persons, members of the congregation are free to move about as they please, kissing the ikons or lighting candles before them, frequently crossing themselves, and, in Russian churches, making prostration when so minded. Otherwise everybody stands. Services tend to be long; no one asks for shortened versions of the type prevalent in the West, where the purpose in view is to meet the needs of those who wish to hear Mass on days other than Sunday. In the East the full-length liturgy remains the focus of Christian life by universal consent, and I think it is not going too far to say that participation in it is active in a way that the West would have found it hard to match since some years. Those who felt that the Latin Mass had come to lack something might usefully have studied what happens in Russian churches before embarking on their ill-judged reforms, since this might have given them ideas as to what a genuine liturgical reform might consist of and how it might be promoted. Without copying the Russian model directly (which would be senseless, as the Latin rite is all it should be as regards both form and content), there was still something to be learned concerning the *manner* of conducting the liturgy so as to leave room for spontaneity while preserving order—to reconcile these two interests sums up the liturgical art.

There is no doubt that a Russian liturgy provides the perfect type of Christian participation in the double sense of discipline and freedom—freedom that is spontaneously disciplined and discipline that is free from too set controls. If this applies to the congregation, it also applies to the celebrants; this all comes so naturally to them that it seems as if a Russian priest or acolyte could never put a foot wrong in this respect. In great Latin churches one has often attended impressive services, where the homely disorder to be found elsewhere was noticeably absent—too noticeably perhaps, since performance sometimes has been a little too reminiscent of company drill at Wellington Barracks; this is not said in scorn, but because one feels that here Russians have something precious to teach the West. It is their particular glory to have achieved the perfection of Christian worship: Who then can say that multiplication of set responses, etc., is necessary for an active participation in the Mass? Here are all the signs of sharing, of uninhibited joy in what is going on, of a unanimous recollection associating old and young, men and women, ministers and people. In a sense the Russians can be called the most Christian of Christians today; if in their home country the church has had to pass through the fire, that is where a Christian revival, should it occur, might be expected to start.

However, this matter of the relationship between priest and people raises a question of principle that does not stop short at church services. Nowadays it is far too readily assumed that a position of hierarchical superiority recognized as attaching to a function (i.e., the priestly function) and expressed by various outward signs such as a special dress constitutes a barrier hindering communication in either direction. This is really the crux of the innovators' argument as outlined above. Individual defects apart, does this assumption rest on any solid grounds in logic or experience?

The answer is that hierarchical differences—differences of "caste," as a Hindu might say—provided they be intelligible and not arbitrary ones, can help to promote communication, not the opposite. Particular respect on the one side answers to pastoral care on the other; neither of these attitudes runs counter to love, and still less to truth. It is in fact the existence of such hierarchical distinctions together with their implications that makes it possible for individually imperfect men to exercise functions for which, by definition as one might say, "fallen" man as such is unworthy. This is the characteristic position in any traditional community such as the Catholic Church. It is only a weakening of the traditional bond that causes people to value the relation of priest and parishioners, or any analogous relationship, no longer in terms of respective vocations implying different attitudes to and fro, but in a merely individual sense, according to which Father O'Leary is a man of limited capacity and his people have now found this out and won't accept his authority any longer. Once this state is reached, everything becomes a matter of likes and dislikes and mostly the latter. A man of very modest powers invested with a traditional status can offer much to his hearers, many of whom may be his intellectual superiors. A man who is both personally gifted and learned but lacks the traditional aura will too easily be written off even by those whose intelligence is far below his own.

Speaking for myself, I very much doubt if an average decent rector in a Catholic parish, or an Anglican parish for that matter, has in the past been anything like as cut off from his people as the new thinkers affect to believe. It is in the nature of things that extreme types should be rare: Both saintly souls and villains are to be found in the ranks of the clergy, but a relative mediocrity is bound to prevail here as in every other profession. To exercise so exalted an office, the aid of tradition is indispensable; it is his voicing of a traditional (i.e., objective) element that makes acceptable the vicar's humble attempts at preaching the Word, for eloquence as such is a subjective talent granted only to the few, and it would be unrealistic to expect things to be otherwise. These are points that the author seems to have overlooked when discussing the question of sermons in church, past or present; the criteria he applies take an individualistic turn for the most part. He says it is hard to understand the fact that many recorded medieval sermons read boringly yet evidently appealed to audiences of the time. One can only repeat: Insofar as those old preachers made themselves mouthpieces of tradition even in a relatively routine way, they had a power to convince far in excess of their own meager capacity. This illustration may be extended to cover many other activities of a priest.

It came as something of a surprise to find the author making considerable concessions to the kind of thinking critized above, since in regard to the new liturgical and scriptural texts his own comments are by no means lenient. He deplores their flatness by comparison with the ancient versions, as also the disappearance of the Gregorian chant in favor of indescribably trivial forms of music designed to pander to all that is most vulgar and sentimental in the human soul: another step toward religious suicide. Given this clear position, one cannot help a feeling of paradoxical inconsequence when one comes to the passage where the author sketches the form that a Mass might take when celebrated in a private house by a part-time priest—a proceeding likely to become frequent if the falling off in the number of priestly and monastic vocations continues at its present rate. The only apparent way out, as Father Sewell reasonably argues, is to provide a shortened course of training open to men who feel a strong vocation to the sacred ministry while being willing to earn their own livelihood in other fields. Their readiness to devote their weekends to the central service of the church, and other spare time when possible, will be the measure of these part-time priests' devotion. Where one is minded to join issue with the author, however, is for needlessly going out of his way to create an artificial atmosphere of informality by excluding from his type-Mass whatever might serve to dignify the occasion or make of it a recognizable parallel with what would take place in a church.

That the conditions themselves would impose their own simplifications is evident enough; an improvised service held in someone's living room need not differ all that much from what commonly takes place on board ship, if a Catholic priest happens to be traveling by sea on a Sunday. Simplification of a ritual can come about in a perfectly natural manner without losing any of its intrinsic solemnity thereby; an affected simplification is quite another thing, for it savors of parody. To say, as some have done, that after all the Last Supper itself was but a simple meal taken in common, or that in the catacombs during the early centuries celebrations of the Eucharist must have been of the simplest—all this does not get us very far both because the parallelism is far-fetched and also because no account is taken of the passage of time with all the modifications in regard to forms and attitudes that this is bound to bring. Insofar as these modifications embody an organic experience of the church in action, they cannot be written off as mere accretions without significance, for most of them have a positive value. The day the Christian Church finds itself again facing the kind of conditions that called the catacombs into existence—not an impossible state of affairs in the world as it is going—on that day the sacred liturgy will automatically undergo a reduction to its barest essentials; meanwhile there is no reason to anticipate on events that may come about sooner than we suppose.

In connection with the domestic Mass it is worth instancing the fact that in Tibet prior to the Chinese Communist occupation every home, however humble, had its consecrated corner where, at the family altar, a visiting lama or monk could be asked to celebrate a rite or teach or lead the family in worship. Why could not many Christian homes do likewise, in which case the practical needs of the domestic liturgy would be permanently met without the part-time priest having to do otherwise than say his Mass in the normal way? There is no need in all this for a self-conscious "mateyness" taking itself for Christian fellowship; compared to such a devaluation, even the most crusted of conservatisms would be preferable, though evidently falling short in respect of the saving intelligence.

Chapter V of *The Vatican Oracle*, dealing with monasticism, is a particularly happy one. While avoiding a too romantic appeal Father Brocard Sewell puts the case for the contemplative life with heartfelt eloquence. A number of well-turned quotations collected from many directions serve to reinforce what his own Carmelite heart has prompted the author to say. He deals firmly with the common prejudice that would have us believe the monastic life to be a selfish or lazy flight from responsibility, and he shows how a life of recollectedness and prayer in pursuance of "the one thing needful"—the unitive love of God—is a service done to all men both by the example it sets and also in a more direct sense, inasmuch as the love of God contains the love of neighbors "eminently," as cause contains effect. The monastic life, when truly achieved, causes this "love within love" to radiate in all directions, and in so doing, it becomes the living exemplar of selfhood subdued, insofar as selfhood is ego, and of selfhood fulfilled, insofar as this reveals the presence of the Divine at the center of each being.

Obviously, only saints find this total effacement of self in Self; regarded as an institution of the church, the contemplative life can but provide a framework and set a pattern. All this is brought out by the author in a few words, while he also offers passing warnings against certain dilutions of the monastic ideal that have become conventional, such as the rather too comfortable "poverty" that is felt by many young aspirants as an obstacle to their entry into one of the monastic orders. In this connection I think the author would be interested in a practice commonly followed in the Theravada Buddhist countries of Burma and Siam, namely for young laymen to spend a certain period as temporary monks, wearing the yellow robe, shaving their heads, and keeping the rule strictly under supervision by fully ordained bhikkus in their local monastery. On completion of the appointed period the young men return to the lay estate in order to follow whatever profession happens to be theirs. A result of this experience, however, is that these people will never be quite like laymen again; the order will have laid its imprint upon their soul in a manner difficult to efface altogether. One could well imagine some such system finding a place in the Christian Church, thus leading to a rekindling of that contemplative fervor that is the greatest need of Christian society today, when an unbridled activism is threatening to erode all truly human qualities.

At the end of this chapter the author mentions a point often missed by those who regard monastic life as being primarily a withdrawal from the world—which it is in a sense, but not in all senses. He remarks that under some circumstances a man wedded to contemplation may feel impelled to issue from his retreat in order to associate himself with some particular activity that will temporarily require his presence in the world, such as dealing with some crying evil of the moment. The author might have added that in this case his contemplative experience, far from unfitting that man for effective action, will on the contrary be found to have endowed his capacity for action with a fresh dimension, by drawing on latent powers that contemplation itself accumulates and releases. One could also speak here of the power of prayer. The lives of saints offer many examples of this kind of contemplative excursion into the active life, and this, for the person concerned, will in no wise imply a lowering of his spiritual sights.

In the last two chapters of *The Vatican Oracle* the author again takes up his main thread concerning the exercise of authority in the church in order to draw certain conclusions of a provisional kind—with the crisis as yet far from resolved, he could hardly hope to do more. Of particular importance for his argument are the proceedings of the reforming Council of Constance held in A.D. 1414–1418, to which a whole appendix is devoted. As we know, the attempt to get the authority vested in general councils recognized as overriding, even to the point of deposing an erring pope if need be, did not really get off the ground despite influential support at the time; it is the contrary view that won de facto acceptance in the Western church. Nevertheless, the author gives his reasons for considering this question as still pending in a de jure sense, chief of which is the fact that ever since the rift between the Eastern and Roman points of view became virtually unbridgeable, a normally constituted council has never actually met, the Easterners being absent; this of course applies to Constance as to all other purely Roman-orientated gatherings. The author therefore accepts the view that the last council to merit the epithet "ecumenical" in an unqualified sense is the second Council of Nicaea in A.D. 787, and this is also the position of the Orthodox. On this assumption, it would be reasonable to argue that the question of where exactly the limits of conciliar and papal authority respectively lie is still an open one, despite all that has happened since in the West, so that to discuss it further does not violate any traditional rights.

In connection with Constance and after, the author several times mentions the decree *Frequens* of that council, in which it is stated that councils should be summoned at regular intervals, and this, as the author sees it, would be a highly desirable thing; presumably, the recent emergence of the idea of "collegiality" could be taken as a cautious move in the same direction. Whoever now wishes to invoke the precedent of *Frequens* by way of readjusting the balance of Catholic authority must, however, take note of the following point: If the idea of the conciliar authority were in its turn to become the subject of legalistic fixation on the same lines as the papal function in 1870, it would not be long before it too became a cause for embarrassment to its own sincerest advocates; a fixation of "democratic" appearance might well prove unwieldy and divisive in ways the advocates of the older conciliarism could never have imagined. Machinery for better and wider consultation could doubtless help the church at the level of practical affairs, but this must not be confused with the special (and providential) function attaching to an ecumenical council as such.

The persuasive power of that function lies in the fact that its intrinsic reality—the church's protection from error by the Holy Spirit at times of doctrinal emergency—is not amenable to juridical, and more especially to quantitative, criteria such as the number and representative range of its attendance and so on. The ecumenical council next following Nicaea I, that of Constantinople in A.D. 381, was a fairly small gathering of mostly Greek bishops, whereas the Arianizing councils of Ariminum and Sirmium were impressively large gatherings— packed assemblies are notoriously well attended. In fact, though in the long course of the church's history councils have been many and various, the "ecumenical" status of any one of them has only been determinable a posteriori; it is tradition operating freely in its own season that has confirmed the fact that here, and not there, the mind of the Christian Church has expressed itself in the plenary sense.

It is undeniable that the Christian civilization of Western Europe in the Middle Ages (distressing features notwithstanding) had a genuinely traditional structure with the forms of the Latin Church providing its spiritual clothing and its idiom of expression—no one looking at Gothic and still more at Romanesque art can possibly doubt the fact—but it is also true to say that the force of Christian tradition was often vitiated to a greater or lesser extent by a too juridical and moralistic bent inherited from pre-Christian Rome. Our author's sympathy for the Orthodox Church with its predominantly Greek patristic background partly arises from an instinctive perception that such was the trouble in the West. Assuredly human beings are fallible beings, half corrupted before they start—the doctrine of the fall expresses the situation clearly—and this inevitably affects their institutions. A perfect society or government or church is not a possibility at the level of (fallen) human existence in this world. Even the sincerest attempts to remedy surrounding injustices and sufferings at any given time will largely consist of choosing the lesser evil. One therefore has to distinguish between a sacred tradition regarded intrinsically and its workings through the agency of men; even at the best of times a certain gap between professions and performance is bound to occur and should be duly allowed for.

Nevertheless, it is empirically right for one's mind to invest the traditional institutions—dogmatic, ethical, and other—with relatively absolute authority (if such a contradictory expression be permissible) matching the intensity of faith. Given the intellectual precaution mentioned above, it can be said of tradition in the Christian world that it is the providentially endowed regulator of the church, whereby the original revelation is perpetuated across time as a stream perpetuates its parent spring across the land, while the spring, for its part, perpetuates the rain from heaven—the divine grace—that keeps the whole circuit in being. Thus tradition is continually at work carrying out its providential mission of spiritual balancer, confirming this or eliminating that, and ever adapting the original message so that it may remain intelligible to each successive generation involved in the current of change. One is speaking of adaptation, not betrayal either of the essential truths or of the characteristic forms with which those truths have become clothed traditionally, thus providing men with a coherent dialect of the spirit. So long as a given religion remains in existence these forms will persist. Allowance has to be made for the natural process of change, while excluding any affectedly revolutionary attitudes. As for legislative precautions against error in both the doctrinal and the ethical fields, these have their place in the church and are indeed unavoidable wherever there is organized religion under any traditional form; it may be added that an overanxious multiplication of safeguards can create its own dangers, by putting genuine vigilance to sleep under a blanket of fictitious immunity.

It is tempting to speculate on what might have been the destiny of the great Christian heresies (or what eventually became such) had they arisen in an Indian setting. Typically, a heresy has its point of departure in some aspect of truth which, by dint of unilateral stressing, begins to oppose itself in an irreducible manner to some other aspect of truth, equally necessary, till finally contact is lost with the metaphysical principle in the light of which the two aspects in question would ultimately find their reconciliation. It is moreover evident that a too rationalistic turn of mind will tend to hasten this result because of its proneness to reduce every question to one of "either . . . or"; such a mentality is almost bound to become heresy-ridden (and therefore also obsessed with a fear of heresy) just because it lacks the means of arriving at a genuine synthesis embracing terms that remain opposed at another level of perception: a want of spiritual "skill," as a Buddhist would say. This kind of intellectual deficiency easily explains why heresies have teemed in the Greco-Roman world, while remaining comparatively exceptional happenings in the Indian world: In fact, they began to multiply there also after a Western-type education got a hold on Indian minds during the nineteenth century with disruptive results.

A potential heresy (every partial truth could become such) will never become actualized so long as it does not develop to the point of denying some other aspect of truth that is complementary to the one it wishes to bring out. It can ignore the latter more or less completely and offer itself as a quasi-independent doctrine, and it can even be critical in regard to various other views, always provided explicit denial be avoided—this is the Indian attitude. It is therefore easy to imagine how Hinduism, for example, faced with an Arian or Monophysite or perhaps even a Lutheran view in its early stages, might have found a way to seize on whatever was positive there in order to make of it yet another *darshana*, or viewpoint, within the framework of Hindu orthodoxy, thus enabling that view to be turned to good account for the benefit of those human temperaments to whose spiritual needs such a view was particularly suited.[1] This does not mean, however, that Hinduism is prepared to tolerate any view whatsoever. Power to reject what is incompatible with its own premises belongs to every

[1] Like Hinduism, Buddhism has given birth to a large variety of schools (ill described as "sects") each of which corresponds to a difference, not of doctrine, but of method *(upāya)*. The anticonceptualist bias that has characterized the Buddhist tradition from its inception requires that whatever differences may develop within its fold should be judged, not in reference to set principles, but empirically in relation to the sole purpose of delivering beings from suffering by directing them toward enlightenment. Beings being diverse, so must their paths be diverse; herein lies the justification for the coexistence of methods which, at first sight, might well seem incompatible in terms of a single orthodoxy. Take for instance Zen and Pure Land (Jodo) Buddhism, to give them their Japanese names: Could two ways be more opposed in appearance? Zen provides the most extreme example of a "self-reliant" *(jiriki)* way; it admits of no other motive but the firm intention to realize "the Kingdom of Heaven within you." Jodo, on the other hand, is as exclusively wedded to the idea of "other-reliance" *(tariki);* one could also say to "the Kingdom of Heaven without." Its primary postulate is the helplessness of the human ego: Only the Grace of Amitabha Buddha avails, this is our lifeline to which we must cling, and this we do through the nembutsu, the unremitting invocation of Amitabha's saving name. Yet both these schools have their anchorage in the same fundamental teachings of the Buddha; they belong to the same orthodoxy and make no sense outside it—a fact that modern exponents of Zen often try to forget. These examples show how far divergences can go without detriment if the parent tradition be strong enough to contain and situate them.

revealed tradition, be this even something undoubtedly inspired but providentially alien in a vital respect (as Buddhism
was for Hinduism), and a fortiori any downright error.

Those who have already read *The Vatican Oracle* may wonder
why this review turned full-scale article has made no mention
of the encyclical *Humanae Vitae,* which provided the author
with a test case from which to develop his argument in the first
place. The fact is, he has discussed the ethical and social aspects
of birth control with great thoroughness; little purpose would
be served by recapitulating his various points here. Assuredly,
this question also carries with it some much wider implications,
both because of its obvious bearing on the problem of mass
proliferation of the human species and its consequences, and
also inasmuch as it inserts itself logically in the cardinal question of the proper (or improper) relationship of man to nature.
This has all along been Christianity's weakest spot, and it
might well be found, could we see far enough, that many of
the troubles that now afflict us have their roots in an initial
failure to integrate the natural order in the Christian perspective, with a consequent imbalance that is still waiting to be
righted.

To give an inkling of what happened, it may be pointed out
that when Christianity emerged as victor from its protracted
struggle with paganism, a violent reaction set in against what
had come to be regarded, rightly or wrongly, as a divinization
of physical phenomena; a certain antinatural bias was thereby
imparted to Christian feeling and thinking that has persisted
ever since.

That many Christian saints have enjoyed a far more positive
outlook on nature is not in doubt. The Desert Fathers, the
Celtic hermits, Saint Francis, and many others passed their life
in primordial harmony with their environment and its nonhuman inhabitants. The precedent is there only waiting to be
cited and applied, but exoteric commentators have been slow
to profit by it, when they have not been at pains to discount
it altogether with the aid of pseudotheological sophistries
summed up in the all-too-familiar dictum "These animals do

not feel; they have no soul." If it be thought by some that the Renaissance, when it came, could have pointed the way to an eventual synthesis of the Christian and the natural orders thanks to the Hellenic, and especially to the Platonic, ideals it recalled to the attention of the West, all one can say is that this overrated revival did not in fact lead to any such result; the metaphysical insight of a Meister Eckhart would have been needed to bring this about, but the mood of the time was not inclined that way.

The Renaissance mind was frantically fruitionist, outgoingly adventurous, combining extreme refinement and extreme toughness in a manner hard for us to imagine; it is not on such a soil that will readily grow the intuitive type who has only to behold a flower or an ant in order to find himself in the presence of God. This is the intellectual stuff architects of synthesis are made of. What the Renaissance did was to give a vast impetus to human interest in all the things of nature while setting the stamp of profanation upon them, and this, for Europe, was the decisive factor. From that time on, the natural sciences moved right outside the orbit of Christian consciousness: the joint effect of a previous Christian negativism versus nature and of giving free rein to what the medieval theologians called *turpis curiositas* was a net view of the created universe that saw in it nothing but an illimitable field for exploitation from any and every motive, be it the most trivial or base. In this picture nature herself figures in the role of the enemy to be overcome; we enter the era of successive human "conquests," Everest yesterday, the moon today, what next tomorrow? In such a vision of the world what room is left for pity, humility, contemplation? Yet there are not wanting Christian leaders who identify themselves with just this point of view and who even claim it for Christianity as its historical outcome, which is only true inasmuch as without the decay of Christianity such a view would not have come to be and that, such being its origin, it still bears recognizable marks of that which it now denies.

This explaining of the facts, however, does not make it any less sad when one finds churchmen utterly unobservant of such matters as the wholesale ravaging of God's creation, land, sea, and air together, and the disappearance of so many forms of life (the rarer and lovelier, the worse the danger), to say nothing of the almost total elimination of beauty from human life itself as industrialism and urbanization creep on their all-devouring way. Few are prepared to connect these sacrilegious happenings with the essential question of what man owes to God in return for his existential prerogative as central being and, in function of this and not apart from it, of what he owes his neighbors, human and nonhuman, having regard to the divine quality that each reflects in its own unique way, thus acting as a witness of God's presence without which the world becomes so much the poorer. That our author is not a victim of this mortal blindness is proved, among other things, by several remarks made in passing where he alludes to the inhuman treatment of helpless animals in the interests of space research or from other similar motives; these remarks of his bespeak the anguish of a fervently compassionate heart, the heart of a Christian man for whom divine, and therefore also human, mercy remains unfragmentable by any subterfuge of "double-think."

On this sympathetic note our survey of a most thought-provoking book can appropriately be ended. If comments on the whole have been noticeably mixed in character, this fact corresponds to the many oscillations of viewpoint apparent in *The Vatican Oracle* itself; for it is evident that two currents of thought have converged in the author's mind, the traditionally Christian and the liberal-humanitarian, without its ever being quite decided which was to have the upper hand. The author himself in his introduction disclaims both the "progressive" and the "conservative" label in order to take up his stance, at least in intention, at the "extreme center" (his own term); but the question can be asked, How far has this intellectually demanding intention been fulfilled? A clear-cut answer to this question is not easy to find. Quite frankly, were someone to try to find the answer by feeding all the relevant passages culled from the 216 pages of the book into a computer, it is difficult to see how the author could avoid being classified among the "progressives" despite his own disavowal of the epithet. But then, the statistical findings of a mindless robot are not the same as the considered opinion of a living person (fallible as he cannot help being), and for this reason Father Brocard Sewell's reviewer wishes it put on record that he rejects the above summary classification. Admittedly, the conservatives have a rough time of it from Father Sewell's pen, yet I suspect that his own heart is not too far removed from them; the modernists are treated by him with indulgence, and sometimes with approval, yet his own feeling for the Eastern Church is anything but modernistic.

In a way, it could be said that the author is living the very crisis he has set out to investigate; his own apparent uncertainties are the uncertainties of a church that has reached a crossroads. To go forward or back, to the right or to the left, this is the question. But to find the extreme center, has one to go anywhere?

This is surely the most pressing question for us all.

The Veil of the Temple

A Study of Christian Initiation

BY MARCO PALLIS

J ESUS, when he had cried again with a loud voice, yielded up the ghost. . . . And, behold, the veil of the temple was rent in twain from the top to the bottom . . ." (Matt. 27:50, 61). This occurrence, which is attested by the three Synoptic Gospels, marks the end of Christ's human ministry, in the ordinary sense of the word, since all that follows, from the Resurrection till his final Ascension, is of a miraculous order. Like all sacred events, the portent at the moment of Christ's death on the cross can be regarded from both a historical and a symbolical angle, since the two views do not exclude one another; in the present case it is the symbolism of the occurrence that will chiefly be considered.

It is important to be reminded of what the veil of the temple of Jerusalem served to mark, namely the boundary between the main portion of the sacred building, where all Jews were admitted and which contained the seven-branched candlestick and the altar of sacrifice, and the Holy of Holies, which was quite empty and into which only the officiating priest could enter. When he did so, the priest had to divest himself of his clothes. Voidness of the place and nakedness of the man are both highly significant indications of what the Holy of Holies stood for in the Jewish tradition, namely "the mysteries" or, in other words, *that* of which the knowledge, formless and inexpressible, can be symbolized only "apophatically," by an emptying or divestment, as in the present case. Esoterically speaking, this knowledge can refer only to God in His suchness, the divine Selfhood transcending even being.

Whatever lay on the hither side of the veil, on the other hand, represented the tradition in its more exoteric aspects, which are multiple and formally expressible in various ways.

81

All three evangelists stress the fact that the veil parted "from the top to the bottom," as if to indicate that the parting was complete and irremediable and that henceforth no definable boundary would exist between the "religious" side of the tradition and the mysterious or, if one so prefers, between the exoteric and esoteric domains. As far as the human eye was able to discern they were to be merged—which does not mean, of course, that their interpenetration would in any way detract from the reality of each domain in its own order, but that any formal expression of their separation was precluded once and for all. For this to be true, it would mean, among other things, that the central rites of the tradition must be such as to serve this comprehensive purpose and that, with any spiritual "support," its context alone, and not its form, would provide the clue as to which domain it pertained to in given circumstances.

This gives the key to Christian spirituality as such; it starts from there. Moreover, it can be seen that if the unicity of revelation has needed to be given increasingly diversified expression parallel with the downward march of a cosmic cycle, each traditional form deriving from this necessity must affirm itself, above all, in those particularities that distinguish it from other comparable forms. Thus Islam remains the prophetic tradition par excellence; though the prophetic function itself is universal and though in other cases one may speak of such and such a prophet or prophets, whenever one refers to *the* Prophet without epithet, one means Mohammed and no one else. Similarly, if one speaks of Enlightenment with a capital *E*, it is of the Buddha one is thinking; which does not mean, however, that enlightenment does not belong to every avataric founder of a religion—obviously this function will always imply the supreme knowledge—but its presentation under the form of "supreme awakening," *sammā sambōdhi*, nevertheless remains the keynote of Buddhism in a sense not shared by other traditions. With Christianity it is *the* Incarnation that provides its specific note; in all other cases, one can only speak of such and such *an* incarnation; emphasis on the word will be relatively more diffuse. The particularity of the Christian tradition, namely its *eso-exoteric* structure, is closely bound up with this all-absorbing role of Christ as the Incarnate Word, in whom all essential functions are synthetized without distinction of levels.

Apart from this special character attaching to Christianity, it is evident that an authentic and integral tradition could at no time be equated solely with its collective and exoteric aspects. Whatever the nature of the formal framework, the presence (latent or explicit) of the esoteric element is necessary; otherwise the tradition in question would be—to use a common Tibetan expression—"without a heart." Similarly, a tradition is never reducible to an esoterism alone: hence the need to be firmly anchored in an orthodox exoterism, speaking its scriptural language and making use of such ritual and symbolical supports as it provides; an esoterism trying to function minus its normal exoteric framework would be like a heart without a body, to use the same comparison as before. Belief in the possibility of a quasi-abstract and wholly subjective spiritual life, one in which tradition and the formal expressions of revealed truth do not count, is a typical error of various neo-Vedantist and other kindred movements that have seen the light of day in India and elsewhere in recent times.

Different ways in which the relationship "mysteries-religion" or "esoteric-exoteric" can be given effect to may be profitably studied by comparing some of the principal traditions in this respect. For instance, in the Islamic tradition, where the two domains are defined with particular clarity, "the veil of the temple" has been present from the origins and remains intact to this day; both the law *(shariah)* and the esoterism *(tassawuf)* are traceable back to the Prophet himself. This is why the Islamic arrangements have so often been quoted as a model when this subject has come up for consideration.

With Christianity, as we have seen, a rending of the veil previously extant in Judaism marks the final affirmation of the New Covenant in the face of the Old and, with it, the birth of a wholly independent tradition. In the case of Buddhism, on the other hand, the nonexistence of any such veil is laid down from the start. The Buddha's saying that "I have kept nothing back in my closed fist" means that in his tradition the purely spiritual interest alone really counts. Although in Buddhism, as elsewhere, an exoteric organization becomes unavoidable from the moment that the number of adherents begins to increase, the fact itself will always remain, from the Buddhist point of view, a matter for regret—something to be accepted *contre coeur*, under compulsion of events, but never in principle.

Something similar can also be said of Christianity: If Christ's kingdom, by his own definition, is "not of this world" [1] and if the penalty of casting the pearl of great price before swine is that they "will turn and rend you," then one of the consequences of the removal of the veil between the Holy of Holies and the more accessible part of the temple (to return to our original symbolism) has been a certain blurring of the distinction between the two domains even where it really applies—the shadow, as it were, of an overwhelming grace. This confusion has expressed itself in the life of the Christian church under the twofold form of a minimizing of what, in spirituality, is most interior and of an excessive focusing of attention on the more exterior and peripheral manifestations of the tradition, and especially on the collective interest treated almost as an end in itself. Carried to extremes, this tendency amply accounts for the fact that it was within the Christian world, and not elsewhere, that the great profanation known as "the modern mentality" first took shape and became, as time went on, the vehicle of "scandal" among all the rest of mankind. If this happening, like everything else of a disastrous kind moreover, comprises its providential aspect, as bringing nearer the dark ending of one cycle and the bright dawning of another, it nevertheless does not escape—by force of karma as Buddhists would say—the curse laid by Christ Himself on all "those by whom scandal cometh." The pain of the cross, in which all must be involved, is there, in anticipation of its triumph.

To return to our original thesis: The special attention called by the evangelists to the fact that the temple veil was split

[1] Islam says this in its own way, when it declares that Jesus was the bringer of an esoterism (*haqiqah*) only, whereas the Prophet Mohammed endowed his followers both with the things of this world and with the things of the other world.

"from top to bottom" shows that this feature of the great portent was an essential one; the veil once torn asunder can *never* be sewn together again. To attempt to do so, on any plea whatsoever, would amount to an arbitrary proceeding, one deserving the epithet "heretical" in the strictest sense of the word. The condemnation by the church of "gnosticism" has no other meaning.[2]

Moreover, the fact that the Christian revelation was, before all else, a laying bare of the mysteries had been widely recognized even by theologians having no pretensions to a particularly inward view of things. We have known an ordinary Greek priest say to his congregation that "the entire liturgy is a mystagogy," using a word belonging to the vocabulary of the ancient Hellenic mysteries and also figuring in the text of the liturgy itself, which does not mean, however, that the man himself will have possessed clear notions of what it really stands for; nevertheless even such a passing reference is in its way significant. Nor is it devoid of interest to point out in the same connection that the Eastern Church, by comparison with the Latin Church, has preserved both in its rituals and in its usual mode of expression a certain "archaism" that anyone who has attended a celebration of the liturgy in a Greek or Russian church could hardly fail to notice; it is not surprising, then, that in the Eastern rite the sacraments are referred to as "the mysteries," a word that, here again, is charged with associations taken over from the esoteric side of the pre-Christian tradition in the ancient world.

For the sake of greater precision it will perhaps be useful at this point to refresh one's mind as to the characteristics that

[2] It is probable that even in the early days of the church the label "gnostic" was sometimes applied to things not really meriting the intended reproach but appearing to do so by reason of superficial similarities that belied their true nature. In our time the accusation of new-fangled gnosticism has provided an all too convenient weapon against those who have suggested that the gift of intelligence is a vocational qualification for the fullest understanding of the Christian dogmas. This gratuitous confusing of intellectuality with "pride" marks a suicidal tendency of which the concordant reaction is the association, in the profane mind, of the word "religion" with an attitude of perfunctory conformism and credulity.

serve to delineate the esoteric realm and to distinguish it from
the exoteric. One might also have said: those that delineate the
initiatic realm, since in principle the two things make but one;
this second term, however, represents a somewhat more particularized aspect of the same reality, since it is concerned with
the methodic realization of what the esoterism represents in the
realm of theory.[3] In seeking an adequate definition one can
safely turn to René Guénon when he said that whereas an
exoteric view of things concerns itself with the individual human interest in the largest sense of the word but stops short
there, an esoteric view reaches beyond the individuality in
order to embrace all the superior states of the being and even
aspires to the supreme state—if what really transcends all possibilities of comparison may be so described, by an unavoidable
concession to the insufficiency of human language.

If we accept the above definition, then the touchstone of
discernment, in the present case, is the *finality* respectively
envisaged, whether individual and limited, that is to say, or else
universal and unlimited by any condition whatsoever. In other
words, the finality of a religious exoterism will be the realization (or "recovery," if one takes into account the Adamic doctrine of the Fall) of the state of "true man," *Chen-jen* of the
Taoists;[4] whereas esoterism, for its part, will envisage as its
ultimate aspiration the realizing of "transcendent man," goal
of the Taoist way, or Universal Man, if one prefers the more
familiar term taken from Sufism. It is noteworthy that the

[3] According to its primitive meaning, the Greek word $\theta\epsilon\omega\rho\iota\alpha$ should
be rendered as "contemplation"; but today this use of the word hardly
survives outside the ranks of those following the Hesychast way. In
modern Greek, as in other European languages, "theory" has become
a sadly impoverished term, with purely mental associations and opposable, as such, to "practice" with a bias in favor of the latter; and as for
"contemplation," this is well-nigh untranslatable into current speech.
[4] In practice, a point of view that a priori limits its own scope to a
human finality is unlikely to realize the perfection of the human order
itself, for a habit of taking the short view tends to restrict a man's
horizon within ever narrower limits; the end of this road is an out-
and-out profane mentality. The esoterist, on the other hand, through
focusing his aim beyond all limitations, is able to take the finality of
religious exoterism "in his stride," as it were, and this is the surest way
to realize it.

realization of the Two Natures, which is the goal of Christian endeavor, to be truly complete would have to include both of the above finalities after the model of Christ Himself, who was "true man" or "second Adam" at the same time as "true God"; the term "christification" might well be used to express this supreme ideal.

When it comes to "initiatic method," designed to foster spiritual realization at all its degrees, it is important not to lose sight of the very wide range of variation in initiatic practice, as between different traditions. In this field, no less than in others, each tradition exhibits its own peculiarities, a fact that does not affect the general principles governing initiatic life but that nevertheless forbids one to drive analogy, as from one to another, too far; and still less does it encourage one to systematize a given pattern of initiation to the point of making of that pattern an absolute test of authenticity or otherwise. Provided one does not exceed the limits of fair comparison, however, there is undoubted profit to be derived from a parallel study of initiatic procedure as found in different traditions; when doing so we shall chiefly be concerned with those features that have a direct or indirect bearing on the question of Christian initiation to which we have gradually been leading up.

Turning first to the Buddhist world: In Tibet it can be said that practically every spiritual activity, down to the smallest detail, is geared to an initiatic purpose, either directly or else indirectly as in the case of "scholastic" studies in the Gelugpa Order, for instance, to which the Dalai Lama belongs. Anything directly relating to *method*, however, will involve an initiatic act of some kind; even to open a book concerned with method requires its initiatory *lung* or ritual authorization imparted by a lama of the spiritual family to which the prospective initiate intends to be attached, and each subsequent stage in the process will likewise be marked by its appropriate *lung*. In Tibet everything is calculated to foster and facilitate the initiatic life for those who aspire to it; the supremacy of this ideal is recognized by all, from the head of the government down to the beggar at the street corner.

Over and above the normal initiatic arrangements, which in

essentials do not differ from what is to be found in India or
other places, Tibetan spirituality includes a large number of
special initiations known as *wang-kur* (from *wang* = power and
kur-wa = to confer), each of which gives access to one particular
form of methodic meditation focused on a *mandala* or symbolical diagram disposed around a central divinity, a combination
of sacred geometry and traditional iconography of forms, colors, gestures, letters, and the like. Visualization of such a *mandala,* under the direction of one's guru, is one of the common
features of tantrik technique; it is not everyone, however, who,
after receiving the *wang* empowering him to meditate on such
and such a *mandala,* actively puts this into effect. Many try to
amass such *wangs* simply as a means of stimulating their own
pious fervor; such a "quantitative" attitude to the acquisition
of *wangs,* though not contrary to the letter of the traditional
rules, does evidently depart from the spirit of the institution,
and for this reason it is condemned by informed opinion both
on the score of "spiritual diffuseness" and also as liable to produce, in extreme cases, dissonances of an unpredictable order.

In any case, this shows that in Tibet, as elsewhere, a sharp
distinction has to be made between the *mutabarik* (to borrow
a convenient Sufic term meaning "blessed"), the man who receives initiation from mixed motives not fully in tune with its
intrinsic purpose, and the *salik* (traveler), namely the man who
proceeds with full intent, keeping the end of the road in view.
All one can say is that in Tibet prior to the Chinese Communist
irruption the number of *salikun* was relatively high as compared with most other places; there was little sign of decadence
in this respect.

Returning to the *mutabarik* type as commonly found in the
Tibetan world, an important thing to be noted is that the initiatic act, though clearly recognized as such and though its
virtuality always remains what it is in an objective sense, is
nevertheless envisaged subjectively in a *quasi-exoteric* sense and
with a view to benefits that do not exceed the individual
sphere—such as piety in this life and a "happy rebirth" in the
next—a fact that by definition forbids one to apply the epithet

"esoteric" to the religious manifestation in question. Yet the initiatic possibility is undeniably there, if unexploited.

This discrepancy of attitude is carried to its furthest point in the great mass *wang-kurs* that take place from time to time. At these gatherings, which thousands may attend, the initiating lama goes through the motion of conferring the *wang* and preaches the appropriate doctrine before the crowd, though few of the participants will be known to him personally either before or after the event; no question of "qualification" can possibly arise under these circumstances. A case in point was the conferring, by the Dalai Lama when he was staying close to the Indian border in 1950, of the "initiation of the Great Compassionate," an eleven-faced form of Avalokitēswara, whose *māndala* is specially associated with the Gelugpa, the "Yellow-Hat" Order of Monks. Vast numbers of people from all the country round and from both sides of the border journeyed to Dung-kar (White Conch) Monastery, where the sacred sovereign was staying, in order to receive the *wang* in question; I myself would gladly have accompanied them, but by that time the political obstacles had become insurmountable. The fervor aroused among the people was tremendous, and to this extent it was no small spiritual occasion. Nevertheless, it must be admitted that those who received the initiation were, almost without exception, simple *matabārikun;* if an odd *sālik* was to be found among them, his presence could not have been detected by any recognizable sign.

But even so, the initiation itself was perfectly regular according to all traditional canons; it was open to any of those who, on that occasion, received the *wang* of the Great Compassionate to present himself then or at any subsequent period to a competent lama in order to put into effect the method pertaining to that particular *māndala*. No question of validity could possibly arise in this connection, nor was even the humblest *mutabārik* in the crowd unaware of the fact that this was an initiation and not something else and that the possibility existed of its being someday turned more fully to account. We have described this happening at considerable length, as shedding a certain light

on the ambivalent use of an undoubtedly initiatic act and therefore also on certain aspects of the Christian tradition.

We must next consider one or two features of Japanese Buddhism that are of special interest from the point of view that
concerns us here; but first we must notice a fact of a general
nature, namely that in Japan, despite the obviously initiatic
character of so much to be found there, it is only the tantrik
sects,[5] of which Shingon and Tendai are the chief, that adminis-
ter an initiation under the form most familiar to us, specifiable,
that is to say, in terms of time and occasion, of "before initiation" and "after." As regards method, Shingon is closely akin
to Tibetan spiritual practice, a common feature being the use
of *māndalas* composed of divine portraiture, Sanskrit letters,
and other symbols also found in Tibet. Apart from the cases
just mentioned, the remaining Japanese sects do not confer a
formal initiation when attaching a new disciple to the line or
subsequently; a spiritual master may admit or reject a prospective disciple, and he may also terminate his discipleship at any
time if dissatisfied with his progress. Otherwise the disciple,
once accepted, will be swept, as it were, into the spiritual current more or less quickly and completely but without this fact
having to be confirmed by a set ritual act of any kind. It is the
process as a whole that constitutes initiatic participation, the
rest depending upon the aptitude of the disciple and the grace
of his master, in which respect Japanese practice does not differ
from that of other traditions.

Coming now to the best-known (and least understood by
Europeans) of the Japanese sects, namely Zen, we find there
a method in which an extreme stringency of discipline and the
use of apparently senseless conundrums (koans) are combined
for the purpose of ridding the mind of the habit of conceptual-
ism, thus allowing the intuitive faculty to be released. That a
spiritual training carried out on these lines constitutes an ini-

[5] For much of the information to be found in this article we have to
thank Miss Carmen Blacker, lecturer in Japanese at Cambridge and
herself a Buddhist; through her kind help we were able to obtain
directly from Japan authoritative answers to a number of questions that
otherwise would have remained in doubt.

tiatic process, in the most rigorous sense of the word, will have
become plainly apparent to anyone who has read, for instance,
Herrigel's account of his own training in archery under a Zen
master.[6] The same applies to other forms of Zen training, as
described in various books; they one and all display a character
that by no stretch could be described as "exoteric," but without
this entailing a rite of access of the kind that would be deemed
indispensable elsewhere—unless one is to regard acceptance by
the master and the administering by him to the disciple of his
first koan as tantamount to "initiation" as we know it; this,
however, was not the view of my informant. Rather would it
seem as if the whole process is to be described as "initiatic,"
without any particular incident in the course of it being singled
out as being more essential than others. In a sense this absence
of a specific initiation goes with the attitude of *jiriki* (own
power) extremism apparent in Zen.[7] Though the spiritual master and the method he imparts are everything in fact, the theoretical emphasis remains always on the personal effort of the
pupil—hence the abysmal misunderstandings to which Zen so
readily lends itself in the minds of Occidentals with their
habitually individualistic bias. Privileged are those few who
have found the way to becoming naturalized in Japanese wisdom to the point of overcoming their own congenital self-
obsession as well as the ratiocinative habit that Zen in
particular sets out to eradicate. We are not among those who
believe that "Zen for the West" corresponds to a widespread
possibility. Attempts to publicize Zen methods, by Western-
ized Japanese, have only resulted, in most cases, in an increase
of the existing intellectual disorder in the West; while a number of earnest souls, lured into the pursuit of a, by them, unreal-

[6] One can contrast with this the initiatic practice in the Corporation
of Archers in ancient Turkey. There initiation took a perfectly normal
form according to the Sufic model, with the shaikh of the corporation
whispering the Name in the ear of the disciple while at the same time
placing his fingers on the "grip" of the bow, where the two halves from
which the Tartar type of bow (including the Japanese) is constructed
are "unified"; the symbolism needs no explaining!

[7] For the *jiriki* (own power) and *tariki* (other power) types of Japanese
spirituality to which Zen and Jodo respectively belong see the appendix
of my book *The Way and the Mountain* (London: Peter Owen, 1960).

izable ideal, have been deterred thereby from seeking other ways, in Buddhism or in traditions nearer home, better suited to their own temperamental needs.

We must now consider the case of another Japanese sect that has still more to tell us than Zen in relation to the subject of the present article. We are referring to Jodo (Pure Land) and its associated sects, in which Invocation of the Buddha of Light, Amitabha (Japanese *Amida*) is the principal, and indeed the only essential, support used. Here again there is no formal initiation, though one would have expected that a conferring of the formula to be invoked, known as nembutsu and enshrining the Name of Amida, would be just the occasion for such an initiatic rite. In point of fact, however, any person may invoke with this formula at will whether he be resorting for instruction to a guru of the line or not. On the doctrinal side it is noteworthy that Jodo and its sister sect Jodo Shinshu (Pure Land true religion) of which Shinran was the Patriarch, have often been compared to Christianity because of their devotional character and because of the role of Savior attributed to Amida thanks to whose "vow" and by whose grace alone the disciple hopes to enter the Pure Land after his earthly life is over. Painted scrolls showing the Buddha Amida and his heavenly attendants on their way down to welcome his devotee into paradise rank among the most deeply moving examples of Japanese art.

Despite the fact that the Pure Land schools display this strongly devotional character, it would nevertheless be a mistake to label them without more ado as a way of bhakti (to use a well-known Hindu term), not only because all branches of Buddhism, whatever may be their outward form, remain in principle ways of knowledge, as laid down in the beginning, but also because the Pure Land teachings, if one looks at them more closely, represent a synthesis of devotional and sapiential elements that fully satisfies the needs of a spirituality having an intellectual goal in view.[8] The Pure Land itself, symbolizing

[8] We have it on the authority of a distinguished priest of Jodo Shin, the Venerable Shojun Bando, that in Shin Buddhism the guru-chela relationship has been strongly upheld in the case of those who wish to

the goal, admits of interpretation at two levels: In a more outward sense it is the Western Paradise of Amitabha, sojourn in
which both is blissful and does not entail further wandering
in the Round of Existence, samsara; what it envisages is a "de-
ferred liberation" comparable to the *krama-mukti* of Hinduism.
But the very name "Pure Land" and the fact that this was
substituted for the more usual form "Western Paradise" shows
that something more lies behind this first interpretation, for
where total purity is to be found, there is *selfhood*—the two
things are really identical. It is admixture with its resulting
internal stresses that necessitates samsaric existence. On this
showing, the Pure Land can only mean Nirvana—anything less
is excluded by the very form of the name.[9] Otherwise put, one
can say that the Western Paradise represents a relative purity,
which from the point of view of the impurity of the world
appears quasi-absolute, whereas the Pure Land as such is pure
in an unqualified sense.

This dual interpretation implicit in the name "Pure Land"
inevitably evokes a similar possibility of transposition as applying to the Christian term "salvation," since this too is habitually described as a passage to paradise; this state beyond all
suffering and in "proximity" to the Divine corresponds very
closely to the Western Paradise of the Buddhists. Nevertheless,

proceed far along that road. For our benefit he quoted Rennyo, a saint
of the fifteenth century, as saying: "Your faith is not consummated
without the guru's guidance," and also, "Five factors are required for
your rebirth in the Pure Land, namely anterior (good) karma, guru,
light, faith, and Name." All the evidence, positive and negative, goes
to show that in this branch of the Buddhist tradition the line of demar-
cation between a fully esoteric and initiatic and a bhaktic and even a
frankly exoteric participation remains pretty indefinite; nevertheless,
in any given case it would be easy to say to which category a man's
spiritual activity really belongs.
[9] A single telling quotation from the Patriarch Shinran himself will
suffice to clinch the point: "Rebirth [in the Pure Land] . . . is complete
unsurpassed enlightenment." We have it on good authority that in
Japan nowadays the intellectual level among Shin followers is, on an
average, rather low; little more than worldly benefits is envisaged in
many cases. Nevertheless, the highest possibility is there for the seeking; but men must have eyes to see and ears to hear or this ever-present
opportunity will pass them by.

in the Christian case, as in the other and with equal logic, the "salvation" that is offered admits of two interpretations, the one indicating a state that is more or less conditioned (depending on which paradise the soul that has been "saved" is called upon to occupy) and the other referring to an entirely unconditional realization, one where it is no longer possible to think of an individual being at all, but only selfhood in the transcendent sense; this has been pointed out before by other writers. Admittedly, the word "salvation" for practically everyone nowadays, and probably for the majority even in primitive times, does carry a more or less restricted meaning in fact, but this does not authorize one to conclude that it does so in principle. It must be remembered that "salvation" is the term Christians have always used; its authority goes back to the Scriptures and to Christ Himself. It would be surprising indeed if it implied any restriction of finality in an absolute sense. There is really nothing to astonish us in the equivocal usage to which the idea of "salvation" has given rise, seeing that this agrees with the bivalency of the Christian spiritual language under all its forms consequent upon the rending of the temple veil.

We have referred to primitive times, but even in later times can one imagine a Meister Eckhart using the word "salvation" with any thought but its transcendent meaning? For such as he, *a* paradise would indeed be "the sage's prison," as the Sufis say. Those who have seen as far as Eckhart may have been comparatively few, but their mere existence is enough to prove the case. All one need say really, in this connection, is that for those for whom the veil is truly parted "from top to bottom" salvation will bear the sense of total deliverance, while for those (the many) whose more or less obscured minds still cause them to imagine a veil where none really is, the same word "salvation" will evidently bear the limited connotation we have become accustomed to take for granted as the only possible one—somewhat abusively, however, both because this restricts scriptural and traditional usage and also because we have thereby been led into systematizing what by rights should remain undefined, instead of allowing the context to tell us which meaning is the one intended. Spiritually this opportunity for discernment is beneficial by reason of the greater "mindfulness" it fosters (to use a favorite Buddhist term) by comparison with a more cut-and-dried solution.

With Hesychasm we find ourselves at last over the threshold of Christian initiation as such, by which we mean, not that this form exhausts the possibilities implied in the name to the extent of providing a single type to which all else can be referred, but that this spiritual current of the Eastern Church represents a perfectly normal "specification" of initiatic activity according to the Christian idiom, one that is neither the result of absorbing elements of foreign origin, as in the case of Hermetism for instance, nor confined to some exceptionally enclosed organization like the Fede Santa and certain other medieval initiations, nor yet the appanage of a vocational institution like the guilds of cathedral builders or the knightly orders. All these things have existed in the Christian world, but none of them conforms to conditions, in terms of finality, doctrine, and method, such as would allow one to identify it without further qualification with "Christian initiation" in an all-inclusive sense. Seeing that Hesychasm is the only extant example of something satisfying the required conditions in a sufficient degree to answer our present purpose, we are left no choice but to take this for our starting point and afterward to build from there.

The chief points to note about Hesychasm are as follows: (1) its basis in Scripture and the Fathers, (2) its invocative formula, (3) the position in it of the "geront" (Slavonic *staretz*), (4) its declared goal, and (5) the absence of any specifically initiatic rite.[10]

Let us take these headings in order and enlarge, where necessary, on various points of technical detail.

1. Scriptural and patristic authority: This has always been strictly maintained, thus providing all that was needed by way of theoretical foundation for the practices of Hesychasm from

---

[10] This and other facts relating to Hesychasm have been carefully checked in consultation with a follower of this way who has spent much time on Mount Athos and been in touch with some notable geronts belonging to the Greek islands.

the earliest times of its existence under that name till nowa-days. In the eighteenth century an anthology of extracts from the Greek Fathers was compiled, known as the *Philokalia*, and this is regarded as containing all the essential doctrinal material required by a follower of this way. This collection exists in both Greek and Russian.[11]

2. The short sentence known as The Jesus Prayer here pro-vides the one and only formula to be invoked, though there is much to be said regarding the manner of its use. It runs as follows: "Lord Jesus Christ, Son of God, have mercy upon me." It will be immediately apparent that these words, as far as their rational understanding takes one, are the common property of all Christians without distinction; no ritual authorization is required, and it would indeed be surprising if such were the case. A precisely comparable case is the nembutsu in "Pure Land" Buddhism which also never has become an object of ritual communication to the disciple.

When it comes to a use of the Jesus Prayer as *mantram* in virtue of the presence in it of the Holy Name, its rational connotation, though still evident, takes second place. In Hesy-chasm, as in other traditions where the inherent power of a name becomes the operative factor in a method, the novice is warned from the outset against using the formula except under direction of a qualified master. To find his spiritual master is therefore, for him, an urgent task. If, however, after persistent searching he is unable to discover such a master, the would-be disciple is permitted to apply the prescribed method as best he can with the aid of books while casting himself on the mercy of Christ as the one unfailing source of instruction. The whole method is closely akin to the Hindu *japa-yoga* or the Sufi dhikr; if some Orthodox apologists, out of a quite uncalled-for desire to safeguard a Christian originality no one threatens, have tried to deny this analogy, this only serves to show into what contra-dictory positions a perverted sense of loyalty is able to lead otherwise quite intelligent people.

[11] A selection from the *Philokalia* in two volumes, excellently translated into English by E. Kadloubovsky and G. E. H. Palmer, has been pub-lished by Faber and Faber (London).

3. The Hesychast "geront" *(staretz)* when found will discharge all the normal functions of a guru according to the Indian conception of the word. In Hinduism one's spiritual master is acknowledged as the direct representative of the supreme *Sad-guru,* the Divine Self. In Buddhism the same holds. The present writer was repeatedly told, in Tibet, that he should look on his lama as if he were "the Buddha himself." Hesychasm says the same: The disciple should behave toward his "geront" as if he were in the presence of Christ. One function only the "geront" will not assume—that of "initiator." According to the Christian spiritual economy Christ, as synthesizing the avataric function exclusively in his own person, is the only possible initiator[12]—hence the sacraments Christ instituted are the only conceivable supports in the initiatic, as well as the exoteric, path from its inception until the goal is reached. A man may envisage these supports with greater or lesser understanding—he may use the opportunity they provide to the full or only by halves—but in principle they remain objectively all-sufficing and indivisible at the level of form, and no subjective qualification or its absence can modify the fact. Hence a human teacher, though representing Christ in a certain way, will always efface himself in principle by stressing the indirect character of the function he exercises.

4. As regards the ultimate purpose of spiritual endeavor, Hesychasm makes use of a word found in the Fathers—namely, "deification." Plainly, this term stands for something far exceeding the individual realm and its possibilities; one is in undoubtedly esoteric country here. It must not be supposed, however, that deification is opposable in principle to the more usual word "salvation," for reasons already fully explained;

---

[12] An exception, more apparent than real, might be made in the case of the Latin rosary, if this were ever taken as the support of a fully initiatic way, which it certainly could be by one endowed with the proper understanding and dispositions; in that case, it would be logical for the Holy Virgin, as original communicator of the rosary to Saint Dominic, to appear in the role of initiator, a privilege due to her in her capacity of *Coredemptrix,* and which no other creaturely figure can possibly share. Evidently, there is no departure from Christian principle here.

rather should it be taken as throwing light on the highest possibilities that salvation intrinsically comprises.

5. Concerning the absence of any special initiatic rite in
Hesychasm, and in Christianity as such, we have already commented sufficiently, both in previous sections and in the present section under headings (2) and (3). All one can add to the
above is to say that those who have searched for an initiatic rite
supposed to operate over and above the sacraments have been
losing their time. So far as Christianity is concerned, the hour
that saw the veil of the temple rent in twain saw the end of any
such possibility forever.[13]

To complete the present survey, a brief discussion concerning the nature of the Christian sacraments is called for, regarded from the initiatic point of view.

Two of them, baptism and confirmation (called Chrismation
in the Eastern rite), can conveniently be grouped together in
this context,[14] if only for the reason that they are the ones that
most evidently display the character of initiatic rites. In baptism there are two aspects to be noted, the first of which is
essential and the second accessory. The essential purpose of
baptism is to give back to "fallen" man the virtuality of "true
man," or of Adam when still in Eden. This finality can hardly
be accounted a purely exoteric interest, though treated thus in
practice and even though admittedly it does not look beyond
the plenitude of the individual possibility as represented by the
state of Adamic innocence, which, moreover, corresponds to
the human nature of Christ, the second Adam. The accessory
aspect of baptism, which might also be called its "aggregatory"
aspect, is its effect of making a man into a member of the
Christian community, a plainly exoteric purpose when re-

---

[13] In the course of the present study of Christian initiation a number
of unacknowledged references have been made to the work of Frithjof
Schuon, several of whose books treat of the same subject in more
extended form. I gladly acknowledge my indebtedness to this source.
[14] In the Eastern rite both sacraments are given together, one after the
other, by the priest; the postponing of confirmation to a later age and
its conferring by a bishop belongs to the Latin rite. Evidently, no
doctrinal implication attaches to this difference.

garded in isolation from the higher possibility that goes with it.

Chrismation, on the other hand, the Pentecostal grace, though it includes the general purpose of confirming a man in all the functions pertaining to Christian life (questions of special vocation apart), is more predominantly turned in the direction of supraindividual aims; the gift of the Holy Ghost could not in principle envisage an individual realization only, even if it be treated perfunctorily in most cases, as a means of increasing piety and no more. If Chrismation can be said to "amplify" the grace already received in baptism, it would be still more true to say that it transposes that grace in the sense of "exaltation"; in other words, its normal finality, despite exoteric shortsightedness, cannot but be the state of "transcendent man" or "deification," to give it its Christian label. Thus the two natures of Christ are covered, in intention, by the two sacraments jointly; the Eucharist is there to render operative this double fulfillment.

At this point it is advisable to answer a possible objection: In view of the fact that baptism has long been imparted to all without distinction and even imposed on them in infancy whether they wish it or not, it might be asked whether this is not *per se* contrary to the initiatic principle, since this normally will imply "qualification" in the recipient, therefore also a selective character to the imparting itself; the same objection would apply to Chrismation.

We think, however, that enough has already been said to show why this objection does not apply in the present case, because of the bivalent character attaching by definition to all essential elements in the Christian tradition as from the very outset. A baptized person may remain unaware of the fact that the rite he went through had more than an aggregatory meaning; the teaching he receives on the subject of baptism's power to neutralize "original sin" may mean to him little more than a quasi-moral benefit, in which case—this is the case of the majority—his participation in the fruits of baptism will necessarily remain exoteric and largely passive. Let, however, an awareness of the greater possibilities likewise comprised in the sacrament he has received but dawn on his mind and that man will be able, from that moment, to view his own baptism and confirmation retrospectively as having opened the gate to a realization far exceeding the exoteric domain. No one will have compelled him to do so, nor is there any presumption as to how many others will or will not follow suit, so that distinctions of qualification, as mentioned above, will not have been disregarded in any essential way, nor will the condition of intellectual aptitude for such a path have been disregarded either. The theoretical position should be clear enough; as for an effective realization of all that baptism and Chrismation offer between them, that is another matter, and it is that which constitutes initiatic life in the Christian sense.

Three of the remaining sacraments, matrimony, ordination, and unction, need not long detain us. In fact the only one of these three that might concern us here is unction, to which the Latin Church adds the epithet "extreme," since the other two explain themselves sufficiently by their form. The nature of unction, on the other hand, seems rather difficult to define from our present standpoint. Inasmuch as it is designed as an instrument of divine healing, it might be placed in a class of its own. In Eastern Christianity not only sick people but also all the faithful are able (but not obliged) to partake of this sacrament. This happens once a year, on the Wednesday in Holy Week, when all who so wish come to receive this medicine for their souls.

This brings us to the remaining two sacraments, penance, or confession, and the Eucharist; like baptism and Chrismation, they belong together, the one being a preparation for the other. The only description that seems to fit the sacrament of penance is by calling it a rite of psychic purification, in the highest sense of the word, and this is doubtless how a Hindu, for instance, would classify it. The Eucharist, on the other hand, would count for him as a sacrificial rite *(yajña)*, which it is in the first instance, but it is many other things besides—every aspect of Christian spirituality finds its focus here, so that the Eucharist can justly be called "the axial mystery," the one that synthesizes all that the other mysteries have to offer. That it is not "an exoteric rite" (however human ignorance may treat it on occasion) is surely obvious—could anything conceivably be more "inward" than the body and blood of the avatara? Its partaking is, for a Christian, what the Tibetans describe as *lamai nendjor* (spelled *blamai rnalbyor*) = union (yoga) with the "guru," a sense that the word "communion" is also intended to convey.

The two elements, bread and wine, figuring in the rite correspond, as many are aware, to the two great "dimensions" of spiritual life, "the exterior" and "the interior,"[15] and therefore also to the two natures of Christ, human and divine, the realization of which the Eucharist is above all designed to being about. When the bread is broken, the sacrifice is accomplished. When the elements are mingled in the chalice, exterior and interior become merged in a single overflowing of the divine compassion—fused but not confused, to quote Meister Eckhart's pregnant saying. The symbolical message is exactly the same as that of the temple veil and its parting, which the mixing of the consecrated elements reproduces here. That is why the Eucharist is food and drink unto salvation, taking this word not merely in its usual restricted sense but also in that unqualified sense that all authentic traditions give to whatever word they use to indicate the ultimate goal of man's spiritual voyage.[16]

This completes our attempted recapitulation of the evidence relating to "Christian initiation" within that "eso-exoteric" structure that the Christian form of tradition characteristically displays. The ambiguities that have revealed themselves in the course of Christian history are to a large extent traceable to this ambivalence of structure; this fact should not, however, be

---

[15] The two names of God corresponding, in Islam, to these dimensions are *az-Zahir* and *al-Bātin*.

[16] The withdrawing of the chalice from the laity in the Latin Church at a certain time in the Middle Ages, though it does not destroy the sacrament in a technical sense (each consecrated element implying the other as with the two natures of Christ), does in a certain symbolical sense appear to restrict man's spiritual finality to the "exterior"; it foreshadows the general exoterization that took place in practice. We are not the first to have pointed out this analogy.

taken for a mere reproach, since it also translates a positive value in that "bursting of all bounds" by the mysteries, which the descent of Christ into the world marked from the outset. Its negative effects are also apparent enough, in the extreme exteriorization that took place later; for if the Holy of Holies, with the parting of the curtain, overflowed into the outer portion of the temple, the reverse was also true. It is a price that had to be paid in practice but which can still be neutralized by spiritual realization and by that alone.

One final message must be addressed to the Christian aspirant who, even when fortified with the assurance that his tradition has (human obtuseness notwithstanding) conserved the virtuality of its inner life, will yet not find his own spiritual problem solved overnight—indeed far from it. The Christian way, under today's conditions, is beset with difficulties for those who are not content to accept whatever an exoteric participation offers them and no more; not the least of these difficulties is an apparently total absence of qualified spiritual instruction—able, that is to say, to harness whatever resources are provided by the tradition to the service of an initiatic method. In a monotonously general picture of spiritual indigence, Hesychasm marks the one noteworthy exception, but this source of guidance too might one day dry up (God forfend it!) as a result of the increasing alienation from the contemplative ideal that has gone with the spread of modern secularism in the Orthodox countries themselves, especially among the young.[17]

---

[17] The eight hundredth anniversary of the founding of the Athonite community was to be marked, so we have read, by the construction of a motorable road onto the peninsula in order to render it more accessible to visitors wishing to attend the celebration. It is to this well-worn tune that the first big inroad into the privacy of the great monastic fastness is being inaugurated, a privacy that the Muslim Turks, in the days of their mastery, never failed to respect. All over Asia road-making, by opening a way for hurried, thoughtless visiting by all and sundry, has been the means of depriving places of pilgrimage of their traditonal raison d'être; the argument of facility is everywhere the same—*facilis descensus Averni!* If Christians only knew their own interest, the whole Christian world would be up in arms to defend the inviolability of Athos. According to a more recent report, the authorities of the Holy Mountain, alarmed by the fact that so many young

In the Catholic West, despite the relative popularity of monastic institutions, the situation is, if anything, still more difficult, since what passes nowadays for a "contemplative life" would hardly earn that epithet from the mouth of, say, an average Tibetan lama or Hindu *sannyasin*. We say this, not in order to discourage the devotee bent on getting his Christian virtuality turned into a reality—indeed the opposite is our purpose—but because when once a man is committed in intention to the "unseen warfare" under any form, for him to underrate the extent of the opposing forces is itself a danger. One has to size up a challenging situation accurately, but without dismay. This is a prior condition to any spiritual victory.

Without venturing on any slick solution to this vexed question of spiritual method and its adequate communication within the Christian world, one can at least say one thing (Hesychasm apart and without allowing for any as yet unverified possibilities in the Western tradition itself), namely that a Christian aspirant enjoys one particular advantage inasmuch as he is able to profit by any unexpected opportunity of spiritual guidance without needing to be provided, even when entering on the most inward quest, with any spiritual "support" beyond the ones he already possesses by right. One is thinking always of Christianity under its still traditional form and not of various residues of its fragmentation where the indispensable means of grace are evidently lacking. If on the one hand a Christian has a number of special difficulties to contend with—and no religious form can be wholly free from such—on the other hand he can confidently claim for himself this unexpected fruit ripened from the original parting of the temple veil, a strange paradox in its way—but then spiritual life is full of paradoxical happenings. There is really nothing to be surprised at here.

---

tourists are coming there simply for the sake of a cheap holiday in romantic surroundings, have requested the Greek government to tighten the regulations for issuing permits of entry. A timely precaution, some will say; but then what becomes of the age-long freedom of pilgrimage itself?

The Spiritual Function of Civilization

BY ABU BAKR SIRAJ AD-DIN

(An address given in Arabic at the Azhar University, Cairo, during the Islamic Conference of 1964.)

WE HAVE HEARD many times during this conference the words "development"[1] *(taṭawwur)* and "progress" *(taqaddum)* and "renewal" *(tajdīd)* and "renaissance" *(nahḍah)*, and perhaps it will not be a waste of time to pause and consider what they mean. "Development" means moving away from the principles, and although it is necessary to move a certain distance from the principles in order to make applications of them, it is of vital importance to remain near enough for contact with them to be fully effective. Development must therefore never go beyond a certain point. Our ancestors were acutely conscious that this danger point had been reached in Islam hundreds of years ago; and for us, who are so much further removed in time than they were from the ideal community of the Prophet and his companions, the danger is all the greater. How then shall we presume not to be on our guard? How shall we presume not to live in fear of increasing our distance from the principles to the point where development becomes degeneration? And indeed it may well be asked as regards most of what is proudly spoken of today as development: Is it not in fact degeneration?

As for "progress," every individual should hope to progress, and that is the meaning of our prayer *Lead us along the straight path*.[2] The word "development" could also be used of individu-

[1] The conference in question was officially held "in response to the spirit of development," and there are reasons to think that it was intended to be something of a parallel to the Vatican Council.
[2] Quotations from the Koran are in italics.

104

als in the same positive sense. But communities do not progress; if they did, what community was better qualified to progress than the first Islamic community in all the impetus of its youth? Yet the Prophet said, "The best of my people are my generation; then those that come after them; then those that come after them." And we must conclude from the Koran that with the passage of the centuries a general hardening of hearts is inevitable, for it says of one community, *a long length of time passed over them so that their hearts were hardened;* and this same truth is to be understood also from what the Koran says of the elect, that they are *many in the earlier generations and few in the later generations.* The hope of communities must lie, not in "progress" or "development," but in "renewal," that is, restoration. The word "renewal" has been used so far throughout this conference mainly as a rather vague synonym of "development," but in its traditional, apostolic sense,[3] renewal is the opposite of development, for it means a restoration of something of the primordial vigor of Islam, and it is thus a movement of return, that is, a movement in a backward rather than a forward direction. Renewal has taken place from time to time, often more or less suddenly, when a renewer has been providentially sent to arrest development and to pull back the community to a closer contact with the principles.

As to "renaissance," it might in itself be used in the same sense as "renewal," but this word "renaissance" has very inauspicious associations, because the movement that is called the European Renaissance was nothing other, if we examine it carefully, than a renewal of the paganism of ancient Greece and Rome; and that the same "renaissance" marked the end of the traditional Christian civilization and the beginning of this modern materialistic civilization. Is the "renaissance" that we now hear of as taking place in the Arab states different from that one, or is it of the same kind?

There is not one of us, whether he be Arab or non-Arab, who does not rejoice in the independence of the Arab states and of Islamic countries in general, and it was to be hoped that this

[3] The Prophet said, "God will send to this community, at the head of every hundred years, one who will renew for it its religion."

independence would bring about a return to the noble civilization of Islam. But what do we see? We see the doors flung wide
open to everything that comes from Europe and America without the slightest discrimination. And it is to be noticed that the
terms *mandūb* (strongly recommended) and *makrūh* (strongly
discouraged)[4] have changed their significance. Thus, in the eyes
of the champions of this "renaissance" that we are now supposed to be enjoying, what is to be "strongly discouraged" is
everything that is left of the Islamic civilization in the way of
customs[5] such as wearing the turban and not shaving off the
beard, whereas what is "strongly recommended" is everything
that comes from the West. It may well be that only a very few
actually go so far as to say that this or that is to be discouraged
because it belongs to the civilization of our pious ancestors or
that a thing is to be recommended because it comes from the
West. But to judge by the facts, one might imagine that such
words were on every tongue, such thoughts in every head. And
what is the result of this? The result is that the rising generation is more ignorant of the practices of the Messenger of God,
and more cut off from those practices, than any generation that
has come into existence since the dawn of Islam. How then
shall we augur well of the present situation? And how shall we
not shrink from the word "renaissance" as from an evil omen?

All this was foreseen by the Prophet. He said, "You will
follow the ways of those that were before you [6] span for span
and cubit for cubit until if they went down into the hole of a
poisonous reptile you would follow them down." That descent
is now taking place; and it is called development and progress.

More than one delegate has mentioned, during this conference, that Islam embraces the whole of life, and no one doubts

[4] In Islam—and the same must be implicitly if not explicitly true of all
religions—every earthly possibility falls into one of five categories,
being either obligatory *(farḍ)*, strongly recommended *(mandūb)*, allowed *(mubāḥ)*, strongly discouraged *(makrūh)*, or forbidden *(ḥarām)*. It
is against the second and fourth of these that a subversive movement
will direct its efforts, at any rate to begin with, for since they are less
absolute than the first and the fifth, it is easier to break through their
defenses.
[5] *Sunan* (singular *sunnah*), that is, customs of the Prophet.
[6] The Jews and the Christians.

this. But what is actually happening today in many if not most Islamic countries is that life is embracing Islam—embracing, no, for it is a stranglehold rather than an embrace! Life is crowding religion out, pushing it into a little corner, and stifling it more and more so that it can scarcely breathe.

And what is the remedy?

By way of answering this question, let us recollect certain outer aspects of our civilization—I mean, the Islamic civilization—aspects whose function was, and can be again, to act as a protective shell for the kernel, that is, for the religion itself. The fabric of our civilization is woven out of the example set by our Prophet; and particularly significant in this connection is the fact that his house was a prolongation of his mosque. Thus for twelve hundred years—and more in many Islamic countries—the houses of his people were prolongations of the mosques. The Muslim would take off his shoes when he entered his house just as he would take them off when he entered the mosque; he would sit in his house in the same manner as he sat in the mosque; he would put such ornaments on the walls of his house as he saw on the walls of the mosque; nor would he put in his house any ornaments that would not be suitable for the mosque. Thus he was continually surrounded by reminders of the spiritual dignity and spiritual responsibilities of man, and he dressed himself according to the same principles. His clothes were in keeping with the dignity of man's function as representative of God on earth, and at the same time they made it easy for him to perform the ablution, and they were in perfect conformity with the movements of the prayer. Moreover they were an ornament to the prayer, unlike modern European clothes which rob the movements of the prayer of all their beauty and impede them, just as they act as a barrier between the body and the ablution.

All that I have mentioned is outward, but the outward acts upon the inward, and a man's clothes and his home are the nearest of all things to his soul, and their influence on it is perpetual and therefore incalculably powerful. There can be no doubt that these outward things were one of the secrets of the depth of piety among Muslims, for twelve hundred years;

and this brings us back to the saying that Islam embraces the whole of life. Thanks to the outer aspects of the Islamic civilization the whole of life was in fact penetrated by religion, and I see no other remedy for our present religious crisis but a return to that noble civilization whose function it is to create a worthy setting for the spirit of the religion, a setting that makes relatively easy the fulfillment of our ritual obligations. Nor can the community dispense with the help of anything that makes this spiritual life easier, for *man was created weak*. But this return can be accomplished only by the widespread setting of examples.

Arabs, you are in the abode of Islam,[7] where after your independence you are free to do what you will; and we look toward you from outside that abode and place our hopes in you. Do not disappoint us.

[7] *Dār al-Islām*, strictly speaking that part of the world that is under Islamic law, but here used more loosely to include any state that is officially Islamic.

Signs of the Times

BY MARTIN LINGS

In the Uncreated Principial Substance, which Hinduism terms *Prakriti*, there is perfect equilibrium between the upward, the expansive, and the downward tendencies, *sattva*, *rajas*, and *tamas*. The creation itself breaks this equilibrium, being in a sense a "victory" of *tamas* over *sattva*. This is inevitable, for creation means separation, and *tamas* is the tenebrous downward separative pull of manifestation away from the Principle. "Darkness was upon the face of the deep," says Genesis. The balance is partly restored, though still as it were within the framework of *tamas*, by the *Fiat Lux*. But "the rest on the seventh day," after the creation of man, celebrates the restoration of equilibrium at a higher level, for this final creation goes beyond separativity and introduces an element of reintegration. It is through the human species that this world is connected with the higher states of being. Through the heart of man alone lies the path of return; through this center manifestation "flows" back to its Principle in conformity with *sattva*, the luminous upward tendency that counterbalances the tamasic impetus with which all creation is penetrated. Hence the enmity, so much stressed in sacred texts, between man and Satan who is a personification of unbridled *tamas*, the "desire" inherent in manifestation to be separate from the Principle and to remain separate in an illusory self-sufficient independence.[1] Hell is the special domain of Satan because it is situated at the outermost edge of creation where the illusion of separate existence, that is, of the absence of God, is sharpest; and the domain of man is paradise because he is inwardly one with God, while

---

[1] Skepticism as to the possibility of creation is nothing other than a prolongation or projection of this desire. The same may be said of the belief that the material world has always existed and will always continue to exist.

outwardly, as a tree growing out of that root of union, he is a living witness to the divine presence. He can say "I" and mean "God," for his supreme quality is his capacity for individual extinction.

After the Fall, which again breaks the equilibrium, the human species is no longer sufficiently true to itself to be able to counterbalance the downward pull of *tamas*. The balance is partially restored by the establishment of religion on earth, which inaugurates the Golden Age; and the continuance of religion is ensured, when it becomes endangered, by subsequent divine revelations.[2] The downward impetus is thus checked for many individuals and for some, an ever decreasing number, is overcome altogether; it nonetheless continues as a general tendency down to the end of the cycle when the world as a whole reaches its maximum of "separation" from its divine origin and when man reaches his most abject state of submission to the powers of darkness.

The outlook that governs modern civilization and that characterizes anyone who can be described as "a typical product of the twentieth century" may be considered as a "sign of the times" in that it represents no less than man's capitulation to his archenemy—a capitulation that is all the more total for being unconscious. That is indeed the crux of the matter, for instead of being bent on revenge, the loser has finally been induced to believe that he has suffered no loss whatsoever, that his enemy is nonexistent, and that man, having evolved from next to nothing, is now better than he has ever been.

So total a defeat would have seemed impossible, even in a relatively near past. But the parable of the talents explains how the apparently impossible can be realized in a downward as well as in an upward direction. For just as the spiritual path, that is, the path of excelling oneself, is only practicable because "unto every one that hath shall be given, and he shall have

---

[2] The spiritual path, that is, the path of return to the Principle, is also in a sense a chain of losses and restorations of equilibrium. But there it is always a question of sacrificing a lower equilibrium in order to gain a higher one, whereas in the unfolding of the cycle of manifestation it is the inverse that takes place.

abundance," so also because "from him that hath not shall be taken away even that which he hath," the unspiritual man is liable to find himself suddenly lacking in those very endowments that seemed most securely his. Thus, for example, the rationalist and the modern scientist, having closed themselves to the spirit by demanding rational and scientific explanations of transcendent truths, are liable to find themselves deserted by logic and by science in the hour of greatest need. Still bristling with antireligious arguments, they have meekly let themselves become the dupes of one of the most subrational persuasions and one of the most unscientific theories that have ever trespassed upon the mind of man.

Though in many respects they overlap, rationalism and scientism may be considered as the two poles, subjective and objective, of the pseudoreligion of the modern world. Rationalism, with its false logic, wishful thinking, and warped sense of values supplies the pseudofaith, namely, the belief that man has progressed throughout the ages and that he will inevitably continue to progress in the future. The error here is almost entirely subjective: Progressism is rooted in complacency, and it depends, not on false data, but on a false interpretation of certain facts coupled with a perpetual readiness to turn a blind eye to other facts. In scientism, which supplies the pseudodoctrine of evolution, the error is mainly objective, at any rate as far as the "layman" is concerned. Here the scientist, who is the "high priest" of the modern world and who alone has power to speak ex cathedra, misleads his flock with a false object of faith. This is by far the greatest triumph of the enemy,[3] for the question of progress must always remain a matter of opinion, but evolution is presented as a scientific fact that "transcends" all discussion; and whereas truly transcendent doctrines lend wings to the intelligence, the pseudotranscendent paralyzes it and sets up a stifling "dictatorship" in the soul.

As to the "layman," it must be admitted that he is subject to considerable pressure. He is pounded by a battery of scien-

---

[3] It is typical of his tactics to allow certain lesser truths—that "discovered" by Copernicus, for example—to pave the way for an enormous lie.

tific terms he does not understand, and on the face of it there would seem to be no reason why the scientist—dry, matter-of-fact, purely objective, and infallibly accurate, as he is supposed to be—should wish to deceive as regards evolution. The public is not to know that the scientist is evolutionist, not in virtue of his science, but by "religion"; but though this secret is not always well kept,[4] the victims of the deception are for the most part only too eager to be deceived. Progressism is, for evolutionism, the most fertile of soils.

In this context the theories of evolution and progress may be likened to the two cards that are placed leaning one against the other at the "foundation" of a card house. If they did not support each other, both would fall flat, and the whole edifice, that is, the outlook that dominates the modern world, would collapse. The idea of evolution would have been accepted neither by scientists nor by "laymen" if the nineteenth-century European had not been convinced of progress, while in this century evolutionism has served as a guarantee of progress in the face of all appearances to the contrary. To those who refuse to see these appearances and who continue to believe in progress "because of all that man has achieved in the last hundred years" and "because there is such promise for the future," there is clearly nothing to be said. But for those whose progressism is propped up only by evolutionism and leans with all its weight on the teaching that evolution is "a scientifically proved fact," it can be a relief comparable to waking up after a bad dream to read an objective assessment of evolutionism by a scientist who is not an evolutionist. One such assessment is Douglas Dewar's book *The Transformist Illusion.*[5] More recent is Evan Shute's *Flaws in the Theory of Evolution.*[6]

The title of the latter is an understatement, for the book is

[4] Some evolutionists make it very clear in their writings and broadcast talks that their case is an outstanding illustration of the truth that man is nothing if not religious, and that if he gives up his religion he inevitably transfers his religious sentiments to something else, endowing it with all those rights and privileges that are the due of religion alone.

[5] Murfreesboro, Tenn.: DeHoff Publications, 1957.

[6] Nutley, N.J.: Craig Press, 1961.

a demonstration that the theory in question is pure conjecture: The only evolution that has been scientifically attested is on a very small scale and within narrow limits. To conclude from this "micro-evolution," which no one contests, that there could be such a thing as "mega-evolution"—that, for example, the class of birds could have evolved from the class of reptiles—is not merely conjecture but perverse conjecture, for as Shute points out, micro-evolution demonstrates the presence in nature of all sorts of unseen barriers that ensure the stability of the various classes and orders of animals and plants and that invariably cause transformation, when it has run its little course, to come to a dead end.

The realm of conjecture is always the realm of disagreement. Moreover some evolutionists are more scientific and more objective than others, and when their sense of science has been outraged beyond measure, they have not always been able to resist pouring scorn on some of the more fantastic ideas of their fellow evolutionists. As a rule such sallies are isolated and have little effect, if indeed they do not pass unnoticed, but when gathered together, as they are in this book, their weight is considerable, and by quoting from the evolutionists themselves[7] Shute has been able to show that the theory of mega-evolution is no more than a shell inside which its champions have demolished each other's conjectures until there is nothing left.

To sum up his thesis, the more science delves into the amazing intricacies of nature, the more overwhelming is the evidence that piles up against evolutionism. As he himself puts it: "Mega-evolution is really a philosophy dating from the days of biological ignorance; it was a philosophic synthesis built up in a biological kindergarten."

Looking at the question from quite a different angle—one that is closer to that of our main theme—it must be remembered that only by escaping from time can man escape from

[7] By way of example, he quotes from the American paleontologist Professor E. A. Hooton: "You can, with equal facility, model on a Neanderthaloid skull the features of a chimpanzee or the lineaments of a philosopher. These alleged restorations of ancient types of man have very little, if any, scientific value, and are likely only to mislead the public."

the phases of time. The spiritual path escapes from these phases because only its starting point lies within time. From there onward it is a "vertical" upward movement through supra-temporal domains as represented in Dante's Purgatorio and Paradiso. But modern science does not know of any such move-ment, nor is it prepared to admit the possibility of an escape from the temporal condition. The gradual ascent of no return that is envisaged by evolutionism is an idea that has been sur-reptitiously borrowed from religion and naïvely transferred from the supra-temporal to the temporal. The evolutionist has no right whatsoever to such an idea, and in entertaining it he is turning his back on his own scientific principles. Every pro-cess of development known to modern science is subject to a waxing and waning analogous to the phases of the moon, the seasons of the year, and the different periods of man's life. Even civilizations, as history can testify, have their dawn, their noon, their late afternoon, and their twilight. If the evolutionist out-look were genuinely "scientist," in the modern sense, it would be assumed that the evolution[8] of the human race was a phase of waxing that would necessarily be followed by the comple-mentary waning phase of devolution; and the question of whether or not man was already on the downward phase would be a major feature of all evolutionist literature. The fact that the question is never put, and that if evolutionists could be made to face up to it most of them would drop their theory as one drops a hot coal, does not say much for their objectivity.

All religions agree that we are passing through the final phase of one of the great cosmic cycles. The end of a cycle means that the possibilities that were contained within it from

---

[8] There could be no question of any such evolution from the standpoint of ancient natural science, which did not claim to have everything within its scope, that is, within the temporal domain. It could therefore admit to being transcended by the origins of earthly things. For these origins it looked beyond temporal duration to the divine creative act that places man (and the whole earthly state) on a summit from which there can only be a decline. The same applies to the different religions that also have their origins outside time. If civilizations wax and then wane, it is because each represents the temporal development of the religion on which it is based. (For a fuller treatment of this question, see Martin Lings's *Ancient Beliefs and Modern Superstitions*, Chap. 2.)

the beginning have reached their extremity of development, that is, their extremity of separation from the Principle. Such a period is one of "remoteness" from God, and one of its necessary characteristics is a world largely peopled by men and women who have no conception of man's true nature and responsibility. He is, for them, not the representative of God on earth, but merely the summit of the animal kingdom. With their backs turned to that center that is man's rightful place as mediator between heaven and earth, their "orientation" is entirely outward, in the direction of the boundary that separates humanity from the lower orders. The centrifugal tendency of modern man is often written on his face so clearly that if an evolutionist were at the same time something of a physiognomist,[9] he would indeed see reason to suppose that mankind, having reached its highest point of evolution, was already well advanced in the complementary phase of devolution.

Although such a supposition would bring him, as we shall see, far nearer the truth than he is now, he would nonetheless be wrong to suppose that the dividing line that separates humanity from the lower orders, as far as life on earth is concerned, could be crossed by anything but a miraculous suspension of the laws of nature. Sacred texts tell us of men having been transformed suddenly into apes by an overflow of divine anger, but mankind could never, by any natural course, devolve into apekind any more than the reverse process could take

[9] An unlikely combination, for physiognomy presupposes the knowledge of what man is and, above all, what God is. The Prophet of Islam said: "When anyone of you strikes a blow [in battle] let him avoid striking the face [of his enemy], for God created Adam in His image." This somewhat elliptical *Hadīth* demands, by way of commentary, the addition: ". . . and it is in the face that the image is especially concentrated." The human face is a mirror that reflects the divine qualities. The human hand is also such a mirror, but to be read, it requires knowledge of a special science, whereas the face is an open book to be read by effortless intuition; and physiognomy is nothing other than the ability to see, in any given face, how full and direct (or, as the case may be, how fragmentary and oblique) the reflection is. Traditionally, physiognomical powers are associated with faith (the Prophet said: "Beware of the believer's power to read the face"), and in fact the man best qualified to judge of the quality of a mirror, that is, to judge how faithfully it mirrors an object, is the man who has the clearest vision of that object in itself, apart from the mirror.

place. Such transformations would require organic changes that, miracles apart, could be effected only by drastic surgical operations.[10] But a man can, after death, "become an ape" in the sense that he can pass on into another state of existence in which, having lost his centrality, he might occupy a position analogous to that of an ape in this world; and an ape could "become a man" in the sense that through some mysterious working of divine grace[11] he might, after his death in this world, be born at the center of the world that comes "next" to it on the rim of the samsara, the great wheel of universal existence. But there is nothing collective about such possibili-

---

[10] Evolutionist texts continually rely on the ignorance or unobservance of the layman. Dewar (pp. 219–241) gives many outrageous examples from which we may quote Darwin's remark: "With some savages the foot has not altogether lost its prehensile power, as is shown by their manner of climbing trees, and of using them in other ways." The truth is, as Darwin must have known, that any human being can develop with practice, if driven by circumstances, certain powers of grasping with the feet. But such development can be only within very narrow limits, for organically the human foot, unlike the human hand, is not made for grasping. It is made to serve as a basis for man's upright posture and gait, whereas the "foot" of an ape is organically as prehensile as a hand. In the human foot the transverse ligament binds together all five toes, whereas in the ape it leaves the big toe free like a thumb. Let any reader of this article look at his own hand, which in the above respect is similar to the foot of an ape, and ask himself whether it is imaginable that even in millions of millions of years the ligament that binds together the four fingers could ever come to throw out a kind of noose, lassoo the thumb, and bind it up together with the fingers, all this, presumably, taking place under the skin. When Darwin says, "the foot has not altogether lost its prehensile power," does he mean "the lassooing has already taken place but the roping in has not quite been effected"? But he relies on such questions not being asked.

[11] Generally speaking, the most desirable destiny in this life for a peripheric being is to be intimately associated with a man who fulfills his centrality enough to be, in some degree, pontifex. It is also as pontifex that a man sacrifices an animal, and it is typical of our times that societies for the prevention of cruelty to animals should so confuse the issue as to include among their many admirable aims the deplorable one of seeking to "save" some animals from being sacrificed ritually (the most truly evolutionary fate that could befall them) and to consign them instead to the profane slaughterhouse. As to ascents made at lower levels in the hierarchy, from one peripheric degree to another, it is clearly auspicious for a lower being to be overwhelmed and absorbed by a higher one. The law of the jungle would seem to be woven upon the hidden mercies of such evolutions.

ties. The threads of which the universe is woven are individual existences moving divergently, as it were at different angles, throughout the samsara, some steeply ascending, others steeply descending, others moving more horizontally in a gradual descent or a gradual ascent. But though the threads cross each other's paths, each must be considered entirely alone in its relationship with the Absolute. Consciousness of this solitude, which every religion insists on, is an indispensable starting point for any spiritual path, and one of the attractions of progresso-evolutionism is that it blurs the "terrible" (to some) fact of this solitude by sugaring it over with a comforting illusion of collective security.[12]

It is partly the function of religion to convey to man as much knowledge as he can assimilate with profit; religions differ in exactly what they convey and what they withhold because of the difference of human collectivities. The scope of this article clearly will not allow us to dwell on the question at any length, but it may be remarked in passing that the doctrine of the samsara, which was not unknown to pre-Christian Europe but which is no more than implicit in Semitic monotheism, has become once more accessible to the Western world from Hinduism and Buddhism—accessible, that is, to anyone who feels impelled to make a serious study of religion; and in fact this doctrine is becoming more and more necessary because the present state of the world, especially in one of its already mentioned aspects, is for some minds so unintelligible as to be a real stumbling block. Without the doctrine of the samsara, how is one to explain the thousands of souls that are being born day after day into conditions spiritually so unfavorable as to offer no apparent hope of salvation? But if one knows that our position in this state was "earned" in our previous state upon the great round of existences, the problem no longer looms so large. The state of those countless people in the modern world who do not seem to have been given "a fair chance" can only be the result of their having already developed a centrifugal impetus in one of the samsara's other worlds, and since God is just, they

[12] Teilhard de Chardin, with his "point Omega," is one of the worst offenders in this respect.

must be said to have developed it willfully. But since He is also long-suffering, the process of losing centrality may be spread over more than one state of existence. The people in question are born into this world at the outside edge of humanity because they were "already" well on their way out of the central state, yet at the same time, since they have not actually left that state, there is always, despite appearances, an element of hope.

The doctrine of the samsara is bound to lead to the idea of reincarnation, for it is difficult to speak of other worlds except in terms of the one world we know. Everything depends on what may be called the "spiritual imagination" of the one who receives the doctrine. The statement that a man could be born in his next life as a lower animal or even as a vegetable or a mineral conveys adequately a truth, provided that the imagination of the hearer is large enough to take in all the terrible implications and sharp enough to galvanize him into the determination to make the most of the inestimable privilege of a central state, "so hard to obtain."[13] The danger of the doctrine is always that an unimaginative wishful thinker will abstract from it the notion that he will be given "another chance" and turn a blind eye to all the rest. But this danger is as nothing compared with the danger of believing that there is no life of any kind after death, a danger that hangs like a shadow over every child that is born into all but the most traditional parts of the modern world.

In any case, the error of reincarnationism cannot be put on a level with the error of evolutionism. The word "reincarnation" as currently used expresses metaphorically, if not literally, what does actually take place. But evolutionism, together with its inseparable complement of progressism, is nothing but a satanic parody of the spiritual path of escape from the samsara, a parody that flattens the vertical to the horizontal and, for having "played one's part," offers as prize, to be awarded not posthumously but "humously"—that is, not to a blessed spirit but to a corpse—an ever-receding earthly "welfare" of doubtful possibility and doubtful desirability. To come back

[13] See Marco Pallis, "Is There Room for 'Grace' in Buddhism?" in this volume.

almost to our starting point, what worse thing could be desired for man by his worst ill-wisher than this twofold pseudoreligion of the modern world that systematically eliminates everything that its victim has an imperative need to know and to do?

And what of God? In Communist countries, where the modern pseudoreligion is de facto and de jure the state religion, God is officially excluded, which is logical and consequent enough, for what function can Divinity have in an entirely flat, "horizontal" universe? In so-called Christendom the pseudoreligion prevails de facto but not de jure. In consequence, God is tolerated, and some would maintain that faith is even encouraged. "And," they add, "it is sincere belief in God that matters; all the rest is of no importance." But supposing that all or some of "the rest" colors their conception of God? Let us consider what sort of faith is "encouraged" by the modern Western world. What place, in other words, does its educational system allot to Christianity? Generally speaking, and always allowing for exceptions, it would be true to say that in most of their lessons, partly through what they are taught and partly owing to the general outlook that all too clearly prevails among the teachers, the pupils are indoctrinated with the modern pseudoreligion; and in the hour or two a week set aside for the study of the Bible they are given a glimpse of an opposite perspective, though the contradictions are presented as "tactfully" as possible, always at the expense of religion. In some cases the first chapters of Genesis are omitted; in others they are taught without comment; in others they are taught as "myths" (in the modern ignoble misuse of that noble word); but one may be certain that the pupils' attention will never be drawn to the fact that Christianity has some of its deepest roots in these very chapters. In short, the whole implacable "either . . . or" is put into the mind of every pupil as if it were a "both . . . and," with its sharp edges so wrapped up that they appear to be round. But the sharp edges are nonetheless there, and a little reflection will cause them to work their way out. Nor does religion, lukewarmly, fragmentarily, apologetically presented as it is, stand much chance when the pupils are faced with a sharp choice between it and modernism. The result is that those who cling to their already precarious faith instinctively block their own channels of spiritual thought, and by a kind of self-imposed mental paralysis, scarcely daring to think about their religion, they sacrifice a vital aspect of sincerity as defined by Christ in his first commandment: "Thou shalt love the Lord thy God with all thy mind"; and it is precisely this part of the commandment that depends most on human initiative, that is, that we should be best able, by our own efforts, to fulfill, though the question of grace can never be absent.

Keeping well within this framework of mental paralysis, Teilhard de Chardin also blocks the main and obvious channels of thought. His appeal lies in his providing certain ingeniously devised side channels which relieve the paralytic by keeping up an illusion of normal mental activity. In other words, with an extraordinary capacity for turning a blind eye and a deaf ear to this and that, he creates a kind of mental hubbub in order to drown the voice of reason, refusing altogether to put to himself the following questions which, for anyone who has received a modern Western education, loudly cry out to be asked:

"If God exists, as we are taught to believe, and if evolution is a scientific fact, as we are forbidden to doubt, what sort of being can God be? Why did He choose to turn mankind back toward the past in longing for a lost paradise, and to leave them so turned, in all parts of the world, for thousands of years, if He knew that the truth lay in just the opposite direction? Why could He not have taught them about evolution to begin with? Or at least brought them gradually to it, instead of allowing religion after religion to repeat and confirm the same old way of thinking? And why did He allow this to culminate, at any rate for the Western world, in a religion that, perhaps more inextricably than any other, is bound up with the doctrine of the fall of man?[14] And why, having prevented all His prophets from divulging evolution, did He allow a mere layman to stumble upon it and to propagate it in defiance of all the spiritual

---

[14] Islam is just as explicit about the fall as Christianity is, but unlike Christianity, it is not centered on any historical redeeming sacrifice in view of the fall.

authorities of the day, thereby causing millions of people to lose their faith in religion and in Him?"

"God moves in a mysterious way," some will argue, in a frantic attempt to retain both God and evolutionism. But you cannot sew up a gaping chasm with such a needle and thread. Seek to retain these two incompatibles, and you will be left with a deity who is not the Lord of All Mystery but a subhuman monster of incompetence, which is precisely what Teilhardism implies of God. But outside the very special climate of this pseudomystical fantasy, one only needs to be able to put two and two together to see that either evolutionism or God must go; and modern education begins to tip the scale in favor of evolutionism at an increasingly earlier age. Many Westerners, even before they have left school, have already opted if not for atheism at least for an agnostic reserve of judgment that they, like their parents, will probably never see fit to unreserve. But a normally functioning mind, which is just what they are systematically deprived of—that is, a mind neither warped by rationalism nor spellbound by materialist scientism—would have no difficulty, when faced by the above questions, in finding the right answer and in razing the whole "card house" of modern ideology to the ground.

Cosmology and Modern Science

BY TITUS BURCKHARDT

I

IN WHAT FOLLOWS attention will be drawn to certain gaps in modern science, and these will be judged by means of the criteria provided by cosmology in the traditional sense of that term. We know that the Greek word *cosmos* means "order," implying the ideas of unity and totality. Cosmology is thus the science of the world inasmuch as it reflects its unique cause, being. This reflection of the uncreated in the created necessarily presents itself under diverse aspects, and even under an indefinite variety of aspects, each of which has about it something whole and total, so that there are a multiplicity of visions of the cosmos, all equally possible and legitimate and springing from the same universal and immutable principles.

These principles, by reason of their very universality, are essentially inherent in human intelligence at its most profound; but this pure intellect becomes "disengaged," generally speaking and for the man who is predisposed thereunto, only with the aid of supernatural elements that an authentic and complete spiritual tradition alone can supply. That is to say, all genuine cosmology is attached to a divine revelation, even if the object considered and the mode of its expression are situated apparently outside the message this revelation brings.

Such is the case, for instance, with Christian cosmology, the origin of which appears at first sight somewhat heterogeneous, since it refers on the one hand to the biblical account of creation even while being based, on the other hand, on the heritage of the Greek cosmologists; if there seems to be a certain eclecticism here, it should be stressed that this is providential, since the two sources in question complement one another in a harmonious way, the first being presented in the form of a myth and the other under the form of a doctrine expressed in comparatively rational terms, one that is therefore neutral from the viewpoint of symbolism and of a spiritual perspective.

Moreover, there can only be question of a syncretism where there is a mixture, hence confusion, of planes and modes of expression. Now, the biblical myth of the creation and the Greek cosmology do not present any formally incompatible perspectives, nor do they duplicate one another, as would be the case if one attempted a mingling of Buddhist cosmology, for example, with the figurative teaching of the Bible. The biblical myth assumes the form of a drama, a divine action that appears to unfold in time, distinguishing the principial and the relative by a "before" and "after." Greek cosmology, for its part, corresponds to an essentially static vision of things; it depicts the structure of the world, such as it is, as "now and always," as a hierarchy of degrees of existence, of which the lower stages are conditioned by time, space, and number, while the superior degrees are situated beyond temporal succession and spatial or other limits. This doctrine thus presents itself quite naturally—and providentially—as a scientific commentary on the scriptural symbolism.

The biblical myth is revealed, but neither is the Greek cosmology of purely human origin; even with Aristotle, that distant founder of Western rationalism, certain basic ideas, like his distinction between form *(eidos)* and matter *(hyle)*, for example, undoubtedly spring from a knowledge that is suprarational and therefore timeless and sacred. Aristotle translates this wisdom into a homogeneous dialectic. His dialectic is valid because the law inherent in thought reflects in its own way the law of existence. At the same time he demonstrates reality only in such measure as it is able to be logically determined. Plato and Plotinus go much further; they reach beyond the "objectivized" cosmology of Aristotle, restoring to symbolism all its suprarational significance. Christian cosmology borrowed the analytical thought of Aristotle, but it is from Plato that it drew the doctrine of archetypes that vindicates symbolism and confirms the primacy of intellectual intuition over discursive thought.

The keystone of all Christian cosmology and the crucial element that renders possible the fusing of the biblical myth with the Greek heritage is the evangelical doctrine of the Logos as source of both existence and knowledge. This doctrine, which in itself exceeds the plane of cosmology—the Gospels contain hardly any cosmological elements—constitutes nonetheless its spiritual axis; it is through this doctrine that the science of the created is connected with the knowledge of the uncreated. It is thus, through its link with metaphysics—comprised in this case in the Johannine doctrine of the Word—that cosmology is reconciled with theology; before becoming an *ancilla theologiae* it is an extension of gnosis.

The same might be said of all traditional cosmologies and in particular of those belonging to Islam and Judaism; their immutable axis will always be a revealed doctrine of the spirit or intellect, whether the latter be conceived as uncreated (as in the case of the Word) or as created (as with the primary intellect) or as having two aspects, the one created and the other uncreated.[1]

We know that there were frequent exchanges between the Christian, Muslim, and Jewish cosmologists, and the same certainly occurred as between the Hellenistic cosmologists and certain Asiatic civilizations; but it goes without saying (as Guénon pointed out) that generally speaking, the traditional cosmologies have no kinship with historical borrowings, for in the first place there is the nature of things, and, after that, there is intuitive knowledge. This knowledge, as we have said, must be vivified by a sacred science, the written and oral repository of a divine revelation. Be that as it may, all is contained definitively in our own soul, whose lower ramifications are identified with the realm of the senses but whose root reaches up to pure being and the supreme essence, so that man grasps in himself the axis of the cosmos. He can "measure" its whole "vertical" dimension, and in this respect his knowledge of the world can

---

[1] Ibn-Arabi uses a similar expression when speaking of *ar-Ruh*, universal spirit, in accordance with certain Koranic formulations. As for the primary intellect *(nous)* of Plotinus, it can likewise be regarded under these two aspects; moreover, the Plotinian doctrine of divine emanations does not introduce the distinction created-uncreated.

be adequate in spite of the fact that he will necessarily be ignorant of much, or even nearly all, of its "horizontal" extension. It is thus perfectly possible for traditional cosmology to convey, as it does, a knowledge that is real and incomparably vaster and more profound than that offered by the modern empirical sciences, even while entertaining childish, or more precisely "human," opinions about realities of the physical order.

Western cosmology fell out of favor from the moment when the ancient geocentric system of the world was replaced by the heliocentric system of Copernicus. For that to be possible cosmology had to be reduced to cosmography alone; thus the form was confused with the content, and the one was rejected with the other. In reality the medieval conception of the physical world, of its ordonnance and its extension, did not correspond only to a natural, and therefore realistic, vision of things; it expressed, at the same time, a spiritual order, in which man has his organic place.

Let us pause, for a moment, at this vision of the world, known to us particularly through the poetic works of Dante.[2] The planetary heaven and the heaven of fixed stars that surrounds it were presented as so many concentric spheres, "all the more vast inasmuch as they possess more virtue," as Dante explains, and of which the extreme limit, the invisible heaven of the empyrean, is identified both with universal space and pure duration. Spatially it represents a sphere of unlimited radius, and temporally, it is the background of all movement. Its continual rotation bears along with it all inferior movements, which are measured in relation to it, though it cannot itself be measured in an absolute way, since time cannot be divided except in reference to the marking out of a movement in space.

These spheres symbolize the superior states of consciousness

[2] There has been much discussion round the question of whether the *Divine Comedy* was influenced by an Islamic model; though the thing is possible in itself, this is not necessarily the case, given that the symbolism in question results both from spiritual realities as already described and from the Ptolemaic system that is common to the Christian and Muslim civilizations of the Middle Ages.

and, more exactly, the modalities of the soul that, while still contained in the integral individuality, are more and more irradiated by the divine spirit. It is the empyrean, the "threshold" between time and not-time, that represents the extreme limit of the individual or formal world. It is in crossing this limit that Dante obtains a new vision, one that is to some extent inverse to the cosmic order. Up to that point the hierarchy of existence, which goes from corporeal to spiritual, expresses itself through a gradual expansion of space, the container being the cause and master of the contained. Now the divine being reveals itself as the center around which the angels revolve in ever closer and closer choirs. In reality there is no symmetry between the two orders, planetary and angelic, for God is at one and the same time the center and container of all things. It is the physical order alone, that of the starry firmament, that represents the reflection of the superior order.

As for the circles of hell, which Dante [3] describes as a pit sunk into the earth as far as the "point toward which all heaviness tends," they are not the inverse reflection but the contrary of the celestial spheres. They are those spheres overturned, as it were, whereas the mountain of purgatory, which the poet tells us was formed from the earth cast up by Lucifer in the course of his fall toward the center of gravity, is, correctly speaking, a compensation for hell. By this localization of hell and purgatory, Dante did not intend to establish a geography; he was not deluded concerning the provisional character of the symbolism, although he obviously believed in the geocentric system of Ptolemy.

The heliocentric system itself admits of an obvious symbolism, since it identifies the source of light with the center of the world. Its rediscovery by Copernicus,[4] however, produced no

[3] Concerning the symbolical location of the hells, medieval authors differ and seem to contradict one another. For Dante, the hells are situated beneath the earth, which means that they correspond to inferior states; for others, and especially for certain Muslim cosmologists, they are to be found "between heaven and earth," that is to say, in the subtle world.

[4] For it is not a case of an unprecedented discovery. Copernicus himself refers to Nicetas of Syracuse as also to certain quotations in Plutarch.

new spiritual vision of the world; rather was it comparable to the dangerous popularization of an esoteric truth. The heliocentric system had no common measure with the subjective experiences of people; in it man had no organic place. Instead of helping the human mind to go beyond itself and to consider things in terms of the immensity of the cosmos, it only encouraged a materialistic Prometheanism which, far from being superhuman, ended by becoming inhuman.

Strictly speaking, a modern cosmology does not exist, in spite of an abuse of language whereby the modern science of the sensible universe is called cosmology. In fact, the modern science of nature expressly limits itself to the corporeal domain alone, which it isolates from the total cosmos while considering things in their purely spatial and temporal phenomenality, as if suprasensible reality with its differing levels was nothing at all and as if that reality were not knowable thanks to the intellect, in which it is analogically inherent in virtue of the correspondence between the macrocosm and the microcosm. But the point we wish to stress here is the following one: "Scientism" is an objective knowledge that would have itself mathematical and exclusive. By virtue of this fact, it behaves as if the human subject did not exist or as if that subject were not a subtle mirror indispensable for the phenomenal appearing of the world. There is a deliberate ignoring of the fact that the subject is the guarantor of the logical continuity of the world and also, by virtue of its intellectual essence, the witness of every objective reality.

In fact, a knowledge that is "objective" and therefore independent of particular "subjectivities" definitely presupposes immutable criteria, and these could not exist, if there were not in the individual subject itself an impartial background, a witness transcending the individual—that is to say precisely, the intellect. After all, knowledge of the world presupposes the underlying unity of the knowing subject, so that one might say of a voluntarily agnostic science what Meister Eckhart said of the atheists: "The more they blaspheme God, the more they praise him." The more science affirms an exclusively "objective" order of things, the more it manifests the underlying unity of the spirit; it does this indirectly and unconsciously and in spite of itself—that is to say, contrary to its own thesis—but when all's said and done, it proclaims in its own way that which it intends to deny. In the perspective of scientism the total human subject who is at the same time sensibility, reason, and intellect is replaced in an illusory way by mathematical thought alone. According to a distinguished scientist of our century,[5] all true progress of natural science resides in the fact that it disengages itself more and more from subjectivity and that it brings out more and more clearly what exists independently of human conceiving, without troubling itself about the fact that the result has only a distant likeness to that which the original perception took for real. According to this declaration, which is considered authoritative, the subjectivity from which one is trying to break loose is not reducible to the intrusion of sensorial accidents and emotional impulsions into the order of objective knowledge. It is the entire "human conception of things," that is to say, both the direct perception by the senses and its spontaneous assimilation by the imagination, that is in question; only mathematical thought is considered to be objective or true. The latter allows in fact a maximum of generalization while remaining linked to number, so that it can be verified on the quantitative plane. It does not, however, include the whole of reality as communicated to us through our senses; it effects a selection of that reality, and the scientific prejudice we have just been speaking of treats as unreal all that this selection leaves out. Thus it is that those sensible qualities called "secondary," such as colors, odors, savors, and sensations of hot and cold, are considered to be subjective impressions implying no objective quality, or possessing no other reality than that which belongs to their indirect physical causes, as for example, in the case of colors, to the various frequencies of the luminous waves: "Once it be admitted that in principle the sensible qualities cannot as such be considered to be qualities of the things themselves, physics offers us an entirely sure and

[5] James Jeans, *Die neuen Grundlagen der Naturerkenntnis* (Stuttgart, 1935).

homogeneous system, one which answers all questions as to what really underlies those colors, sounds, temperatures, etc." [6] What is this homogeneity but the result of a certain reduction of the qualitative aspects of nature to quantitative modalities? Modern science therefore asks us to sacrifice a good part of that which makes for us the reality of the world, and offers us in exchange mathematical schema of which the only advantage is to help us to manipulate matter on its own plane, which is that of quantity.

The mathematical selection of reality does not only eliminate the "secondary" qualities of perception, it removes also what the Greek philosophers and the Scholastics called form—that is to say, the qualitative "seal" imprinted on matter by the unique essence of a being or a thing. For modern science, the essential form does not exist: "Some rare Aristotelians," writes a theoretician of modern science,[7] "still perhaps think they can attain intuitively, through some illumination by the active intellect, the essential ideas of the things of nature; but this is nothing but a lovely dream. . . . The essences of things cannot be contemplated, they must be discovered by experience, by means of a laborious work of investigation." To this a Plotinus, an Avicenna, or a Saint Albert the Great would answer that there is nothing more evident in nature than the essences of things, since these manifest themselves in the very "forms." Only, these cannot be discovered by a "laborious work of investigation" nor measured quantitatively; but the intuition that grasps them leans directly upon sensory perception and upon imagination inasmuch as the latter synthetizes the impressions received from outside.

Moreover, what is this human reason that tries to grasp the essences of things by "a laborious work of investigation"? Either this faculty of reason is truly capable of attaining its object, or it is not. Now, we know that reason is limited, but we also know that it is able to conceive truths that are independent of individuals, therefore that a universal law is manifested in it.

[6] B. Bavink, *Hauptfragen der heutigen Naturphilosophie* (Berlin, 1928).
[7] Josef Geiser, *Allgemeine Philosophie des Seins und der Natur* (Münster i.W., 1915).

If human intelligence is not merely "organized matter"—in which case it would not be intelligence—this means it necessarily participates in a transcendent principle. Without entering into philosophical discussions on the nature of reason, we can compare the relation existing between it and its supra-individual source (which medieval cosmology calls "active intellect" and in a more general sense "first intellect") to the relation of a reflection to its luminous source, and this image will be at the same time more vast and more correct than any philosophical definition whatsoever. A reflection is always limited by the nature of its reflective plane—in the case of reason, this plane is the mind and in a more general sense the human psyche—but the nature of light remains essentially the same, in its source as in its reflection; the same applies to spirit, whatever may be the formal limits that a particular reflective plane lends to it. Now, spirit is essentially and wholly knowledge; in itself it is subject to no foreign constraint, and nothing could in principle prevent its knowing itself and at the same time knowing all the possibilities contained in itself. Therein is to be found a means of access, not to the material structure of things in particular and in detail, but to their permanent essences.

All truly cosmological knowledge is founded on the qualitative aspects of things—that is to say, on "forms" insofar as these are marks of their essence. By this fact, cosmology is at the same time direct and speculative, for it grasps the qualities of things in a direct way, without calling them in question, and at the same time it disengages them from their particular attachments in order to consider them at their different levels of manifestation. The universe thus reveals its internal unity and shows at the same time a rainbow-hued variety of aspects and dimensions. Often this vision of things has something poetic about it, a fact that is evidently not to its detriment, since all genuine poetry comprises a presentiment of the essential harmony of the world; it is in this sense that Mohammed was able to say "Surely there is a part of wisdom in poetry."

If reproach can be leveled at this vision of the world on the grounds that it is more contemplative than practical and that it neglects the material connections of things (which in reality is hardly a reproach), it can be said on the other hand about scientism that it empties the world of all its qualitative sap. The traditional vision of things is above all "static" and "vertical." It is static because it refers to constant and universal qualities, and it is vertical in the sense that it attaches the inferior to the superior, the ephemeral to the imperishable. The modern vision, on the contrary, is basically "dynamic" and "horizontal"; it is not the symbolism of things that interests it, but their material and historical connections.

The great argument in favor of the modern science of nature —an argument that counts for a lot in the eyes of the crowd (whatever may be the reservations made by men of science themselves)—is its technical applicability; this, so it is believed, proves the validity of scientific principles,[8] as if a fragmentary and in some respects problematical efficacy were a proof of an intrinsic and total value. In reality, modern science displays a certain number of fissures that are not only due to the fact that the world of phenomena is indefinite and that therefore no science could come to the end of it; those fissures derive especially from its systematic ignorance of all the noncorporeal dimensions of reality. They manifest themselves right down to the foundations of modern science, and in domains seemingly as "exact" as that of physics; they become gaping cracks when one turns to the disciplines connected with the study of the forms of life, not to mention psychology, where an empiricism that is relatively valid in the physical order encroaches strangely upon a foreign field. These fissures, which do not affect only the theoretical realm, are far from harmless; they represent, on the contrary, in their technical consequences, so many seeds of catastrophe.

From the fact that the mathematical conception of things inevitably participates in the schematic and discontinuous character of number, it neglects, in the immense tissue of na-

---

[8] It is, however, a fact that most of the greatest technical inventions have been effected on the basis of theories that were inadequate or even false.

ture, all that consists of pure continuity and of relations subtly kept in balance. Now, continuity and equilibrium exist before discontinuity and before crisis; they are more real than these latter and incomparably more precious.

II

In modern physics the space in which the heavenly bodies move, as also the space traversed by the trajectories of the minutest bodies such as electrons, is conceived as a void. The purely mathematical definition of spatial and temporal relations between various bodies great or small is in this way rendered easier. In reality a corporeal "point" "suspended" in a total void would be without any relation with other corporeal "points"; it would, so to speak, fall back into nothingness. People speak of "fields of force," but by what are these fields supported? A totally empty space could not exist; it is only an abstraction, an arbitrary idea that but goes to show where mathematical thinking can lead to when artificially detached from the concrete intuition of things.

According to traditional cosmology, ether fills all space without distinction. We know that modern physics denies the existence of ether, since it has been established that it opposes no resistance to the rotatory movement of the earth, but it is forgotten that this quintessential element, which is at the basis of all material differentiations, is not itself distinguished by any particular physical quality, so that it could not offer opposition to anything whatsoever. It represents the continuous ground whence all material discontinuities detach themselves.

If modern science admitted the existence of ether, it might perhaps find an answer to the question whether light is propagated as a wave or as a corpuscular emanation; most probably its movement is neither the one nor the other, and its apparently contradictory properties are explainable by the fact that it is most directly attached to ether and participates in the indistinctly continuous nature of the latter.

An indistinct continuum cannot be divided into a series of similar unities; if it does not necessarily escape from time or space, it nevertheless eludes graduated measurements. This is especially true of the velocity of light, which appears always the same independently of the movement of its observer, whether the latter displaces himself in the same direction or in the opposite direction. The velocity of light thus represents a limit-value; it can neither be exceeded nor rejoined by any movement, and this is like a physical expression of the simultaneity proper to the act of the intelligible light.

We know that the discovery of the fact that the velocity of light, when measured on the one hand in the sense of the rotation of the earth and on the other hand in the direction contrary to that rotation, is invariable has placed modern astronomers before the alternative either of admitting the immobility of the earth or else of rejecting the habitual notions of time and space. Thus it is that Einstein was led into considering space and time as two relative dimensions, variable in function of the state of movement of the observer, the only constant dimension being the velocity of light. The latter would be everywhere and always the same, whereas time and space vary in relation to one another; it is as if space could shrink in favor of time, and inversely.

If it be admitted that a movement is definable in terms of a certain relation of time and space, it is contradictory to maintain that space and time are to be measured in terms of a movement, that of light. It is true that on a quite different plane—when it is a question of the intelligible light—the image of light "measuring" the cosmos and realizing it thereby is not devoid of deep meaning; but what we have in view here is the physical order, which alone is considered, and with good cause, by Einstein's theory. It is therefore in this context that we will put the following question: What is that famous "constant number" that is supposed to express the speed of light? How can a movement having a definite velocity—and its definition will always be a relation of space and time—itself be a quasi-"absolute" measure of those two conditions of the physical world? Is there not here a confusion between the principial and quantitative domains? That the movement of light is the fundamental "measure" of the corporeal world we willingly believe but why should this measure itself be a number and even a definite number? Moreover, do the experiments that are supposed to prove the constant character of the speed of light really get beyond the earthly sphere, and do they not imply both space and time as usually imagined by us? Thus "300,000 km per second" is written to indicate the speed of light, and it is held that here is a value that, if it be not necessarily expressed everywhere in this manner, does nonetheless remain constant throughout the physical universe. The astronomer who counts, by referring to the lines of the spectrum, the light-years separating us from the nebula of Andromeda, supposes without more ado that the world is everywhere "woven" in the same manner. Now, what would happen if the constant character of the velocity of light came to be doubted—and there are plenty of chances that this will happen sooner or later—so that the only fixed pivot of Einstein's theory would fall down? The whole modern conception of the universe would immediately dissolve like a mirage.

We are told that reality does not necessarily agree with our inborn conceptions of time and space; but at the same time it is not doubted for a moment that the physical universe can be in agreement with certain mathematical formulas which, for their part, necessarily proceed from axioms that are no less inborn.

In the same order of ideas must be mentioned the theory according to which interstellar space is not the space of Euclid but a space that does not admit the Euclidean axiom of parallel lines. Such a space, so it seems, flows back upon itself without it being possible to assign to it a definite curve. It would be possible to see in this theory an expression of spatial indefinitude, since in fact space is neither finite nor infinite, as the ancients indicated by comparing space to a sphere whose radius exceeds every measure and which is itself contained in universal spirit. But this is not the way that modern theoreticians understand things, for they declare that our primary conception of space is quite simply false or incomplete, and that we must for that reason familiarize ourselves with non-Euclidean space, accessible to a disciplined imagination. Now, this is in no wise true, since this non-Euclidean space is only indirectly accessible starting from Euclidean space, so that the latter remains the qualitative model for every conceivable kind of space. In this case, as in many others, modern science tries to exceed mathematically the logic inherent in the imagination and to violate that logic by dint of mathematical principles, as if every intellectual faculty other than purely mathematical thought were somehow suspect.

In conformity with this mathematical schematism, matter itself is conceived as being discontinuous, since atoms, as well as their constituent corpuscles, are supposed to be even more isolated in space than are the heavenly bodies. Whatever may be the present conception of the atomic order—and theories put out on the subject change with disconcerting rapidity—it is always groupings of distinct corporeal "points" that are in question.

Let us recall here the traditional doctrine of matter.[9] It is starting out from "primary matter" that the world is constituted by successive differentiations, under the "nonacting" action of the informing essence, but this *materia prima* is not tangible matter; it underlies all definite existence, and even its nearest modality, *materia signata quantitate*, which is the basis of the corporeal world, is not manifested as such. According to a most judicious expression of Boethius,[10] it is by its "form" —that is to say, its qualitative aspect—that a thing is known, "form being like a light by which we know what that thing is." Now, *materia* as such is precisely that which is not yet formed and which by that very fact escapes all distinctive knowing. The world that is accessible to such knowing therefore extends between two poles that are unmanifested as such, the informing essence and the undifferentiated *materia*, just as the range of colors in the spectrum opens out through the refraction of white light—as such colorless therefore—in a similarly colorless medium.

---

[9] *Cf.* René Guénon, *The Reign of Quantity and the Signs of the Times* (Baltimore, Md.: Penguin Books Inc, 1972), Chap. II, *"Materia Signata Quantitate."*
[10] *De Unitate et Uno.*

Modern science, which despite its pragmatism is not behind-hand in claiming to offer a complete and comprehensive explanation of the sensible universe, strives to bring back all the qualitative richness of that universe to a certain structure of matter conceived as a variable grouping of minute bodies, whether these be defined as genuine bodies or as simple "points" of energy. This amounts to saying that all the "bundles" of sensible qualities, all that constitutes the world for us, with the exception of space and time, should be reduced, scientifically speaking, to a series of atomic "models" definable in function of the number, mass, trajectories, and velocities of the minute bodies concerned. It is evident that this reduction misses its mark, for though these "models" still comprise certain qualitative elements—if only their imaginary spatial form—we have here nonetheless a reduction of quality to quantity; now, quantity can never comprehend quality.

On the other hand, the elimination of qualitative aspects in favor of a more and more tight mathematical definition of atomic structure must necessarily reach a limit after which precision will open out on the indeterminate. This is just what is happening with modern atomist science, where mathematical reflection is being more and more replaced by statistics and calculations of probability and where the very laws of causality seem to be facing bankruptcy. If the "forms" of things are lights, as Boethius puts it, the reduction of the qualitative to the quantitative element can be compared to the action of a man who puts out all the lights the better to scrutinize the nature of darkness.

Modern science will never reach that matter that is at the basis of this world. But between the qualitatively differentiated world and undifferentiated matter there lies something like an intermediate zone—this is chaos. The sinister dangers attendant on atomic fission are but a pointer indicating the frontier of chaos and of dissolution.

III

If the ancient cosmogonies seem childish when one takes their symbolism literally (which amounts to misunderstanding them), modern theories about the origin of the world are frankly absurd. They are so, not doubtless in their mathematical formulations, but because of the blank inconsequence with which their authors set themselves up as sovereign witnesses of cosmic becoming, while at the same time holding that the human spirit itself is nothing but a product of that becoming. What connection is there between that primordial nebula, that eddy of matter whence they wish to derive both the earth and life and man, and this little mental mirror losing itself in conjectures—since for the scientists intelligence is but this—with the certainty of discovering in itself the logic of things? How can the effect judge concerning its own cause? And if there exist any constant laws of nature such as those of causality, number, space, and time, and also something that, within ourselves, has the right to say "this is true and this is false," where then lies the guarantor of truth, in the object or in the subject? Is the nature of our spirit only a little foam on the waves of the cosmic ocean, or is there to be found deep within it a timeless witness of reality?

Certain protagonists of the theories in question will perhaps say that they only busy themselves with the physical and objective realm without seeking to prejudge the realm of the subjective; they can, perhaps, refer back to Descartes, who defined spirit and matter as two realities coordinated by Providence but dissociate in fact. Quite plainly, this division of reality into watertight compartments served to prepare people's minds for the setting aside of whatever is not of the physical order, as if man were not himself a proof of the complexity of the real.

The man of antiquity, who pictured the earth as an island surrounded by the primordial ocean and covered by the celestial dome, or medieval man, who saw the heavens as concentric spheres starting out from the earthly center as far as the limitless sphere of the divine spirit, doubtless was misled concerning the true disposition and proportions of the sensible universe. On the other hand, both of them were fully conscious of an infinitely more important fact, namely that this corporeal world is not the whole of reality and that it is as if surrounded and pervaded by a reality both greater and more subtle, which in its turn is contained in the spirit; and they knew, indirectly or directly, that the world in all its extension disappears in the face of the infinite.

Modern man knows that the earth is only a ball suspended in a bottomless abyss and carried along in a dizzy and complex movement and that this movement is governed by other celestial bodies incomparably larger than this earth and situated at immense distances from it. He knows that the earth on which he lives is but a grain in comparison with the sun which, for its part, is but one grain amid myriads of other incandescent stars and that all is in motion. An irregularity in this assemblage of sidereal movements, the interference of a heavenly body foreign to our planetary system, a deviation of the sun's trajectory, or some other such cosmic accident would suffice to make the earth unsteady in its rotation, to trouble the course of the seasons, to change the atmosphere and to destroy mankind. Modern man likewise knows that the smallest atom contains forces that, if unchained, could involve the earth in an almost instantaneous conflagration; all this, the "infinitely small" like the "infinitely great," presents itself from the point of view of modern science as a mechanism of unimaginable complexity of which the functioning is solely due to blind forces.

In spite of this, the man of our time lives and acts as if the normal and habitual unfolding of the rhythms of nature were assured for him. In practice, he neither thinks about the abysses of the stellar world nor about the terrible forces latent in every scrap of matter. He sees the sky above him as every child sees it, with its sun and its stars, but the remembrance of the astronomical theories prevents him from recognizing divine signs there. The sky no longer is for him the natural expression of the spirit enfolding and illuminating the world. Scientific knowing has substituted itself for that vision at once "naïve" and profound, not as a new consciousness of a vaster cosmic order, an order of which man forms part, but one from which he is exiled, an irremediable disorder in the face of abysses with which man no longer has any common measure. For nothing now reminds him that after all this whole universe is contained in him, not indeed in his individual being, but in the spirit that is in him and that is at the same time more than himself and more than the entire phenomenal universe.

IV

Even the least phenomenon participates in several continuities or cosmic dimensions, incommensurable in relation to each other; thus, ice is water by its substance, and in this respect it is not distinguishable from liquid water or water vapor, whereas it belongs by its state to solid bodies. Similarly, when a thing is constituted by diverse elements, it participates in their natures even while differing from them. Cinnabar, for instance, is a synthesis of sulfur and mercury; it is thus in some sense the sum of these two elements, but at the same time it possesses qualities that are not to be found in either of the above two substances. Quantities can be added to one another, but a quality is never only the sum of other qualities. By mixing the colors blue and yellow, green is obtained; this third color is therefore a synthesis of the other two, but it is not the product of a simple addition, for it represents at the same time a chromatic quality that is new and unique in itself.

Herein is to be seen something like a discontinuous continuity, which is even more marked in the biological order, where the qualitative unity of an organism is plainly distinguishable from its material composition. The bird that is born from the egg is made of the same elements as the egg, but it is not the egg. Similarly, the butterfly that issues from a chrysalis is neither that chrysalis nor the caterpillar that produced it. A kinship exists between these various organisms, a genetic continuity, but equally they display a qualitative discontinuity, since between the caterpillar and the butterfly there is something like a rupture of levels.

At every point of the cosmic tissue there is thus a warp and a weft that cross one another, as indicated by the traditional symbolism of weaving, according to which the warp threads, vertically hung on the loom of primitive form, represent the permanent essences of things—and so also qualities and essential forms—while the weft, which binds the warp together horizontally and at the same time covers it with its alternating waves, corresponds to the substantial or "material" continuity of the world.[11]

The same law is expressed by the classical hylomorphism, whereby the "form" of a thing or being, seal of its essential unity, is distinguished from its "matter," namely the plastic substance that receives this seal while conferring on it a concrete and limited existence. No modern theory has ever been able to replace this ancient theory, for the fact of reducing the whole plenitude of the real to one or other of its "dimensions" hardly amounts to an explanation of it. Modern science especially ignores what the ancients denoted by the name of "form," precisely because here there is question of a non-quantitative aspect of things, and such ignoring is not unrelated to the fact that this science discerns no criterion in the beauty or ugliness of a phenomenon. The beauty of a thing is the sign of its internal unity, its conformity to an indivisible essence, therefore also to a reality that can neither be counted nor measured.

It is necessary to point out here that the notion of "form" necessarily includes a twofold meaning. On the one hand, it denotes the delineation of a thing, and this is its most usual connotation; in this respect, form is situated on the side of matter or, more generally, on the side of the plastic substance which, for its part, limits realities and separates them.[12] On the other hand, "form" understood in the sense given it by the Greek philosophers, and after them by the Scholastics, is the association of qualities of a being or thing and therefore the expression or trace of its immutable essence.

The individual world is the "formal" world because it is the realm of realities constituted by the conjunction of a "form" with a "matter," whether subtle or corporeal. It is only in

[11] René Guénon, *The Symbolism of the Cross;* chapter on the symbolism of weaving.
[12] In Hindu parlance the distinction *nāma-rupa*, "name and form," is attached to the idea in question, "name" here standing for the essence of a being or thing, and "form" for its limited and external existence.

connection with a "matter," or plastic substance, that "form" plays the part of a principle of individuation; in itself, in its ontological basis, it is not an individual reality but an archetype, and as such it lies beyond limitations and beyond change. Thus a species is an archetype, and if it is only manifested by the individuals belonging to it, it is nonetheless as real and indeed incomparably more real than they are. As for the rationalist criticism that tries to prove the absurdity of the doctrine of archetypes by arguing that a multiplication of mental notions would imply a corresponding multiplication of archetypes—leading to the idea of the idea and so forth—it quite misses the point, since multiplicity can in no wise be transposed onto the level of archetypal roots. The latter are differentiated in a principial way, within being and in virtue of it, as if being were a single, homogeneous crystal potentially containing all possible crystalline forms whatsoever.[13] Multiplicity and quantity therefore exist only at the level of the "material" reflections of the archetype.

From what we have just said it follows that a species in itself is an immutable "form"; it could not evolve and become transformed into another species, although it can include variants, all these being diverse "projections" of a single essential form from which they will never become detached, just as the branches of a tree never become detached from their trunk.

It has been justly said [14] that the whole thesis of the evolution of species, inaugurated by Darwin, rests on a confusion between species and simple variation. Its advocates present as the start or "bud" of a new species what is really but a variant within the framework of a determinate specific type. This faulty assimilation is, however, insufficient to fill the numberless gaps in the paleontological succession of species; not only are related species separated by profound gaps, but there do not

[13] It goes without saying that all the images one can give of the nonseparative distinction of the possibilities contained in being remain imperfect and paradoxical.
[14] Douglas Dewar, *The Transformist Illusion* (Murfreesboro, Tenn.: Dehoff Publications, 1957). See also Louis Bounoure, *Déterminisme et Finalité*, Collection Philosophie, Flammarion.

even exist any forms such as would indicate a possible thread uniting different orders like fishes, reptiles, birds, or mammals. One can doubtless find certain fishes using their fins to crawl on a shore, but it is in vain that one would seek among them the least beginning of articulation, which alone would make possible the formation of an arm or paw. Similarly, if certain resemblances exist between reptiles and birds, their respective skeletons nonetheless exhibit a radically different structure. Thus, for example, the very complex articulation of its jaws, in a bird, and the connected organization of its hearing apparatus pertains to an entirely different plan from that found in reptiles; it is difficult to conceive how the one might have derived from the other.[15] As for the famous fossil bird *Archaeopteryx*, it is quite certainly a bird, despite the claws at the end of its wings, its teeth, and its long tail.[16]

In order to account for the absence of intermediate forms, the partisans of transformism sometimes have argued that these forms must have disappeared because of their very imperfection and precariousness; but this argument is plainly in contradiction with the principle of selection that is supposed to be the operative factor in the evolution of species. These sketchy attempts should be incomparably more numerous than the ancestors having already acquired a definitive form. Besides, if the evolution of species represents, as is declared, a gradual and continual process, all the real links in the chain—therefore all those that are destined to be followed—will be at the same time resultants and intermediaries, in which case it is difficult to see why the ones would be much more precarious and more destructible than the others.[17]

---

[15] Dewar, *The Transformist Illusion.*
[16] *Ibid.*
[17] Teilhard de Chardin *(The Human Phenomenon)* writes on this subject: "Nothing is by nature so delicate and fugitive as a beginning. As long as a zoological group is young, its characteristics remain undecided. Its edifice is tender. Its dimensions are slight. Relatively few individuals compose it, and these are rapidly changing. Both in space and duration, the peduncle (or the bud, which comes to the same thing) of a living branch corresponds to a minimum of differentiation, expansion and resistance. How then is time going to act on this feeble zone? Inevitably

The more conscientious among modern biologists either reject the transformist theory or else maintain it as a simple
"working hypothesis," being unable to conceive any genesis of
species that would not be situated in the "horizontal line" of
a purely physical and temporal becoming. For Jean Rostand:

> The world postulated by transformism is a fairy world,
> phantasmagoric, surrealistic. The chief point, to which
> one always returns, is that we have never been present
> even in a small way at *one* authentic phenomenon of evolu-
> tion . . . we keep the impression that nature today has
> nothing to offer that might be capable of reducing our
> embarrassment before the genuinely organic metamor-
> phoses implied in the transformist thesis. We keep the
> impression that, in the matter of the genesis of species as
> in that of the genesis of life, the forces that constructed
> nature are now absent from nature. . . .[18]

Even so, this biologist sticks to the transformist theory:

> I firmly believe—because I see no means of doing other-
> wise—that mammals have come from lizards, and lizards
> from fish; but when I declare and when I think such a
> thing, I try not to avoid seeing its indigestible enormity
> and I prefer to leave vague the origin of these scandalous
> metamorphoses rather than add to their improbability that
> of a ludicrous interpretation.[19]

All that paleontology proves to us is that the various animal
forms such as are shown by fossils preserved in successive
layers of the earth made their appearance in a vaguely ascend-

---

by destroying it in its vestiges." This reasoning, which obviously exploits the purely external and conventional analogy between a genealogical "tree" and a real plant, is an example of the "imaginative
abstraction" that characterizes this author's thought.
[18] *Le Figaro Littéraire*, April 20, 1957.
[19] *Ibid.*

ing order, going from relatively undifferentiated organisms—
but not simple ones [20]—to ever more complex forms, without
this ascension representing, however, a univocal and continuous line. It seems to move in jumps; that is to say, whole
categories of animals appear at once, without real predecessors.
What means this order, then? Simply that on the material
plane, the simple or relatively undifferentiated always precedes
the complex and differentiated. All "matter" is like a mirror
that reflects the activity of the essences by inverting it; that is
why the seed comes before the tree and the leaf bud before the
flower, whereas in the principial order perfect "forms" preex-
ist. The successive appearance of animal forms according to an
ascending hierarchy therefore in no wise proves their continual
and cumulative genesis.[21]

On the contrary, that which binds the diverse animal forms
to one another is something like a common model, which reveals itself more or less through their structures and which is
more apparent in the case of animals endowed with superior
consciousness such as birds and mammals. This model is expressed, for instance, in the symmetrical disposition of the
body, in the number of extremities and of sensory organs, as
also in the general form of the chief internal organs. It might
be suggested that the design and number of certain organs and
especially those of sensation simply correspond to the terrestrial surroundings, but this argument is reversible, since those
surroundings are precisely what the sensory organs grasp and
delimit. In fact, the model underlying all animal forms estab-

---

[20] The electron microscope has revealed the surprising complexity of
functions at work in the interior of a unicellular being.

[21] The most commonly mentioned example in favor of the transformist
thesis is the hypothetical genealogy of the equine animals. Charles
Depéret criticizes this view in the following terms: "Geological observation establishes in a formal manner that no gradual passage existed
between these genera"; the last *Palaeotherium* was extinct long since,
without transforming itself, when the first *Architherium* appeared, and
the latter had disappeared in its turn, without modification, before
being suddenly replaced by the invasion of *Hipparion*" (*Les Transformations du Monde Animal*, p. 107). To this it can be added that the supposed
primitive forms of the horse hardly recur in the equine embryology,
though the development of the embryo is commonly regarded as
recapitulating the evolution of the species.

lishes the analogy between the microcosm and the macrocosm. Against the background of this common cosmic pattern, the differences between species and the gaps separating the ones from the others are all the more marked.

Instead of "missing links," which the partisans of transformism vainly seek, nature offers us, as if in irony, a large variety of animal forms which, without coming out of the preestablished framework of a species, imitate the appearance and customs of a species or order foreign to them. Thus, for example, whales are mammals but borrow the aspect and behavior of fishes; hummingbirds have the appearance, the iridescent coloring, the flight, and the mode of feeding associated with butterflies; the armadillo is covered with scales like a reptile while being a mammal, and so on. Most of these animals of imitative form represent superior species that take on the aspect of relatively inferior ones, a fact that excludes a priori our interpreting them as intermediary links of an evolution. As for their interpretation as forms of adaptation to determined surroundings, this seems more than dubious, for what could be, for instance, the intermediate forms between some land mammal or other and the dolphin? [22] Among these "imitative" forms, representing as many extreme cases, we must also include the fossil bird *Archaeopteryx* mentioned above.

Since each animal order represents an archetype that includes the archetypes of its corresponding species, one might well ask oneself whether the existence of "imitative" animal forms does not contradict the immutability of the essential forms; but this is not the case, for the existence of such "mimics" on the contrary demonstrates that immutability by a logical exhausting of all the possibilities inherent in a given type or given essential form. It is as if nature, after bringing forth fishes, reptiles, birds, and mammals with their distinctive characters, wished besides to show that she was able to produce an

[22] On the subject of the hypothetical transmutation of a land animal into the whale, Douglas Dewar wrote: "I have often challenged transformists to describe plausible ancestors situated in the intermediate phases of this supposed transformation" ("What the Animal Fossils Tell Us," Trans. Vict. Inst., Vol. 74).

animal like the dolphin which, while remaining a true mammal, possesses at the same time almost all the faculties of a fish, or a creature like the tortoise, which possesses a skeleton covered in flesh, yet at the same time is enclosed in an external carapace after the fashion of certain mollusks.[23] Thus does nature manifest her protean power, her inexhaustible capacity for generation, even while remaining faithful to the essential forms, which are in fact never blurred.

Each essential form—or each archetype—includes after its own fashion all the others, but without confusion; it is like a mirror reflecting other mirrors, which in turn also reflect it.[24] By its deepest significance the mutual reflection of types is an expression of the metaphysical continuity of existence, or of the unity of being.

Some biologists, in regard to the discontinuity in the paleontological succession of species, postulate an evolution by leaps and in order to render this theory plausible, refer to the sudden mutations observed among certain living species. But these mutations never exceed the limits of an anomaly or a decadence, as, for example, the sudden appearance of albinos or of dwarfs or giants; even when these characteristics incidentally became hereditary, they remain as anomalies and never constitute new specific forms.[25] For this to happen, it would be necessary for the vital substance of an extant species to serve as the "plastic material" for a newly manifested specific form; practically, this means that one or more females of the species qua substance would suddenly bear the fruit of a new species. Now, as was written by the hermetist Richard the Englishman:

[23] It is significant that the tortoise, whose skeleton seems to indicate an extravagant adaptation to the "armored" state on the part of this animal, appears all at once among fossils, without evolution. Similarly, the spider appears simultaneously with its prey and with its faculty of weaving already developed.
[24] This is the image used by the Sufi 'Abdul-Karim al-Jili in his book *al-Insān al Kàmil*, the chapter on the divine unicity.
[25] Bounoure, *Déterminisme et Finalité*.

Nothing can be produced from a thing that is not contained in it; by this fact, every species, every genus or every natural order develops within the limits proper to it and bears fruits according to its own kind and not according to an essentially different order; all that receives a seed must be of the same seed.[26]

Basically, the evolutionist thesis is an attempt to replace not "the miracle of creation" but the cosmogonic process—largely supersensual—of which the biblical narrative is a scriptural symbol; evolutionism, by abusively making the greater derive from the less, is the reverse of that process or that "emanation," which, moreover, has nothing in common with the emanationist heresy, since the transcendence and immutability of the ontological principle are here in no wise called in question. In a word, evolutionism results from an incapacity—peculiar to modern science—to conceive "dimensions" of reality other than those of purely physical sequences; to understand the "vertical" genesis of species, it is worth recalling what Guénon said about the progressive solidification of the corporeal state through the various terrestrial eras.[27] This solidification must obviously not be taken to imply that the stones of the earliest ages were soft, for this would be tantamount to saying that certain physical qualities—and in particular hardness and density—were then wanting; what has hardened and become fixed with time is the corporeal state viewed as a whole, with the result that it no longer receives directly the imprint of subtle forms. Assuredly, it cannot become detached from the subtle state, which is its ontological root and by which it is entirely dominated, but the relationship between the two states of existence no longer has the creative character that it possessed at the origin; it is as when a fruit, having reached maturity, becomes surrounded by an ever harder husk and ceases to absorb the sap of the tree. In a cyclic phase where bodily existence

[26] Quoted in the *Golden Treatise, Museum Hermeticum* (Frankfurt, 1678).
[27] Guénon, *The Reign of Quantity and the Signs of the Times.*

had not yet reached this degree of solidification a new specific form could manifest itself directly starting from its first "condensation" in the subtle or "animic" state; [28] that is to say, the different types of animals preexisted at the level immediately above the corporeal world as nonspatial forms but clothed with a certain "matter," that of the subtle world. Thence, these forms "descended" into the corporeal state, wherever the latter was ready to receive them, and this "descent" had the nature of a sudden coagulation and hence also the nature of a limitation or fragmentation of the original animic form.

Indo-Tibetan cosmology describes this descent—which is also a fall—in the case of a human being under the form of the mythological combat of the devas and asuras. The devas having created man with a body that was fluid, protean, and diaphanous—that is to say, in a subtle form—the asuras try to destroy it by a progressive petrifaction; this body becomes opaque, it gets fixed, and its skeleton, overcome by the petrifying process, is immobilized. Then the devas, turning evil into good, create joints after having fractured the bones, and they likewise open the ways of the senses by piercing the skull, which threatens to imprison the seat of the mind. Thus, the solidifying process stops before reaching its extreme limit, and certain organs in man, such as the eye, still keep something of the nature of the noncorporeal states. [29]

In this story, the pictorial description of the subtle world must not be misunderstood. Howbeit, it is certain that the process of materialization, going from supersensory to sensory, had to be reflected within the material or corporeal state itself, so that one is on safe ground in saying that the first generations of a new species did not leave a mark in the great book of

[28] Concerning the creation of species in a subtle "protomatter"—wherein they still preserve an androgynous form, comparable to a sphere—and their subsequent exteriorization "by crystallization" in sensible matter, heavy, opaque, and mortal, see Frithjof Schuon, *Light on the Ancient Worlds*, Chap. 2, "In the Wake of the Fall," and *Dimensions of Islam* (New York: Fernhill House, Ltd., 1970), Chap. 11, "The Five Divine Presences."

[29] Krasinsky, *Tibetische Medizin-Philosophie*.

earthly layering; it is therefore useless to want to seek in sensible matter the ancestors of a species and especially those of man.

The transformist theory not being founded on any real proof, its corollary and final outcome, namely the thesis of the infrahuman origin of man, remains suspended in the void. The facts put forward in favor of this thesis reduce themselves to a few groups of skeletons of disparate dating. It happens that skeletal types deemed more "evolved," such as the "man of Steinheim," precede others of a seemingly more primitive character, such as the "Neanderthal man," even though this latter example was doubtless not so apelike as tendentious reconstructions would have us believe.[30]

If, instead of always putting the question where humankind begins and what is the degree of evolution of such and such a type counted among prehumans, we were to ask ourselves how far does the monkey go, things might well appear in a very different light, for a fragment from a skeleton, even if it be related to that of man, is hardly enough to establish the presence of that which makes man, namely reason, whereas it is possible to conceive of a great variety of anthropoid apes whose anatomies are more or less close to that of man.

However paradoxical this may seem, the anatomical resemblance between man and the anthropoid apes is precisely explainable by the difference, not gradual but essential, separating man from all the other animals. Since the anthropoid form is able to exist without that "central" element that characterizes man—and that moreover is manifested anatomically by his vertical position, among other things—that form must exist; in other words, there cannot but be found, at the purely animal level, a form that realizes in its own way—that is to say, according to the laws of its own level—the very plan of the human anatomy. It is in this sense that the monkey

[30] In a general way this province of science has been almost smothered by tendentious theories, mystifications, and imprudently popularized discoveries. *Cf.* Dewar, *The Transformist Illusion.*

is a prefiguration of man, not as an evolutionary phase, but in virtue of that law that decrees that at every level of existence analogous possibilities will be found.

One more question arises in the face of the fossils ascribed to primitive men: Did certain of these skeletons belong to men we can look upon as being ancestors of men presently alive, or do they bear witness to the existence of a few groups that survived the cataclysm at the end of a terrestrial epoch in order to disappear in their turn before the arising of our present humanity? Instead of primitive men, it might well be a case of degenerate men, whether these did or did not exist side by side with our real ancestors. We know that the folklore of most peoples speaks of giants or dwarfs who lived long ago, in remote countries; now, among the skeletons in question, several cases of gigantism are to be found.[31]

Lastly, let it once more be recalled that the bodies of the most ancient men have not necessarily left solid traces, either because their bodies were not yet materialized or "solidified" to that point, or else because the spiritual state of those men, conjointly with the cosmic conditions of their time, rendered possible a resorption of the physical "body" into the subtle "body" at the moment of death.[32]

We must now say a few words about a thesis today much in vogue, which claims to be something like a spiritual integration of paleontology, but which in reality is nothing but a purely mental sublimation of the crudest materialism, with all the prejudices this includes, from the belief in an indefinite progress of humanity to a leveling and totalitarian collectivism, without forgetting the cult of the machine that is at the center of all this; it will be apparent that it is about the Teilhardian evolutionism that we intend to speak here.[33] According to Teil-

[31] Like the Meganthrope of Java and the *Gigantopithecus* of China.
[32] In some very exceptional cases—such as Enoch, Elijah, the Virgin Mary—such a resorption took place even in the present terrestrial age.
[33] The materialism of Teilhard is manifest in all its crudity, and also in all its perversity, when that philosopher advocates the use of surgical means in order to accelerate "collective cerebralization" (*The Place of Man in Nature*). Let us also quote some highly revealing words of the

hard de Chardin, who hardly worries over the gaps inherent in the evolutionist system and largely banks on the climate created by the premature popularization of the transformist thesis, man himself would only represent an intermediate stage of an evolution starting with unicellular organisms and ending up in a sort of global cosmic entity, in union with God. The craze for trying to bring everything back to a single univocal and uninterrupted genetic line here exceeds the material plane and launches out wildly into an irresponsible and avid "mentalization," characterized by an abstraction clothed in artificial images which their author ends up by taking literally, as if it were a case of concrete realities. We have already mentioned the imaginary genealogical tree of species, of which the supposed unity is but a snare, being made up by the hypothetical conjunction of many disjointed elements. Teilhard amplifies this notion to his heart's content, in a manner that is purely graphic, by completing its branches—or "scales," as he prefers to call them—and by constructing its pinnacle in the direction of which humankind would supposedly be situated. By a similar sliding of thought from abstract to concrete, from figuration to what is deemed real, he agglutinates, in one and the same pseudoscientific sprouting, the most diverse realities such as mechanical laws, vital forces, psychic elements, and spiritual entities. Let us quote a characteristic passage:

> That which explains the biological revolution caused by the apparition of Man, is an explosion of consciousness; and that which, in its turn, explains this explosion of con-

---

same author: "It is finally on the dazzling notion of Progress and on faith in Progress that today's divided Humanity can reform itself. . . . Act one is played! We have access to the heart of the atom! Now come the next steps, such as the vitalization of matter by the building up of supermolecules, the modeling of the human organism by hormones, the control of heredity and of the sexes by the play of genes and chromosomes, and the readjustment and liberation by direct action of the springs laid bare by psychoanalysis; the awakening and captation of intellectual and affective forces still slumbering in the human mass" (*Planete* III, 1944, p. 30). Quite naturally Teilhard proposes the fashioning of mankind by a universal scientific government—in short, all that is required for the reign of Antichrist.

sciousness, is simply the passage of a privileged radius of "corpusculization," that is to say of a zoological phylum, across the surface, hitherto impermeable, separating the zone of direct Psychism from that of reflected Psychism. Having reached, following this particular ray, a critical point of arrangement (or, as we say here, of enrollment) life became hypercentered on itself, to the point of being capable of foresight and invention. . . .[34]

Thus "corpusculization" (which is a physical process) would have as its effect that "a zoological phylum" (which is only a figure) passed across the surface (purely hypothetical) separating two psychic zones . . . but one must not be surprised at this absence of *distinguo* in Teilhard's thinking, since according to his own theory, the spirit is but a metamorphosis of matter!

Without stopping to discuss the strange theology of this author, for whom God himself evolves with matter, and without daring to define what he thinks of the prophets and sages of antiquity and other "underdeveloped" beings of this kind, we will say the following: If man, under the double relationship of his physical nature and his spiritual nature, were really nothing but a phase of an evolution going from the amoeba to the superman, how could he know objectively where he stands in all this? Let us suppose that this alleged evolution forms a curve, say a spiral. The man who is but a fragment thereof —and let it not be forgotten that a "fragment" of a movement is but a phase of that movement—can that man step out of it and say to himself: I am the fragment of a spiral developing in such and such a way? Now, it is certain—and Teilhard de Chardin recognizes this moreover—that man is able to judge of his own state. In effect he knows his own rank amid other terrestrial beings; he is even alone in knowing objectively both himself and the world. Far from being a simple phase in an indefinite evolution, man represents essentially a central possibility, unique therefore, irreplaceable and definitive. If the human species had to evolve toward another more perfect and

[34] *La Place de l'Homme dans la Nature,* p. 84.

more "spiritual" form, man would not already now be the "point of intersection" of the divine spirit with the terrestrial plane; he would neither be capable of salvation nor intellectually able to surmount the flux of becoming. To express these thoughts according to the Gospel perspective: Would God have become man if the form of the latter were not virtually "god on earth," that is to say, qualitatively central as well as definitive in relation to his own cosmic level?

As a symptom of our time, Teilhardism is comparable to one of those cracks that are due to the very solidification of the mental carapace,[35] and that do not open upward, toward the heaven of true and transcendent unity, but downward toward the realm of the inferior psychism. Weary of its own discontinuous vision of the world, the materialist mind lets itself slide toward a false continuity or unity, toward a pseudospiritual intoxication, of which this falsified and materialized faith—or this sublimated materialism—that we have just described marks a phase of particular significance.

V

"The object of psychology is the psychic; unfortunately it is also its subject." Thus wrote a famous psychologist of our time.[36] According to this opinion, every psychological judgment inevitably participates in the essentially subjective, not to say passionate and tendentious, nature of its object; for according to this logic, no one understands the soul except by means of his own soul, and the latter, for the psychologist, precisely belongs only to the psychic and to nothing else. No psychologist, whatever may be his claim to objectivity, can escape from this dilemma, and the more categorical and general are his affirmations in this realm, the more they will be suspect; such is the verdict that modern psychology pronounces in its own cause, when it is sincere toward itself. Whether it is so or not, the relativism expressed by the aforementioned sentence

---

[35] Guénon, *The Reign of Quantity and the Signs of the Times*, Chap. XV, "The Illusion of 'Ordinary Life.' "
[36] C. G. Jung, *Psychologie und Religion* (Zurich, 1962), p. 61.

is inherent in it. This relativism is also a kind of prometheism that would make of the psychic the ultimate reality of man. It is the root of the manifold divergencies that have arisen in the interior of this discipline, and it dominates it to the point of contaminating whatever that discipline touches: At its contact history, philosophy, art, and religion all become psychological in turn and therefore also subjective, that is to say, devoid of objective and immutable certainties.[37]

But all relativism laid down a priori is inconsistent with itself. Despite the admitted precariousness of its viewpoint, modern psychology behaves like every other science: It utters judgments and believes in their validity, and in this respect it leans unknowingly or without admitting the fact on an innate certitude. In effect, if we are able to observe that the psychic is "subjective"—that is to say, dominated by a certain egocentric bias imposing on it certain limits or a particular "color"— this is because there is to be found in us something that is not subject to the same limits or tendencies, but exceeds and dominates them in principle. That something is the intellect, and this it is that normally provides us with the criteria whereby the fluctuating and uncertain world of the psyche can alone be illuminated; though the evidence for this speaks for itself, it remains totally outside modern scientific and philosophical thinking.

It is important above all not to confuse intellect and reason; the latter is indeed the mental reflection of the transcendent

---

[37] "I do not find that there is occasion for surprise at seeing psychology exchanging visits with philosophy, for is not the act of thinking, basis of all philosophy, a psychic activity which, as such, directly concerns psychology? Must not psychology embrace the soul in its total extension, which includes philosophy, theology, and countless other things besides? In the face of all the richly diversified religions there rise up, as the supreme instance perhaps of truth or error, the immutable data of the human soul" (C. G. Jung, *L'Homme à la Découverte de son Ame* [Paris, 1962], p. 238).

This amounts to replacing truth by psychology; it is being quite forgotten that there are no "immutable data" outside that which is immutable by its own nature, namely the intellect. Besides, if the "act of thinking" is but a "psychic activity," by what right does psychology set itself up as the supreme instance—psychology, which is but one "psychic activity" among others?

intellect, but in practice it is only what one makes of it, by which is meant that its functioning is limited, in the case of the modern sciences, by the empirical method itself; at the level of the latter, reason is not so much a source of truth as a principle of coherence. For modern psychology it is even less than that, for if scientific rationalism lends a relatively stable framework to one's observation of the physical world, it reveals itself as entirely insufficient when it comes to describing the world of the soul; hardly can psychic movements at the surface, namely those whose causes and aims are situated on the plane of current experience, be translated into rational terms. All the chaos of inferior, and mostly unconscious, psychic possibilities escapes rationality, and this is even more true of whatever stands above the rational; which means that the greater part of the psychic world, on the one hand, and the metaphysical realm, on the other, will appear "irrational" according to this measure of thought: hence a certain tendency, inherent in modern psychology, to relativize reason itself, which is a self-contradictory tendency, since psychology could not dispense with rational methods. Psychology finds itself facing a domain that overflows in all directions the horizon of a science built on empiricism and the Cartesian standpoint.

For this reason, the majority of modern psychologists ensconce themselves in a sort of pragmatism; it is in a "committed" experience, coupled with a coldly clinical attitude, that they see some guarantee of "objectivity." In point of fact, the movements of the soul cannot be studied from the outside, as in the case of bodily phenomena; in order to know what they signify, they have in a sense to be lived, and this raises the question of the observer himself, as was justly pointed out by the psychologist we quoted at the outset. As for the mental faculty that "controls" the experiment, what is this but a "common sense" of a more or less arbitrary kind, one that is inevitably colored by preconceived ideas? The would-be "objectivist" psychic attitude therefore changes nothing in regard to the uncertain nature of the experiment, and thus one returns, failing a principle at once interior and immutable, to the dilemma of the psychic striving to grasp the psychic.

The soul, like any other compartment of reality, can only be truly known by that which exceeds it. This is admitted spontaneously and implicitly when people recognize the moral principle of justice, which demands that men should overcome their individual subjectivity. Now, it would be impossible for a man to overcome it if the intelligence, which guides his will, were itself nothing but a psychic reality, and intelligence would not exceed the psyche if in its essence it did not transcend the plane of phenomena, both internal and external. This observation suffices to prove the necessity and the existence of a psychology deriving in some sense from above and not claiming an a priori empirical character. But although this order of things is inscribed in our very nature, it will never be admitted by modern psychology; despite its own reactions against the rationalism of yesterday, it stands no nearer to metaphysics than any other empirical science—indeed quite the contrary, for its perspective, which assimilates the suprarational to the irrational, predisposes it to the worst of errors.

What modern psychology lacks entirely is criteria allowing it to situate the aspects or tendencies of the soul in their cosmic context. In traditional psychology these criteria are provided according to two principal "dimensions," namely, on the one hand, according to a cosmology that "situates" the soul and its modalities in the hierarchy of states of existence, and on the other hand, according to a morality directed toward a spiritual aim. The latter can provisionally espouse the individual horizon; it nonetheless keeps in view the universal principles attaching the soul to an order more vast than itself. Cosmology in some senses circumscribes the soul; spiritual morality plumbs its depths. Just as a current of water reveals its force and direction only when it breaks against an object that resists it, so the soul can show its tendencies and fluctuations only in relation to an immutable principle; whoever wishes to know the nature of the psyche must resist it, and one only resists it truly when one places oneself, if not effectively then at least virtually or symbolically, at a point corresponding to the divine self, or to the intellect which is like its ray.

Traditional psychology has therefore one impersonal and

"static" dimension, namely cosmology, and another personal and "operative" dimension, namely morality, or the science of the virtues, and this is necessarily the case because the genuine knowledge of the soul results from the knowledge of oneself. He who, by the eye of his essence, is able to "objectivize" his own psychic form, by that very fact knows all the possibilities of the psychic or subtle world; it is this intellectual "vision" that is both the outcome, and if need be the guarantor, of every sacred science of the soul.

For the majority of modern psychologists the traditional morality, which they readily confuse with a purely social or conventional morality, is nothing but a kind of psychic dam, useful on occasion but more often a hindrance or even harmful for the "normal" development of the individual. This opinion is especially propagated by the Freudian psychoanalysis, now become of very general application in certain countries, where it has practically usurped the function that elsewhere belongs to the sacrament of confession: [38] The psychiatrist replaces the priest, and the bursting of the complexes that had previously been repressed takes the place of absolution. In ritual confession the priest is but the impersonal representative (necessarily discreet) of the truth that judges and pardons; the penitent, by admitting his sins, "objectivizes" in some sense the psychic tendencies these sins manifest. By repenting, he detaches himself from them, and by receiving the sacramental absolution, his soul is virtually reintegrated in its primitive equilibrium and centered on its divine essence. In the case of the Freudian psychoanalysis,[39] on the other hand, man lays bare his psychic entrails, not before God, but to his fellow. He does not draw away from the chaotic and obscure depths of his soul, which the analyst unveils or stirs, but on the contrary he assumes them, for he must say to himself, "So I am in reality"; and if

[38] It also prospers chiefly in Protestant countries.
[39] One must specify that here it is the method of Freud that is in question, for psychoanalysis in our day knows forms that are more neutral and less pernicious, a fact that from the present standpoint, however, in no wise amounts to a justification.

he does not overcome, with the help of some salutary instinct, this kind of disillusion from below, he will keep from it something like an intimate sullying; in most cases it will be his self-abandonment to the collective mediocrity that for him will play the part of an absolution, for it is easier to endure one's own degradation when this is shared with others. Whatever may be the occasional and partial usefulness of such an analysis in certain cases, the state described above is its more usual result, given that its premises are what they are.[40]

If the medicine of the traditional civilizations knows nothing analogous to modern psychotherapy, this is because the psychic cannot be treated by means of the psychic. The psyche is the realm of indefinite actions and reactions. By its own specific nature, it is essentially unstable and deceptive, so that it can be cured only by resorting to something situated "outside" and "above" it. In some cases, one will act favorably upon it by reestablishing the humoral balance of the body, commonly upset by psychic affections;[41] in other cases it is only by the use of spiritual means, such as exorcism,[42] prayer, or a sojourn in holy places that the soul can be restored to health.

We all are aware of the fact that modern psychology tries to explain in a psychological sense the spiritual means mentioned above. In its eyes the effect of a rite is one thing and its theological or mystical interpretation is another. The effect of the rite, arbitrarily limited to the psychic and subjective domain only, is attributed to psychic dispositions of ancestral origin, which its form is supposed to actualize. There is no question of a timeless and superhuman sense inherent in the rite or symbol

[40] René Guénon has observed that the principle whereby every psychoanalyst needs to have been psychoanalyzed himself before being empowered to analyze others raises the troublesome question of knowing who occupied the first place in the queue.

[41] Usually a vicious circle ensues, with the psychic unbalance engendering a physical intoxication, which, in its turn, causes the psychic unbalance to worsen.

[42] Cases of diabolical possession, such as visibly call for an application of the rites of exorcism, seem to have become rarer nowadays, doubtless because the demoniac influences are no longer "restrained" by the barriers of tradition but are able to range pretty well anywhere, under forms that are to some extent "diluted."

—as if the soul could cure itself through believing in the illusory projection of its own preoccupations, whether individual or collective. There is nothing in the above supposition to shock modern psychology, since the latter goes much further than this in admitting, for example, that the fundamental forms of thought, the laws of logic, merely represent a residue of ancestral habits.[43] This path is one that leads to the outright denial of intelligence and to its replacement by biological fatalities, if indeed psychology can go that far without encompassing its own ruin.

In order to be able to "situate" the soul in relation to other cosmic realities or realms, one must refer to the cosmological scheme where the degrees of existence are represented under the form of circles or concentric spheres. This scheme, which amplifies the geocentric conception of the visible universe, identifies the corporeal world symbolically with our terrestrial surroundings; around this region there extends the sphere or spheres of the subtle or psychic world, enclosed in their turn by the sphere of the world of pure spirit. This representation is naturally limited by its own spatial character, yet at the same time it well expresses the relation existing between these various states. Each of these spheres, considered in itself, is presented as a complete and perfectly homogeneous whole, whereas from the "viewpoint" of the sphere immediately superior to it, it is but a content thereof. Thus the corporeal world, envisaged at its own level, knows not the subtle world, just as the latter knows not the supraformal world, precisely because it only includes that which has a form. Furthermore, each of these worlds is known and dominated by that which exceeds and enfolds it. It is from the immutable and formless background of the spirit that the subtle realities become detached as forms, and it is the soul that through its sensory faculties knows the corporeal.

[43] They will say, for example, that logic is but an expression of the physiological structure of our brain, even while forgetting that the above statement would then be, no less, an expression of the same physiological fatality.

This double relationship of things, which hides itself a priori from our individual vision, can be grasped "alive" when one considers the very nature of sensible perception. On the one hand, this really reaches the corporeal world, and no philosophic artifice will be able to convince us of the contrary; on the other hand, there is no doubt that all we perceive of the world are but those "images" of it that our mental faculty is able to keep hold of, and in this respect the whole fabric made of impressions, memories, and expectations, in short all that for us constitutes the sensible continuity and logical coherence of the world, is of a psychic or subtle nature. It is in vain that one will try to know what the world is "outside" this subtle continuity, since the corporeal world is but a content thereof, even while appearing, when viewed in the mirror of that state, as a materially autonomous order.[44]

It is evidently not the individual soul but the entire subtle order that contains the physical world. The logical coherence of the latter implies the unity of the former, as manifested indirectly by the fact that the multiple individual visions of the sensible world, fragmentary as they are, coincide in substance and are integrated in one continuous whole. The individual soul participates in this unity both by the structure of its cognitive faculties, in conformity with the cosmic order, and also by its nature as a subject containing the physical world in its own way; otherwise regarded, the physical world is "a world" only in relation to the individual subject, in virtue of the cleaving of consciousness into object and subject, a cleaving that results precisely from the "egoic" polarization of the soul. By this same polarization the soul is distinguished from the totality of the subtle state—the "universal or total soul" of Plotinus—without, however, being substantially separated from it. For if it were so separated, our vision of the world would not be adequate to reality; now it is adequate, in spite of the limitations and relativity of all perception.

It is true that ordinarily we perceive only an isolated fragment of the subtle world—the fragment that we "are" and

[44] Nothing is more absurd than the attempts to explain the perception of the material world in material terms.

that constitutes our "myself"—whereas the sensible world reveals itself to us in its macrocosmic continuity, as a whole that seems to include us. The reason is that the subtle world is the very field of individuation; in reality we are steeped in the ocean of the subtle world as fishes are in the water, and, like them, we do not see that which constitutes our own element.

As for the opposition between the psychic world as "internal" and the corporeal world as "external," this becomes actualized only in relation to, and in function of, the latter. In itself the subtle world is neither "internal" nor "external"; at most it is "nonexternal," whereas the corporeal world is external as such, which furthermore proves that it does not enjoy an autonomous existence.

The corporeal state and the psychic state both form part of formal existence; in its total extension, the subtle state is none other than formal existence, but we call it "subtle" insofar as it escapes the laws of corporeity. According to one of the most ancient and natural symbolisms, the subtle state may be compared to the atmosphere surrounding the earth and pervading all porous bodies and acting as a vehicle of life.

A phenomenon of whatever kind can only be truly understood through its relations, both "horizontal" and "vertical," with total reality. This truth applies in a particular, and in a certain sense practical, manner to psychic phenomena. A selfsame psychic "event" can simultaneously occur in answer to a sensory impulsion, to the manifestation of a wish, as a consequence of an interior action, or it can appear as the trace of the typical and ancestral form of the individual, as the expression of his genius, or, again, as the reflection of a supraindividual reality. It is legitimate to consider the psychic phenomenon in question under one or other of these aspects; but on the other hand it would be abusive to try and explain the notions and motives of the soul by a single one, or by several, of these aspects exclusively. In this respect let us quote the words of a psychiatrist who has shown himself to be well aware of the limits of contemporary psychology:

There is an ancient saying of the Hindus the psychological truth of which can hardly be contested: "What a man thinks, that he becomes." If one steadfastly thinks of good deeds, one will end by becoming a good man; if one always thinks of weakness, one will be weak; if one thinks of how to develop one's strength (bodily or mental), one will become strong. Similarly, if for years one is almost daily engaged in stirring up Hades,[45] explaining systematically everything higher in terms of the lower, ignoring at the same time all that in mankind's cultural history (in spite of its lamentable errors and misdeeds) has been regarded as valuable, the danger can scarcely be averted that discrimination will be lost, imagination (a fountain of life) will be leveled down, and the mental horizon will shrink.[46]

Ordinary consciousness serves to illuminate only a restricted portion of the individual soul, and the latter represents but a minimal part of the psychic world. Nevertheless, the soul is not isolated from the remainder of that world, its situation is not that of a body rigorously limited by its own special extension and separated from other bodies. That which distinguishes the soul from the aggregate of the vast subtle world is solely its own particular tendencies, whereby it is defined (to employ a very simplified image) as a given spatial direction defines the ray of light that follows it. By those same tendencies the soul is in communion with all the cosmic possibilities pertaining to analogous tendencies or qualities; it assimilates them and is assimilated to them. For this reason, the science of cosmic tendencies (the gunas of Hindu cosmology) is fundamental for the knowledge of the soul. In this order of ideas it is not the external context of a psychic phenomenon, the accidental occasion

[45] Allusion to the quotation from Virgil, *Flectere si nequeo superos Acheronta movebo* ("If I cannot bend the Gods, I shall stir up hell"), that Freud placed at the head of his *Interpretation of Dreams*.
[46] Hans Jacob, *Western Psychology and Hindu Sadhana* (London: Allen and Unwin). The author of this work is a former disciple of Jung, who later discovered the doctrine and method, immeasurably greater, of the Hindu sadhana, which thus enabled him to submit Western psychotherapy to a just criticism.

for its manifestation, that matters essentially, but its connection with sattva, rajas, or tamas—the "upward," "expansive," and "downward" tendencies—which confers its rank on that phenomenon in the hierarchy of internal values.

The motives of the soul being perceptible only across the forms that manifest them, it is on these forms or manifestations that a psychological assessment must needs be founded. Now, the part played by the gunas in any form whatsoever can be measured only in a purely qualitative manner, therefore in reference to precise and decisive, and in no wise quantitative, criteria such as are entirely lacking in the quite profane psychology of our time.

There are some psychic "events" whose repercussions traverse all the degrees of the subtle world "vertically," since they touch the essences; others—these are the ordinary psychic movements—only obey the "horizontal" coming and going of the psyche; lastly, there are those that derive from the subhuman depths. The first of these do not lend themselves entirely to expression—they include an element of "mystery"—and yet the forms they evoke occasionally in the imagination are clear and precise, such as those characterizing the true sacred arts. The third kind, the demoniac "inspirations," are unintelligible by their very forms; they "ape" true mystery by the nebulous, obscure, and equivocal character of their formal manifestations, of which examples can easily be found in contemporary art.

When studying the formal manifestations of the soul, one must, however, not forget that the psycho-physical organism of man can display strange caesuras or discontinuities. Thus, for instance, in the case of certain states of the soul as found among that somewhat "anarchical" category of contemplatives known as "fools in God," the spiritual states in question are hardly being manifested normally and harmoniously and do not make use of the reason. Inversely, an intrinsically pathological state, dominated as such by infrahuman and chaotic tendencies, may incidentally and by accident comprise openings toward supraterrestrial realities; this is but saying that the human soul is of an unplumbed complexity.

Viewed as a whole, the subtle world is incomparably vaster and more varied than the corporeal world. Dante expresses this by making the entire hierarchy of planetary spheres correspond to the subtle world and only the earthly surroundings to the corporeal. The subterranean position of the hells, in his system, merely indicates that the states in question are situated below the normal human state; in reality, these likewise form part of the subtle state, and it is for this reason that certain medieval cosmologists place the hells symbolically between heaven and earth.[47]

Experience of the subtle world is subjective—except in the case of certain sciences quite unknown to the moderns—because consciousness, in identifying itself with subtle forms, is affected by their tendencies, just as a light is turned from its course by the form of a wave that it happens to traverse. The subtle world is made up of forms—that is to say, it comprises diversity and contrast—but these forms do not possess, in themselves and outside their projections in sensible imagination,[48] spatial and defined contours as in the case of corporeal forms. They are entirely active or, to be more exact, dynamic, since pure activity belongs only to the "essential forms" or archetypes, which are to be found in the world of pure spirit. Now the ego or individual soul is itself one of the forms of the subtle world, so that the consciousness that espouses this form is necessarily dynamic and exclusive; it realizes other subtle forms only insofar as these become modalities of its own egoic form.

Thus it is that in the dream state individual consciousness, even while being reabsorbed in the subtle world, nonetheless remains turned back on itself. All the forms it lives while in that state present themselves as simple prolongations of the

[47] In Islam, it is said that the throne of the devil is to be found between earth and heaven, a statement that also indicates the temptations to which those who follow the "vertical path" expose themselves.
[48] If certain masters have compared the subtle world to imagination, it is the imaginative activity and not the images produced through the imagination that they had in mind.

individual subject, or at least they appear so in retrospect and inasmuch as they verge on the state of wakefulness. For in itself and despite this subjectivism the consciousness of the dreamer is evidently not impermeable by influences originating from the most diverse "regions" of the subtle world, as is proved, among other things, by premonitory or telepathic dreams such as have been experienced by many people.[49] In truth, if the imagery of dream is woven from the very "substance" of the subject—a "substance" that is none other than the progressive actualization of his own psychic form—it nonetheless manifests, incidentally and at varying degrees, realities of a cosmic order.

The contents of a dream can be considered under several relationships. If one analyzes the *materia* of which it is made, one will find that it is constituted by all sorts of memories, and in this respect the current psychological explanation, making of the dream an expression of subconscious residues, is largely right. It is not, however, excluded that a dream might also comprise "materials" that in no wise proceed from the personal experience of the dreamer and that are like traces of a psychic transfusion from one individual to another. There is also question of the economy of the dream, and in this respect one may quote the following description of C. G. Jung, which is exact despite the radically false theses of that author:

> The dream, deriving from the activity of the unconscious, gives a representation of the contents that slumber there; not of all the contents that figure in it, but only of certain ones among them which, by way of association, are actualized, crystallized, and selected, in correlation with the momentary state of the consciousness.[50]

As for the hermeneutic science of dreams, this eludes modern psychology in spite of its efforts in this direction, for it

[49] Also empirical psychology no longer ventures to deny this phenomenon.
[50] *L'Homme à la Découverte de son Ame,* p. 205.

would not be possible to interpret validly the images reflected by the soul without knowing to what level of reality these refer.

The images one retains on waking from a dream generally represent only a shadow of that which the psychic form one lived in the state of dream amounted to in itself. At the time of passage to the state of wakefulness a sort of decantation takes place, of which one can, however, take note, insofar as something of the reality inherent in the dream evaporates more or less rapidly. There exists, nevertheless, a certain category of dreams, well known to the traditional oneirocritic science, the remembrance of which persists with incisive clearness, and this can happen even if the profound contents of these dreams appears to conceal itself. Such dreams, which most often occur at dawn and which finally lead to awakening, are accompanied by an irrefutable feeling of objectivity; otherwise put, they comprise a more than merely mental certainty. But that which characterizes them above all and independently of their moral influence on the dreamer is the high quality of their forms, disengaged from every kind of turbid or chaotic residue. These are the dreams that come from the angel—that is to say, from the essence connecting the soul with the supraformal states of the being.

Since there are dreams of divine or angelic inspiration, there must also exist their contrary, namely dreams of satanic impulsion, containing palpable caricatures of sacred forms. The sensation accompanying them will not be made of cool and serene lucidity, but of obsession and vertigo; such is the attraction exerted by the abysses. The infernal influences sometimes ride on the wave of a natural passion, which opens a way for them, so to speak; they are, however, distinguishable from the elementary character of passion by their arrogantly negative tendency, accompanied either by bitterness or else by sadness. "He who tries to play the angel will play the beast," said Pascal, and in effect nothing is so apt to provoke caricatures, both in dreaming and elsewhere, as the unconsciously pretentious attitude of the man who mixes God with his own highly particularized ego—the classical motive of many of the psychoses studied and exploited by the post-Freudian psychologism.[51]

It was starting from the analysis of dreams that C. G. Jung developed his famous theory about the "collective unconscious." Observation of the fact that a certain category of dream images cannot be explained simply in terms of residues from individual experiences led Jung to distinguish, within the "unconscious" domain whence dreams are fed, between a "personal" zone whose contents after all represent the other face of individual psychic life, and a "collective" zone made up of latent psychic dispositions of an impersonal character, such as never offer themselves to the direct grasp of the consciousness, but manifest themselves indirectly through "symbolic" dreams and "irrational" impulses. At first sight, this theory has nothing extravagant about it, except its use of the term "irrational" in connection with symbolism. It is easy to understand that the individual consciousness centered on the empirical ego leaves on its margin or even outside itself all that which, in the psychic order, is not effectively attached to that center, just as a light projected in a given direction decreases toward the surrounding darkness. But this is not how Jung understands the matter. For him, the nonpersonal zone of the soul is unconscious as such; that is to say, its contents can never become a direct object of the intelligence, whatever its modality or however great its extension may be:

> . . . just as the human body displays a common anatomy, independently of racial differences, so also the *psyche* possesses, beyond all cultural and mental differences, a common *substratum*, that I have named the collective unconscious. This unconscious *psyche*, which is common to all men, is not made up of contents able to become con-

---

[51] In a general way, contemporary psychology delves in the observation of pathological cases and views the soul largely through this clinical perspective.

scious, but solely of latent dispositions giving rise to certain reactions that are always identical.[52]

The author goes on from there to insinuate that here one has finally to do with ancestral structures having their root in the physical order:

> The fact that this collective unconscious exists is simply the psychic expression of the identity of cerebral structures beyond all racial differences. . . . The different lines of psychic evolution start out from one and the same trunk, of which the roots plunge through all the ages. It is here that the psychic parallelism with the animal is situated.[53]

One notices the plainly Darwinian turn of this thesis of which the disastrous consequences, in the intellectual and spiritual order, announce themselves in the following passage: "It is this which explains the analogy, and indeed the identity, of mythological motives and of symbols as means of human communication in general." [54] Myths and symbols would therefore be the expression of an ancestral psychic fund that brings man near to the animal! These have no intellectual or spiritual foundation, since

> from a purely psychological viewpoint, it is a matter of common instincts of imagining and acting. All conscious imagination and action has evolved on the basis of these unconscious prototypes and remains constantly attached to them, and this is especially the case when consciousness has not yet attained a very high degree of lucidity, that is to say, as long as it is still, in all its functions, more dependent on instinct than on conscious will, as long as it is more affective than rational. . . .[55]

[52] C. G. Jung, *Das Geheimnis der goldenen Blüte (The Secret of the Golden Flower)* (Munich, 1929), Introduction.
[53] *Ibid.*
[54] *Ibid.*
[55] *Ibid.*

The above passage clearly shows that, for Jung, the "collective unconscious" is situated "below," at the level of physiological instincts. It is important to bear this in mind, since the term "collective unconscious," in itself, could carry a wider and in some sort more spiritual meaning, as certain assimilations made by Jung seem to suggest, especially his utilizing—or rather in point of fact his usurping—of the term "archetype" in order to indicate the latent, and, as such, inaccessible contents of the "collective unconscious." For though the archetypes do not belong to the psychic realm but to the world of pure spirit, they nevertheless are reflected at the psychic level—as virtualities of images in the first place—before becoming crystallized, according to circumstances, in images properly so-called, so that a certain psychological application of the term "archetypes" could at a pinch be justified. But here it is that Jung defines an archetype as "an innate complex" [56] and describes its action on the soul: "Possession by an archetype makes of man a purely collective personage, a kind of mask, under which human nature can no longer develop but degenerates progressively." [57] As if an archetype, which is an immediate and supraformal determination of being—and non-limitative by that very fact—could in any sense "cast a spell" on and vampirize the soul! What is really in question in the more or less pathological case envisaged by Jung? It is simply a question of a dissociation of the possibilities inherent in the subtle form of a man, a form that includes multiple aspects each of which has something unique and irreplaceable about it. In every nondegenerate human individual there is to be found in potency a man and woman, a father and mother, a child and elderly person, as also various qualities or "dignities" inseparable from the original and ontological position of man, such as the priestly and royal qualities and those of a creative artisan, a servant, and so forth. Normally, all these possibilities complete one another; here there is no question of an irrational fund of the soul, for the coexistence of these diverse possibili-

---

[56] See *L'Homme à la Découverte de son Ame*, p. 311.
[57] *Die Beziehungen Zwischen dem Ich und dem Unbewussten* (Zurich, 1963), p. 130.

ties or aspects of the human "form" is perfectly intelligible in itself and can be hidden only from the eyes of a mentality or civilization that has become one-sided and false. Every "genial" development of one of these multiple possibilities or dispositions inherent in the human soul moreover requires the integration of the complementary possibilities; the true man of genius is a balanced being, for where there is no balance there is no greatness either. The contrary of such a development is the barren and pathological exaggeration of one of the soul's possibilities in disregard and at the cost of the others, leading to that kind of moral caricature compared by Jung to a mask; and let it be added that it is the carnivalesque mask one must think of here, and not the sacred mask, which, for its part, precisely does express a true archetype and therefore a possibility that does not bewitch the soul but on the contrary liberates it.[58]

Psychic dissociation always produces a fixation as well as a tearing apart between opposing poles, and this is rendered possible only by the clouding over of that which, in the soul, corresponds to the archetype. At the antipodes of this imbalance productive of hypertrophies, perfect virility, for example, in no wise excludes femininity, but on the contrary includes and adapts it, and the same is true of the opposite case. Similarly the genuine archetypes, which are not situated at the psychic level, do not mutually exclude but comprise and imply one another. According to the Platonic and hallowed meaning of the term, the archetypes are sources of being and knowledge and not, as Jung conceives them, unconscious dispositions toward acting and imagining. The fact that the archetypes cannot be grasped by discursive thought has no connection with the irrational and obscure character of the supposed "collective unconscious," whose contents could be known indirectly only through their "eruptions" on the surface. There is not only discursive thought but also intellectual intuition, and it is the latter that attains to the archetypes starting out from their symbols.

[58] See my article "Du Masque Sacré," *Etudes Traditionnelles*, November–December, 1963.

Doubtless the theory according to which ancestral structures constitute the "collective unconscious" imposes itself all the more easily on the most modern thinking inasmuch as it seems to be in agreement with the evolutionist explanation of the instinct of animals. According to this view, instinct would be the expression of the heredity of a species, of an accumulation of analogous experiences down the ages. Thus it is that they explain, for instance, the fact that a flock of sheep hastily gathers together around the lambs the moment it perceives the shadow of a bird of prey or that a kitten while playing already employs all the tricks of a hunter or that birds know how to build their nests. In reality, it is enough to watch animals in order to see that their instinct has nothing of an automatism in it. The formation for such a mechanism by a purely cumulative and consequently vague and accidental process is, moreover, something highly improbable, to say the least. Instinct is a nonreflective modality of intelligence; it is determined not by a series of automatic reflexes, but by the "form"—the qualitative determination—of the species. This form is like a filter through which the universal intelligence is manifested. Nor must it be forgotten that the subtle form of a being is incomparably more complex than its bodily form. The same thing holds for man too: by which is meant that his intelligence also is determined by the subtle form of his species. This form, however, includes the reflective faculty, which allows of a singularization of the individual such as does not exist among the animals. Man alone is able to objectivize himself. He can say, "I am this or that"; he alone possesses this two-edged faculty. Man, by virtue of his own central position in the cosmos, is able to exceed his specific norm; he is also able to betray it and sink lower—*corruptio optimi pessima*. A normal animal remains true to the form and genius of its species; if its intelligence is not reflective and objectifying, but in some sort existential, it is nonetheless spontaneous. It is assuredly a form of the universal intelligence even if it be not recognized as such by some men who, from prejudice or ignorance, identify intelligence with discursive thought exclusively.

As for Jung's thesis that certain dreams, which cannot be

explained as personal reminiscences and which seem to arise
from an unconscious fund common to all men, contain motives
and forms that are also to be found in myths and in traditional
symbolism, the thing is possible in principle; not that there is
in the soul a repertory of types inherited from distant ancestors
and witnessing to a primitive vision of the world, but because
true symbols are always "actual" inasmuch as they express
nontemporal realities. In fact, under certain conditions the soul
is able to take on the function of a mirror that reflects, in a
purely passive and imaginative manner, universal truths contained in the intellect. Nevertheless, "inspirations" of this nature remain fairly rare; they depend on circumstances that are,
so to speak, providential, as in the case of dreams communicating truths or announcing future events, to which allusion has
previously been made. Moreover, symbolic dreams are not
clothed in just any traditional "style"; their formal language
is normally determined by the tradition or religion to which
the individual is effectively or virtually attached, for nothing
arbitrary is to be found in this domain.

Now, if one examines examples of supposedly symbolical
dreams as quoted by Jung or by other psychologists of his
school, one notices that in most cases it is a matter of false
symbolism, of the kind commonly met with in pseudospiritual
circles. The soul is not only a sacred mirror; more often it is
a magic mirror that deceives him who views himself in it. Jung
should have known this, since he himself speaks of the tricks
of the anima, indicating by this term the feminine aspect of the
soul; and some of his own experiences, as described in his
memoirs,[59] should have told him that an investigator of the
unconscious depths of the psyche exposes himself, not merely
to the wiles of the egocentric soul but also to psychic influences
coming from elsewhere, from unknown beings and entities,
especially when the methods of analysis used derive from hyp-

[59] The kind of introspection practiced by Jung by way of psychological
investigation as mentioned in his memoirs, as well as certain "parapsy-
chological" phenomena he provoked by this method, takes one into a
plainly spiritualistic ambience. The fact that the author in question
proposed to study these phenomena "scientifically" changes nothing
in regard to the influence they in fact had on his theory of "archetypes."

nosis or mediumship. It is in this context that must be placed certain designs executed by sick patients of Jung and which the latter tries to palm off as genuine mandalas.[60]

On another side, there exists a symbolism of very general character and underlying language itself, as for instance when one compares truth to light and error to darkness, or a progress to an ascent and a moral danger to an abyss, or when one represents fidelity by a dog or craftiness by a fox. Now, to explain the occurrence of a similar symbolism in dreams, of which the language is naturally figurative and not discursive, there is no need to refer to a "collective unconscious"; it is enough to note that rational thought is not the whole of thought and that the consciousness in the waking state does not cover the whole region of mental activity. If the figurative language of dreams is not discursive, this does not necessarily make it irrational, and it is possible, as indeed Jung has properly observed, that a dreamer shows himself more intelligent during his dreams than in his waking state. It even would seem as if this difference of levels as between these two states is fairly frequent among men of our own time, doubtless because the frameworks imposed by modern life are particularly unintelligent and incapable of conveying in a normal way the essential contents of human life.

This has evidently nothing to do with the function of purely symbolic or sacred dreams, whether these be spontaneous or evoked through rites; here one is thinking of the example of the Indians of North America, whose whole tradition, as well as their vital ambience, favors a kind of dream-nourished prophetism.

In order to neglect no aspect of this question, the following may be added: In every collectivity that has become unfaithful to its own traditional form, to the sacred framework of its life, there ensues a collapse or a sort of mummification of the symbols it had received, and this process will be reflected in the psychic life of every individual belonging to that collectivity and participating in that infidelity. To every truth there corre-

---

[60] *Cf.* the Introduction to *Das Geheimnis der goldenen Blüte.*

sponds a formal trace, and every spiritual form projects a psychic shadow; when these shadows are all that remain, they do in fact take on the character of ancestral phantoms that haunt the subconscious. The most pernicious of psychological errors is to reduce the meaning of symbolism to such phantoms.

As for the definition of "unconscious," it must never be forgotten that this is eminently relative and provisional. Consciousness is capable of gradation like light and is similarly refracted in conformity with the media it meets. The ego is the form of individual consciousness; it could not be its luminous source. The latter coincides with the very source of Intelligence. In its universal nature, consciousness is in a sense an existential aspect of the intellect, and this comes down to saying that nothing is basically situated outside it.[61] Whence it follows that the "unconscious" of the psychologist is merely all that, in the soul, lies outside ordinary consciousness—that of the empirical "I" orientated toward the corporeal world—that is to say, this "unconscious" is made to include at the same time the inferior chaos and the superior states. The latter (which Hindus compare to the bliss of deep sleep, the state of *prajñā*) irradiate from the luminous source of universal spirit; the definition of "unconscious" therefore in no wise delimits a given concrete modality of the soul. Many of the errors of "depth psychology," whereof Jung is one of the chief protagonists, spring from the fact that it operates with the "unconscious" as if with a definite entity.

One often hears it said that Jung's psychology has "reestablished the autonomous reality of the soul." In truth, according to the inherent perspective of this psychology, the soul is neither independent nor immortal; it is merely a kind of irrational fatality situated outside any intelligible cosmic order. If the moral and mental behavior of man were secretly determined by a collection of ancestral "types" issuing from a fund that is entirely unconscious and entirely inaccessible to the intelligence, man would be as if suspended between two irreconcil-

---

[61] Let us recall here the Vedantine trinity of *Sat-chit-ānanda* (being, consciousness, bliss).

able and divergent realities, namely that of things and that of the soul.

For all modern psychology, the luminous pinnacle of the soul or its existential summit is its consciousness of the "I," which evolves in such measure as it is able to disengage itself from the darkness of the "unconscious." Now, according to Jung, this darkness contains the vital roots of the individuality. The "collective unconscious" would then be endowed with a regulatory instinct, a kind of somnambulant wisdom of a biological nature doubtless; from this fact, the conscious emancipation of the ego would comprise the danger of a vital uprooting. According to Jung, the ideal is a balance between the two poles of the conscious and the unconscious, one that can be realized only by the help of a third term, a sort of center of crystallization which he calls "the self," this term being borrowed from the doctrines of India. Here is what he has written on the subject:

> With the sensation of the self as an irrational and indefinable entity, to which the "I" is neither opposed nor subordinated, but to which it adheres and round which it evolves in some sort, like the earth going round the sun, the aim of individuation is attained. I use this term "sensation" to express thereby the empirical character of the relation between I and self. In this relation there is nothing intelligible, for one can say nothing about the contents of the self. The "I" is the only content of the self we know. The individualized I feels itself to be the object of another subject, unknown and superior to itself. It seems to me that psychological observation here touches its extreme limit, which one can certainly justify psychologically, but could not prove satisfactorily. The step beyond science is an absolute requirement of the psychological evolution described here, for without the postulate in question I could not formulate sufficiently the psychic processes established by experience. From this fact, the idea of a self possesses at least the value of a hypothesis after the likeness of the theories about the structure of the atom. And if it be true

that here also we are prisoners of an image, this is in any
case an eminently living image, the interpretation of
which exceeds my capacities. I scarcely doubt that it is a
case of an image, but of an image which contains us.[62]

Despite a terminology too much bound up with the current
scientism, one might be tempted to grant full credit to the
presentiments expressed in the above passage and to find in it
an approach to the traditional metaphysical doctrines if Jung,
in a second passage, did not relativize the notion of the self by
treating it this time not as a transcendent principle but as the
outcome of a psychological process:

> One could define the self as a sort of compensation in
> reference to the contrast between interior and exterior.
> Such a definition could well be applied to the self insofar
> as the latter possesses the character of a result, of an aim
> to reach, of a thing that only was produced little by little
> and of which the experience has cost much travail. Thus,
> the self is also the aim of life, for it is the most complete
> expression of that combination of destiny we call "an in-
> dividual," and not only of man in the singular but also of
> a whole group, where the one is the complement of the
> others in view of a prefect image.[63]

There are some realms where dilettantism is unforgivable.

It is the balance to be realized between the conscious and the
unconscious, or the integration, in the empirical "personality,"
of certain forces or impulsions emanating from the unconscious, that Jung paradoxically labels as "individuation," using
a term by which was traditionally designated, not some psychological process or other, but the differentiation of individuals
starting from the species. That which Jung understands
thereby is a kind of definitive pronunciation of the individuality which is taken as an end in itself. In such a perspective the

[62] *Die Beziehungen Zwischen dem Ich und dem Unbewussten,* p. 137.
[63] *Ibid.*

notion of "self" plainly loses all metaphysical meaning, but this is not the only traditional notion that Jung appropriates in order to debase it to a purely psychological and even clinical level; thus he compares psychoanalysis, which he uses precisely to promote this "individuation," to an initiation in the proper and sacred meaning of the term, and he even declares that psychoanalysis represents "the only form of initiation still valid in the modern age!" [64] Whence proceed a whole series of false assimilations and intrusions into a realm where psychology is devoid of competence.[65]

Here it is not a case of the involuntary ignorance of some isolated seeker, for Jung carefully avoided all contact with the representatives of living tradition. During his travels in India, for example, he did not wish to see Sri Rāmana Mahārshi—al-

---

[64] *Cf.* psychological commentary on the *Tibetan Book of the Dead.*

[65] Jung's psychological interpretation of alchemy has been expressly refuted in the author's book *Alchemy: Science of the Cosmos, Science of the Soul* (Baltimore, Md.: Penguin Books Inc, 1971). Frithjof Schuon, after reading the present chapter, sent me the following reflections in writing: "People generally see in Jungism, as compared with Freudism, a step toward reconciliation with the traditional spiritualities, but this is in no wise the case. From this point of view the only difference is that, where Freud boasted of being an irreconcilable enemy of religion, Jung sympathizes with it while emptying it of its contents which he replaces by the collective psychism, that is to say by something infra-intellectual and therefore also antispiritual. In this there is an immense danger for the ancient spiritualities, whose representatives, especially in the East, too often are without critical sense in regard to the modern spirit, and this, by reason of a complex of 'rehabilitation'; also it is not with much surprise, though with grave disquiet, that one has come across echoes of this kind from Japan, where the psychoanalytical balancing has been compared to the satori of Zen; and there is little doubt that it would be easy to meet with similar confusions in India and elsewhere. Howbeit, the confusions in question are largely favored by the almost universal refusal of people to see the devil and to call him by his name, or in other words by that kind of tacit convention formed of optimism to order, of a tolerance that in reality hates truth, and of compulsory alignment with scientism and the official tastes, without forgetting a 'culture' which swallows everything and engages one in nothing if it be not in a 'neutralism' of complicity; to which must be added a no less universal and quasi-official contempt for all that is, we will not say 'intellectualist,' but truly intellectual and for that reason tainted, in people's minds, with 'dogmatism,' 'scholasticism,' 'fanaticism,' and 'prejudice.' All this agrees perfectly with the psychologism of our time and is in large measure its result."

leging a motive of insolent frivolity [66]—doubtless because he feared instinctively and "unconsciously" (it is a case for saying it) a contact with a reality that would disprove his own theories. For him, metaphysics was but a speculation in the void or, to be more exact, an illusory attempt of the psychic to reach beyond itself, comparable to the senseless gesture of a man who tries to pull himself out of a mudhole by his own hair. This conception is typical of modern psychology, and this is why it is mentioned here. To the absurd argument that metaphysics is only a production of the psyche, one could easily object that the above-mentioned judgment itself is but a similar production. Man lives by truth; to admit any truth whatsoever, however relative this may be, is to admit that *intellectus adequatio rei.* To say "this and that" is to affirm at the same time the very principle of adequation, therefore the presence of the absolute in the relative.

Jung breached certain strictly materialistic frameworks of modern science, but this fact is of no use to anyone, to say the least—one would have liked to rejoice over it—because the influences that infiltrate through this breach come from the inferior psychism and not from the spirit, which alone is true and alone is able to save us.

[66] *Cf.* the preface of the book by Heinrich Zimmer on Sri Rāmana Mahārshi.

Discovering the Interior Life

BY MARCO PALLIS

(Talk given at a conference of Catholic religious headmistresses in January, 1968. The Venerable Lama Trungpa, who was to have delivered the lecture, being prevented from keeping the appointment, asked the present author to act in his stead. Given the nature of the audience, no attempt was made to stick to a Buddhist terminology; Pali and Sanskrit words have been replaced by expressions more familiar to Christians. Both sources have been freely drawn on in the shape of quotations and other illustrative material. Emphasis all along has been less on antithesis than on intelligible dialogue.)

WHEN THE Venerable Lama asked me to stand in for him at this conference, I confess to having felt some dismay at the prospect of replacing one whose whole training, from early childhood, was conditioned by the aim of developing the interior life to the fullest possible extent. Schooled in the tradition of Tibetan Buddhism under its most contemplative form, your chosen lecturer was well qualified to discourse on the means whereby a human soul may be opened to its own latent possibilities of illumination—to the "Kingdom of Heaven that is within you," to quote the phrase used by Christ Himself. It is a real pity that a conjunction of unforeseen causes prevented him from attending your meeting, but this could not be helped; he wishes me to say how sorry he is to have disappointed you. He had, however, told me something about the line he intended to take when addressing you, and this evidently has been some guidance to me. I can only express the hope that what I am going to say ties up sufficiently with the specific question raised in your conference prospectus, namely how to help the young people placed under your care to form themselves in the love and knowledge of the Lord in a manner that will be not merely conceptual but also effective.

This in fact is a question that concerns us one and all, be we young or old, clever or simple, European or Asian, religious or lay; quite simply, the supplying of an answer to this question is the purpose of religion under all its forms. Buddhism expresses this truth by saying that for any human enterprise to be brought to proper fulfillment, wisdom and method must operate together, as one conjoint principle. They must keep in step with one another; otherwise the enterprise will be frustrated as a result of its own inherent unbalance. The Tibetans convey this lesson by the following parable: Two men were both trying to get to the City of Nirvana, but neither of them could make much headway because the one was blind while the other was lame, so they decided to join forces. The lame man climbed on the blind man's back and pointed out the way (this is wisdom) while the man who had sound legs (this is method) carried his companion along the road. This sets the pattern of every spiritual life; all the rest is but a matter of variable circumstance and detail.

The same idea is expressed traditionally by saying that method and wisdom are husband and wife, who may never be divorced. In the Buddhist iconographical symbolism method is always depicted as a male figure, wisdom by a female. When the two appear together on the same ikon, they are usually shown in conjugal embrace, a fact that in the past has often been misinterpreted in an obscene sense by uninformed European observers. Had they but known it, it was their own minds that were thus affected, since these particular ikons illustrating what might be called the "mystical marriage of wisdom and method" are regarded by Buddhists as conveying a message of austerest purity; to suspect anything different would, for them, savor of blasphemy.

It is noteworthy that though method is represented as playing the male part in the divine alchemy, that is to say in the process of transmuting the lead of our creatural ignorance into the gold of the saving enlightenment, it is wisdom, female counterpart of method, who will first be encountered by the human aspirant, and the reason for this is evident. There must be some kind of initial vision of the truth, a first glimpse of wisdom, before any man will feel impelled to alter the direction of his life by turning his back on the world and its manifold allurements in order to seek God. This change of direction, which the word "conversion" by its etymology expresses, itself implies an initial grace thanks to which one suddenly becomes aware of the futility of one's present state and, by the same token, becomes aware of the possibility of reaching a better and happier state. This grace, the gift of faith, marks the first awakening of wisdom in the soul; automatically it will give rise to the question "What must I do (or avoid) in order to reach a goal I now discern in the dim distance? What road am I to follow?" This very word "what" implies a prayer for method; all the prescriptions, positive or negative, of religion can in fact be grouped under one or other of our two main headings. Its doctrinal formulations indicating what is to be realized and why correspond to wisdom under various aspects, whereas the ritual, moral, and artistic equipment provided by religion may properly be grouped under the heading of "methodic supports" at various levels. The supreme instrument of method is the life of prayer, taken in the widest sense; Buddhists would rather say "the practice of meditation," a matter of terminology that indicates a certain difference of viewpoint but certainly not any essential incompatibility.

In this same connection it should be pointed out that from a Buddhist standpoint a too preponderantly abstract presentation of theological truth is dangerous inasmuch as this can easily degenerate into mere philosophizing, into a mental art for art's sake. A theology offered without its concurrent means of active verification in the soul, that is to say as an isolated wisdom, will at best lead the mind into an intellectual dead end; at worst, it will engender its own opposite, since typically the world's heresies have all arisen from an unbalanced presentation of some truth or other. Error—a failure in respect of wisdom—will always imply a parallel failure in respect of method and vice versa. One cannot afford to forget for a minute the essential interdependence of the two great spiritual factors. The great value of tradition is that it serves to maintain the polar balance between theory and practice, between wisdom and its effective realization, through calling into play the appropriate spiritual means. If wisdom is by definition concerned with *knowing*, method for its part is concerned with *being*. In fact, one can only really claim to know something by being that thing; to mistake a merely mental appreciation for knowledge is the classical trap of the philosophers. Realization can be said to take place at the moment when being and knowing coincide.

If one were called upon to describe the process of spiritual regeneration or enlightenment as a whole, one could perhaps best qualify it in terms of a circuit, with wisdom calling forth its appropriate method at each stage of the way, with the result that this same wisdom will become integrated in the soul as a henceforth inalienable element of one's being. The way starts from wisdom and ends in wisdom. Buddhism by its own showing offers itself as a series of methods calculated to lead suffering beings more or less directly to enlightenment; this is Buddhism's specific "note."

To give the parallel version: Christ offers Himself to men both as "Light"—another name for wisdom—and as "the Way." "I am the Way." He could equally well have said, "I am the Means." The prayer "Light up our way, O Lord!" sums up man's most essential needs. What we call the interior life is but an answer to that prayer.

Before entering on a discussion of method under its more technical aspects, it would be well to give our attention briefly to two important conditions attaching to any form of contemplative discipline if it is to be fruitful. The first of these conditions relates to the attitude a man should take up versus nature and the things of nature, whereof he himself is one thing among others; the second relates to what may be called "the mythological mantle of truth," this being one among several means whereby divine wisdom has chosen to reveal its secrets in intelligible form, either in certain parts of Holy Scripture or else through the medium of a traditional folklore, for both these ways of conveying certain truths have been in evidence throughout the world. If our own rationalistic education has rendered us largely impervious to this mode of communication, then it is important for us to reanimate the missing faculty, since a mind that has become closed in this respect will certainly be gravely hampered in its discovery of the life within.

To take the question of man's place in nature first of all: Quite obviously mankind, in order to exist, are compelled to draw on the things around them for their sustenance and in various other ways. As far as that goes, man does not differ greatly from the cow or the tiger or any other living thing, except that his ingenuity in procuring what he wants exceeds theirs, and so do his appetites, a fact that, religiously speaking, is hardly a cause for self-satisfaction; rather should it be deemed a cause for self-questioning.

To suggest, as has been far too commonly the case, that the right to use the fruits of this world's garden, as recorded in Genesis, can be equated with permission to indulge an irresponsible and limitless cupidity, destructiveness, and even cruelty toward our nonhuman fellow creatures is an insult to the Creator, first because it makes nonsense of the statement that "God hateth nothing of what He has made" and second because it restricts the idea of the usefulness of things to their material possibilities alone, and even to only a part of these. Their illuminative uses, as signs or reminders of God's merciful presence, are ignored. The beauty of animals and plants, for instance, and the intrinsic qualities that make of each created thing a unique and irreplaceable witness to one or other divine aspect—all this is food for the intellect, chosen instrument of intuitive contemplation wherewith man is enabled to behold mysteries far beyond the reach of his discursive reason. It is this transcendent faculty, which since Adam's fall has been as if asleep, that needs reawakening in such a way as to allow all our other faculties of perception and action to group themselves harmoniously around it: The word "Buddha," which means "the wake," testifies to this crowning need. For Buddhists, goodness is first of all *intelligent*, since it leads to God. Sin, on the other hand, is stupid; it proceeds from ignorance and leads back to ignorance, and its mere "badness" pales beside its principal disadvantage, which is to thicken the veil between ourselves and the Divine. Buddhism always tends to see in sin a greater or lesser degree of incompetence and in virtue a proof of skill. A Buddhist would readily agree with the statement that Christian "love," that which makes a man yearn to know God and experience His constant presence already here in this world, is firstly and lastly an activity of awareness. As for the love of neighbor, in which Buddhism includes all that shares in man's capacity to suffer—itself a consequence of separation from the divine center—this is both a logical and indispensable condition of deliverance from suffering through a clear discerning of its root cause; Christ's words "Inasmuch as ye have done so to the least of these, ye have done it unto Me" will always find a ready echo in any Buddhist heart.

A compassionate attitude in both thought and practice toward all that lives is one of the keys of a true contemplation. It is preceded in a Buddhist religious training by intense meditation on the theme of the *impermanence*, including suffering and death, that man and all other creatures have to share. This thought is inculcated early in the Buddhist child; such a remark as "Look at that horrid moth, let's kill it" would be quite unthinkable in a Buddhist home. In Tibet, to swear at a horse or a mule, let alone to beat it, was a thing unknown. Wild animals and birds were mostly half-tame because they had so little cause to fear their human neighbors, and their peaceful proximity was in fact a particularly powerful factor in molding the spiritual outlook of the people at large—an object lesson in what Eden must have felt like for Adam.

Let me quote you one passage from the writings of a great saint which perfectly sums up the attitude I have just been describing:

> What is a charitable heart? It is a heart aflame with charity for the whole of Creation, for men, for birds, for beasts, for devils, for all creatures. He who has this heart will be unable to remember or see a creature without his eyes filling with tears because of the compassion that grips his heart; and that heart is softened and cannot endure to see even a slight pain inflicted on a creature or to hear of it through others; this is why such a man does not cease praying also for animals, for the enemies of the Truth, for

those who do evil to him, so that they may be protected and purified; he even prays for reptiles, moved by an infinite pity which is awakened in the heart of those who assimilate themselves to God.

Surely a world so schooled would be a world far less contentious and destructive than the one we know. But now I must make a confession, since I have been playing something of a spiritual practical joke on you all, if such an expression be not far-fetched! The quotation I have just read out to you does indeed well express the Buddhist spirit, but it is in fact taken from a Christian saint, Isaac the Syrian. The Desert Fathers, the Celtic hermits, and Saint Francis all represent a similar trend. Contemplation of the divine mysteries and a fellowship with nature go hand in hand; this is the point I have been trying to make. And now for the second condition alluded to above, the function of "mythological communication." This need not occupy us long, yet some mention of the subject is indispensable.

Latterly a widespread movement has made itself felt in the Christian West the aim of which, as its supporters put it, is to "demythologize" the church's teachings. This is a most sinister development, one fraught with peril both to faith and to the object of faith, which is none other than truth. This antimythological bias proceeds from two evident causes: first, a feeling of defeatism versus modern science, its discoveries and its gibes, and second, an inability to see that it is quite in the nature of things for revelation to use various means of communicating its message, traditions with a mythological form exemplifying one kind of means among others and indispensable in their own place. Every religion contains this element to some extent, and in certain religions—Hinduism, for instance—this enters in very largely, as I was myself able to observe when living in the hills of North Bengal. My gardener, for instance, had a strongly developed sense of the omnipresence of God of which the evidence, for him, was for the most part vehicled by scriptural narratives of a mythological and therefore also timeless character; historical considerations hardly entered in.

Like Christianity and Islam, Buddhism has a strongly affirmed historical framework. The life of the founder can be timed and featured, and its episodes provide the prototype whereon a man's spiritual life is to be modeled. However, even in these traditions there are to be found other concordant ways of conveying the saving message, and the respective Scriptures all include portions that are ascribable neither to the historical unfolding of the religion in question nor to its purely doctrinal side; they narrate mythological happenings which, to be understood, have to be read not physically but metaphysically. This does not mean, of course, that these stories are of human invention and therefore lacking in truth—indeed quite the contrary. Their place in the corpus of revealed truth is guaranteed by the fact that certain lessons can best be conveyed by this means and thanks to the very fact that they take one into a metaphysical dimension that is as real today as yesterday and will remain equally so tomorrow.

The Old Testament, in particular, is rich in this kind of ever-actual narrative; a mind that can respond aright to such a teaching has to be free of a certain self-imprisonment in time and space. Many people are apt to confuse the miraculous with the mythological, which is wrong inasmuch as a miracle, whenever it occurs, belongs by definition to the order of historical happenings; a miracle is an exceptional manifestation in this world of an influence of a transcendent order on a particular occasion. Those who say they wish to remove the mythological element from the church's inheritance may not admit, even to themselves, that after mythology miracles will be their next target; a false mental association of these two elements will nevertheless make this likely. Where possible, miraculous happenings will be explained away, as by saying of the Virgin Birth that the mother of Jesus was so pure a soul that her purity was "tantamount to virginity" or some such thing. I fully expect this to happen—if this warning proves to have been needless, so much the better! Common prudence, however, requires us to be prepared for this and other similar attempts, for pointers in this direction are now too many to be overlooked by anyone who is not blind.

In the case of happenings that could properly be qualified

as pertaining to a sacred mythology, such as the story of the Ark or the Tower of Babel, those who wish to discredit them start off from an assumption that such happenings are either historical or else mere fiction; they can discern no other choice. What they fail to see is that even if these stories be accepted as literal fact, as was the case with our ancestors, this in no wise deprives the stories of their power to convey truth. Where a genuine myth is concerned, its illuminative effectiveness operates outside the alternative "belief or disbelief"; whosoever cannot receive it thus will fail to understand it.

Let the two aforementioned examples from the old Hebrew mythology tell us what they can. First, the Ark. From its description in Genesis 11, complete with measurements given in cubits, it is obvious that a person in the Middle Ages, for instance, had he felt so minded, could easily have found out that a vessel of that size could not possibly have accommodated all the known kinds of animals, let alone the food needed to keep them and also Noah's family alive for forty days or more. Since there is not the slightest reason for supposing that people were more stupid then than nowadays, and good reason for believing the contrary, one has to explain their apparent lack of interest in certain questions of probability or otherwise by the fact that, for them, the dimension of sacred happenings was accepted as a whole, for what it plainly told them; its intrinsic truth shone too brightly to require corroborating through a meticulous canvassing of details. The medieval mind, for all the presence there of human defects as well as virtues, was a *whole* mind, and so was its view of the cosmos; the Gospel references to receiving the truth "as a little child" well describe this attitude. For such a mentality the story of the Ark retains all its intrinsic validity quite apart from any possibility that at a certain moment in time an extensive flood might in fact have overwhelmed part of the inhabited world and thus given rise, in retrospect, to this marvelous story. Its lesson is for all time, for the flood (or its equivalent) is always on the point of overwhelming some section of humanity—today it might well be humanity as a whole that is thus threatened—and escape from the disaster is always by way of an ark of sorts to which only those who fear the Lord can gain admission, because this very fear spells intelligence. The fate of those who become oblivious of God (they may appear to be quite kindly people) is always to be drowned in the consequences of their own forgetfulness.

The Tower of Babel is another such universal myth, also peculiarly applicable to our own time, as it happens. Here again, it is irrelevant whether some ruler in ancient Mesopotamia may or may not have inaugurated an ambitious project of constructing an edifice bigger than ever before and describable as "reaching to heaven." The Empire State Building in New York almost answers to that description, especially on days when the top is swathed in cloud while the street below is clear—in this respect it can emulate many a natural hill. All this remains beside the point, however, because the spirit of Babel is something that is repeating itself continually in human history, in the form of megalomaniac plans wherein man sees himself as the "conqueror of nature" and as the archplanner who can manipulate the future at his own sweet pleasure. The day some Russian or American spaceman first sets foot upon the moon you can be sure that the world will be treated to a babel of blasphemous boasting exceeding all that has been heard hitherto; for the "confusion of tongues" one has but to substitute "confusion of minds" and the Bible story will be lived over again with almost literal similarity.

It is moreover noticeable that those who have taken part in recent cosmonautical exploits have been alike in one thing, namely that their comments relayed from the heights of space have been of a uniformly abysmal triviality that contrasts disconcertingly with the supposed greatness of their achievement, let alone with the courage these people undoubtedly have shown. This is the story of Babel repeating itself with a vengeance! Who then shall say that this story has lost its relevance for us moderns and should now be "demythologized" into oblivion?

As you doubtless are expecting, the latter part of this discussion will contain some reference to the question of "method" in its positive sense of aiding concentration or, to give it also its negative sense, of overcoming distraction. Needless to say, this is where the Venerable Lama will be most sadly missed by us today, for though still young he has already had a wide experience of handling this matter of practical training in the contemplative art, both in relation to the ever-varying needs of individual disciples and, at a more external level, when offering general guidance to groups. Though I cannot hope to emulate him in this respect, I can at least suggest that considerable profit may be derived through reading his book *Born in Tibet*. Though this is presented as a personal account of the lama's early life and training leading gradually to his adventurous escape with a band of refugees in 1959, the book episodically contains much that throws light on the power of a steady contemplation to regulate action even under the utmost stress of danger and hardship—a lesson to our contemporary activists. Whoever will but read between the lines will find in this book much that speaks to his condition.

Since we are on the subject of books, I take this opportunity of drawing your attention to another book by a contemporary Catholic author, Dom Aelred Graham, an English Benedictine who spent many years in America as director of a large boys' school. As a result of experience in the practice of meditation in company with some Buddhist friends, Dom Aelred wrote a book [1] to show how certain current Buddhist techniques might be adapted advantageously for Christian use, with the aim of deepening the contemplative awareness of Christians at a time when the pull is mostly in the opposite direction. As you see, his motives and your own are much the same in this respect.

With much sagacity, Dom Aelred Graham has arranged his material according to the plan that is traditional in the Buddhist East; that is to say, he has presented it under the twofold heading of theory or wisdom and of practice or method whereby that same wisdom may be experienced in one's inmost being—the only way to know, as has been said already. Every initiatic teaching, in Tibet or Japan, has always rested on the

[1] *Zen Catholicism* (New York: Harcourt, Brace & World, Inc., 1963).

authority of a particular sutra or group of sutras, that is to say, on certain inspired treatises or selected portions of the Scriptures related directly to the method in question and from which the method itself draws its technical apparatus in appropriate form; normally these sutras would be memorized before embarking on the corresponding course of meditation. In Dom Aelred's book this wisdom function is filled by a quite remarkable series of quotations mostly drawn from Saint Thomas Aquinas and disposed in such a way that the subsequent comments about ways and means will at once be recognizable as "enactments" (if one may so use the word) of the truths expressed specifically by those quotations. I feel sure that this book will be helpful to many of you here.

Incidentally, in a talk on this same subject given by Dom Aelred Graham to the Anglican Congregation of Saint John the Divine in Boston he mentioned one fact that will surely interest you greatly. In his school, quite unprompted by himself, a number of the boys came and asked to be allowed to join in a session of what they called "Catholic Zen meditation" each Sunday for half an hour of their free time. Dom Aelred said this had been one of the most moving experiences of his life at the school. What this shows above all is that the young, given the right example exerted through the presence of a revered teacher even more than through any spoken exhortation, may well discover in themselves that very possibility of contemplation that provides faith with its inward dimension and with an unshakable defense. This does not mean, of course, that the spoken or written word has ceased to count, where these profound matters are concerned; what it means is that wherever wisdom at any degree is content to shine with its own light, by an "activity of presence," its communication will be both more clear and more far-reaching.

To return to Buddhists and their practices: Certain methods of inducing a habit of attention or "mindfulness," as it is most commonly called, have been in current use since the beginning, whereof an example is the practice of watching the alternate incoming and outgoing breaths over a longer or shorter period; this method remains classical where beginners are concerned, and it has many variants. Similarly in Hinduism exercises in breath control are in common use, as also a whole body of quasi-gymnastic movements and posturings whereby rhythm and poise are promoted in body and mind together. A number of instructors in these methods have found their way to the West, many of whom, however, offer them as a means of promoting bodily and psychic health apart from any religious purpose. Whatever benefits may accrue from such a restricted application of these methods, the results will always suffer from a taint of profanation, as indeed happens with many things familiar to us today—tobacco smoking, for instance, started as the profanation of a sacramental rite of the American Indians which the white settlers in America prostituted to a mere luxury of the senses. Carried out under proper direction, however, this kind of physical or psychological adjunct to meditation can have great uses, provided the indispensable link with a traditional wisdom is maintained from start to finish.

It is not, however, about this kind of method that I wish to speak today, not being expert in this field. Nor is there much point in discoursing on some of the more elaborate meditative schemes belonging to the Tantric form of spirituality, as found in India and Tibet, for the simple reason that these methods require conditions such as would not easily be realizable in a Western framework, save by exception. I do not think these methods would easily transpose into a Christian medium just as they stand, though theoretically the possibility of adaptation in certain cases need not be excluded altogether. What can be said, however, in a more general way is that in a time of growing alienation and disbelief apparatus of a very complex kind hardly fits the need, which calls for a discipline that is at once "central," that is to say expressive of the most central truths of the tradition, and at the same time extremely concise as to the instruments it sets in motion, thus allowing of their methodic exercise under all kinds of circumstances, be it even the most unfavorable.

Such an instrument is typically represented by the invocation of a sacred name (the Indian *japa*) or else of a short formula in which a sacred name is found enshrined. All the great traditions are agreed in saying that this way of concentrating attention and pervading a person's whole being with continual reminders of God is a spiritual means particularly suited to the needs of the Dark Age, when religion is at a low ebb and the forces of godless subversion seem to be a mounting tide. In Buddhist Japan, for instance, this method is associated with the school known as Jodo, or "Pure Land," in which the name of the Buddha Amitabha (meaning "Infinite Light") is the invocatory means provided. In Tibetan Buddhism a similar means exists in the form of the six-syllabled phrase *Om mani padme hum,* of which the manifold and complex mystical correspondences have caused it to be described as "the quintessence of the wisdom of all the Buddhas"; but time does not allow of more than a bare mention of the sacred formula in question. In the Islamic tradition the name of God (in Arabic *Allāh*) is recognized as the spiritual means par excellence. Its invocation, in the Sufi confraternities that exist for the sole purpose of fostering the inward life, is known as dhikr, remembrance; the Sufi initiations, instituted for this purpose of bringing about the "divine encounter" in the heart, all trace back their lineage to the Prophet himself.

Perhaps some inkling of how an invocatory method is intended to operate in the soul may be afforded by recalling the words of a lama whom I met near Shigatse in Tibet when I was staying in the district in 1947. After describing some other methods of a more specialized kind, he offered the following advice: "If a man has been given a particular task to accomplish, this should be carried out with diligence according to the needs of the moment. This having been done, one's remaining time should be filled up with the invocation, leaving no gaps."

Thinking afterward about that lama's advice, it came into my mind that here was a case for applying the lesson of the Gospel story about the man whom an unclean spirit had just quitted. The text goes on to relate how this unclean spirit wandered away through dry places vainly seeking rest until it began to feel homesick for its previous haunt within the man, so it came back there to find the place empty and nicely tidied up—the text says "swept and garnished"—as if awaiting a new occupant. Then that evil spirit proceeded to recruit seven more wickeder than itself, and they all came to dwell there so that the last state of that man was worse than the first.

Here we have a perfect picture of the process of distraction in the mind. If one distracting thought be expelled, a horde of other distracting thoughts will crowd in to fill the vacant place, for willpower alone will not suffice to fight them off. What is needed is a wholesome presence that will leave no room for anything else of a harmful kind. This presence is the Name and its continual invocation. So long as the Name is there, no unclean spirit can gain access to that soul; let this state become an established habit of unbroken attention, and the agents of distraction will give up the struggle, leaving the man in peace.

After what has been said about the Oriental religions, it will be no cause of surprise to find an analogous spiritual method in the Christian tradition itself; indeed it could scarcely be otherwise, since such a way corresponds to a basic human need, outside all questions of religious form. In fact a quintessential formula of the kind referred to above exists in the churches of the Eastern rite under the name of the Jesus Prayer, being invoked there in much the same way as in the traditions of the farther East and giving rise to a whole spiritual method that goes under the name of Hesychasm, from the Greek word *hesychia*, meaning "tranquillity," that peace in Christ that is the recompense of saints in this world and the next.

Probably a good many of those here present will have read a small book published under its English title of *The Way of a Pilgrim*, its author being an unidentified Russian of the mid-nineteenth century. At that time the Jesus Prayer and its invocation was the lamp lighting up the way of salvation for many pious men and women in both Russia and the Balkan countries. Monastic centers or hermitages where eminent masters of this spiritual art were known to reside attracted a continuous stream of pilgrims drawn from all sections of the population. Such a master was called *geron* in Greek and *staretz* in Russian, both of which mean "old man." The "Elder" Zosima, in Dostoevski's *Brothers Karamazov*, is a somewhat fanciful portrait of such a master. The most famous center where the Hesychast methods were practiced and taught was the Holy Mountain of Athos, having been so since Byzantine times; but the roots of this form of Christian yoga, as it may well be called, can be traced much further back, to the hermit communities of the Desert Fathers in Egypt and other parts of the Christian East.

In the eighteenth century a specially selected collection of Greek texts from the Fathers was compiled and first printed in Venice under the name of *Philokalia*, its purpose being to provide the appropriate sapiential foundation for those following the Hesychast way. This collection was soon translated into Russian, being also slightly modified in the process. Two sizable volumes of extracts from this book exist in English, translated by E. Kadloubovsky and G. E. H. Palmer. I recommend this book to your notice with all my heart.

The Jesus Prayer itself consists of a single sentence, which runs as follows: "Lord Jesus Christ, Son of God, have mercy on me" (or "on us" or "on me a sinner," since all three variants exist). Quite evidently, this formula sums up the essentials of the Christ-given wisdom in relation to human need; as a Buddhist would say, this is an *upāya*, or spiritual means, of the greatest efficacy and power. It is equally evident that as far as the prayer itself goes, it is accessible and appropriate to every baptized person as such; moreover its conciseness makes it suitable for all possible occasions—even in the presence of scoffers and persecutors it can be pronounced unobtrusively, just as it also lends itself to being whispered by the dying with their last conscious breath.

Seeing that the Jesus Prayer belongs historically to Eastern Christianity, it may be asked by some whether its transplantation to the West at this late hour would be entirely appropriate, using it of course in its Latin translation of *Domine Jesu Christe Fili Dei miserere nobis*. Could not the rosary, as an existing Western form, fill the same purpose? This is a question I do not feel prepared to answer outright. All one can say is that "invocation," in the methodic sense given to its practice in the East, seems to require a maximum of concentration in the form so used, so that a more extended formula, though not inferior per se since it relates to the same wisdom, may not in practice lend itself quite so well to the purpose the invocation is intended to foster. According to one spiritual master, the natural equivalent for a Western follower of the method might well be either *Christe eleison* (which in effect is a compressed form of the Jesus Prayer) or else simply the twofold name *Jesu-Maria*, whereof the concentration of both light and power is too evident to require comment. Another point to note in this connection, one that has an important "technical" bearing on this whole method, is that the less the formula used lends itself to rational analysis, the better will it match that inward synthesis of which it is destined to become the operative support. It is the holy name, sonorous presence of the divine grace enshrined in the formula, that is both the source of its power to illuminate and a sharp sword to cut off ignorance and distraction at the root. The name when treasured in the heart may be likened to a spark of that same uncreated light that shone into the faces of the three Apostles on Mount Tabor and out of which, as the Hesychast tradition itself teaches, the crowns of God's saints both here and hereafter are made.

In point of fact, a number of Catholics known to the writer have long been using one of the above forms of invocation, and there is no reason why others should not follow their example, if so minded. In Greece and Russia the Jesus Prayer can be invoked on a rosary or else aloud or silently according to circumstances; with those in whom the invocation becomes fully operative, the formula begins to repeat itself spontaneously in the heart, by night as well as day. Christian saints have testified to this fact, and so have Hindu, Buddhist, and Muslim saints who have followed corresponding methods; in every case it is a divine name that is at the center of the process, being first the apparent object of invocation and then becoming its subject, until finally the subject-object distinction disappears altogether. This, as Buddhists would say, is the consummation of the marriage of wisdom and method in the heart—but here words fail entirely, and only silence remains to express this supreme experience.

One question relating to the invocation is likely to be put by some; those who have written from actual knowledge in this connection have been almost unanimous in emphasizing the need to practice this method under direction of a spiritual master who has himself proceeded far along this way. As in the case of those following one of the Indian forms of yoga, an intending Hesychast disciple is warned of dangers that might arise from an unguided use of a spiritual instrument of such great inherent potency, for instance through the development of unusual psychic powers whereby attention might be diverted from "the one thing needful" to the ego of the person himself, as proud possessor of the powers in question; this is always a danger, especially when a man is passing from the elementary to the more advanced stages of a spiritual training, when the bodily faculties have been considerably disciplined but the far more elusive psychic faculties are still half out of control. For this reason, it is far better to work under direction of a qualified master who thus becomes, for the disciple, the earthly representative of Christ in relation to the method and should, as has been said again and again, be treated as if it were the Savior Himself who was imparting the instruction. Given this need for qualified direction, it may well be asked where today is such direction to be sought? For it is in no wise to be supposed that qualification for this spiritual office somehow goes with the priestly office, the latter being sacrificial and ritual but not per se connected with the initiatic function of a "director of souls." If the sacerdotal office represents the organized side of the tradition, the office of spiritual master represents "the spirit that bloweth where it listeth"; if the spiritual master happens to be a priest and monk (as in fact has usually been the case in practice), this must nevertheless be accounted an "accident" in respect of his special vocation.

When I was preparing this talk, I often put to myself the question "What shall I answer if I am asked where qualified guidance may be found by a Christian seeker today?" This is admittedly a difficult question, but in fact, the Hesychast Fathers had already foreseen this contingency long ago, for after dwelling at length on the imperative need to find a master and put oneself under his direction, they add that if despite all efforts no master is found, the aspirant is not to despair but is to practice the Jesus Prayer with fear and love, instructing himself where possible through reading. As they say, he must throw himself confidently upon the mercy of Christ the Lord, imploring him to be his instructor, and if the aspiration be a genuine one, surely God's grace will come to the man's aid. One is never justified, however discouraged one may feel, in behaving like the man in the parable who only received one talent; one cannot compel the grace of God, but one can always keep oneself in the disposition of responding to it if and when it chooses to manifest itself.

Properly speaking, it is the interior life itself that chooses the man, not the contrary—let this also be remembered. To wait upon the Lord by day and by night is already to be well on the way. There is no time or place where man is left devoid of all spiritual opportunity, unless it be that he himself refuses or ignores the divine mercy that surrounds him.

Remarks on the Enigma of the Koan

BY FRITHJOF SCHUON

ANYONE who has taken an interest, however slight, in Zen Buddhism knows that the koan is an intentionally absurd formula that is destined to bring about a kind of liberating explosion in the mind of the person meditating on it, the mind in this instance being considered with regard to its hardness and blindness. All too frequently, however, the koan has been represented in a more or less unsatisfactory manner: People like to pretend, not without a hint of relish at the expense of common sense in general or of logic (that allegedly Western peculiarity) in particular, that koans are there to confer a new vision of the world and of life, an aim in itself completely devoid of interest; or else they make out that Zen is all of a piece with practical life of the most everyday sort, a view that takes no account of spiritual values at all. This is not to say that such assertions and flattering claims are altogether lacking in reality; it should, however, be emphasized that they do not constitute definitions and that if they did so, they would not be of a sort to convey a high idea of spirituality as embodied in Zen.

Obviously it is quite inadequate to declare that the purpose of the koan is to produce a particular mental change and that this is achieved purely thanks to its absurdity. Such an opinion fails to explain why one koan differs from another, nor does it account for the trouble taken to assemble a collection of koans, a traditional work deriving all its canonical authority from the fact that the koans were given by the greatest masters. Were it sufficient for a koan to be absurd for it to be able to bring about a state of illumination, one could confine oneself to the remark that two and two make five, and there would be no need to resort either to a traditional koan or to one koan rather than another.

The fact that koans do not deliberately include a statement

198

of metaphysical doctrine and that it is impossible to explain their meaning verbally does not imply that they have no meaning at all. People are not encouraged century after century to meditate on complete and utter absurdities. Moreover, the traditional character of the koan as well as its illuminative result proves that this formula is not just anything. But if the koan possesses no intentional doctrinal content, what can its content be? Both the specific character of Zen itself and the replies of the masters provide us with the explanation: The koan expresses the spiritual experience of a given master in a symbolical—and intentionally paradoxical—form, the significance of which is only verifiable by actually undergoing the self-same experience. At the moment of that rupture that is satori, or illumination,[1] the koan is suddenly "understood," its data are identified; and if one koan differs from another, this is not because the effect of satori is multiple but because its aspects are multiple. There can be no doubt that the koan has a metaphysical meaning if it has any meaning at all, or rather because it has a meaning; but its justification lies precisely in its referring to the inexpressible aspect of the experience of awakening. The objection could be raised that in such a case the koan has no right to exist, having no place in language since language implies intelligibility; this objection is in itself pertinent, but the occasional exception must also be given its due, allowing that paradox can have a catalytic function in the economy of maya.

The above observations call for some further remarks on the intentions and means of Zen in general. What Zen wants is the supernatural recovery of the perception of things sub specie

---

[1] Satori is not absolute illumination; it amounts already to a degree of bodhi, but is not yet the *Samyaksambodhi* of the Buddha. If the profane state is separated from that of the Awakened Buddha as the circle is separated from its center, satori would be the sudden realization of the ray that, without itself being identical with the center, is as it were a prolongation of it. In relation to the profane state one may say that satori "is" illumination in itself; distinctions between degrees of illumination have a meaning only on the spiritual plane, not in relation to the world.

aeternitatis or in the "eternal present"; having neither the ability nor the need to come outside relativity, the spirit from that moment on finds itself rooted in the Absolute, both intellectually and existentially. But Zen also comprises another dimension, complementary to the first; this is its aspect of "simplicity" or "equilibrium," a returning to primordial nature. The complement of lightning and of breaking out, or of satori, is found in the peace that dwells in the nature of things, as revealed in the stillness of a pool reflecting the moon or in the truly contemplative grace of the waterlily, or, yet again, in the calm and precise elegance of the tea ceremony. The sober turning toward nature together with its somewhat iconoclastic element is no mere luxury in the Zen tradition; whoever wishes to recall the human spirit to that "intuition of eternity" for which it was made, but which it has lost through its decadence—the fruit of a curiosity that disperses and a passion that compresses—must needs also recall soul and body to their primordial simplicity by freeing them from the artificialities superimposed on them by civilization.[2] The one thing does not go without the other; the lightning's perfection evokes that of the lotus. In this second dimension Zen was able to profit from the ground prepared by Shinto, just as the presence of Taoism had rendered similar service with regard to the first dimension. This, however, must never lead to our losing sight of the fact that all was given from the beginning: The origin resides in the Buddha's gesture, his smile, and the flower held in his hand.

Given that one takes as one's starting point the elementary idea—even simply with a certain effectiveness in view—that the world is none other than impermanent, that it is composed of impermanent and changing "categories" or "atoms" and that

---

[2] The posture in Zen meditation, *zazen*, is revealing in this respect: erectness and motionlessness, balance between effort and naturalness. Zen has developed an "art of gesture" extending to various professions, including the profession of arms. All kinds of decorative and relatively feminine activities are also included, in which, however, is to be seen the very antithesis of the would-be "sincere" and pseudonatural indecency of today.

Nirvana alone possesses permanence, one is surprised at the extent to which people forget—assuming they have ever thought about it—that escape from impermanence or even the mere conception of the idea of impermanence and deliverance would be impossible if no trace of permanence existed within the impermanent or of absoluteness within the relative. Inversely and a priori, there must be an element of relativity in the absolute; otherwise the relative would not exist, let alone the notion of relativity and escape from the relative. The yin-yang symbol represents this truth in its own particular way, as has been pointed out by the author on many different occasions.

Now, it is precisely this element of absoluteness or of permanence at the very heart of the contingent or of the impermanent that constitutes our own essence, our "Buddha nature"; to rediscover our own true nature is to realize permanence and to escape from the "round of existence." It is by basing itself on this idea of immanence that Zen sets out to detach itself, not from tradition of course, since it is Buddhist, but from concepts as such; its very foundation is the fact that everything that revelation offers is to be found principially within ourselves. Zen teaches its disciples, by means of various signs and attitudes, to perceive and to become everything that gives its sufficient reason to words and ideas and to tradition.

While holding no special brief for Aristotelianism, it goes without saying that Aristotle is a thousand times preferable to a pseudo-Zen divorced from its roots and so deprived of its justification and its effectiveness. If the point is stressed here, this is because modernistic Zen all too readily overlooks the fact that Zen is "neither with nor without forms" and that, besides rigorous introspection and what may be termed the cult of voidness, it includes, at least a priori,[3] an attitude of devotion,

---

[3] This reservation implies that the devotional virtues are looked upon as becoming absorbed ultimately in an inward extinction which, while surpassing them, is in no wise opposed to them; from another point of view one may say that in Zen the various attitudes are found side by side, everything having its proper place.

of humility and gratitude, which it shares in common with all spirituality worthy of the name.[4] From whatever angle one views it, a spiritual method is not something that is freely dispensable to all and sundry. To the very extent that it is subtle or esoteric it becomes transformed into poison when not practiced within the framework of canonical rules, "in the name of God," therefore, as one would say in the West; in the case of Zen this framework is above all the triad "Buddha-Law-Community" (Buddha-Dharma-Sangha). Zen is a function of everything implied by this triad, or else it is nothing.[5]

[4] Zen monks recite the sutras every morning, which proves they are far from despising texts; they also repeat the prayer of Ta-Hui, which contains a series of spiritual and material demands and is addressed to "all the Buddhas and Bodhisattva-Mahāsattvas of the past, present and future in the ten quarters [of the universe], and to Mahāpraj-nāpāramitā," the Shakti of the Adi Buddha—Vajradhara—with whom she is sometimes identified. One should also note that every meal is accompanied with prayers and that the principal building of the monastery contains an image of Shakya-Muni.
[5] Moreover there is nothing in common between Zen and the theories of men like Jung or Krishnamurti or any other form of psychologism.

Who Is Man?

The Perennial Answer of Islam

BY SEYYED HOSSEIN NASR

(A Noranda Lecture delivered at Expo 67 in Montreal on September 4, 1967.)

IN A WORLD exhibition whose theme is "Man and His World," "La Terre des Hommes," and which is devoted to a display of the different aspects of man's life and activities, it is perhaps not futile to pause for a moment and pose the question who is this man to whom the world is said to belong, the world or the "earth" that he has conquered yet is on the verge of destroying at the very moment when his conquest seems most complete. Modern man feels at home on earth, or rather would like to feel at home completely in this world, in contrast to the traditional Christian man or men of other civilizations who nearly always felt as a traveler in this world and a stranger upon the earth, which they considered as but a temporary abode. Yet even modern man cannot totally evade or forget his inner yearning for the abode beyond, his urge for the transcendent, or remain oblivious to the fact that the more he tries to become a completely terrestrial being, a creature of this earth, the more does the earth seem to crumble from under his feet and the more does he seem to fall out of harmony with the earthly environment. It is a paradox that the more man has tried to become "natural" during the postmedieval period, the more has he lost harmony and contact with nature to the extent of endangering his own existence within it.

Let us not forget that today the predominant axis of man's knowledge of things, his science, is earthly and terrestrial. Modern man learned the laws of the physics of the earth from celestial physics and astronomy. The laws of motion of Newton were based on the laws of planetary motion established by a Pythagorian Kepler who significantly enough spoke of these laws, specially the third law, in a work entitled *Harmonice Mundi*. And once these heavenly laws were relegated to the level of terrestrial physics, this physics itself became the model of other forms of knowledge. Today it is this "earthly" physics that seeks to understand the constitution of the "heavens" and therefore to obliterate the meaning of heaven, at least physically. Today all of modern man's science is "terrestrial," yet he cannot obliterate the metaphysical and symbolic significance of "heaven," of the "celestial" whose imprint he bears deep within himself. And so when man no longer makes spiritual flights or ascensions into the heavens in the manner of a Dante, he has the mystique to fly with a capsule into planetary space—in the same way that when he no longer climbs spiritual mountains, he tries to desecrate and debase physical mountains by "conquering" them. Or when the majority of men no longer practice those authentic spiritual disciplines that make the veritable vision of the transcendent world possible, they use mescalin and LSD with the hope of gaining such a vision without undertaking the necessary travail, self-negation, and discipline. Although outwardly now a complete creature of the earth and its master, and no longer the "half angel–half man" of traditional Christianity, this urge is deeply engraved in the very texture of man's existence and manifests itself in one way or another, sometimes even violently, when the natural and normal means are not open to it.

Man feels himself as the possessor of all things, as the unquestionable conqueror and master of all of nature as if he had created it himself. But this sense of possession and power is only too often combined with a remarkable lack of responsibility and realization of the right to life of other creatures. Man's domination is too often a prostitution of nature rather than its legitimate use. The voice of conservationists is raised here and there but is usually drowned in the much louder voice that in the name of human welfare wants to make man's mastery over the earth total and complete, irrespective of what this may mean for the earth itself and its creatures. It is here that one is faced with the tragic situation in which the very assertion of the unlimited rights and power of man over the earth makes man's life on earth ever more difficult and dangerous, leading in a direction that if pursued further might mean the very termination of both this domination and man's very life. One is reminded of the Koranic verses: "But the Devil whispered to him, saying: O Adam! Shall I show thee the tree of immortality and power that wasteth not away?" (20:120, Pickthall translation), referring to a Faustian power that not only appears not to waste away but is always posing the danger of destroying him who would wield that power. Being no longer the custodian of the earth, and yet wielding power, man is in the danger of losing his mastery over it as well. It seems that man cannot really live peacefully on earth and be just an earthly creature. The loss of the transcendent dimension has made terrestrial life itself precarious.

Could one but conclude that a secular humanism of the type first cultivated during the Renaissance is basically contradictory and fallacious? That is, one cannot speak of man and defend his dignity and right independent of the "divine image" that has made him man and bestowed upon him both dignity and freedom. Otherwise, humanism is only a halfway house from the theomorphic conception of man to the infrahuman into which man is being dragged today through many of his own inventions and creations. He who wishes to speak about man better concern himself about the whole of man or not speak at all. And he who wishes to speak about man and his world must of necessity first consider who is man and in reality *whose* world one is speaking about. Without penetrating into these questions and discovering the appropriate answers the hope for a harmonious relation between man and his world is dim indeed, and so many pictures of the further and more complete conquest of nature in the future become nothing but a chimera and dream, for within man lie forces that no "earthly" science, even if it is extended to the Pleiades, can ever understand or unravel or control.

Modern science may enable man to know how he is constituted chemically or biologically or where he is in galactic space. But this form of science cannot tell man who he is, where he was before his earthly existence, and where he will be after it. It cannot reveal to man where he stands in what has been called existential space, in the hierarchy of universal existence. It therefore cannot provide for man "orientation," for to orient man's life means to know where he comes from, where he is to go, and most of all who he is.

In this situation in which the knowledge of man is urgently needed and is yet well-nigh impossible to discover through normal channels of learning available today, where even the traditional Christian theological teachings concerning man have in certain cases succumbed to the lure of the microscope and the telescope, giving rise to a pseudowisdom that strikes at the very root of the Judeo-Christian concept of man and his dignity, it is not perhaps unwise to turn to the teachings of Islam on this question. For in Islam, as in other revealed religions, the truth of the nature of things and especially of man is to be found, and Islam reaffirms explicitly and fully the truths expressed in another fashion in Christianity and other revealed traditions. Moreover, Islam, belonging to the same spiritual tree as Judaism and Christianity, presents a doctrine of man not so far removed from the Occidental world view as to be considered by oversophisticated and so-called realists as merely "exotic" but irrelevant and is yet original and distinct enough to be of interest for the Westerner who seeks to answer the question "Who is man?" One could in fact say that in the teachings of different religions man can discover different elements of his own universal nature, aspects of the "universal man" himself, of which every man is an image.

If some religions are based on the incarnation of God in human history or the God-man, Islam is based on the encounter between God considered in His absoluteness and man in his full nature as the theophany of God's names and qualities. All creatures reflect some aspect of the divine, as an image is reflected in a mirror. Only man reflects all of the divine names and qualities and this moreover in a central and conscious manner. By virtue of this relation that he possesses vis-à-vis

God, he is a "central being" in this world, always located in an "existential space" in which the vertical, transcendent dimension is present. Whether he is aware of it or not, man's situation in this "space" is not just horizontal and material. The vertical, spiritual axis stands always before him. Reality for man is always three-dimensional, whether man chooses to live in a two-dimensional, material world devoid of the dimension of depth or height *(al-ṭūl)* or whether he realizes fully the infinite third dimension beyond the limited horizontal surface of existence with which he usually associates himself, and today more than ever before, whether he flies to the galaxies or swims to the depths of the sea. This centrality is intrinsic to the human situation, and man cannot evade it any more than he can evade being born in a particular time and space. That is why he is called the vicegerent of God on earth *(khalīfat Allāh)*.

Man was taught the name of all things as the Koran states: "And He taught Adam all the names" (2:31), meaning that he was given power and dominion over all things by virtue of being God's vicegerent *(khalīfah)* on earth. But with this function of *khalīfah* was combined the quality of *'abd*, that is, the quality of being in perfect submission to God. Man has the right to dominate over the earth as *khalīfah* only on the condition that he remains in perfect submission to Him who is the real master of nature. The mastery and power of man over nature is only a borrowed power given to man because he reflects the divine names and qualities.

Islam does not accept the idea of incarnation or filial relationship between God and man, but it does stress the theomorphic nature of man, the fact that God breathed into man of His spirit and created a being in which His names and qualities are fully reflected, for as the Prophet said: "God created man upon His image." Nor does Islam accept the idea of original sin. It appeals, not to the will of man, which has been warped since that event or act that Christianity so profoundly describes as original sin, but to his intelligence, which lies within the primordial nature of man *(al-fiṭrah)*, the inner nature that man possessed before his fall on earth *(hubūṭ)* and that man still carries deep within himself.

In his primordial nature man is always the perfect *khalīfah* of God, but man is forgetful of this nature and therefore always in need of divine revelation and grace as also confirmed by Christianity. Being forgetful, man is prone to seek to take advantage of the power and privilege afforded to him as the *khalīfah* of God while neglecting to remain His *'abd*. From the Islamic point of view the plight and tragedy of modern man consists in that he wishes to make use of his intelligence and power as a theomorphic being to dominate the earth and even the heavens, without accepting the fact that he *is* a theomorphic being or realizing the responsibilities that issue from the occupation of such a central and seignorial position on earth. Man wants to play the role of God, to create and destroy, to dominate and rule, without realizing that he is not God but an image and reflection of His names and qualities. It is as if a shadow would want to play the role of the object of which it is the shadow or as if noise would be sufficient to conquer the heavens. The great disequilibrium existing between man and nature as well as man and himself today, could be summarized in Islamic terms by saying that man wishes to remain the *khalīfah* he was created without being the *'abd* that he was also created, given that mysterious freedom to rebel against even that which he really is. In fact indirectly the most evident proof of man's theomorphic nature is that he can rebel against himself, against his own nature, and stop being, at least for a time, what he really is.

Yet man cannot fully forget his inner being, his theomorphic nature, for however hard he tries to float on the surface of his being and run away from the center, he carries the center within him, and sooner or later the center manifests itself in one way or another in the periphery and the surface. For to be made in the image of God in the sense of being the theophany of His names and qualities is a reality that lies in the human state itself. Islam affirms the primordial character of man's theomorphic nature and his special situation in the cosmos and vis-à-vis God by referring to a covenant made between God and man even before the creation of the world. For as the Koran states: "And [remember] when thy Lord brought forth from the Children of Adam, from their reins, their seed, and made them testify of themselves [saying]: Am I not your Lord? They said: Yea, verily." (7:172). In this "yea" is to be found the secret of human destiny, because by iterating it man accepted the burden of trust *(amānah)* which none in creation but he dared accept. "Lo! We offered the trust unto the heavens and the earth and the hills, but they shrank from hearing it and were afraid of it. And man assumed it." (33:72).

This trust from whose acceptance all of creation shied away is precisely the burden of vicegerency of God on earth, of faith itself in its profoundest sense. To have accepted this trust means to have accepted freedom and also responsibility toward both God and all creatures. It means the freedom to transcend all degrees of existence and reach the divine presence even above the state of the angels, as Islamic texts assert. But it also means the possibility of rebellion, of the negation of the very reality upon whose image man is made. The grandeur of the human state is precisely in the sublimeness of the goal that can be achieved and the abysmal terror of the risk that is inherent in the situation. Whatever path he chooses, man cannot evade the grandeur of his state, the fact that he is placed at the intersection of the "horizontal" and "vertical" dimensions of reality. Even when he tries to forget this nature and consider himself only as an animal that somehow happens to think, he cannot evade the cosmic dimension of his being, except that in such a case he risks bringing destruction to the whole terrestrial environment and even to the cosmic environment about him.

Man then cannot evade the consequences of that original covenant by virtue of which he accepted the trust *(amānah)* from God, receiving certain rights as well as being charged with certain responsibilities. Tradition or religion in its universal sense *(al-dīn)* is then inherent to the human state. The spiritual anthropology of Islam considers *dīn* as a necessary condition of full manhood. For man to live without *dīn* is to be only accidentally human, for it is to be deprived of that very essential condition, the acceptance of the burden of *amānah*, that defines the human state. One could thus again reconfirm the point already mentioned that humanism without the realization of the theomorphic nature of man is, from the Islamic point of view, no less than a contradiction and absurdity. And perhaps the experience of the past two centuries in the West has, to put it mildly, at least not contradicted the Islamic view. Cut from his transcendent and spiritual archetype, man has the greatest difficulty in remaining just human and not being dragged into an infrahuman world created by secularized man himself.

The Islamic conception of man is summarized in the doctrine of *al-insān al-kāmil*, the universal or perfect man, a doctrine whose essence and full manifestation is to be found in the Prophet of Islam and whose doctrinal exposition and formulation was left to later sages and saints such as ibn-Arabi and Jalal-ud-din Rumi. In fact Islamic gnosis *(al-ʿirfān)* revolves nearly always around the two axes of unity *(al-tawḥīd)*, dealing with God and His names and qualities, and *al-insān al-kāmil*, dealing with man and the cosmos. The first is concerned with the origin and source of creation and the second with manifestation and the return of things to the source. Or one could say that the first corresponds to the first "witness" or *Shahādah* of Islam, *Lā ilāha ill'-Allāh* (there is no divinity but the Divine), and the second to the second "witness," *Muḥammadun rasūl Allāh* (Mohammed is the Messenger of God). Mohammed is the universal man par excellence and also the quintessence of all creation, of all that is positive in cosmic manifestation. The universal man contains all degrees of existence within himself and is the archetype of both the cosmos and man. Therefore, metaphysically and of course not physically and quantitatively, there is a profound correspondence between man and the cosmos. Although outwardly a small part of the cosmos, man contains inwardly and within himself a reality that is the source of the cosmos itself—and that is why even fallen man, he who has forgotten his own true nature, has the power to dominate nature.

From the pure star-bright souls replenishment is ever coming to the stars of heaven.

Outwardly we are ruled by these stars, but our inward
   nature has become the ruler of the skies.
Therefore, while in form thou art the microcosm, in reality thou art the macrocosm.
Externally, the branch is the origin of the fruit; intrinsically the branch came into existence for the sake of
   the fruit.[1]

The spiritual man, although outwardly dominated by nature,
inwardly rules over things most of all because he has conquered
his own inner nature. Might one not add that today when man
boasts most about conquering nature, the reverse process has
taken place, namely an apparent and outward conquest of nature combined with complete lack of asceticism, spiritual discipline, and self-negation, which therefore makes man more than
ever a prisoner of his own passions and natural inclinations.
But the spiritual man who has overcome his passions and who
is the reflection of universal man and its realization and embodiment is the pole toward which the universe itself is attracted, to the extent that Jalal-ud-din Rumi, that supreme poet
of the spirit, could say:

Wine in ferment is a beggar suing for our ferment;
Heaven in revolution is a beggar suing for our conscious-
   ness;
Wine was intoxicated with us, not we with it;
The body came into being from us, not we from it.[2]

The universal man, whose full metaphysical doctrine cannot
unfortunately be expounded here, is then the sum of all degrees
of existence, a total mirror before the divine presence and at
the same time the supreme archetype of creation. It is the
prototype of man, the reality that man carries potentially
within himself and can always realize if there is aspiration,
persistence, and of course divine succor. It is enough for man

[1] Jalal-ud-din Rumi, in R. A. Nicholson, *Rūmī, Poet and Mystic* (London:
Allen and Unwin, 1950), p. 124.
[2] *Ibid.*, p. 141.

to realize the total possibility of his own existence, to become fully conscious of himself, to gain that treasure of true felicity and peace that he seeks outwardly here and there but never seems to find.

> You who wander in deserts away from your own con-
>   sciousness,
> Come back to yourself to find all existence summed up in
>   you.
> You are the way and reality of perfection.
> One in whom the great consciousness of God dwells.[3]

One is here reminded of the advice of medieval sages in the West: "Above all to thine own self be true."

The cosmic dimension of man may bring certain protests from theologians that this would obliterate the distinction between grace and nature and reduce man to simply "natural man." Christianity, having expanded in a world that suffered from too much emphasis upon rationalism and naturalism, had to draw a sharp distinction between nature and grace, at least in its official theology. But Islam was not faced with the same situation. For this and for other reasons its doctrines are such that it considers nature itself as a handiwork of God in whose arteries flows the grace issuing from the Creator Himself. Man also is from a certain point of view a "natural being," yet without being deprived of grace. He is natural without being reduced to the natural man of the Renaissance or of Rousseau and the French encyclopedists. The whole question of natural law, original sin, the role of nature in spiritual realization, and the like is approached in a different light in Islam, and these questions have of course their bearing on the understanding of man and his function in the world. By considering man in his primordial nature *(al-fiṭrah)* and bestowing upon each Muslim the priestly and sacerdotal function, Islam removed the sharp distinction between the religious and secular, or sacred and profane, making of man a natural being who yet is the most

---

[3] Abu 'l-Mawāhib al-Shādhilī, in M. Smith, *The Sufi Path of Love* (London: Luzac and Co., 1954), p. 72.

direct symbol of the spiritual world in nature and in direct contact with that world.

Furthermore, by virtue of being the *khalīfah* of God on earth and occupying the central position he does hold, man is the channel of grace for nature. The spiritual man is the means whereby nature breathes of the spiritual life and is prevented from suffocation and destruction, as also confirmed by Western hermetical and alchemical writers like Flamel and Jakob Böhme. Were man to cease completely to follow the spiritual life and lose his contact with the spiritual world, he would also cease to be a source of light for nature and in fact would turn toward the destruction and vilification of nature. The relation between modern industrial societies and virgin nature should provide an occasion to pause and meditate on this relationship.

The constitution of man and his relation with God and nature cannot be fully understood without analyzing the meaning and role of intelligence and reason, by means of which man seeks to master the world. First of all a clear distinction, often forgotten today, must be made between the intellect, the faculty that knows immediately and totally, and reason, whose Latin root *(ratio)* reveals its function of analysis and division. Islam appeals to the intellect in man, whose function it is to know the principles of things and which will arrive at the basic Islamic doctrine of Unity *(al-tawḥīd)* if it functions normally and is wholesome *(salīm)*. In fact the role of revelation is to remove those obstacles that prevent the intelligence from functioning in a wholesome manner. Otherwise the intellect within man confirms the revealed truths of religion, and Islam bases itself on a truth that is evident and in the nature of things.

As for reason, it is like the shadow and reflection of the intellect. If it remains subservient to the intellect and also to revelation, which likewise issues forth from the Supreme Intellect or Logos, then it is a positive instrument that can aid man to journey from multiplicity to Unity. But if it rebels against its own source, against both the intellect and revelation, then it becomes the source of disharmony and dissolution. Other creatures have intelligence in the sense that they reflect certain aspects of the divine and also cosmic intelligences. But only man possesses this subjective polarization of true intelligence that we call reason. And that is why only he can destroy the natural harmony of nature.

If modern man has been able to dominate but at the same time destroy nature and himself more than men of all other civilizations, it is precisely because with him more than ever before reason has been made independent of its principle. In such a condition reason becomes like an acid burning through the tissues of the cosmos and at the same time is powerless before the infrahuman and irrational forces that revolt against it from below, in the same way that it has rebelled against the intellect above it. The relation between rationalism and the spiritual and intellectual heritage against which it rebelled on the one hand, and the irrationalism of modern times on the other, is very similar and in fact nearly the same thing as the humanism that rebelled against the theomorphic concept of man only to end in being threatened by infrahuman forces it has itself liberated. Islam, while considering man as essentially an intelligence that has also willpower and performs actions, and emphasizing knowledge as a means of salvation and deliverance, yet rejects the position of rationalism and its limiting of the intellect to its reflection, which is reason as ordinarily understood. For Islam the world of the mind is much more vast than we usually envisage. It is in fact the locus of the presence of the divine spirit, but man must penetrate beneath the surface of the mind with which he usually identifies himself in order to become aware of this presence. Again to quote Rumi:

> What worlds mysterious roll within the vast,
> The all-encircling ocean of the Mind!
> Cup-like thereon our forms are floating fast,
> Only to fill and sink and leave behind
> No spray of bubbles from the Sea upcast.
> The Spirit thou canst not view, it comes so nigh.
> Drink of this Presence! Be not thou a jar
> Laden with water, and its lip stone-dry;
> Or as a horseman blindly borne afar,
> Who never sees the horse beneath his thigh.[4]

[4] Nicholson, *op. cit.*, p. 106.

It is the very centrality and totality of the human state that makes any "linear" and "horizontal" evolution of man impossible. One cannot reach a more central point in a circle than the center itself. Once at the center one can always move either upward or downward but no further in the horizontal direction. The evolutionary view of man as an animal, which even from the biological point of view is open to question, can tell us little as to the real nature of man; no more than can the theories of many anthropologists who discuss anthropology without even knowing who man, the anthropos, is and without realizing the complete states of universal existence that man carries with him here and now.

Once it was asked of Ali, the cousin and son-in-law of the Prophet: What existed before Adam? He answered Adam, and to the question what existed before that Adam he again answered Adam, adding that were he to be asked this question to the end of time, he would repeat Adam. This saying means that irrespective of when he appeared in the time-space matrix of this world, the metaphysical reality of man, of the universal man, has always been. It could not become but is, because it transcends time and becoming. It is, furthermore, this eternal archetype that determines the meaning of the human state and that man always reflects and bears potentially within himself in all time and space. Those who speak of the future evolution of man perhaps do not realize that higher possibilities of existence do not lie in some future time ahead of man but here and now above him, yet within his reach. Frankly, it must be said that the way man is "evolving" today makes it ever more difficult for him to attain these higher states of consciousness and being, whose very existence he has begun to doubt in general, while a certain number of people in this very climate of doubt seek to reach these states through the shortcut of drugs and pills rather than through spiritual discipline. One might say that the total and central nature of the human state, deriving from man's theomorphic nature, makes his relation with other states of being not a temporal one but a spatial one. Man stands at the crossing of the vertical and horizontal dimensions containing the amplitude and breadth of universal existence within himself here and now. It is for him to delve into himself in order to realize who he is, to realize these states that comprise his full nature. No development in time, especially in a process during which man lives increasingly on the surface of his being, fleeing from himself and the needs of his inner nature, will ever automatically bring an evolution to higher planes for the human species.

Rather, the urgent problem today is to prevent man from falling into an infrahuman world, which he faces because he has rejected his own transcendent origin and prototype. Modern man wants to kill the gods, without destroying himself. He wants to reject the Divine and yet remain fully human. Islam has considered this question fully and has provided an answer with which we shall conclude this discussion. In several places in the Koran mention is made of the term "Face or Countenance of God" *(wajh Allāh),* for example the verses: "There remaineth but the Countenance of thy Lord of Might and Glory" (55:27) and "Everything will perish save his Countenance" (28:88).

Nearly all Muslim sages have agreed that "the Face or Countenance of God," which alone endures and persists, is the spiritual aspect of man's nature. Ultimately the body dies, and even the inferior psychic elements perish or at least are integrated into a higher degree of being, namely that of the spirit. It is only the spiritual element that is eternal. It is the face that man has turned toward God. But it is also the face that God has turned toward man. The "Face or Countenance of God" embraces a total reality one aspect of which is man's spiritual countenance and the other God's countenance toward his creation and especially his vicegerent on earth, man. And it is this same reality that in Shi'ite Islam comprises the inner nature of the imam. The imam is the link between God and man, a spiritual being in whom the divine and the human orders meet.

To meditate on the theme of the "Face of God" is to realize that man cannot destroy the divine image without destroying himself. The poetical cry of Friedrich Nietzsche in the nineteenth century that "God is dead," a cry that has now been turned into a theological proposition in certain quarters and is advertised far beyond its purport and significance by those who seek after the sensational and who seem to have little reverence for the belief of those living and dead for whom God is eternally present and alive, cannot but have its echo in the assertion that man is dead, man as a spiritual and free being. Man cannot destroy the face that God has turned toward him without destroying the face that man has turned toward God, and therefore also all that is eternal and imperishable in man and is the source of human dignity, the only reality that gives meaning to human life. The inexhaustible richness of the symbol of the "Face or Countenance of God" should possess much meaning for modern man who seeks desperately for meaning in human life and the preservation of human dignity, but is too rarely concerned with the other half of this reality, namely the "Countenance of God," that aspect of the Divine that has turned toward us as human beings.

To know himself, man must come to know the "Face of God," the reality, that determines him from on high. Neither flights into outer space nor plunges beneath the seas nor changes of fashions and modes of outward living alter the nature of man and his situation vis-à-vis the Real. Nor can biological or conventional psychological studies that deal only with the outward aspects of human nature reveal to man who he is and how he should "orient" himself in that journey whose end is the meeting with the Real. Man can know himself only by realizing his theomorphic nature. It is only in remaining conscious of the divine imprint upon his soul that man can hope to remain human. Only the attraction of the celestial can prevent man from being dragged by gravity to the abysses of subhuman existence. And it is a remarkable feature of the human state that no matter where and in what condition he may be, man always finds above him the sky and the attraction that pulls him toward the infinite and the eternal.

The Seven Deadly Sins
in the Light of
the Symbolism of Number

BY MARTIN LINGS

IN THE SERIES of single-figure numbers there are two that stand out from the rest as having an essentially divine significance, namely one and seven; between them, as between alpha and omega, is enacted the whole drama of existence. One is the Creator; two signifies the spirit,[1] three heaven,[2] four earth, and five man, whose place is as a quintessence at the center of the four elements, the four points of the compass, and the four seasons of the year, which characterize the earthly state. But man cannot fulfill his function as mediator between heaven and earth without the transcendent dimension of depth and of height and the vertical axis that passes through the center of all the degrees of existence, which is none other than the tree of life. This superhuman dimension is implicit in the central point of the quintessence but does not become explicit until the number five is transcended. It is through six that the center becomes the axis, that the seed becomes the tree, and six is the

---

[1] That is, according to the Islamic conception, as the summit and synthesis of all creation, opening to the Uncreated and therefore possessing, implicitly if not explicitly, the Uncreated Aspect that is none other than the Third Person of the Christian Trinity. According to Shaikh al-Alawi, in his treatise on the symbolism of the letters of the alphabet, the letter *ba,* which has the numerical value of two, is a symbol of the spirit. See *A Sufi Saint of the Twentieth Century* (University of California Press, 1972), Chap. 7.

[2] This applies not only to three in itself, but also to its intensification three times three, nine being in some respects the most celestial of all numbers.

number of primordial man in the state in which he was created on the sixth day. As universal mediator [3] he measures out, with his six directions, the whole of existence; and beyond six lies that from which existence proceeds and to which it returns. "And God blessed the seventh day, and sanctified it, because that in it He had rested from all his work."

Seven thus signifies repose in the divine center. From that point of view it is the symbol of absolute finality and perfection, appearing in this world as a divine seal upon earthly things, as in the number of the days of the week, the planets, the sacraments of the church, and many other septenaries the mention of which would take us too far from our subject. But despite these considerations—or rather because of them—there is, as we shall see, a profound reason why the deadly sins should be seven in number.

In quest of the key to this paradox, the first thing to be remembered is the underlying continuity that exists between Edenic man and fallen man. At the fall there was no new creation; virtually man is still a central being. If he were not, there would be no nostalgia in his soul, and the first human perfection, instead of being a norm and an ideal, would be out of reach and as it were alien. But in fact it has never been superseded, whence the doctrine of original sin, which is itself an affirmation of the continuity we are considering. Moreover, a doctrine of sin means a doctrine of atonement: Where there is a question, not of irrecoverable loss, but of dormancy and perversion in the soul, there can be reawakening and reintegration. This reversible continuity between primal norm and present fact means that however prone to guilt certain powers of the soul may have become, they were originally innocent. We must remember also in this connection the axiom *corruptio optimi pessima*, the best when corrupted becomes the worst; and if it be asked, "What is the worst?" we may answer, with regard

---

[3] In Arabic the letter *waw* and in Hebrew the letter *wāw* both have the numerical value of six, and each constitutes, in its respective language, the linguistic mediator, namely the word "and."

to the human soul, "The seven deadly sins." At any rate, these sins may be taken as landmarks [4] in the domain of all that is most evil; and the three words *seven deadly sins* in a sense "add up" to *corruptio optimi pessima*, for the number seven betrays the mysterious presence of an *optimum* in the context of deadly sin, *pessima corruptio*. Here also lies the key to the paradox of the correspondence of the deadly sins to the planets, including the luminaries. Taking them in their traditional order, *superbia* (pride) is related to the Sun, *avaritia* (avarice) to Saturn, *luxuria* (lust) to Venus, *invidia* (envy) to Mercury, *gula* (gluttony) to Jupiter, *ira* (anger) to Mars, and *accidia* (sloth) to the Moon. It would be wrong, however, and even sacrilegious, to invert this manner of expression and to say that sins are actually represented by these celestial bodies after which, in virtue of their exaltation and luminosity, the very heavens themselves are named. All that can be said is that the planets are symbols of what is "best" in the soul; and when these *optima* are corrupted, they still continue to be related to the planets, just as they still continue to bear the seal of seven. In other words, those psychic powers or tendencies that have become the vehicles of deadly sin were numbered before the fall, when they held in the soul a place analogous to that of the planets in the firmament. Seven may thus be considered as a mark of identity used by a shepherd that it may continue to show, when a sheep has strayed, the fold to which it rightly belongs and to which it may be brought back.

In considering how it is possible for the "sheep" to stray so far, let us begin with a fact about one of the sins that is generally known but seldom weighed and that is not without its implications as regards other sins. A feature that all religions have in common is the concept of anger as an unholy rupture of equilibrium side by side with the concept of holy anger, which is exemplified in Christianity by Christ's driving out the

---

[4] This reserve is perhaps necessary because the septenary in question appears to be arbitrarily incomplete, unless we take some of the specified sins to include implicitly others that are not explicitly mentioned but that are nonetheless closely related.

merchants from the temple and of which the sin itself⁵ seems
like a parody. Analogously, although the term "holy avarice"
is not used, could it not be said that a miser is a caricature of
an ascetic and in rare cases perhaps even potentially an ascetic?
The traditional representation of a miser as a half-starved man
dressed in rags and carrying a bag of gold would have an altogether different meaning if the gold were to be taken symbolically and not literally. Some misers have been known to endure
what would be described, in the case of a saint, as "heroic
deprivations." But since "acts are according to intentions," the
two "poverties" are as remote from each other as hell is from
heaven. Nonetheless—for with God all things are possible—if
a great spiritual master were to take a miser and turn him into
a saint, the avarice, though necessarily rejected, would not have
to undergo an absolute rejection; but the word "turn" is used
here advisedly, for the tendency in question would need to be
completely reorientated. Thinking along parallel lines, could
not something analogous be said of the sin of lust, for example?
And in connection with another deadly sin, we may remember
the words of the Decalogue: "I the Lord thy God am a jealous
God." Not that "jealous," as used here, is a synonym of "envi-
ous," but the two may be said to have a common root, namely
the refusal to accept that another should have or be given something that one feels should come to oneself. Similarly, as regards the worst sin of all, it is significant that in Islam one of
the ninety-nine divine names is "the Proud." The Koran uses
exactly the same word to glorify God as to condemn Pharaoh;
and if God is Proud, then pride must also be an aspect of human
perfection, made in His image. We have here a virtue and a vice
that bear the same name even though they lie at opposite poles
of human possibility; and the truth *corruptio optimi pessima*

---

⁵ Needless to say, there are many degrees of anger that lie between the
two extremes; more precisely, though anger is seldom holy, it is often
just and therefore often not sinful. The sin implies an extremity of
violence out of all proportion to its cause, a more or less total loss of
self-control and therefore of centrality, a momentary suspension of all
higher consciousness, whereas holy anger is as it were an overflow of
higher consciousness, a flooding of the periphery by the center.

stands as a bridge across the gulf that appears to separate them. It remains to be seen how it is possible for this bridge to be crossed, both by way of corruption and also, from the other side, by the path of redemption.

As regards corruption, we may take our key from the symbolism of another number traditionally associated with the deadly sins, that is, the number eight,[6] for if seven denotes simply the best, eight in its positive sense [7] denotes the precise degree that this particular best, the best of the corruptibles, holds in the universal hierarchy. In his article on the symbolism of the octagon Guénon mentions that in sacred architecture an octagonal structure often serves as support for a dome, thus marking the transition from the square foundation to the circular summit, that is, from the terrestrial number four to the celestial number nine.[8] In other words, eight denotes the intermediary region between earth and heaven or, microcosmically, between body and spirit; and the octagon supporting the dome is particularly relevant here as a symbol of that "best" part of psychic substance that is the vehicle of spiritual light symbol-

[6] The doctrine of the *peccata capitalia* can be traced back as far as Serapion, who was bishop of Thmuis in the Nile delta in the middle of the fourth century. Having given the number of the deadly sins as eight, he enumerated only seven, and on being asked about the eighth, he said that it was the elementary condition of the soul under the influence of sin, the condition symbolized by the captivity of the Israelites in Egypt. Now, this captivity was an intermediary state between two freedoms, and eight is in fact a symbol of the intermediate or the transitional, which may be negative, as in this particular case, but which can also be positive or merely neutral.

[7] As regards what might from a certain point of view be called its negative sense, eight has a "mortal" effect upon "five" (man), for the number obtained by their multiplication is forty, which in many diverse traditions is the number of death. Moreover, in astrology, of the twelve houses that make up the full circle of the heavens, it is the eighth that signifies death; and in this connection we may remember that the eighth sign of the zodiac is Scorpio, whose hieroglyph, the letter *M* with a barbed final stroke, is doubly symbolic of death, by the reason of the sting in its tail and because the letter itself stands for *mors*. But death is not necessarily negative, and if it be considered as the transition from one state to another, the "mortal" symbolism of eight may be included in the number's overall significance as a symbol of the "intermediate," which is what we are considering here.

[8] *Symboles Fondamentaux de la Science Sacrée*, Chap. 42.

ized by the dome itself. This octagon has in fact a triple symbolism, for not only is it a vehicle of the dome but also, by being immediately adjacent to it, it expresses the nearness to heaven of the psychic elements in question, and by being almost circular in form it expresses their all but spiritual nature. Moreover, eight is the number of the winds, which signify the inspirations that it is the function of these elements to receive. But being of the soul, not of the spirit, these relative summits are by definition corruptible; and not only has the devil access to them but it is here above all that he intervenes,[9] for he can do no far-reaching harm to a human soul unless he can first pervert one or more of its highest elements, which otherwise, continuing to fulfill their intuitive function, will remain like vigilant sentinels, ever ready to give the alert. It was certainly not to any lower faculties that Satan's original temptation was addressed, but rather to those that constitute man's leanings toward the next world, his hopes of immortality, his longings for the untransitory. This is brought out clearly in the Koranic account of the fall (20:120): "Then Satan whispered unto him,[10] and said: 'O Adam, shall I show thee the Tree of Immortality and a kingdom that fadeth not away?'" Let us quote also the following comment on this:

> All his deception of mankind throughout the ages[11] is summed up in the above verse; he ceaselessly promises to show man the Tree of Immortality, gradually reducing by this means the highest and most central faculties into the

[9] As, for example, when he succeeds in drawing Moses and Joshua away from the very brink of the Waters of Life (Koran 18:61–63).
[10] The Koran here represents Satan as tempting Adam not through Eve but directly, and in other passages he addresses them both together.
[11] It is unrealistic to maintain that no one can be held responsible for anything that took place in this world before his birth, for a man *is*, in a sense, his ancestry. Less elliptically, the chain of occurrences that since the beginning of the world has produced the particular heredity and environment into which he is born corresponds exactly to the total "earnings" of his previous states. Thus even if a religion does not explicitly recognize these previous states, that is, if it does not have the doctrine of the samsara, reality nonetheless compels it to consider everyone as if he or she had actually succumbed to the original temptation that brought about the fall.

outer part of the soul so that he may imprison them there in attachment to the counterfeit objects which he has forged for their perception. It is the presence here of these perverted faculties, either in discontent that they can never find real satisfaction, or finally in a state of atrophy in that they are never put to their proper use, which causes all the disorder and obstruction in the soul of the fallen man.[12]

To take particular examples, it could be said that the sin of gluttony is caused by the erring presence, in the outer or lower part of the soul, that part that is nearest the senses, of a perverted psychic element whose rightful place is at the threshold of heaven and whose normal function is to represent, for the individual in question, what might be termed the sense of the infinite. True to its nature, it looks for infinite satisfaction in the domain of the finite. A similar erring presence can be said to lie at the roots of the sin of lust.

On the other hand, the "static" or "contractive" sins of sloth and avarice can be traced to a perverted sense of eternity. The one is the attempt to realize eternal peace in a domain that is divinely willed to be in a state of movement and vicissitude. The other is the attempt to keep eternally that which is, by its very nature, ephemeral; it is also the blindness of attributing to "treasure upon earth" the absolute value that belongs only to "treasure in heaven."

Eternity and infinity are dimensions of the Absolute, and the perverted sense of the Absolute, either directly or through one or other of these dimensions, may be said to lie at the root of all deadly sin. It is "reverberation" of the Absolute, however remotely, that alone can account for the monstrousness of the semi-insane exaggerations in question.

The sin of anger presupposes as much lack of sense of proportion as avarice does, though in an altogether different mode; either could be described as the "absolute" effect of a relative cause. But avarice is the deification of a material object, whereas

[12] Abu Bakr Siraj Ad-Din, *The Book of Certainty* (New York: Samuel Weiser, 1970), p. 42. See also pp. 35–39.

anger, like the sins of envy and pride, implies a certain deification of the ego, its endowments with rights that belong only to the Absolute, that is, to the Supreme Self. But at the summit of the soul of the saint there are necessarily elements of sublime "thunder and lightning," just as there are necessarily elements that may be said to participate in the divine jealousy inasmuch as they "begrudge," through their discernment, the attribution of any absolute value to other than the self. Similarly, having realized the answer to the question "Who am I?" [13] the saint cannot fail to participate in the divine pride, which will be reflected in the outer part of the soul, not as the sin of pride, but as the virtue of dignity and sometimes even of majesty.

The intuitive part of the psychic substance, the part through which the soul may be said to have the sense of the Absolute, the Infinite, and the Eternal, can be fully operative only if all its elements are in their rightful place. The soul of the saint is perfect order and harmony; fallen souls are in a state of disorder that varies incalculably from individual to individual. Needless to say, it is possible that part of the higher substance should remain relatively unfallen. Otherwise there could be no initial other-worldly aspirations, and the individual in question could never become a novice for the spiritual path. But as to those elements that are disintegrated and fallen, in that soul as in other souls, their chaos is caused by the higher elements being buried beneath the lower ones or, which amounts to the same, by the inner elements having strayed into the outer part of the psychic substance, where they cause perversion or obstruction according to whether they are virulent or dormant.

In connection with the widespread dormancy of psychic elements, it is particularly ironical that the notion of sincerity—or rather the word, for it is scarcely more than that—should loom so large in twentieth-century complacence, for sincerity, which implies an integral vigilance, is just what modern man most lacks. The often heard words "sincerity is all that matters" express, if duly weighed, a profound truth; but it is nearly always forgotten that sincerity cannot be assessed without ref-

[13] The reference is to the methodic question that formed the basis of the teaching of Sri Rāmana Mahārshi.

erence to what one is sincere about. In other words, the quality of the subjective reaction is inextricably dependent on the quality of the object. To take particular examples, it is really no less than a contradiction in terms to speak of a "sincere humanist" or a "sincere communist" if the word "sincere" is to retain its sense of "total dedication." Enthusiasm, everyone now knows, is no guarantee that the subject is sincere. This century, especially in its second half, is witnessing without respite the most violent orgies of enthusiasm, and as often as not the object is so worthless that the "enthusiast" can be no more than a small fraction of a soul, a fraction that has, perhaps momentarily, declared itself independent of reason, memory, and other faculties. Such cases may not be too dangerous in themselves, but they are alarmingly symptomatic of a widespread psychic disintegration. To revert to less paroxysmal but much more chronic and therefore more dangerous enthusiasms of the humanist and the communist, we have only to consider what man is to see that neither humanism nor communism has anything whatsoever to offer to the higher reaches of the human soul. If such an enthusiasm is nonetheless able to gain a lifelong grip of any given individual, it can do so only without the assent of his higher psychic elements; and the negative presence of these elements in his soul, whether they be dormant or atrophied, precludes all questions of sincerity. It may be objected that in some cases the elements in question are perverted without being dormant and that the soul can be something of a chaos but nonetheless "all there" and therefore sincere; and there can be no doubt, as regards the two enthusiasms in question, that they are able to gain their formidable impetus only by drawing, to a considerable extent, on the soul's latent treasuries of idle and unused spiritual fervor. But such thefts can never be total; perversion is always fragmentary. Fervor is, in its highest sense, no less than the thirst for the Absolute, the Infinite, and the Eternal, and there can be no common measure between the psychic vehicles of this fervor when in their rightful place at the summit of a normal soul and a mere fraction of them that has been perverted and dangerously bottled up as part of an enthusiasm for some finite and ephemeral object.

Only religious orthodoxy at its fullest—that is, when endowed with the full range of its third dimension of mysticism —is large enough to engage the whole psychic substance of man and coordinate it into a sincerity worthy of the name. The truth is indivisible totality and demands of man that he shall be no less than one undivided whole; and it is a criterion of orthodoxy that it should stake a claim in every element of our being.

But how does mysticism bring about the inverse of *corruptio optimi pessima*, that inverse that is expressed by "The stone which the builders rejected is become the head of the corner" [14] and also by "Joy shall be in Heaven over one sinner that repenteth more than over ninety and nine just [15] persons which need no repentance"? The first phase of the spiritual alchemy of repentance is "the descent into hell," so called because it is first necessary to penetrate into the depths of the soul in order to regain consciousness of the "worst" which by "repenting" is to become once more the best. In this connection some reference to psychoanalysis is no doubt opportune, and the author may perhaps be excused for simply repeating here what he has already formulated in a similar context elsewhere:

[14] Not in their highest sense, as quoted by Christ and commented by Saint Paul, but in a more relative sense, according to which they are akin to the parable of the prodigal son. Their original context in the Psalms (118:22) is directly though not exclusively suggestive of this more relative interpretation:

> The Lord hath chastened me sore: but he hath not given me over to death.
> Open to me the gates of righteousness: I will go into them, and I will praise the Lord. . . .
> I will praise thee: for thou hast heard me, and art become my salvation.
> The stone which the builders refused is become the head stone of the corner.

[15] This "justice" is exactly analogous to the symmetry of the majority of the stones. On the other hand, the lack of symmetry for which the keystone was rejected, and which is by ordinary standards a deformity, is shown to be an extension of celestial supraformality once this stone has taken its rightful place at the summit of its arch which is, like the octagon we have been considering, an architectural symbol of the threshold of Heaven.

The modern development of psycho-analysis makes it necessary to explain that this first phase of the mystic path is radically different from any psycho-analytical descent into the subsconscious. Psycho-analysis is largely a case of the blind leading the blind, for it is simply one soul working upon another without the help of any transcendent power. But initiation, followed up by the devotional and ascetic practices implicit in it, opens the door to contact with the perfecting and unifying power of the Spirit whose presence demands that the psychic substance shall become once again a single whole. The more or less scattered elements of this substance are thus compelled to come together; and some of them come in anger, from dark and remote hiding-places, with the infernal powers still attached to them. From this point of view it is truer to say that Hell rises than that the mystic descends; and that the result of this rising is a battle, with the soul as battle-field. . . .

At the outset of the path the perverted psychic elements are more or less dormant and remote from the centre of consciousness. They must first of all be woken, and then redeemed, for they cannot be purified in their sleep; and it is when they wake in a state of raging perversion that there is always the risk that they will overpower [16] the whole soul. [17]

The first phase of purification is rejection. The battle is fought in order to rout and put to flight those elements that

[16] Here lies the great danger of the spiritual path, and this is why the esoteric methods have always been kept more or less secret, for it is incomparably better not to set out at all than to follow the path for a certain distance and then abandon it. In fact, it would be no doubt true to say that no man runs the risk of becoming a personification of one or more of the deadly sins so much as does an initiate who breaks his pact.

[17] *Shakespeare in the Light of Sacred Art* (London: Allen and Unwin), pp. 51–52. These last two paragraphs were written with reference to Angelo in *Measure for Measure* and to Leontes in *The Winter's Tale*, and there can be no doubt that in his maturer plays Shakespeare was deeply preoccupied with the questions that are being considered here.

have become the soul's lowest possibilities, for it is only through banishment and exile that they can be cut off and isolated from the relativities to which they have become all too absolutely attached and disencumbered from the false associations which have stunted them and warped them. Rejection is thus ultimately a liberation.

The rejected "stones" have then to be reminded of their true nature and brought back in honor through "the gates of righteousness." This phase of love and recall may be said to follow that of fear and rejection, for "fear of the Lord is the beginning of wisdom"; but the two phases are partly simultaneous in the alchemy of purification, for love means consciousness of the bonds of the Absolute, and it is above all this consciousness that has power to loosen the bonds of relativity. The spirit, vehicled by the rites, may be said to address the soul's fallen elements with exactly the same message as that which originally seduced them; but this time the message is true, and a true message is infinitely more powerful than a false one: "O Adam, shall I show thee the Tree of Immortality and a Kingdom that fadeth not away?" By the implacable rhythmic regularity of the performance of rites, which is an essential feature of the spiritual path, this promise of the transcendent is "drummed" ceaselessly into the soul; and since the elements chiefly concerned, those that were made for nothing but the transcendent, are merely being asked to conform to their own true nature, this promise is bound to prove, sooner or later, irresistible—whence the exaltation, by spiritual masters in all ages and in all religions, of the virtues of perseverance, patience, and reliance.

Is There a Problem of Evil?

BY MARCO PALLIS

WHEN WE POSE the question "Is there a problem of evil?" we are not doing so with the intention of charming away evil with words; still less of relieving our minds of the sense of sin, as modern psychology is more and more tending to do; nor are we concerned with any kind of comforting mental "adjustment" nor with what people refer to as "happiness," to which moroever they suppose themselves to have a "right."

On the contrary, for us, evil corresponds to a reality at the level of the world, and so does "sin," in the religious sense of a voluntary disregard of a revealed law. Likewise "goodness," in the ordinary sense, though often vaguely conceived and expressed, corresponds to a reality at this level. In fact, the two things belong together, as members of a duality, as shadow belongs to light and cannot help doing so. All this may be taken for granted in the present instance.

What, however, we are now concerned with is whether or not evil constitutes a "problem," one that supposedly is still awaiting a satisfactory solution. It cannot be denied that this opinion has often been put forward, consciously or, still more often, unconsciously—the phrase "problem of evil" is one of the commonest clichés in the language—and furthermore religious writers, especially in the Christian church, have frequently felt constrained to offer more or less satisfying solutions to this supposed problem, of which a typical example is the statement, theologically valid but vulnerable to sentimental stultification, that God "permits" evil in view of a greater good. "Why does the world not contain only good, only joy?" is a question constantly cropping up through the ages. "Why was it not created free from evil, pain, and anxiety?"

When shorn of all accessory considerations, the alleged problem reduces itself to the following dilemma: God is said to be almighty and all good; He is also called the creator of the world. If He is good but yet created a world as evil and unhappy as the one we see around us, then He cannot be almighty; if on the other hand He is almighty and still created the world thus, then He cannot be all good.

In their time, the Manichaeans and kindred sects known to early Christian history, on the basis of such reasoning, concluded that the demiurge, the world's creator, must be an intrinsically evil being, certainly not God Himself. Trying thus to shift the blame, they still left the essential problem unsolved, since they did not tell us how or why the demiurgic tendency itself either arose in the first instance, in the face of God, or was able to operate. In fact these sects were obsessed with this particular problem, and their attempts to find an answer satisfying to human feeling often led them into strangely contradictory enunciations. It is not with these desultory attempts, condemned by the church, that we are concerned today, for in the religious crisis through which the world is now passing the basic dilemma takes a different and more far-reaching form; in fact, behind it lurks the thought, as an implicit conclusion, that if things are so, then God is neither almighty nor good nor creator, for He does not exist. The world is a blind place then, a field of blind forces whose playthings we, and all our fellow beings, are and must needs remain. If during past ages, when faith was relatively general, people hesitated to draw the conclusion in this naked form and therefore resorted to various intellectual subterfuges in order to avoid it, that conclusion was there all the same potentially, a seed waiting to germinate whenever it found itself in a soil conditioned to receive it; the unuttered thought was like a perpetual chink in the armor of belief, and the various dialectical expedients resorted to during times when the human mind was still predisposed to accept the theological premises were never quite sufficient to plug this gap in man's spiritual defenses. We are speaking, of course, chiefly of the Christian world (in the Indian traditions the problem, if indeed it existed at all, never assumed this acute form, for reasons to be explained later), but as we are living in an environment formed on the basis of Christian concepts and still predominantly governed by Christian values, it is necessary, and indeed inevitable, for us to concern ourselves with the consequences of Christian thought, or lack of thought, on this vital subject. We are living through an age of doubt, if not of "counterfaith," and this makes it more than ever imperative for us to think clearly, if we are able, concerning a question with which the spreading attitude of doubt is causally bound up, at least in large measure. Before we can think of discovering an answer, however, we must first make sure if the question itself has been properly put; for unless such is in fact the case, it would be idle to expect a proper solution.

Indeed, many of the unresolved problems that plague men's minds, and especially those of a metaphysical order—the ultimate questions concerning selfhood and existence—are not merely unsolved but insoluble because they have in fact been faultily set. There is a catch in the statement of the problem itself, and this precludes the possibility of an answer. A question badly put—to quote one eminent commentator of our time, Frithjof Schuon—does not call forth light any more than it derives from light. Half the urgent questions that keep tormenting us would evoke their own answer spontaneously, if only they could once be correctly framed.

Such is the question now before us. What we are presently attempting to do is in fact to improve the framing of this question of evil, as an indispensable prelude to any eventual answering of it.

Before proceeding with our discussion, however, there is one remark to offer: The evidence that will be laid before the reader, doctrinal, illustrative, or dialectical, is drawn from many different sources. Little is attributable to myself personally, except the manner of presenting it. In any case the truth belongs to all equally, in proportion to each man's power—and willingness—to assimilate it (this was said by René Guénon); there is no room for claims of human originality in respect of the truth itself, except in this sense, namely that whoever succeeds in expounding any aspect of truth is original in virtue of that very fact, and necessarily so. It is also good to remember that the effective realization of truth in any circumstances will always entail more than an operation of mere thought. Such a realization, as saints and sages are forever reminding us, will always imply an equating of being and knowing; it must never be supposed that the thinking faculty amounts to the total intelligence of a being, though it is a mode of intelligence in an indirect sense and useful in its own sphere, which is that field of relativities whereof the manifested world consists. True intelligence, which alone deserves the name of intellect unqualified, is a faculty that, if it be not hindered as a result of insubordination by the lesser faculties, its appointed handmaids, will fly straight to the mark. It does not "think"; it sees. The catalyzing of this power to see, which everyone bears within himself whether he be aware of it or not, is the aim of all spiritual method, its only aim. Correct framing of a necessary question, so that the evidence supplies itself and hence also the answer or proof, can act as such a catalytic agent. That is why a discussion like the present one can on occasion be fruitful; otherwise it were better to keep silent. Of purposeless discussion the world has more than enough.

But let us now go back to the dilemma concerning the Creator's power and His goodness, as propounded above. We said that behind it lay concealed the thought that this apparent contradiction was tantamount to a dethroning of God, to be replaced, as the ultimate and only principle in the universe, by a blind becoming, a view from which a theory of complete determinism would moreover seem to follow inescapably.

It is, then, a rather startling fact that at the very time when theories of this kind seemed to be gaining ground in the world of science and among the educated classes generally—I will not call them intellectual—and in a more diffuse and instinctive form among the urban masses, another type of theory should have gained credence whereby something like an optimistic bias was attributed to the course of the universe and to the shaping of its contents, a bias working in a (to us) pleasing direction, by a passage from simple to complex (complex being equated with superior) and culminating, up to date, in mankind as we know it, though, of course, with the implication that further developments in the same sense are to be expected in an indefinite future. I am referring to the body of theories that come under the heading of evolutionism, of which the Darwinian theory was but one specification among others, one that created the stir it did largely because of its timing, as having supplied just the kind of explanation people were looking for at the moment, especially in the sociological sphere where the doctrines in question are associated with the name of "progress." It provided, as it were, a scientific sanction, supported by much tangible evidence, to an already existing wish, and this conjunction carried it far on the road to general acceptance within a very short time.

Evolution, whatever truths or fallacies the word may enshrine, has become, to all intents and purposes, a dogma of the modern age—in some countries its open denial might even land a man in jail—and though scientists themselves may discuss its premises in this or that context, the public at large takes it as much for granted—a glance at the daily press shows this—as any medieval public took for granted certain dogmas of the church, even while oversimplifying their meaning. As Gai Eaton wrote: "The ages of faith are always with us, only their object changes." Here the word "faith," of course, must be understood loosely, as meaning belief, since faith in its deeper (and more accurate) sense is far more than that, indicating that indirect and participative knowledge that must fill the gap between knowing and being, theoretical assent and realization, so long as the two exist apart; once they are unified, by the miracle of intellection, there is no more seeing in a glass darkly, but only face to face, in the noonday of truth.

Now, this mention of the evolutionary doctrines has a purpose that ties up with the subject of this essay. I am not concerned to discuss the applicability of these doctrines as such. What I wish to illustrate, by this passing reference, is that they imply, under all their differing forms, acceptance of a kind of universal trend toward the better, which here is represented as an inherent property of becoming, the good itself being always an ideal perceived some distance ahead but presumably never actually attainable, since this would terminate the evolutionary process in a seemingly arbitrary manner. It is noteworthy that with every fresh discovery of science, every invention and especially those that present a sensational aspect as with rockets to the moon, etc., this idea of the upward evolution of humanity is evoked as a kind of mystique, and the same occurs in respect of the more important social developments. If it be objected that some of these happenings are by no means so certainly beneficial as their sponsors would have it, this is not the point, since what we are trying to observe is a certain trend in the general mentality, very marked in our time, which, because of its reading of an optimistic bias into the unfolding of the universe, runs flatly counter to the other logical implications of a materialist determinism, of a universe conceived as functioning minus God. That two such opposed assumptions should be able to coexist in a self-same mind, as they so often do, is a highly significant piece of evidence, since it shows, for one thing, that the "problem" of good and evil, or superior and inferior if one so prefers, is still very much with us and as far from a solution as ever.

There is really no logical reason for believing in a survival value attaching to what is good, rather than to what is evil (one cannot avoid using these terms here, imprecise as they are); nor is there any evident basis for the supposition that a blind universe, one that reflects no principle superior to its becoming, somehow carries within itself a preference in favor of what we men regard as "good"—on the basis of our own feelings—indeed there is a very considerable weight of evidence against such an opinion, at least sufficient to preclude any facile assumption in its favor. Hence it is reasonable to conclude that behind the belief in question there lies some kind of sentimental motive, such as has influenced both the selecting and the reading of the evidence in a manner that cannot be described as purely "scientific"—scientific implies above all impartiality—and this again goes to show that man is still tormented with the pressing problem of his present unhappiness, for which he tries to compensate by projecting onto the future his own yearning for a universe organized so that he will not suffer; in other words a "good" world or a happy world.

The picture that this calls up, if one pauses to think, is so reminiscent of the carrot swinging in view of the donkey to make it pull the cart ever farther that one cannot help asking oneself who, in that case, is the driver of the cart, the one who placed the carrot where it is? This also is a pertinent question in its way.

The stage has now been sufficiently set to allow us to come to grips with our initial question: Is there a problem of evil, as the saying still goes? It is best to leave aside individual speculations and turn, for light, to the teachings of the great traditions and see what they have to offer by way of an answer. In treating their sacred narratives and other symbolical expressions, however, we must be ready from the start to look beyond the letter, to read between the lines, to find, side by side with the more literal interpretation (valid at its own level), that deep-searching interpretation that Dante called "anagogical" as pointing the way to the heights of mystical realization. (The word "mystical" here must be given its root meaning of "silent," of a knowledge inexpressible because escaping the limits of form.) To this knowledge the sacred forms—forms, that is to say, drawing their spiritual efficacy from the fact that they are founded upon true analogies between different orders of reality—serve as provisional pointers. Their providential usefulness is to provide keys to the mysteries; as such, they are not to be decried, as so often happens, in the name of some mental abstraction or other that would have itself "pure spirit," but rather they must be treated as the good craftsman treats the tools of his trade, by guarding them against such impairment as a straitlaced literalism, on the one side, or profane denigration, on the other, may have wished upon them. This all has a close bearing on the currently imputed failure of religion and the consequent neglect, by disheartened men, of means provided for the sake of the only task that matches the human condition—means that have to be formal by the very fact that we ourselves are beings endowed with form.

In order to illustrate our chosen theme, it is fitting, with an audience largely composed of Christians or of people molded more or less by Christian thought, that we should turn first of all to the evidence contained in the earliest chapters of the Book of Genesis, those that give the story of Adam and Eve. No more illuminating symbolical narrative is to be found in all sacred literature.

Here we see the Tree of Life, corresponding to the axis of the universe, standing in the midst of the garden in which Adam, primordial man, dwells at peace with all his fellow beings, the animals and plants of the garden. Through him they participate in the center, represented by the tree; so long as his attention remains focused there, there is no disharmony or fear anywhere, and as far as anyone can tell, this state of affairs will continue indefinitely. Here we see the image of *perfect participation in passive mode*. (Of participation in active mode we shall have something to say later.)

But now there comes along the serpent, offering to Adam a hitherto untasted experience, that of fragmented unity, of things unreferred to the center and valued for their own sake as if they were self-sufficing entities. This was, and still remains, the characteristic lure of the Tree of Knowledge of Good and Evil. Adam, persuaded by Eve at the instance of the serpent, tastes of the fruit, and behold in a moment his pristine purity of intent is lost, and he and Eve suddenly become conscious of all that divides them from themselves and from one another and consequently also from each and every thing around them. From that moment on they feel imprisoned each within his own fragmentary consciousness, his empirical ego, and this fact is evidenced by their shame at their own nakedness, which they try to cover up with an artificial selfhood of their own contriving, the fig leaves that have become the prototype of all human disguise.

And as for the Tree of Life, what has become of it? For it no longer is, as far as Adam and Eve are concerned. Looking where they expect to behold it, they can discern only that other tree, the Tree of Good and Evil, bowing under the weight of its fruits light and dark, containing the seeds of indefinite becoming. Advisedly we said "that other tree," since for the first time they feel an acute sense of otherness, of *I* and *you*, and by this very fact they are cut off from those other beings with whom they formerly had communed on free and fearless terms.

What they fail to perceive, however, is the real identity of the tree itself; this is a vital point in this highly symbolic story. Indeed, I myself remember as a child at school feeling much puzzled by this unexplained appearance in the garden of a second tree; it was not till years after I was grown up that it dawned on me that there never had been a second tree but that it was the same tree seen double, through the distorting glass of ignorance. Regarded from the viewpoint of ignorance, the Tree of Life *becomes* the Tree of Knowledge of Good and Evil; regarded from the viewpoint of true knowledge, the Tree of Becoming (as it might just as well be called) *is* the Tree of Life.

Here we have a complete metaphysical doctrine, in its essentials, expressed through the biblical narrative. And how effective to communicate is this concrete symbolism of a tree, or trees, in comparison with the abstractions dear to the philosophic mind!

But now we have been led back to our initial dilemma. Apologists who have wished to defend God (!) against an accusation of being "the author of evil"—and many have felt constrained so to defend Him—have missed one vital point: The paradise, happy as it was, *contained the serpent.* Nothing is said in the narrative itself to account for this startling fact, which occurs almost casually at the moment when the fatal event is about to take place.

Yet if one pauses to look really closely into the premises of creation, one must surely wake up to the truth that a paradise —any paradise—to be a paradise *must contain the serpent.* I admit I did not discover this for myself; it was pointed out to me. The perfection of a paradise without the presence of the serpent would be the perfection, not of paradise, but of God Himself. It would be, in Sufic terms, "the paradise of the Essence." Therefore when one says of a paradise (or anything else) that it is created good or perfect, this can only mean that it is good or perfect *as far as a paradise* (or other created thing) *is able to be perfect.*

Moreover, the same principle will apply in the case of a hell. A hell, to be a hell, must contain a trace of the Tree of Life concealed in it somewhere; it cannot be a place of absolute evil or absolute imperfection or absolute anything. That is why, in the Tibetan iconography, for instance, when hells are depicted, a Buddha is always also shown there, as a necessary, if latent, witness to the omnipresent truth.

The essential principle to grasp is that wherever one is dealing with a *relative* perfection, one that has existential limits, one has implicitly accepted a degree of imperfection in respect of the absence of whatever lies outside those limits. This privative character of the limit is manifested, within any limit, by a proneness to change and consequent suffering. This is a basic thesis of Buddhism, but it is not less a thesis, if differently expressed, of the Semitic tradition. Let it be remembered that even Christ on occasion said, "Why callest thou me good?" What He was in fact affirming by these words was the genuineness of His own human state, in the presence of His essential divinity. When it is said of Christ that He is "true God, true Man," this necessarily implies, in respect of the second term, an existential limitation, therefore also a certain aspect of imperfection inseparable from the relative as such. Were this limit not there, as expressed in the fact that the Son of Man, Jesus, was able to become and to suffer, the humanity of Christ would have remained a mere phantom—there have been sects holding this view—and the incarnation would have been meaningless. In the human person of Christ we see therefore the perfect figure of humanity including its limitations. By definition the suchness of man is not the suchness of God; hence it cannot be called "good" in its own right but only inasmuch as it reveals the divine perfection, first by existing at all and second by its symbolism.

In purely metaphysical terms this truth of Christianity can be expressed most succinctly by saying that in Christ absolute perfection and relative perfection meet. The intersection of the cross is the symbol of their perfect coincidence.

From all this it can be seen that our original question, "Is there a problem of evil?" by dint of closer scrutiny, has undergone a shift of emphasis, since enough has been said to show that what manifests itself as "evil" relatively to our human situation has its roots, cosmically speaking, further back in an imperfection inseparable from all manifestation as such, be it in the shape of a world, an individual being, or even a paradise. When the Sufis declare that "paradise is a prison for the Sage just as the world is a prison for the believer," they are voicing their ultimate dissatisfaction with all that is not God while at the same time claiming to be something in itself.

It would then appear as if the question to be put should rather take the form of asking, "Why does God create at all? Why is there any manifestation, any world? In fact, why need we exist?"

Now, before deciding whether such a question is a proper one or not, it is important to stress the fact that whenever divine action is spoken of, that action must be regarded as *necessary* as well as *free; in divinis* the two attributes coincide at every point, whereas, with us, existence, which relativizes everything, renders them more or less incompatible in any given set of circumstances. God's infinity implies absolute liberty; where there is no limit, there can be no constraint either. Likewise God's absoluteness implies limitless necessity; it is absurd to speak as if God's ordinances bore an arbitrary character, though the anthropomorphic symbolism sometimes may seem to suggest such an interpretation, a matter of expression only, which ought not to deceive any reasonable mind.

If then the creative act has been described, theologically, as "gratuitous," this is intended to affirm God's absolute freedom and certainly not to deny His infinite necessity. The best one can say, therefore, about manifestation is that the infinite nature of the divine possibility evidently includes it and therefore also requires it; were it not so, the infinite would not be itself. This must, however, never be taken as meaning that the world, by existing, has added something to God or that its eventual disappearance will indicate a proportional privation concerning the Divine, for the relative in itself amounts to nothing in the presence of the real, though by its own limited reality it manifests the real at a given level, failing which it would not exist. As for the question why things exist, it is intrinsically devoid of sense; our existence is not something to which the question "Why?" can validly be attached in expectation of a solution conformable to human logic, itself an appanage of the existence in question. Existence is something one can accept only for what it is. All argument about things starts from there; it cannot be pushed further back thanks to some more than usually ingenious subterfuge of the discursive mind. Only the eye of intellect—the "third eye" of Indian traditional symbolism—is able to pierce beyond the existential veil (if grace will have it so) because something of what lies beyond is already to be found in its own substance; it is not for nothing that Meister Eckhart called it "uncreate and uncreatable." But here we are outside the discursive realm altogether.

The only comment to be offered—and it constitutes a perfectly adequate answer to a question in itself senseless—is that as long as existence (or creation) is a possibility (as it evidently is at its own level), that possibility will, in due course, be called to manifestation, for the reason we have already given, namely that the divine all-possibility cannot be limited in any manner whatsoever. This is enough to account for the existence of the relative, the cosmic unfolding in all its indefinitude of becoming, including that apparent opposing of relative to real, of world to God, that constitutes, for beings, their separative dream. Better reply we cannot find, but this one surely is good enough.

It now remains for us to consider in turn, though very briefly, what the chief traditions have to say on the subject of evil, since each will inevitably look at it from its own angle, offering comment attuned to its own spiritual dialect and technique. The unanimous testimony is to be found at the center, where all ways meet.

So far, we have chiefly drawn examples from the Christian tradition for obvious reasons, with passing references to the sister traditions. Here, all that needs to be added on the subject of Christianity is that the idea of "a problem" of evil originated there and is largely confined to that field. This idea is closely bound up with the anthropomorphic presentation of the relationship between human and Divine, which, if pushed too far or insufficiently corrected by commentaries of a more purely sapiential kind (as in the sermons of Meister Eckhardt, for instance), can easily become invaded by sentimental and moralistic influences. To say this is in no wise to blame the anthropomorphic symbolism as such, which has not only proved its usefulness in the course of ages but also offers certain undoubted advantages for many souls. If it has its dangers, this is true of every form of expression, however hallowed; the serpent will be there, in some form or other.

There is only one defense against the kind of doctrinal abuses we are thinking of, those that, in the Christian world, especially in modern times, have troubled and even alienated many minds, and this is by a return to the central themes of the doctrine, to its metaphysical heart. Sentimental and rationalistic confusions invariably arise in the periphery of a tradition; it is an excessive preoccupation with marginal matters that tends to provoke them. Too many rather trivial considerations habitually occupy Christian minds to the neglect of the essential. Christian theology has been relegated dangerously to the status of a "speciality," a matter for professionals and experts, instead of being regarded as the daily food for every soul which it really is. In this respect the Eastern traditions, despite the degeneration of the times which has not spared them, have much to teach regarding the day-to-day practice of religion. At Kalimpong, in the northern hills of Bengal, where I lived for three years, my gardener (who was no saint) possessed a metaphysical and theological sense that many a bishop might have shared with advantage. The things he saw around him were far more transparent to his intelligence than is usually the case among religious people here. In that sense he could see God everywhere; theology was, for him, both a living and a practical pursuit. His devotion, such as it was, had an undoubted intellectual quality.

Only too often Christian devotion has been kept starved of intellectual nourishment, with the result that it has readily slipped into sentimentalism, and this, in its turn, has tended to drive out of the Christian fold many of the more intelligent minds, with disastrous results for themselves and for the world;

but the fact is that though these people may have been, in one sense, too intelligent to accept the heavily sweetened food that their religion thought they wanted, yet in another sense they were not quite intelligent enough to detect, through the sugar, the salt that was still there waiting to be tasted.

One can only repeat it: A Christian revival, without a renewal of intellectual penetration of the central truths, is a chimera. Collective sentimentality will not bring it about, if indeed it does not hinder it further. It is time the leaders of the church recognized this; otherwise, they will remain blind leaders of the blind, despite their sincere wish to serve. There is no substitute for knowledge.

To return to the Christian attitude toward evil: Exoterically and in conformity with the anthropomorphic symbolism, Christian teaching has largely been content to say that God "is not the author of evil," which, for its part, came about thus and thus. This view, though it contains flaws, is nevertheless justified, inasmuch as God does not will evil qua evil, evil as it appears to us. He is the creator of the relative, as required by His infinity; of that relative the thing we call evil is a necessary function, being in fact the measure of the world's *apparent* separation from its principle, God—an illusory separation inasmuch as nothing can exist side by side with the infinite, however real it may claim to be at its own relative level. To quote Frithjof Schuon, who has thrown the greatest light upon this question—his books are treasuries of spiritual knowledge— "One cannot ask of God to will the world and at the same time to will that it be not a world." A world is a whirlpool of contrasts—the Indian word "samsara" expresses this—it is not a unity in its own right. It is no limitation on the Almighty that He cannot produce another Himself, a second Absolute. The world is there to prove it.

Passing now to another Semitic tradition, Islam, we will find that it follows a somewhat different line. The central testimony of Islam is the unity and absolute transcendence of God, a truth that it shares with Christianity but stresses, if anything, in a more exclusive way than in any other tradition; hence it is obliged to declare, without turning to one side, that whatever exists in any sense whatsoever is unequivocally the creation of God and therefore that evil, since it exists, is to be numbered among God's creatures.

If Christian theology on the whole shrank from such a plain statement and wished to wrap it up for the reasons we know of, Islam did not avoid it for another good reason—both reasons are valid but relative, hence their mutual exclusion. Indeed, where relativities are concerned, such divergencies are unavoidable and moreover necessary, since truth is one and discernment is a function of intelligence as such, in the light of truth. In this way, differentiation of witness, as between the various traditions, serves to reveal the converging nature of the various spiritual paths and their meeting at the center, in the heart of truth.

The existence of the relative has this positive merit, offsetting its limiting or negative function, namely that it precludes our taking ourselves or the world for absolute, in other words, for God. The same applies in the field of doctrine. To attribute an absolute character to a form or other relativity is of the very nature of error, by fixing or "petrifying" a limit and its attendant oppositions. Hence the teaching of Islam that "the variety of the interpreters is also a blessing." This statement contains no condemnation of orthodoxy, or of forms as necessary and legitimate instruments, but it bears witness to that variety in testimony that is one of the factors guaranteeing the unity of revelation.

The Muslims have also said: "When the gates of Paradise were opened the gates of Hell were opened at the same time." How often do we hear a wish expressed that God had made heaven but no hell; how many people expressing their belief in heaven couple this with a refusal to entertain any belief in hell? Here again is a case of failing to recognize that two things belong together, as correlatives pertaining to the same order. To deny this is implicitly to deny the Absolute, by wishing to endow one particular relativity with an absolute character while refusing relative existence to its normal partner; it is but another form of the error that would have God create a paradise minus the serpent.

All relativity can, and indeed must, ultimately be transcended, not by arbitrary denial, but by integration. The world cannot just be charmed away, but it can be rendered transparent so that the light, ever shining, may illuminate our existential darkness. The center is everywhere, this room included; and where the center is, there is the beatific vision.

Passing now to the Indian traditions, it will be found that the viewpoint is somewhat different, inasmuch as the general concept of "manifestation" is not linked to the more particular concept of "creation," as in the Semitic religions. The Hindus, when they attribute creative activity to the Divinity under one or other of its aspects, liken this to a "divine playing," which is a way of affirming the unqualified freedom and transcendence of the Godhead in its unmanifest and impersonal essence, versus those dynamic, creative, and therefore qualifiable aspects of Divinity that correspond to the personal God of our own spiritual parlance.

In Buddhism, where the idea of creation is practically absent, the personal aspect is as if "bypassed" in the case of both the divine prototype and the human being. The "nontheistic" (not atheistic) character of the Buddhist wisdom and its insistence on the "nonselfhood" of all things belong together, a fact that moreover explains Buddhism's marked preference for apophatic enunciations. Dogmatic affirmations, by lending to ideas a kind of fixed self, are, from a Buddhist point of view, always suspect, if not in practice avoidable altogether. The Hindu tradition, on the other hand, with the maternal exuberance that characterizes it, is able to accommodate all manner of doctrines such as, in other traditions, would tend to exclude one another; thus, for example, the Vedanta stands near to Buddhism in the rigorously impersonal nature of its appeal, while Vishnuite Hinduism and the bhaktic doctrines generally come much nearer to a personal religion in the Western sense. In practice

Hinduism is able to associate both the personal and the impersonal approach in a synthesis that allows of an almost endless variety of combinations.

The manifested world, or worlds, as viewed through Indian eyes, does not, as we have said, require in principle to be given the character of a willed making or "creation." In Buddhism, where this idea (as we pointed out) practically finds no place, samsara, the Round of Existence, is described as having "no beginning" but as "having an end"; in other words, the process of continual passage from cause to effect is left undefined in terms of origin, but that process and its associated possibility of suffering can be neutralized by integration into the center "where the wheel of rebirth is not turning." Negatively regarded, this will be nirvanic extinction or self-naughting; positively regarded, it is the awakening to enlightenment, Buddhahood. Compare with this the Christian view representing the other extreme, namely the description of the world as having "a beginning" (in creation) but as able to become "world without end," in salvation through Christ. One metaphysical paradox is worth another, since, strictly speaking, beginning and ending belong to the same duality; their dissociation in either direction is metaphysically inconceivable. The paradoxical character of both the above-mentioned enunciations is explainable in terms of a spiritual purpose, a call to realization; neither of them should be driven too far in literalism, but each expresses truth in its own way.

The mentality fostered by both Hinduism and Buddhism is not such as to see a problem in evil or suffering, as has happened elsewhere, because a sense of the relative and its ambivalent character, at once of a veil over the absolute and a revealer thereof, of a reality at one level and an illusion at another, is too strongly ingrained in Indian thought to allow of evil being regarded as anything more than a particular case of the relative, viewed from its privative angle. Suffering in all its forms is then accepted as a measure of the world's apparent remoteness from the divine principle. The principle is absolutely omnipresent in the world, but the world is relatively absent from the principle; this apparent contradiction between "essence" and "accidents" is paid for in "suffering." By identifying ourselves, consciously or unconsciously or by our actions, with our "accidents," whereby a specious selfhood is both created and nourished, we invite an inescapable repercussion in the form of the good and evil that consequently shape our lives for us while we are swept along by the stream of becoming. So long as that stream continues to flow, in the passage from action to concordant reaction, suffering will be experienced in positive or negative form, as unwanted presence of the painful or else as absence of the desirable. The nature of samsara, the world's flow, is such, and no effort or contrivance on our part can render it otherwise. One can shift given evils to one side (life in this world often compels one to do so), or one can promote certain good objects—often at the price of neglecting others—but the process itself we never touch by this means; our many attempts to abolish given evils will necessarily remain a treatment of symptoms, leaving the deepest causes of unhealth untouched, because intellectual discernment, the essential diagnosis, is wanting. Fundamentally, religion is concerned with such a diagnosis, and in the light of it, with the remedies to be applied; it is directly concerned with nothing else.

While we are on the subject of cosmology, something must be said about the theory of cosmic cycles, highly developed in Indian tradition but also known to Western antiquity with its golden, silver, bronze, and iron ages, the first-named corresponding to a period of primordial purity, of which the terrestrial paradise gives the type, the lattermost indicating a period of general obscurity due to the neglect or loss of the essential knowledge, leading to a catastrophe that, for the humanity concerned, will appear as a final discrimination or judgment. When one considers the process of cosmic development in relation to human existence, individual and collective, it is apparent that there are times and occasions when a kind of cumulative bias in one or other direction takes place, like a spring or neap tide which nevertheless leaves the ocean itself essentially as it was. In a minor way recorded history is full of examples of this kind; but it is possible also to recognize oscillations on a much larger scale in which the tendency to-

ward enlightenment or toward infatuation becomes so pronounced as to justify the use of the broader classification of
cyclic phases mentioned above. Each of these great divisions
of time represents a piling up of positive or negative factors
which the beings who experience the results will interpret in
terms of quasi-universal good or evil, though in point of fact
the process of cosmic flux goes on uninterruptedly, nothing of
this world being intrinsically permanent or satisfying. For man
to seek his real home amid these ever-shifting quicksands seems
like asking for disappointment; and yet this is precisely where
his quest must start, from the very situation, that is to say,
determined for him by antecedent karma, which he has the
power neither to choose nor to refuse. The gate of deliverance
can be found only here and now, not elsewhere or otherwhen.

By now enough will have been said to show that if there be
a question that urgently concerns us—the word "problem" was
unhappy—it is neither the existence of the world nor our idea
of what a world might have been like had we been asked to
create one, but solely the question of how best to rejoin our
own center, which is also the center of all things, the Tree of
Life, the axis uniting heaven and earth. The word "religion"
by its derivation means "to unite," and so does the word
"yoga"—the same root as "yoke."

In effect we have somehow to retrace the steps of our forefa-
ther Adam, but in inverse order. For him it was an outgoing
path that lured him, from center to periphery, a consequence
of the illusory duplication of the original unity, whereby the
Tree of Life became mysteriously clothed in the semblance of
the Tree of Good and Evil; this gives us the very pattern and
principle of distraction in this world.

For the posterity of Adam, nourished as we are day after day
on the fruits, white or black, of the dualistic tree, the process
of return must start out from here, as we said once before,
which means that it is the Tree of Good and Evil this time that
must be caused to yield up its secret by revealing its identity
with the Tree of Life, even while remaining itself at its own
level.

This brings us to the point where it is possible to speak of *realization in active mode,* which we promised to discuss when speaking of the Adamic innocence. This innocence is always a perfection in its own way, like that of the newly born—hence the injunction to enter the Kingdom as a little child—but its existential passivity leaves it vulnerable to the egocentric urge that lets men feel themselves "as gods" and places them under the law of mortality by that very fact. For unequivocal security it needs to be completed by the active realization, full awareness of the essential identity, across their relative distinction, of the Tree of Life and the Tree of Contrast, Nirvana and samsara. It is only this transcending of all the dualities and their oppositions that can render one immune to the serpent's sting, because then the serpent itself, like everything else, will in the light of knowledge have been recognized for what it is, namely a property of existence and no more. Light therefore takes priority among all our needs; the Buddha in placing "right view" at the beginning of the Noble Eightfold Path that leads to deliverance paid full tribute to this first requirement. Though passive and active realization have both been mentioned in turn, it is necessary to make a third point by saying that reintegration in the center, to be complete and in balance, will in fact be active and passive at one and the same time, the former in virtue of knowledge that is active by its own nature like the intellect that communicates it, and the latter in virtue of the living gift of grace, the spontaneous attraction of the center itself, which cannot be commanded but can only be accepted freely or else ignored; in which case, as Schuon said in one of his most telling passages, it is always man who is absent, not grace. To follow the spiritual way, the ingoing path, a two-directional traffic will therefore always be implied, whatever may be the apparent emphasis in any given case, as between human initiative on the one hand and divine gift on the other; it is the very disproportion between a necessarily limited human effort, however intense, and the transcendent and unlimited object to be encompassed that shows why this must be so.

The traditional image of the Buddha—perhaps the most

miraculous form of ikon in existence—perfectly exemplifies the synthesis of attitudes required of man by the circumstances. As he sits in lotus posture at the foot of the Tree of Enlightenment—the Tree of Life it might just as well be called—the Buddha, the fully awakened, touches with his right hand the earth calling her to witness; an active attitude toward "the world" is indicated by this gesture. His left hand, for its part, supports the begging bowl held in readiness to receive whatever may be cast into it from above; this gesture indicates passivity toward heaven, perfect receptiveness. The incomparable eloquence of this symbol beggars all comment.

For a Christian, the realization in active mode is represented essentially by the redemption inaugurated by Christ Himself. To compensate for the fall, the path of reintegration has to pass through the sacrifice—the ego must suffer transformation in the fire of Shiva, as a Hindu would put it. Virtual reintegration into the Adamic state of innocence, in passive mode, is operated through baptism. Virtual reintegration in active mode, into the Christic state, is operated through the Eucharist, the eating and drinking of Christ in order to be eaten and drunk by Christ. Herein is to be seen all the difference separating "the sinner that repenteth" from "the just person that needs no repentance." It is the former that corresponds to the active realization: The bird that has escaped from the cage will never again be caught. The innocence represented by the passive participation is indubitable, but it is the other that calls forth the greatest joy in heaven.

Incidentally, the foregoing citation provides an excellent illustration of the polyvalent character of revealed Scripture, in virtue of which the same words, while retaining their literal applicability at one level of understanding, are transposable into a more universal sense at another. Here is a case of that method of exegesis referred to once before under the name of "anagogical," as pointing upward to the threshold of the mysteries. The immense stress laid by all the great traditions on scriptural memorizing and recitation is explained by this property of the sacred text to vehicle superposed aspects of the truth, whereby it is able to provide a support for meditation and concentration that is practically inexhaustible.

The twofold virtuality, covering all possibilities both passive and active, has to be *actualized* through the life in religion; religious doctrines and methods, whatever their particularity of form, have no other purpose but this.

Moreover, the same is the unique purpose of human life as such, "human life hard to obtain," as the Buddhists say, and therefore not to be frittered away in irrelevant, profane pursuits. Again and again the various traditional paths rejoin one another in this urgent plea to man to fulfill his human destiny, which is none other than deliverance—or salvation, if the Christian term be preferred, always provided it be given the sense, not of some individualistic compromise or other, but that given it by Christ's own words when He said, "Be ye perfect even as your Father in Heaven is perfect," surely the most awe-inspiring injunction to be found in Scripture!

The transcendent nature of the human vocation and of its finality is evidenced, above all, by the presence, in man, of a sense of the Absolute. The name of God is indelibly inscribed in the human heart; all the profane overlayings due to inattention and consequent ignorance are unable quite to extinguish its remembrance, though they may at times come near to doing so in practice. Even man's infidelities betray themselves by their inconsistency. As Meister Eckhardt put it, "The more he blasphemes the more he praises God." At any degree, the state of forgetfulness will always carry with it a gnawing sense of privation, which will not be stilled until its one real object, instead of many fancied ones, has been found again. Did we but know it, all the desires beings experience, all their attempts to snatch satisfaction from this thing or that thing, are but signs of a deep-seated homesickness for the Tree of Life, man's true homeland.

The one and only "problem," in our situation, is to find the way home, in which case we can show it to others. One who has missed his own way makes a poor guide; to have ignored this fact is what vitiates so much so-called service in the world, a typically humanitarian delusion. In the long run, only the saints can offer efficient service, those who know the way by walking it.

The way itself involves two conditions, namely a direction—the sacred tradition provides this direction—and a method of concentration appropriate to each person's relative capacity; but whatever form this may take in practice, in principle method is reducible to the unbroken remembrance of God, perfect mindfulness in the Buddhist sense. The Prophet of Islam, speaking with the fierce eloquence of the desert, has cried out: "All in the world is accursed except the Remembrance of God." Whatever is attachable to that remembrance is acceptable; whatever is incompatible is for rejection. This is the law governing the whole spiritual enterprise.

Man is human by his vocation; he is subhuman in proportion as he disregards it. The animals and plants who follow their own destiny are superior to the man who betrays his. To spend the precious gift of human existence on anything but "the one thing needful," as Christ described it while in the house of Martha and Mary, is to condemn oneself to the fate of the Flying Dutchman and sail the ocean of existence interminably to and fro, buffeted by its gales and deluded by its calms, while always seeking a haven. Divine grace always leaves us this one hope: God who now seems so distant is ever close at hand—"closer than your jugular vein," as the Koran has it. The Tree of Life is standing in this room, as certainly as it stood in Eden; it is a pity if we will not use our eyes.

Living One's Karma

BY MARCO PALLIS

THE CONCEPTION of existence as samsara, cosmic flux, together with its parallel conception of karma, "concordant action and reaction" as the determinant of each being's part in that flux, is an essential feature of all the traditions directly or indirectly deriving from India. Though the subject is here being considered from a Buddhist angle, most of what will be said could apply to Hinduism equally well.

Let us first consider the Round of Existence through its symbolical representation, said to go back to the Buddha himself, as a circle subdivided into six sectors, each containing one of the typical classes of sentient beings. These sectors can be arranged in three pairs, as follows:

> our world: (1) human (the central state), (2) animals (peripheral states)
> supernal worlds: (3) gods, or devas, (4) titans, or asuras
> infernal worlds: (5) tantalized ghosts, or pretas, (6) hells

This symbolic scheme is familiar wherever the Buddhist tradition prevails.

Let us examine each of the six components in somewhat greater detail. Quite evidently, the human sector, which was mentioned first, has been given a disproportionate share in the whole if one considers it solely from the point of view of the number of beings concerned. As compared with the vast multiplicity of their nonhuman neighbors, men represent a very small number indeed, apart from the fact that they form but one species as compared with an immense variety extending to genera, families, and natural orders. The reason for this privileged treatment is twofold: First, being men ourselves, it is natural for us to single out for study our own kind and manner of existing; second, the human species is the chosen field of avataric descent, of Buddhahood, and this, qualitatively speaking, entitles it to privileged consideration.

Passing to the animal sector: This contains a large number of different species situated at the same level of existence as man, but varying in respect of their nearness to, or remoteness from, the human position. It might then be asked: Where do plants and minerals come in, since they do not seem to figure by name in any sector? The answer can only be that here one is not dealing with a chart of biological or geological statistics; one must not expect a meticulous consistency in regard to details. All the traditional picture of the Round is intended to do is to serve as a broadly sufficient guide to an understanding of the universe, one that is based, all along, on qualitative factors rather than on "facts" or quantitative considerations such as enter into the purview of natural sciences in the usual sense of the word.

Regarded from the human point of view, the supernal states are those that in greater or lesser measure escape the physical and psychic limitations of our own state of existence. The two sectors grouped in the supernal class may, however, themselves include quite a number of different degrees that we, in our present state, are hardly concerned with. It is said of gods, or devas, that theirs is a state full of delights such as "wishing trees" able to grant any boon at the mere thought and other picturesque amenities of a similar kind; no pain can enter into this state while it lasts, which makes the moment of change when it strikes at long last all the more painful for the beings in question, as they suddenly wake up to the fact that their state of bliss is not eternal but remains subject to birth and death like every other existential state. As one Mongolian monk said to the writer: "The long-lived gods are stupid." Lulled into overconfidence by sheer absence of contrast in their present condition, they are wholly unprepared for the fatal moment when it comes, and they may sink as low as hell itself, a truly lamentable fate.

Not all the gods, however, display this lack of intelligence. Many of them play a creditable part in stories of the Buddha.

Some, such as Vishnu's hawklike steed Garuda, are constant attendants on the Buddha's person whose canopy they provide; others again, and especially Brahma, king of the devas, after the Buddha's enlightenment persuade him to preach the doctrine lest the world be utterly lost. This overcoming of the Buddha's "reluctance" at the instance of the gods features in the history of every teaching Buddha and is meant to convey symbolically that the knowledge possessed by an enlightened one is so profound as to be virtually incommunicable to men in their present state of ignorance. The Buddha, however, consents to teach, thus showing that ignorance notwithstanding, the Light is not unattainable. For this we have to thank the persuasion of the gods.

Titans, or asuras, for their part, though superior to men in virtue of their possession of various powers, are always represented as contentious beings, full of envy for the gods and their felicity and ever plotting to dethrone them. Typically they are beings who through "austerities," intense work carried out in various fields, have been enabled to extend their own natural faculties to the point of threatening heaven itself. Sometimes titanic ambition even wears an altruistic mask, as when Prometheus stole the fire from the gods in order to bestow it on mankind, thus exposing the latter to the consequences of his own act of profanation. It is typical of an asuric or Promethean temperament to promote recklessly the use of abnormal powers from every kind of motive except the essential one, the one that could lead a being to Buddhahood. Lacking this motive, it lacks all; such is the asuric sign in beings.

The two infernal sectors of our symbolism, the land of tantalized ghosts (pretas) and the hells, are places whence joy and comfort are entirely banished. The first-named is a realm wherein reigns the most intense feeling of want, an insatiable hunger and thirst. Pretas are pictured as having huge, inflated bellies and pinpoint mouths, so that enough nourishment can never find its way through the tiny inlet to meet the excessive cravings of the belly, and thus the being remains in a constant state of misery, which only a change of state may eventually relieve, could he but awaken to this possibility. The hells, on the other hand, more or less explain themselves: They are places of sheer expiation, hot or cold according to the nature of the offenses committed (or opportunities disregarded) in the course of previous life. In this respect they hardly differ from the conception of hell as found in the Semitic religions except in matters of detail and, more especially, in the absence of any perfunctory attribution of "eternity" such as does not belong anywhere in the Round.

This last is the most important point to grasp. The keynote of samsara is *impermanence*, the primary theme to meditate upon for every Buddhist. All that the world's flow brings into being is unstable. This is true of heavens or hells, happier states as well as more unhappy; the former admit of no complacency, the latter are never entirely without hope. For everything, in the fullness of becoming, when its particular possibilities have spent themselves, must change to something else. This is the universal law of existence in the Round.

The number and variety of beings extant in the universe is incalculable. The same holds for world systems; they are indefinite both in their incidence and in the variety of conditions to which each world system is subject. But whatever the conditions governing a given world may be, the sixfold grouping can still be applied to it, with suitable allowance made for differences of detail. Thus every world must have its "central" or "axial" state which, by analogy with our world, may well be called human; just as there will also exist superior and inferior states classifiable as such from the standpoint of that state that provides the median term.

The essential characteristics of each world are integrally reflected in the being that is central to that world and in a more or less fragmentary manner in the various beings occupying peripheral positions. The central state, being a totality in its own order, constitutes something like an autonomous world of its own, a microcosm, and this is the case with man in our world system. Knowing the state of man at a particular time, one can almost say one knows the state of the world, so closely are the two interests bound together. A transposition of the sixfold symbolism from the greater world in all its extension to the human microcosm follows logically from this interrelationship; thus certain properties of human nature can be said to correspond to certain classes of beings, in the sense that in proportion as a man identifies himself with such a property rather than with such another, he will display, in his human life, something of the character of one or other of the nonhuman classes. To give one instance, it is easy to recognize the type conforming as nearly as possible to a state of "human animality," that of men regarded chiefly in the mass as feeders and reproducers in a quantitative sense; needless to say, no disparagement of animals is intended by the above allusion, for animals and plants in a state of nature live out their karma with sure instinct and exhibit qualities of dignity and beauty that man, for his part, can emulate only by remaining faithful to his own vocation, which is of another order just because of his central position in the world.

To take another example, modern "economic man" oscillates between the animal and preta types, the latter being the one that is most consonant with his professed ideal of an indefinitely expanding production and of a so-called high standard of living. A vast machine of propaganda exists for the sole purpose of exacerbating an appetite for possessions, with the proviso, however, that the happiness these are supposed to procure must never be quite reached, for if man rested satisfied at any point, the wheels would stop going round there and then, and this would mean economic ruin, so inextricably have the two motives been geared to one another. Therefore man must keep on being tantalized into fresh desires—a far cry from Buddhism.

If this be not a picture of a Pretaland, it is the next best thing to one. And to what kind of rebirth are men schooled in this way likely to attain? Might it be to rebirth as pretas perhaps?

As for the hells, they are surely discernible among those dark reservoirs below the level of human consciousness wherein our psychologists so often like to fish. Sometimes their contents also overflow: An utterly subhuman type is not uncommon in our midst, even without mentioning what he himself calls art, a devilish appliance in its way. Naturally, one has been referring to extremes. The purer types are relatively rare; mostly one has to do with various blends and hybrids.

There is one other kind of man, however, the one who alone is able to realize the plenitude of the human possibility, and this is the man who identifies himself, in intention and practice, not with some samsarically conditioned human faculty, but with the axis of the human microcosm itself, the thread of Buddha-nature passing through the heart of every being, every world. For peripheral beings this identification can only be indirect and eminently passive; but with man, because he is an axial being by definition, this can also take place in active mode, without restriction of scope or finality. This, in fact, is the possibility of full awakening, Buddhahood, and justifies the statement, found in the Semitic Scriptures, that man has been made "in the divine image." Whether we call man "theomorphic" or "buddhamorphic," it makes little difference in this context.

Lastly, let us return to the traditional portrayal of the Round of Existence, as originally described, in order to point out that like every true symbolism, it derives from the *nature of things* and not from some arbitrary contrivance of the human mind as if it were just a poetic allegory. Its purpose is to serve as a key to a heightened awareness; it has no other use.

A symbolical classification like the present one is not meant to be read in the sense of a compact formula: It has to be freely interpreted and intelligently applied, for samsara as such is *indefinite;* it does not admit of systematization. The sutras in fact describe it as "without beginning" (i.e., undefined in terms of origin) but as "having an end" (in deliverance, Nirvana)—a paradoxical description, since, metaphysically speaking, what has no beginning cannot have an end either, and vice versa. One can compare with this the similar (but inverse) Christian paradox of a world "with beginning" (in creation) yet able to become "world without end" (by salvation through Christ).

In both the above cases the object is to communicate a saving truth, not a nicely rounded-off philosophical thesis, hence an apparent disregard of logic.

We said at the outset that in samsara the determinant of any coming into being or "birth" is antecedent action, with its consequent reaction. This is the doctrine of karma and its fruits, which, ripening in their season as results, are fated in their turn to become causes containing, as they do, the seeds of further becoming. The continual intercrossing of numberless strands of causality goes to make up the skein of samsara; the conception is *dynamic,* a continual passage from state to state, with each birth marking a death to some preceding state and each death marking a fresh birth and so on indefinitely.

Since everything is in a state of ceaseless flux, any event or object one chooses to observe has to be *abstracted* from the whole process in a more or less arbitrary manner, with the result that whatever one observes will necessarily have a certain character of *ambiguity:* Both the object itself and the observing subject are changing all the time, which means that any judgment passed on the basis of an empirical examination of objects found in the world will remain approximate, provisional, relative, fluid, and ambivalent. The empirical approach precludes any conclusion qualifiable as "exact" and "complete."

Having said this much, it is necessary also to mention the complementary aspect of the same doctrine, lest one be led unconsciously into a relativism that will itself assume a quasi-absolute character, to the point of doing away with all idea of truth itself; in these days of far-fetched and one-sided subjectivism, a dissolution of all objective values and criteria in a kind of psychoanalytical penumbra is a real danger and must be guarded against. A judgment is inadequate, insofar as it claims to judge the whole absolutely from a particular standpoint likewise treated as absolute; this is the error of "dogmatism," i.e., of an abusive stretching of relative formulations that are true as far as they go. A judgment is valid, however, insofar as, starting out from criteria duly recognized to be relative, it judges a phenomenon whose relative limits are likewise recognized. Given that one is vigilantly heedful of these conditions, a judgment can be perfectly exact, to the point of being called relatively absolute within its proper context.

A Buddha is called an awakened one just because his knowledge owes nothing to the world or to the empirical ego that jointly provided the focus of his previous dreaming. When a man wakes from sleep, we do not say he is someone else despite an apparent change in the nature of his consciousness; this analogy gives an inkling of the passage from the state of an ignorant being to Buddhahood. Knowledge is only possible inasmuch as the "eye of bodhi" (the pure intellect), in the subject, perceives, in the object, the "bodhi message" (i.e., its symbolism). When these two coincide, there is instant awareness—"eternal awareness," as one might say, inasmuch as what pertains to bodhi belongs per se to the intemporal and the changeless. The awakening to knowledge, at any degree, is like the flashpoint reached by the rubbing together of two sticks; the satori of Zen is of this nature. Were things otherwise, enlightenment would not be a possibility for beings.

In samsara it is evident that one can only judge fragments from standpoints no less fragmentary; in Nirvana such a question does not arise. Awareness of samsaric differences and our own response to them on the strength of that awareness detracts in no wise from the intrinsic reality of phenomena considered as a whole. Their totality then brings us back to samsara as such, and this, in essence, brings us back to Nirvana. Here we meet a basic Buddhist principle, namely that he who really understands samsara (or karma, which comes to the same) understands Nirvana. To see a single grain of dust in full awareness is to see the universe; no more is needed for enlightenment, wherein absolute and relative knowledge, the Buddha's two modes of truth, make but one.

What one always needs to bear in mind is that the world with its phenomena amounts to a *play of compensations* in such fashion that though every part is ever shifting and therefore out of balance and ungraspable in itself, yet the whole, qua whole, remains unchanged across all its vicissitudes, as does the ocean in spite of its many waves and currents. If we try to define one of those waves in fixed terms, it will elude us, yet each reveals the unchanging in its own way. Hence the statement that a Buddha is to be found in every drop of water, every grain of sand.

This "nongraspable" nature of all things in existence is what has given rise, in the Buddhist spiritual economy, to another basic idea, one that people have found especially difficult to understand, namely the idea of anatta, "nonselfhood," as applying to beings at all levels and to the manifested universe itself.

We have seen that the basic "notes" of existence are relativity, impermanence, and becoming, to which we must add "suffering," which is the characteristic that expresses the preceding three in the consciousness of beings. Universal possibility being unique, it excludes repetition in existence. In the cosmos there can be likeness or analogy at every degree but never absolute identity or selfhood.

What does the word "selfhood" really convey to our minds? It conveys unequivocal *purity*, total nonadmixture. A substance can be called pure only when it is nothing else but itself, being free from any trace of "otherness." Being such, it carries no incentive to change. It is the ambivalent character of the relative that is the root of change, for where there is more than one pole of attraction (or repulsion), there instability will prevail in some degree. What is wholly free from internal tensions cannot die, for what should there be to make it die? Whatever is liable to death, therefore, implies a dualism, the presence of forces pulling different ways, a composition of things partly incompatible, and this, by definition, is other than selfhood. It is the sharpening, in the course of becoming, of its internal contradictions that eventually causes a thing to fall apart, at the moment we call death.

When we are led to fix our attention, not on the process of becoming as a whole, but on an abstracted part of it (which may be our own person or any other thing), we are thereby easily led into attributing to that thing a fixed character. The same applies to a situation or an act when so regarded for its own sake. This is the error of *false attribution*, the congenital ignorance attaching to all extant beings as such. The specifically Buddhist doctrine of anatta is a way of dispelling this ignorance.

Let us now pass over to the more detailed consideration of karma, the impelling force behind every rebirth or redeath, that is to say *action* taken in the broadest sense of the word (including its negative aspect, *omission*) together with its inseparable accompaniment, the reaction it inescapably provokes, the two being strictly proportioned to one another. The physical principle that action and reaction are equal and opposite is but one example of this universal cosmic dispensation.

Now, like everything else the mind is concerned with, this law of karma were best contemplated in a purely detached, impersonal way, as if we ourselves were standing outside the Round of Existence and looking at it from the vantage point of a lofty and distant peak. But in point of fact such is not the case. We are deeply involved at every moment of our earthly sojourn, and consequently, insofar as we feel ourselves to be "this person so-and-so," distinct from all the beings who, for us, fall under the collective heading of "other," we cannot help assessing this cosmic play going on all around us in terms of plus or minus, profit or loss, pleasure or pain, "good" or "evil," as we call them. This it is that accounts for the fact that in religious life karma has been explained, more often than not, in terms of moral sanction, as reward for good deeds and punishment for ill deeds, and this is how the matter is regarded, almost always, by the popular mind.

Such a view is not in itself false; indeed it can be salutary. The only falseness is if one imagines this to be the whole story, the first and last word to be said on the subject. A full awareness of the implications of karma will carry one outside the circle of moral alternatives (and of the attachments that a personally biased view inevitably will foster in the long run); but nevertheless, for the common run of mortals, the view of karma as *immanent justice,* in the moral sense, is not unwholesome, since it inclines a man at least to take the lessons of karma seriously and apply them in his day-to-day life. All ethical laws, in every religion, have this character; they are *upāyas,* "means," far-reaching but still relative in scope, a fact that incidentally explains why the most hallowed moral laws sometimes will not work, so that even in this sphere one must expect the occasional exception, if only "to prove the rule."

Immanent justice, in its fullest sense, is nothing else but the equilibrium of the universe, that state of balance between all the parts that the quivering scales express but do not visibly

achieve; but here again, we have come outside the moral perspective that, though included in the general panorama of "justice," no longer needs to be given privileged emphasis in view
of a particular human interest.

It is a commonplace with Buddhist controversialists, out to
criticize what they look on as the arbitrary explanations offered
by the theistic religions, to argue that the doctrine of karma,
by accounting for the apparent irregularities of fate in terms
of antecedent action leading to present sanction, is "more just"
than other views relating to the same facts. It is well to point
out that once such an argument becomes clothed in a moral
form, it becomes every whit as anthropomorphic as the teachings about "the will of God" in relation to sin current in the
Christian and kindred religions. The use of this kind of language and all arguments taking this form can be justified empirically, as satisfying the need of certain minds, and, if so, it
is no small profit. However, any simplification of this kind
must always be accounted an expression of "popular apologetics" rather than of deep awareness of what really is at stake.
It is nevertheless a mistake to laugh at such a view of things;
if one is able to see the fallacy behind the argument, one is free
to transcend it in deeper understanding of the same truth,
without taking up a patronizing attitude toward the simple
souls for whom this argument has provided a stepping stone
in the way.

Speaking more generally, the important thing when comparing doctrines as propounded by different traditions is to find
out, by an examination conducted with insight—scholarly
scrupulousness in comparing the material is not by itself
enough—whether the seeming divergences betray a genuine
opposition or only a divergence of spiritual dialect, since both
things are possible. Every religion resorts to certain accommo-
dations in the doctrinal field in order to bring various truths
within the purview of an average mind; it is left to the saint
and the sage to see beyond these somewhat garbled versions in
order to find the truth they nevertheless convey in their own
fashion. Here we see the difference between religion under its
"exoteric" aspect, adequate to a collective need, and under the

aspect qualifiable as "esoteric," where no such concessions have a place. This distinction rests, not on a rigid compartmenting of religious truth, but rather on the need for a graded approach to that same truth, the bright light of which has to be tempered to men's varying capacities of vision. The two broad categories we have mentioned explain themselves sufficiently in the light of this principle, which is an *upāya* of general applicability to every spiritual path.

An instance of how·popularized interpretations can lead to a certain amount of doctrinal distortion is provided by current beliefs in Buddhist countries concerning the possibility of "rebirth as a man." People all too readily assume that a human rebirth, provided they keep leading fairly ethical lives (often at a lowish level) is there for the asking. I could mention several examples of this kind of attitude from my own experience, by no means all of them drawn from among the simple and uneducated. People find it easy to imagine that it is but a matter of a little careful moral accountancy on their part, and their next human life will be as good as assured! With these people "merit," good karma, comes to be regarded wholly in a quantitative sense, rather as if it could be meted out by the pound, a matter of manipulating a neat double-column balance sheet in such a way as not to leave oneself too heavily in debt. They forget the common dictum about "human birth hard to obtain" or the Buddha's parable about the purblind turtle swimming in a vast ocean where there is also a piece of floating wood with a hole in it. He estimated any particular being's chances of obtaining a human birth as about equal to the likelihood of that turtle pushing its head through that hole!

By this far-fetched parable he evidently wished to impress on people the extreme precariousness·of the human chance, warning them thus against the folly of wasting a precious opportunity in trivial pursuits. In a world that likes to think of itself as "progressive" how many people, I wonder, make even a slight attempt to follow this advice?

Let everyone only ask himself the question "Do I give the Buddha and his teachings (or Christ and his teachings, for that matter), say, half an hour's worth of attention per day of my life?" and if the answer is in the negative, is it then reasonable to expect, under the law of karma, to receive another human chance in this or other worlds? And if one is prepared to give an honest answer to this question, one must surely go on to ask oneself another, namely, "Why then do I so unaccountably hang back?" The opportunity lies here and now, this is certain; what sense is there in banking on some dubious future, on the strength of a naïve attempt to strike a bargain with God?—if we may here permit ourselves a turn of phrase that is not strictly Buddhist.

The essential thing to remember about the human state or any state describable as "central" is that it marks the point where exit from the fatal round of birth and death is possible without the prior need to pass through another state of conditioned existence. The door is there, whereas if one has been born into some more peripheral situation, it is indispensable, before one can aspire to deliverance, to gain a footing on the axis, in other words to find the way to a human birth. Once on the axis, the path lies open trodden by all the Buddhas; what is essential is not merely to occupy one's human position *passively*, thanks to the karma that placed one there, but to realize it *actively*, and this is the express concern of a spiritual life.

If we pause to consider our present state of existence attentively, we will soon discover that it is, after all, not every man born who can be said to possess true humanity; we have already touched on this point when speaking of the human microcosm. In practice most human beings lead more or less subhuman lives, by which is meant, not that they are all great criminals— the Macbeths and Iagos of this world are comparatively rare— but that so much of their time and attention goes in trivialities utterly incompatible with a human status; if life on earth were fated to last a thousand years, they could hardly be more wasteful of it. Certainly few escape this reproach altogether, even among those claiming some sort of religion for themselves. There is nothing more salutary than self-examination on this issue; a detailed diary if honestly kept would make cruel reading for many of us.

What everyone needs to remind himself of in the first place

(if he gets so far) is that before he can even begin to ascend the axial mountain that leads toward Buddhahood, he has first to become "true man" (as Taoism puts it), which, in our world, is the station from which the mountain itself begins to rise; and that is why religion, in general, starts off by propounding the need for a purposeful life of virtue, because this chiefly is a means of regaining the missing human norm, the one we all bear in name but rarely possess in fact.

So far, karma has chiefly been considered under its cosmic aspect as the determinant, for beings, of their fate. Plainly, when taken in this sense, karma can be accepted only in passive mode, since the nature of a being's existence in a given world is something that being is impotent to alter, wish as he may; in this sense, "the hairs of our head are all numbered." There is, however, side by side with this involuntary and imposed passivity, a possibility of living the same karma in *active* mode— that is to say, mindfully and intelligently—and here the human will, which allows us to choose this second way or to neglect it, counts decisively, since, without its active concurrence, all we have to do is to let ourselves drift to and fro like logs floating on the surface of samsara's swirling waters; but this attitude hardly befits those who, by virtue of their human quality, already stand at the wicket gate of freedom.

For a way to be justly describable as "active" it must be clearly related, under the double heading of intention and method, to the promoting of enlightenment. A way that does not look beyond samsara, even though some active elements may be called into play incidentally in the course of gaining merit, remains essentially passive in respect of its finality, and by this criterion it falls short.

For karma to be utilizable as an instrument to serve the greater purpose a number of "technical" conditions have to be satisfied, three of which are of particular importance, so that they can fittingly provide the conclusion to this essay. The three are as follows: First, there must be conscious self-identification with one's karma. Second, there must be just discernment as to what really constitutes "good karma." Third, one's karma must be recognized as the determinant of vocation, of one's own specific dharma.

Let us take each of these points in order:

1. The basis of self-identification with one's karma is the clear recognition that it is essentially just—just in principle and just in the particular, including that particular we call "myself." Similarly one's future karma has to be accepted, as if by anticipation; one must expect to reap as one has sown and not otherwise.

What must be remembered at every turn is that karma is the expression of the inherent equilibrium of the universe, which is always present in toto, with every apparent disturbance of balance automatically entailing its compensating reaction whereby the total balance is maintained; karma is therefore not only just, it expresses the very principle of justice, which is *even balance*.

For man, an attitude of acceptance in the face of his state of existence, as determined by antecedent karma, as also in the face of the unavoidable happenings of his existence while that state lasts, the fruits of karma, is both realistic in itself and morally sound. This attitude has often been stigmatized as "fatalistic," especially when displayed by Orientals, but the intended criticism starts out from a faulty premise, namely from a confusing of mere passivity versus one's fate with *resignation*, which is an intellectual attitude, active therefore and allied to detachment; it rests on an understanding of a real situation by a mind free from wishful thinking.

Fatalism, which also exists among men, can be imputed only where someone adopts a helpless attitude in respect of elements still indeterminate and therefore still offering openings for the free exercise of willing and acting in some degree or other. If, for instance, the house catches fire or if one's child is taken ill, these are results of karma and must, so far as that goes, be accepted; but there is no evidence to prove that standing by and letting the fire consume the house or failing to call in the doctor (whose existence in the neighborhood, incidentally, is also a fruit of karma) is an already predestined fact, and it would be straining the doctrine of karma to hold back from an obviously reasonable, as well as possible, action on the strength of a pessimistically prejudged result. Lack of initiative and a spirit of resignation are two very different things.

Admittedly the kind of attitude we have been describing is sometimes to be found among simple people, especially in the East, so that the accusation of fatalism is not unjustified in some cases. Equally often, however, the attitude decried as fatalism is not such, but springs from true resignation in the face of unavoidable ills, in which case it is wholly justifiable and sane; just as, on the other hand, a congenital readiness of Western people to fight an apparently losing battle is often rewarded by an unexpected success and represents realism of another kind, namely a willingness to challenge fate as long as the least hope remains of altering a bad situation for the better. Each of the two attitudes has its proper place in human affairs, and each goes with its characteristic abuse; as between an unthinking fatalism and a tendency to kick obstinately against the pricks there is not much to choose.

The point to grasp is that though the dispensations of karma, once declared, have to be accepted for what they are, as inherently just—therefore also without resentment, which would in fact be futile—yet at the same time the use of such resources as lie to hand (also thanks to one's karma) is justified pending a final declaration of the result. Within these limits remedial action is in no wise opposed to resignation.

The all-important thing, however, when undertaking any action aimed at promoting human welfare, whether at an individual or a collective level, is not to lose sight of the essential truth of impermanence, as pertaining to the action itself and its eventual consequences. Whatever degree of success or non-success may appear to attach to the latter, this will never be definitive in either sense, such being precluded by the very nature of that samsaric process in which both action and its fruits appear but episodically. The pathetic hope, fostered by the mystique of "progress," that by a successive accumulation of human contrivances samsara itself will somehow be, if not abolished, permanently tilted in a comfortable direction is as incompatible with Buddhist realism as with historical probability. Among obstacles to enlightenment there can be none greater than to forget samsara and our own inescapable place in it—in other words, to forget the first of the Four Noble Truths, enunciated by the Buddha, namely the necessary association of existence with suffering in some degree or other.

Though we have spoken at some length about acceptance of one's karma, as marking an important stage, a full self-identification with it takes one much further. For such to be realized it is necessary to recognize what should be an obvious fact, though often overlooked, namely that a man *is* his karma in the sense that all the various elements that together have gone into the composition of his empirical personality, what he and others take for his "self," are one and all products of karma, and so are the modifications through which that personality passes in the course of its becoming: family, possessions, occasional happenings, illness, old age, or what you will. Apart from these "accidental" products of becoming, that personality would not exist, and when they fall apart, it no longer is. Therefore there is a real identity between the process and the product, and once this is clearly recognized, it should be possible to go a stage further and make friends with one's karma as Sāvitri made friends with Death when he came to fetch her husband and conquered him by so doing.

2. Now for our second question: What constitutes good karma?

An average layman would probably answer something like this: Merit, good karma, accrues to him who leads an upright, pious life, keeping the precepts, showing compassion to fellow creatures of every kind, and contributing duly to the support of the sacred congregation, the sangha; if the man is a monk, he may add one or two items to the list, but broadly speaking this is the answer one will get. If one also asks him what are the fruits of meritorious karma, he will probably say, "a healthy and happy life, a painless death, with rebirth into a state of felicity among gods or the like, or else again as man." Now, this kind of answer, which is conventional, though acceptable as far as it goes, hardly makes for a far-reaching aspiration. The attitude remains samsaric; there is no touch of Buddha-thinking here.

For one in whom "the mind of bodhi" has begun to stir, be it ever so slightly, a different answer is required. Before he calls his karma "good" or "bad," he will want to know, above all, whether or not it places him in favorable circumstances for encompassing "the one thing needful," as Christ described it; rewards for merit, assessable only according to the scale of samsaric values, hold little attraction for such a man. A beatitude minus the essential opportunity is not far from being, for him, a hell.

Once a man begins to hold such views, his valuation of things around him and also in the world at large cannot but change its emphasis, since it will be influenced, at every turn, by this paramount consideration: Is this conducive to enlightenment, or is it not, and if it is, how far is it so? This thought becomes the touchstone of discernment in things great and small, and nothing will henceforth be immune to reappraisal in the light of it.

By this criterion an unschooled beggar woman in Tibet strong in the faith of Buddha has a more enviable lot than many an eminent professor in other lands whose obsessive pursuit of purely samsaric investigations constitutes an obstacle a hundred times more insurmountable than mere illiteracy and some degree of petty superstition could ever be for that poor woman. On balance, the illiteracy might even count as a gain, since it will have screened her mind effectively from the contagion of cheap literature—or rather would have done so had she been born in Europe, since in Tibet before the Communists came such a thing as profane literature was unknown, all books being attached to the sacred interest in some degree or other. The same of course would apply in any fully traditional society, whether of East or West. As between that woman and the professor, her simple faith, however limited, must count as an elementary knowledge, where colossal erudition, directed, not to the center, but to numberless peripheral phenomena, must count as a peculiarly pretentious form of ignorance. Therefore, rebirth as that beggar woman, for the professor, would spell almost unqualified gain; the reverse, for her, unqualified loss.

An English traveler was once asked by a Tibetan, "What is the good of trying to suppress all superstitions, since, on a final count, whatever exists outside bodhi, outside enlightenment, and whatever does not lead there, is but superstition?" A Mongol also once asked the writer if it was true that the British, as he had been given to understand, were all completely without superstitions of the kind to be found among the people of his own country or Tibet. On being given a few instances of superstitions still current in Europe he said, with evident relief, "Then there is hope for these people after all, since their mind is not completely closed [he might have said "sterilized"] in respect of things that do not meet the eye." The above examples, which can be varied in a hundred ways, should be sufficient to illustrate the principle at play.

People speak of prosperity as if they had a right to it regardless of their karma, and of adversity as if it were something in which they had no stake; but here again it is necessary to discriminate in the light of the respective karmic fruits. For the man of insight, a form of prosperity tending to increase distraction (though this does not always happen, of course) must be reckoned a drawback from the point of view of fruits, whereas an adversity that serves to open one's eyes must be accounted more of a boon than a punishment; merit might earn a blessed pain, where an unfavorable karma would place one in prosperity as a stage on the way to hell.

For instance, would the early Christian martyrs have been gainers if in place of the terrible suffering they were called upon to face they had been born, say, as prosperous businessmen in New York today? Was that monk who was murdered for refusing to preach against religion at the bidding of the Communists or was that humble retainer they also murdered because he persisted in denying that the feudal landowner he served had behaved oppressively a victim of bad, or a gainer of good, karma? On a short view they both suffered; on a long view both earned the crown of martyrdom. It is for oneself to judge which is the overriding criterion in every such case. Remember that in samsara there are no absolute categories;

every criterion can be read two ways. That is why each case that crops up has to be settled on its merits, in reference to the one supreme interest; otherwise one's conclusions will remain both crude and dubious.

One other example drawn from a source very foreign to the Buddhist world will help to clinch the argument. I remember an occasion some years ago when I sat listening to Wagner's music-drama *Die Walküre*. It was the scene where Wotan, chief of the gods, is about to sentence his daughter, Brunhilde, the celestial warrior-maiden, to deprivation of her godhood for having disobeyed his command to side with Hunding, and in his person with the laws of conventional morality, against Siegmund who here stands for the cause of spirit versus the letter and as the exception that proves the rule. This story was taken by Wagner from an ancient German myth, a symbolical narrative, that is to say, charged with a metaphysical message that the composer must have felt instinctively even if he did not consciously penetrate its every meaning.

The crux of the story is that Wotan, to punish his daughter, turns her into an ordinary woman; that is to say, Brunhilde is caused to exchange a state that, though it bespeaks superior powers, remains peripheral, in favor of the human state, which is central. Thus the seeming punishment becomes a real reward. As a further result, according to the myth, Brunhilde, now a woman, becomes the spouse of Siegfried, type of the Solar Hero—and let us not forget that traditionally "solarity" is an attribute of the Buddha himself. If we translate the episode into Buddhist terms, Brunhilde's good karma, due to her having shown true discernment when faced with a crucial choice, won her a place on the axis of deliverance. This is the essential point; the "punishment" is only incidental. This all came to me in a flash, as I sat under the spell of that glorious music, which thus served as an *upāya*, as a catalyst of wisdom hidden in the old German and Scandinavian mythology, which otherwise I might never have discovered for myself.

3. Third and last: concerning karma as determinant of a man's vocation, of his own specific dharma:

We said, when discussing the first of our three headings, that a man *is* his karma inasmuch as he owes to it all the various elements of which his human personality is compounded, nothing being found there that he can call his own in the sense of a personal constant or selfhood.

Now, what is received through one's karma is necessarily delimited; it includes certain elements and excludes others, and these between them mark the positive and negative boundaries of the personality concerned. By the same token one is shown what possibilities of action lie open to one—as also of thought, since this is activity of a kind and limited in its own way. The things one lacks cannot be utilized; each man must work with the tools, mental or physical, he has been given, and this means, in effect, that he will be qualified for certain kinds of activity and not for others. It indicates for each his own vocational trend, and this, when one is striving to find one's center, is already a valuable pointer.

The Buddhas have trodden the path beforehand. They have left a tradition as a compass to keep men facing in the right direction together with various "means of grace" from the Noble Eightfold Program downward. What even the Buddhas do not do, however, is to travel in our place. Each must approach the center of knowledge in his own peculiar way, for the experience of each being is unrepeatable; every possibility in the universe is unique.

Let no one feel discouraged because his knowledge is as yet minute; rather let him think of enlarging it by every means in his power. Minute or not, it is a spark, and with a spark it is possible to kindle a still brighter lamp and thus pursue the way.

May that lamp grow, for each and all of us, till it has reached the brilliance and magnitude of a Vaisakh moon.[1]

[1] According to the Indian calendar, the full moon in the month of May, which marked the Buddha's enlightenment at the foot of the World Tree at Gaya.

Is There Room for "Grace" in Buddhism?

BY MARCO PALLIS

To the question "Is there room for 'grace' in Buddhism?" there are many today who without further reflection would give a negative reply. It is a commonplace of neo-Buddhist apologetics with an eye on the fashionable "humanism" of the Western world to stress both the exclusively self-directed achievement of the Buddha as "discoverer" of the way to enlightenment and also, on the strength of the Buddha's example, the empirical character of the opportunity open to those who would follow in his footsteps. Within its proper traditional context the first of these two statements is valid, whereas the second one rests on more doubtful grounds and certainly needs qualifying in several important respects. However, it can be admitted that a perspective that does not include the idea of a personal God may seem, at first sight, to leave little room for the idea of grace either: How could a merciful action from above, definable in terms of an unsolicited gift offered to men independently of their own effort, be reconciled, so some will argue, with the inflexible determinism ascribed to the manifested universe itself, as expressed in the doctrine of concordant action and reaction, karma and its fruits? Yet this idea of "grace," which translates a divine function, is by no means unintelligible in the light of traditional Buddhist teachings, being in fact implicit in every known form of spirituality, the Buddhist form included. The question, however, is how to situate the said idea in a manner that implies no contradiction, since it must freely be admitted that the Buddhist wisdom has not given to the idea of grace the same form as it has received in the personalist and theistic doctrines of Semitic provenance; nor is such a thing to be expected, inasmuch as the "economy" of the respective traditions rests on very different premises, thus affecting both the doctrines and the manner of their application in practice. Each kind of wisdom determines the nature of its corresponding method. Buddhism has always made of this a governing principle of spiritual life at any degree or level.

Evidently the nature of the Christic revelation was such as to require a strong affirmation of the element of grace from the very outset, which was not the case with Buddhism. Such differences in the line of approach to the saving truth are in the nature of things and should cause no surprise given the diversifying of mankind in the course of its karmic development. The important thing to recognize in this case is the fact that the word "grace" corresponds to a whole dimension of spiritual experience; it is unthinkable that this should be absent from one of the great religions of the world. In fact, anyone who has lived in a traditionally Buddhist country knows that this dimension finds its expression there too, vehicled by the appropriate forms. For us it is of interest to observe these forms and clarify for ourselves the teaching they carry explicitly or else latently. The present essay should be regarded as contributing to this clarification.

The pursuit of enlightenment, which is the purpose for which Buddhism exists, is paradoxical by its own showing inasmuch as this aim appears to require an encompassing of the greater by the less, of the imperishable by the ephemeral, of absolute knowledge by a relative ignorance; it seems to make of man the subject and of enlightenment the object of the quest. Moreover, a similar paradox applies in the theistic forms of religion; people speak of seeking God and of contemplating His perfections even while knowing that in terms of human measurement and however far along the road a man may have proceeded, God lies farther still and that no unilaterally directed human perception or effort is adequate to the divine truth even across one of its aspects, to say nothing of its essence. In Buddhist terms no human powers however stretched can possibly match up to the suchness of enlightenment. Yet Buddhahood, to which we are invited by the teaching and tradition of the Buddha and still more by his example, is just this. Nothing less is offered to us, since it is axiomatic to the Buddhist revelation as such that to reach this transcendent goal does, in principle, lie within the scope of every human being in virtue of that being's place on the axis of Buddhahood—for this is what to be human really means—and also, more indirectly, within the scope of every being whatsoever "down to the last blade of grass," as the saying goes, via the prior attainment of a human birth in this world or, if another world be in question, a birth of corresponding centrality.

For a start, it is worth pointing out that if from the "non-personalist" standpoint of Buddhism, the supreme goal is presented as "a state" (hence the use of a word like "enlightenment"), from the standpoint of the Semitic religions that goal is most commonly clothed in the attributes of personality. Nevertheless, in the latter religions the word "God" will always comprise, be it more or less unconsciously, the idea of the unqualifiable *Godhead,* and this is true even when the word is being quite loosely used. Despite the antimetaphysical bias of much Western theological thinking, it would be a mistake to conclude that the qualifying of God as "person" constitutes a limit in principle. In Islam this particular danger of confusion is in practice far less than in Christianity. Outside the Semitic world, Hinduism reconciles the two points of view, personal and impersonal, with perfect ease.

Where Buddhism is concerned, despite its preference for impersonal expressions, one could yet ask oneself, "Whose is the state of enlightenment?" since the word itself, as used, does not altogether keep clear of anthropomorphic overtones; neither does one speak of a Buddha, once enlightened, as "It"—all of which goes to prove that in this sphere, as in others, it is not the words used but the manner of using them in a given context that counts. Both modes of expression, the personal as well as the impersonal, are possible and therefore legitimate, since each may serve as an *upāya,* or provisional means, to evoke, rather than to define, a reality that is inexpressible in terms of our earthly experience. Provided it has this effect on those for whom it is intended, the means in question becomes acceptable.

Given our common human condition as thinking and talking animals, there is no reason to fight shy of a more or less anthropomorphic terminology when discussing even the most sublime of subjects provided one does not forget the truth that if speech is good, speech nevertheless arises from the rupture of a silence, which is better still. "The Buddha's silence" regarding the nature of the Ultimate is, among his many and various *upāyas*, the most enlightening of all. When the Buddha spoke no word but merely held up a flower, Zen took birth; there is a profound lesson in this story.

Fortified by this precaution, it is now possible to approach our chosen theme by quoting a famous passage from the Pali Canon (Udana 7:1–3) wherein lies concealed a key to the understanding of what "grace" means in a Buddhist setting. Here is the passage in question:

> There is, O monks, an unborn, an unbecome, an unmade, an uncompounded; if, O monks, there were not here this unborn, unbecome, unmade, uncompounded, there would not here be an escape from the born, the become, the made, the compounded. But because there is an unborn, an unbecome, an unmade, an uncompounded, therefore there is an escape from the born, the become, the made, the compounded.

The above quotation is plainly couched in the language of transcendence; any Christian or Muslim could have used these same words when referring to God and the world. This transcendence is propounded by the sutra as providing real grounds for human hope. What it does not do, however, is to define the link between the two terms under comparison; we still need to be shown the bridge over which changefulness must pass to reach the eternal. This link or bridge in fact corresponds to that very function of divine grace that is the object of our present investigation.

The key to the problem lies in a property of transcendence itself. Given the incommensurable gap apparently fixed between enlightenment and the seeker after enlightenment—ig-

norant by definition—it is self-evident to anyone who thinks
at all, and still more so to anyone possessed of a metaphysical
flair, that such a seeking on the part of a human being with his
necessarily imperfect vision and limited powers does not really
make sense when taken at its face value alone. Enlightenment
(or God for that matter) cannot possibly be situated at the
passive pole in relation to man's endeavor; it cannot per se
become object to man as subject. If our human language sometimes makes things seem so, it is high time we became aware
of its inadequacy. Buddhism for its part will add that here is
patent evidence of the illusory character of the human claim
to selfhood, to which all our conceptual aberrations are sever-
ally and collectively imputable.

To put the above argument somewhat differently: Man cannot possibly be the active agent in an operation wherein enlightenment plays the passive part. Whatever may or may not
be suggested by appearances, the truth has to be read the other
way round, since enlightenment, awareness of the divine reality, belongs outside all becoming by definition; it is wholly "in
act," so that wherever one discerns contingency or potentiality,
as in the case of our human seeking, this of necessity pertains
to samsara, to the changing, the impermanent, the compounded. It is this very character of potentiality, experience-
able positively as arising and negatively as subsiding, which
makes samsara, the Round of Existence, to be such as it is.

The consequences of the above observation are momentous;
for if there is to be a wooing of enlightenment by man, it is
nevertheless the former that, in principle and in fact, remains
the real subject of the quest as well as its ostensible object. It
has often been said that in enlightenment the subject-object
distinction is canceled out—a truth to bear in mind even if, in
our present state, this remains more of a puzzling thought than
a verified reality. Metaphysical intuition, however, already allows one to know—or shall we say, to sense—that intrinsically
enlightenment is the active factor in our situation and that it
is man who, for all his apparent initiative and effort, represents
the passive term of the supreme adequation. Meister Eckhart
puts this whole question into proper perspective when he says

that "in the course of nature it is really the higher which is ever more ready to pour out its power into the lower than the lower is ready to receive it," for, as he goes on to say, "there is no dearth of God with us; what dearth there is is wholly ours who make not ready to receive his grace." Where he said "God," you have but to say "enlightenment," and the result will be a Buddhist statement in form as well as content.

The great paradox, for us, is that we still cannot help viewing this situation in reverse; a misplaced egocentricity makes us do so: We all have to suffer the congenital illusion of existence in which every creature as yet undelivered shares in greater or lesser degree. Buddhism invites us to get this thing straight in the first place, prior to showing us that the two viewpoints on reality, the relative and absolute, samsara and Nirvana, essentially coincide, as the Heart Sutra explicitly teaches.

In China the Taoists have always spoken of the "activity of heaven"; for us to speak of the "activity of enlightenment" is in no wise far-fetched. This is in fact the function of grace, namely to condition men's homecoming to the center from start to finish. It is the very attraction of the center itself, revealed to us by various means, which provides the incentive to start on the way and the energy to face and overcome its many and various obstacles. Likewise grace is the welcoming hand into the center when man finds himself standing at long last on the brink of the great divide where all familiar human landmarks have disappeared. Only he who came down from heaven can ascend to heaven, as the Gospel says, but about this mystery it is useless for ignorance to speculate, let alone speak. Till the great leap in the dark is taken, faith in the Buddha's enlightenment must be our lamp, since all that stems from light is light, and even our darkness, did we but know it, is none other than the dazzlement inflicted by a radiance too intense for samsaric eyes to bear.

The attractive influence of enlightenment, experienced as providential and merciful emanation from the luminous center, strikes on human consciousness in three ways, which might be described respectively as: (1) invitation into enlightenment,

(2) companionship of enlightenment, and (3) reminders of enlightenment.

The first-named corresponds to "conversion," the gift of faith. The second corresponds to man's being "in a state of grace," in virtue of which his apparent weakness is enabled to envisage tasks and surmount obstacles far beyond ordinary human strength. The third way coincides with the supplying of various "means of grace," that is to say, *upāyas* consecrated by tradition—scriptural teachings, methods of meditation, initiatic rites, and the like. Moreover, the whole inspiration of an art properly describable as "sacred" issues from this source. In short, whatever serves as a reminder of enlightenment or helps to keep attention in that line of vision is a "means of grace" in the sense here intended. It is worth dwelling on the above three factors of attraction in somewhat greater detail.

Invitation into enlightenment: This phrase has been coined by way of describing a man's first clear experiencing of an overriding call to turn his religious life into a reality. Antecedent circumstances, such as a person's background formation or the degree of his or her intellectual maturity, need not be taken into account in the present instance; all one is concerned with is the nature of the event itself. Until "the thought of enlightenment" has gained a place in one's consciousness, one can hardly claim to be "traveling" in a Buddhist sense. The awakening of faith remains a great mystery; its negative concomitant will always be a certain turning away from the world, and it is only later (save by rare exception) that any question of integrating the world positively, in the sense of the essential identity of samsara and Nirvana as expressed in the Heart Sutra (this was mentioned before), can play an effective part in one's preoccupations. "Nonduality" is not for the beginner; presented as an abstract theory, this idea can even be harmful for a mind insufficiently prepared because it leads only too easily to pretensions of an ego-inflating kind—hence the danger of much that passes for Zen or Vedanta today. The reticence of some religious exoterisms on the subject, which it is the fashion to blame, is by no means unjustified in the light of the results.

An important thing to notice here is that the sense of

spiritual urgency, whether coming to a person suddenly or else by hardly perceptible steps, is experienced as a call to activity whereof the person himself is in the first place the passive recipient, having done nothing particular to bring it about; this is typical and normal and admirably fits in with the description of a grace as being "free gift." All at once a peremptory urge takes root in that man's soul telling him that enlightenment is the only thing of worth in its own right and that all other things, be they great or small, can only be properly valued in proportion as they contribute to that end or else impede its attainment. Once this has happened, the essentials of spiritual life are there, namely discernment between the real and the illusory and the will to concentrate upon the real; this latter definition comes from Frithjof Schuon. However elementary may be one's present awareness of this twofold call, whereof wisdom and method are the respective expressions, it can be said with certainty that a foretaste of enlightenment has been received; it is as if a ray spontaneously emitted from the center has come to effect a first incision in the shell of human ignorance because the Buddha-nature in a man wishes to be delivered. More than this cannot be said about something that baffles all the calculations of the ordinary mind.

Companionship of enlightenment: If invitation into the Way is something of a unique event in a human life, the graces to be experienced in the course of following that way are multiple in the sense that they repeat that first call at various stages of spiritual development in the form of an urge to proceed further, to deepen this experience or that, to eliminate such and such causes of distraction, or to concentrate on this or that aspect of awareness. This process can be illustrated by comparing it to the climbing of some mountain ridge leading to a summit. At the start of the ascent the thought of the summit alone possesses one's mind, but when once one is actually on the ridge, each successive pinnacle or gash needing to be circumvented will engage all one's attention to the point of temporarily eclipsing remembrance of the summit itself. The nearer obstacles do in fact continue to reveal the existence of the summit by implication, but also in a sense they veil it; in other words, each obstacle in turn serves to *symbolize* the summit and thus becomes a factor of awareness in a relative sense. Thus do the things encountered in samsaric existence prove the latent presence of enlightenment even while appearing to hide it. A "symbol" is a key to knowledge; an "idol" is a symbol taken for a reality in its own right: This is a fundamental distinction to bear in mind, because symbolism, properly understood and applied, is the very stuff of the spiritual alchemy whereby the samsaric lead may be transmitted into the Buddhic gold it is in principle. In all this process, be the Way long or short, the companionship of enlightenment is operating like a ferment, an ever-present grace filling the gap, as it were, between our human incapacity and the apparently superhuman task to which we are committed thanks to a human birth.

Seeing that the Way with its stages has just been mentioned in correlation with the effusion of grace, this will provide an opportunity to discuss one question that has often been a cause of confusion, namely how we are to situate our own present life in the general scheme of transmigration as set forth by Buddhism; for this purpose a brief digression will not come amiss.

The question might be put this way: When considering the path to enlightenment, are we to take into account, as some might ask, the extended possibilities implied in successive births (sometimes reckoned by the million), or should we confine our attention to present existence while ignoring the rest except in the sense of a more or less schematic representation of samsara, the world's flow, as conditioned by the continual interplay of action and reaction, karma and its fruits? This is indeed a pertinent question to put, since it touches something quite fundamental in Buddhism, namely the truth that to know samsara's true nature is to know Nirvana, nothing less. The converse also holds good; for if one may be allowed to paraphrase a sentence of Saint Thomas Aquinas, "A false opinion concerning the world will fatally engender a false opinion concerning Enlightenment" (Saint Thomas says "concerning God"); the two awarenesses hang together, reality being one.

Coming as a fresh and unfamiliar idea, transmigration often

makes a strong appeal to a Western mind just because it seems to provide for "a second chance," that is to say, for the possibility of taking the way to enlightenment by easy stages instead of having to stake one's all on a single throw, as the Semitic eschatologies would appear to suggest. For one who takes this complacent view of his human opportunities, it is only too easy to read into the doctrine of samsaric rebirth something closely akin to the current belief in a one-directional "progress"; whether this belief be clothed in the more scientific-sounding phraseology of "evolution" on Teilhardian lines or otherwise makes no matter.

Now, such a view does not square with Buddhism inasmuch as it misses the chief point about transmigration, namely its essential *indefinitude*—this can never be said too often—as also, incidentally, the high degree of improbability attaching to any kind of human rebirth when weighed up in terms of karmic consequence. It is not very logical (to say the least of it) to spend most of one's earthly life in the pursuit, not of enlightenment, but of all that is unnecessary and trivial and then to expect this life to repeat itself in human form; yet this is precisely the life led by a majority of people and not least by those whom the world regards as highly civilized and admires for their manipulative dexterity or their insatiable erudition. What right have these people to expect privileged treatment when the time comes for them to be weighed on the karmic scales? Have they ever given a thought to that saying about "human birth hard to obtain" which runs through Buddhism like a refrain? If one wishes to be honest with oneself, one has to admit that in most cases rebirth as a worm would be a merciful requital; certainly one is being less than prudent if one assumes that the hells of Buddhism are only there to accommodate murderers and gangsters. How many of us would ever have the nerve to commit murder? To what kind of rebirth, then, is it likely that a frittered consciousness will lead, or a persistent lukewarmness in respect of truth?

The Semitic eschatologies, which offer man the single alternative "salvation or perdition," can at least claim an empirical realism for this narrowing of choice on the grounds that such an attitude makes for a sense of urgency in life and is therefore, spiritually speaking, an *upāya* adjusted to its purpose. For the Buddhist, what in fact replaces the Christian's fear of God's wrath is the fear of interminable wandering through samsara, now up, now down, but never free from suffering. Any attempt to read into the samsaric process an idea of something like a uniform cosmic movement endowed with an optimistic trend is as un-Buddhist as it is improbable in itself.

In point of fact, whenever enlightenment is attained, this is always from the vantage point of a particular human life, or an equivalent state if another world system be in question; the individual called Prince Siddhartha who became Sakya Muni Buddha perfectly illustrates the above statement. One must not slip into thinking of enlightenment as if it were the last and sweetest of a long-drawn-out harvest of samsaric fruits. Good karma, any life well spent, contributes to one's enlightenment, first because virtue is dispositive to knowledge while vice does the reverse and second because within the scale of samsaric possibilities good karma promotes the emergence of fresh creations[1] in relatively favorable surroundings as, for instance, in countries where enlightenment is not forgotten, which is no small advantage in this world. To this extent a life well and intelligently spent is not irrelevant to one's attainment of the goal even if one stops short somewhere on the path. To admit this is, however, very different from turning this possibility of good karma into an excuse for postponing one's best efforts till a future life assumed to be better than the present one. This very attitude almost makes it certain that it will be worse. In any case, so long as one remains a samsaric being, any kind of relapse is possible; it is salutary to bear this in mind while putting all one's effort into immediate opportunities consonantly with present grace. Above all it should be remembered that enlightenment, if and when it comes, spells a reversal of all samsaric values or, in a still deeper sense, their integration. If it be currently said of a Buddha that "he knows all his anterior births," this is because he is identified with the heart of

[1] The words "karma" and "creation" derive, by the way, from a common root.

causality, the mysterious hub of the wheel of becoming where no motion ever was or could be. Beings still in samsara do not enjoy this possibility, so that it would seem in every way more practical for them to make the best of a human opportunity while they have it, instead of banking on a future that could be anything from a paradise of devas to an infernal sojourn amid fire or ice.

A most important thing to remember in all this is that the attainer of enlightenment is not "this man so-and-so" but rather that it is by the ending of the dream of one's own "so-and-soness" that enlightenment arises. As far as knowledge of samsara is concerned, what is needed is for each thing to be put in its own place, neither plus nor minus, including one's own person. When all things have become transparent to the point of allowing the Uncreated Light to shine right through them, there is nothing further to become. Becoming is the continual process of resolving internal contradictions, fruits of the dualistic tree, by means of partial compensations leading to fresh contradictions and so on indefinitely. To understand this process with full clarity is to escape its domination. The Buddha has shown the way.

With this question behind us, let us take up the last of our three headings, *reminders of enlightenment,* but this need not long detain us; it is enough to have listed a certain number of type examples of "means of grace" as supplied by the tradition under various forms and in view of various uses. All traditional civilizations abound in such reminders; once one is aware that such exist, it is easy to observe the workings of grace through the medium of these forms. Nevertheless, there remains one example that deserves quite special attention as a supreme reminder and means of grace: this is the sacramental image of the Blessed One found in every corner of the Buddhist world. We will take up this subject in due course.

The next channeling of grace to be offered to the reader's attention is one that takes us into a spiritual dimension close to the heart of things. This is the function of guru, or spiritual master, of him who initiates a man into the path that leads, via the higher states of consciousness, to the threshold of enlightenment itself—so near and yet so far, since the final passage remains pure mystery whereof grace alone holds the key. In a very special sense the spiritual master is the representative of "the spirit that bloweth where it listeth." His qualification for such an office devolves on him outside any determinable test. If he be not yet discovered, his very seeking confers light; when found, his favor may yet be granted or withheld without any reasons given. His displeasure is the bitterest medicine for any man to swallow. In his master's presence the disciple is expected to behave as if the Buddha himself stood before him; in the Christian initiation centered on the Jesus Prayer the same advice is given, with substitution of the person of Christ.

In relation to the sangha the guru stands for its essence; this is true even if the master be not himself a bhikku, though obviously he often is that too. The famous guru of Mila Repa, Marpa, was a consecrated layman with a family, than whom no greater master has existed anywhere; just as, in the matter of discipleship Mila Repa is unsurpassed, to say the least of it. His own poems, the most beautiful in the Tibetan language, ring of the guru's grace at every turn, even though as far as personal effort is concerned Mila Repa's persistence in the face of Marpa's calculated (but ever so compassionate) snubbing is something so unheard of as to make one think that a man must be born a Tibetan to stay such a course.

However, the human guru is not the whole story; there is another guru to be considered, interior this time and whose visible counterpart the outward guru is. "Intellect" is his name, Socrates's *daemon*, though later usage has debased a word that by rights should be confined to the intuitive intelligence indwelling at the heart of every being and especially of man, the immanent grace about which Christ said "the Kingdom of Heaven is within you." When the outer guru has done his work, he hands over to the inner guru, leaving him to do the rest.

Intellect can save us because it is that, in us, which needs no saving seeing that enlightenment is in its very substance. Stemming from light, itself is light, leading back to light. The great puzzle is our egotism, our false sense of selfhood and consequent reluctance to let go what never makes us really happy. Our recurring dissatisfactions are also guru; all we have to do is to trace these dissatisfactions to their primary cause. This is the positive message of suffering, a message that also harbors a hope, one that surely cannot forever remain unheeded. The Buddha's "First Truth" really teaches nothing different.

Let us now take a brief flight out of this suffering world in order to visit the homeland of grace and the source of its bountiful stream. Mahayana Buddhism speaks of three *kayas*, or bodies of Buddhahood, or, if one so prefers, three mansions of enlightenment considered respectively as essence or suchness, fruition or bliss, and Avataric projection into the world; the corresponding Sanskrit names are *Dharma-kaya*, *Sambhoga-kaya*, and *Nirmāna-kaya*, and it is especially of this third body that something must now be said, as relating directly to the question of grace and its manifestation among beings.

A quotation from a short but highly concentrated Tibetan sutra composed in verse, *The Good Wish of Great Power*, will provide us with the essential data: "Uninterruptedly my Avataras [incarnations] will appear in inconceivable millions and will show forth various means for the conversion of every kind of being. Through the prayer of my compassion may all sentient beings of the three spheres be delivered from the six samsaric abodes."

Traditionally, the "revealer" of this sutra is given as the Buddha *Samanta Bhadra*, the "All Good"; significantly his name is preceded by the prefix *Adi*—or primordial—thus stressing the principial nature of the attribution. Concerning the primordial reality whereof this Buddha is spokesman, it is also said that neither the name of Nirvana nor of samsara applies to it, for it is pure "nonduality" *(advaita)* beyond all possible distinction or expression. To realize this truth fully is to be *buddha*, awake; not to realize it is to wander in samsaric existence; the sutra says this expressly. The Vedantine *selfhood* is but another way of conveying this truth.

In their ceaseless warfare waged against men's proneness to superimpose their own concepts on the Divinity as such, the Buddhist sutras have introduced the word "void" to suggest the total absence of positive or negative definability; hence also the Buddha's title of *Shunya-murti,* "Form of the Void"—a contradiction in terms that again serves to underline a truth that eludes all attempts at positive enunciation.

As soon as one passes over to attribution, by saying of Divinity that "it is" or "is not" this or that or else by giving names such as "all good," etc., one is perforce in the realm of being; the merciful epithet mentioned above is, among names, one of the first to impose itself. The visible sign of this merciful presence is to be seen in the stream of avataric revelation (hence the use of the word "millions" in the sutra), the Buddhas and Bodhisattvas who appear in the various world systems and, through their own enlightenment, show the way of deliverance to creatures. Our sutra concludes with the following words: "May beings of the three spheres one and all by the prayer of my contemplation . . . finally attain Buddhahood." This grants the very charter of grace and of its operation in the world; it hardly calls for further comment.

All that can usefully be added is perhaps to point out that if, in Christianity for example, the aspect of "Divine Personality" may sometimes seem to have obscured the Suchness of the Godhead Itself, in the case of Buddhism, though this danger has been sedulously avoided, a certain personal expression of the Divine is nevertheless to be found there in "distributive" form, namely as the heavenly sangha of Buddhas and Bodhisattvas, with the former standing for its static and the latter for its dynamic aspect, as mercy when projected into samsara itself. In the final section of this essay, when the Pure Land doctrine is discussed, this question will be taken up again.

After this excursion to the heights we must come down to earth again and examine one concrete means of grace, mentioned before, which perhaps more than all others has helped to keep remembrance of enlightenment alive among men. This is the image of the Buddha making the "earth-touching" *(bhumi-sparsha)* gesture. No corner of the Buddhist world but knows and loves this image; both Theravada and Mahayana have produced marvelous examples of it. If there be a symbolical representation to which the word "miraculous" properly applies, this surely is the one.

The story of how a Buddha image came to exist at all is instructive, since Buddhism at the beginning did not incline to anthropomorphic imagery, preferring more elementary symbols. It is said that several abortive attempts were made to put the Buddha's likeness on record from motives of a personal kind such as the wish to remember a loved and revered figure and so on; a certain confusing of appearance and reality is always involved in such cases, hence the prohibition of the "graven image" by Judaism and Islam, for instance. However, in this case the compassion of the Victorious One intervened; he was prepared to allow an image of himself provided this was a true symbol and not a mere reproduction of surfaces—this distinction is very important. Yielding to his devotees' prayers, the Buddha projected his own form miraculously and it was this projection that provided the model for a true ikon, fit to serve a purpose other than that of personal adulation such as a sacred theme by definition precludes.

I should like to quote here from *Sacred Art in East and West*, by Titus Burckhardt, in which a whole chapter is devoted to the traditional *Buddha-rupa*. After mentioning the above story about the frustration of the artists and the miraculous projection, the author continues:

> . . . the sacred ikon is a manifestation of the grace of the Buddha, it emanates from his supra-human power. . . . If one considers the matter fully one can see that the two aspects of Buddhism, the doctrine of *karma* and its quality of grace, are inseparable, for to demonstrate the real nature of the world is to transcend it; it is to manifest the changeless states . . . and it is a breach made in the closed system of becoming. This breach is the Buddha himself; thenceforth all that comes from him carries the influx of *Bodhi*.

The enlightening function of the sacred image could not have been better put.

Before going into the various details of the image itself, it were well to refresh our memory about the episode in the Buddha's life which this particular posture is meant to perpetuate. Everyone will remember that shortly before his enlightenment the Buddha-to-be proceeded into the great primeval forest near the place in Bihar now called Bodh-gaya and there found a spreading pipal tree *(Ficus religiosa)* at the foot of which a seat stood ready prepared for one destined to become the Light of the World; the tree itself obviously stands for the world's axis, the Tree of Life as Genesis calls it. Just as he was about to take his seat there, Māra the tempter appeared before him, challenging his right to the adamantine throne: "I am prince of this world," Māra said, "so the throne belongs to me." Then the Bodhisattva stretched forth his right hand and touched the earth, mother of all creatures, calling on her to witness that the throne was his by right, and earth testified that this was so.

In the classical form of this image the Buddha is always shown sitting upon a lotus; the choice of this water plant is in itself significant inasmuch as in the traditional lore "the waters" always symbolize existence with its teeming possibilities, that samsara that the Buddha was to show the way to overcoming, not by mere denial but by showing forth its true nature. As for the figure itself, its right hand points downward to touch the earth as in the story while its left hand is turned upward to support the begging bowl, sign of a bhikku's estate. Just as the bhikku in his bowl catches whatever the passerby may choose to cast into it, be it much or little, not asking for more but letting it serve his own sustenance for the day, so also man has to accept the heavenly grace as the free gift it is. In the two gestures displayed by the Buddha image the whole program of man's spiritual exigencies is summed up.

Toward the earth, that is to say toward the world to which he belongs by his existence, man's gesture is *active;* such an active attitude is always needed where the world and its manifold temptations and distractions are concerned. Toward heaven and its gifts, on the other hand, the spiritual man is *passive;* he is content to receive the dew of grace as and when it falls and to refresh his more or less flagging powers with its aid. As for the ignorant man, he does just the reverse, showing himself soft and accommodating toward the world while making all kinds of conditions of his own choosing where the things of heaven are concerned, if indeed he deigns to give them any thought at all. For the truly mindful man, even his own karma can be both grace and guru, not merely in the sense of reward or sanction imposed by a cosmic law, but because karma is a potent and inescapable reminder of enlightenment as the crying need of man and as the only unequivocably reasonable object of his desires. Accepted in this sense, karma, be it good or evil, can be welcomed as Sāvitri once welcomed Death when he came to claim her husband and by her resignation overcame him. Contemplated rightly, the Buddha's sacramental image tells us all these things: For us, it is the means of grace par excellence.

Sufficient has by now been said (or so one hopes) by way of answering our original question as to whether Buddhism leaves any room for grace. One last illustration, however, will serve to clinch the argument by showing that the idea of grace can play a predominant part in a doctrine that nonetheless remains Buddhist in both form and flavor: This is the Pure Land doctrine (*Jōdo* in Japanese), developed around the vow of the Buddha Amitabha·and using, for its single operative means, the invocation of his name. The name itself means "Infinite Light" and the Buddha thus denoted is the one who presides over the Western quarter where his own "Buddha-land" is symbolically situated. It must be mentioned, in passing, that Europeans who feel drawn to Buddhism have hitherto been inclined to avoid the Pure Land form of it just because of its insistence on grace, described there as *tariki* (other power), which reminded them too much of the Christianity they believed themselves to have left behind. Western seekers have on the whole felt more drawn to *jiriki* (own power) methods, those where personal initiative and heroic effort are greatly stressed—hence their preference for Zen (or what they take for such) or else Theravada interpreted in an ultrapuritanical, not to say humanistic sense; not for anything would these people be mistaken for miserable, God-dependent Christians! I hope, however, to show that the two lines of approach, *jiriki* and *tariki*, are by no means as incompatible as some affect to believe and that, despite contrasts of emphasis, the two belong together and are in fact indispensable to one another.

Taking Zen first, one thing that many of its foreign admirers are apt to lose sight of is the fact that, in its own country, those who feel called into that way will already, since childhood, have been molded by the strict discipline of Japanese tradition in which respect for authority, an elaborate civility, and the acceptance of many formal restraints all play their allotted part and where all the basic assumptions of Buddhism can also be taken for granted. Nor must one forget the Shinto element in the tradition, with its cult of nature on the one hand and its inculcation of the chivalrous virtues on the other; the Japanese soul would not be what it is without both these influences to fashion it. Thus prepared, a man can face both the severity of a Zen training and also that element of the outrageous in Zen which so fascinates minds anxious to react against the conventional values of their own previous background, with its ready-made morality and its conceptual triteness. All these things have to be seen in proportion if they are to be rightly understood.

For those who think that Zen is pure "self-power" without any "other power" admixture it is well to point out that at least one of the manifestations of grace listed in this essay plays a most important part there: this is the guru, or *roshi*, who, since he is not the disciple, must needs represent "other power" in relation to the latter, say what one will. That Zen, despite its constant exhortation to personal effort, does not exclude the *tariki* element was proved to me (if it needed proof) by a Japanese Zen lecturer who came to England some years ago. At the end of his talk I went up to the platform and asked him, "Is it correct to say that, as between 'own power' and 'other power,' each always will imply the other? If one is affirmed, can one then assume the other as latent, and vice versa?" "But of course," the speaker answered. "They are two sides of the same coin. This is self-evident. Moreover, is not Zen a nondual-istic doctrine?"

A story that has provided many Japanese painters with a subject will further serve to illustrate this same point. This is the story of Zen's redoubtable Patriarch, Bodhidharma, and of his crossing the ocean borne on a reed or sprig of bamboo; for "ocean," samsara is to be understood, this being the traditional symbolism of the waters all the world over.

It is said that on one occasion Bodhidharma came to the seashore wishing to cross to the other side. Finding no boat, he suddenly espied a piece of reed and promptly seized and launched it on the water; then stepping boldly on its fragile stalk, he let himself be carried to the farther shore. Now, Bodhidharma was a sage; he knew that "own power" and "other power," dedicated free will and grace, are in essence the same, and his own use of the reed for a vehicle rests on that very awareness. For us onlookers, however, the point to note is that Bodhidharma *found* that reed on the seashore; he neither created it nor brought it with him. Who was it, then, that placed that reed there ready to be discovered? The "other power"; it could be no other. The reed came to the Zen Patriarch as a grace, to which in the first place he could but be passive; then having received it, he responded actively by an appropriate initiative and crossed the waters of samsara to the other shore. Hereby the moral of the Buddha image is pointed once again, if in different form.

By contrast with Zen, the Pure Land doctrine offers itself as a typical way of grace; hence the suggestion put forward by some that Jodo, in its early Chinese days, was influenced by Christian teachings brought to China by members of the Nestorian sect from Syria—a gratuitous hypothesis if ever there was one, since Jodo in all essentials remains a typically Buddhist form of wisdom. The following brief outline of the Pure Land teaching will make its theoretical position sufficiently clear for present purposes.

A certain Bodhisattva of the name of Dharmakāra was about to enter the state of enlightenment when, moved by compassion, he said to himself: "How can I bear to enter Nirvana when

all the multitude of beings have to stay behind, a prey to indefinite transmigration and suffering? Rather than leave them in
that state, I vow that if I am not able to deliver them down to
the last blade of grass, then let me never reach enlightenment!"
But in fact (so the argument runs) he did reach enlightenment
and now reigns, as the Buddha Amitabha, over the Western
quarter; therefore his vow cannot have failed in its object; suffering beings can and must be delivered, if only they will have
faith in Amitabha's vow and call upon his name. This they do
through the nembutsu, the formula "Hail to Amitabha Buddha" (in Japanese *Namu Amida Butsu*). Invocation of this formula in selfless reliance on the vow is, for the Pure Land devotee, his constant means of grace, the sign of his unconditional
surrender to the "other power." To think of effort or merit or
knowledge as "one's own" inevitably implies clinging to a fancied selfhood, disguise this as one will; it violates the first and
last condition of deliverance. Who can speak of self-power
when he lacks the first idea of what self means?

From here, the Pure Land dialectic goes on to say that in the
early days of Buddhism men doubtless were stronger, more
self-reliant; they could take severe disciplines and follow ways
of meditation of the *jiriki* type. But now, thanks to our bad
karma, we are living in the latter days, dark and sin-ridden,
when men have grown weak, confused, and above all, hopelessly passive. Well, then, says the Pure Land teacher, let this
very weakness of theirs be turned to good account; let it offer
itself humbly to Amitabha's grace, yielding before the power
of his vow. If by the force of his vow the righteous can be
delivered, how much more will this be true of sinners whose
need is so much greater! Compare with this the words of Christ:
"I came not to call the righteous, but sinners, to repentance";
in their implications the two statements are not all that
different.

It is of interest to note that in Tibet a method of invocation
exists that is in many ways reminiscent of the nembutsu. It uses
a six-syllable formula of which the mystical associations are too
complex to be discussed in a few words; it is enough to know
that it is called the *Mani mantra* and that its revealer is the

Bodhisattva *Avalokitēsvara* (*Chenrezig* in Tibet) who in the heavenly sangha personifies compassion. For present purposes the significant point to notice is that Chenrezig himself is an emanation of the Western Buddha Amitabha, having taken birth from his head, a mythological feature showing the evident kinship of *mani* and nembutsu. A difference worth noting, moreover, is that whereas Amitabha's mercy, being that of a Buddha, has a "static" quality, the compassion of Chenrezig is "dynamic" as befits a Bodhisattva who, by definition, operates *in the world* as helper of suffering creatures. Every Bodhisattva as such is in fact a living embodiment of the function of grace.

Before concluding this essay I cannot forebear from pointing ut a case of what may be called "spiritual coincidence," as between two widely separated traditions, the Buddhist and the Islamic; this coincidence is attributable neither to borrowing nor to any cause of a haphazard kind but stems from the very nature of things.

The opening line of the Koran is *Bismi 'Lāhi'r-Rahmāni'r-Rahīm*, which has usually been translated as "In the Name of God, the Compassionate, the Merciful"; in Arabic a common root renders the connection between these two names still closer. Now, some well-instructed Muslim friends have explained to me that the difference between the above names consists herein, namely that *Ar-Rahman* refers to God's mercy as an intrinsic quality of the Divine Being whereas *Ar-Rahim* refers to that quality as projected into the creation. It expresses the dynamic aspect of mercy, mercy poured forth and reaching creatures in the form of grace, from which it would appear that a more apt translation would have been "In the Name of God the Merciful, the Compassionate," since compassion always has a dynamic quality—it must find an object for its exercise. It is easy to see that these two names respectively correspond, in all essentials, to Amitabha and Chenrezig: a shining confirmation from an unexpected quarter!

But let not this surprise us unduly; for in the Pure Land of Enlightenment is it not true to say that all ways will most certainly meet?

Symbolic Truth

The Language of the Birds

BY RENÉ GUÉNON

> *Waṣṣaffāte saffan*
> *Faz-zajirāti zajran*
> *Fat-tāliyati dhikran*
> (By those who are ranged in ranks,
> Who repel and rout,
> And who recite the invocation)

THERE IS often mention, in different traditions, of a mysterious language called the language of the birds. The expression is clearly a symbolic one, since the very importance that is attached to the knowledge of the language—it is considered to be the prerogative of a high initiation—precludes a literal interpretation. The Koran, for example, says, "And Solomon was David's heir and he said, 'O men, we have been taught the language of the birds *['ullimnā manṭiq aṭ-ṭayr]* and all favors have been showered upon us' " (27:15). Elsewhere we read of heroes, like Siegfried in the Nordic legend, who understand this language of the birds as soon as they have overcome the dragon, and the symbolism in question may be easily understood from this. Victory over the dragon has, as its immediate consequence, the conquest of immortality, which is represented by some object, the approach to which is barred by the dragon, and the conquest of immortality implies, essentially, reintegration at the center of the human state, that is, at the point where communication is established with the higher states of being. It is this communication that is represented by the understanding of the language of the birds, and, in fact, birds are often taken to symbolize the angels, who precisely stand for the higher states of being. That is the significance, in the Gospel parable of the grain of mustard seed, of "the birds of the air" that came to lodge in the branches of the tree—the tree that represents the axis that passes through the center of each state of being and connects all the states with each other.[1]

In the Koranic text given above the term *aṣ-ṣāffāt* literally designates the birds but symbolically refers to the angels *(al-malā'ikah)*, and thus the first line signifies the constitution of the celestial and spiritual hierarchies.[2] The second line denotes the struggle of the angels against the demons, the celestial powers against the internal ones, that is, the opposition between the higher and the lower states.[3] In the Hindu tradition this is the struggle of the devas against the asuras and also, according to a symbolism that comes very close to the symbolism of our theme, the fight of Garuda against the Naga which is, moreover, none other than the above-mentioned serpent or dragon. Garuda is the eagle, and elsewhere his place is taken by other birds such as the ibis, the stork, or the heron,[4] all

---

[1] In the medieval symbol of the *Peridexion* (a corruption of *Paradision*) one sees birds on the branches of a tree and a dragon at its foot (see my *The Symbolism of the Cross*, Chap. 9). In a study of the symbolism of "the birds of Paradise" Charbonneau-Lassay has reproduced an illustration of a piece of sculpture in which the bird is shown with only a head and wings, a form in which angels are often represented.

[2] The word *saff*, "rank," is one of the many that have been suggested as the origin of the word *ṣufi* and *taṣawwuf* (Sufism). Although this derivation does not seem to be acceptable from the purely linguistic point of view, it is nonetheless true that, like many other derivations of the same kind, it does represent one of the ideas actually contained in these two terms, for the "spiritual hierarchies" are essentially identical with the degrees of initiation.

[3] This opposition exists in all beings in the form of the two tendencies, one upward and the other downward, called *sattva* and *tamas* in the Hindu tradition. It is also what is symbolized in Mazdeism by the antagonism between light and darkness, personified by Ormuzd and Ahriman.

[4] See, in this connection, the remarkable works of Charbonneau-Lassay on the animal symbols of Christ (in *Le Bestiaire du Christ*). It is necessary to point out that the symbolic opposition between the bird and the serpent exists only as long as the serpent is seen in its malefic aspect. In its benefic aspect it is sometimes united with the bird as in the figure of Quetzalcohuatl in the ancient American tradition. On the other hand the combat between the eagle and the serpent is also mentioned in Mexican myths. In connection with the benefic aspect we may recall the biblical text "Be ye therefore as wise as serpents and harmless as doves" (Matt. 10:16).

enemies and destroyers of reptiles. Finally, in the third verse, the angels recite the dhikr, which normally means the recitation of the Koran—not, needless to say, the Koran expressed in human language but its eternal prototype inscribed on the Guarded Tablet *(al-lawḥ al-maḥfūz)*, which stretches from heaven to earth like Jacob's Ladder throughout all the degrees of universal existence.[5] Similarly, in the Hindu tradition, it is said that the devas in their struggle against the asuras protected themselves *(acchandayan)* by reciting Vedic hymns, which, for this reason, were given the name of *chandas*, a word that denotes rhythm. The same idea is contained in the word "dhikr," which, in Islamic esoterism, is used of the rhythmic formulas that correspond exactly to Hindu mantras. The repetition of these formulas is intended to bring about the harmonization of the different elements of the being and to cause vibrations that, by their repercussions throughout the whole hierarchy of the states, are capable of opening up a communication with the higher states. This is, moreover, generally speaking, the essential and primordial purpose of all rites.

This brings us back directly to what was said at the outset about "the language of the birds," which can also be called "angelic language" and which is symbolized in the human world by rhythmic language, for the science of rhythm, which has many applications, is in fact ultimately the basis of all the means that can be brought into action in order to enter into communication with the higher states of being. This is why it is said in an Islamic tradition that Adam, while in the earthly paradise, spoke in verse, that is, in rhythmic language. It is also why the Sacred Books are written in rhythmic language, which clearly makes them something altogether different from the mere "poems" (in the purely profane sense) that the antitraditional prejudice of the "critics" would have them to be; nor was poetry itself, in its origins, the vain literature it has now become as a result of the degeneration that is part of the down-

[5] As regards the symbolism of the book, with which this is directly connected, see *The Symbolism of the Cross*, Chap. 14.

ward march of the human cycle.[6] It had on the contrary a truly
sacred character. Examples can be found as far back as classical
Western antiquity, of poetry being called the "language of the
Gods," an expression equivalent to that we have already used
since the "Gods," that is, the devas,[7] represent, like the angels,
the higher states of being. In Latin, verses were called *carmina*,
a name connected with their use in the accomplishment of rites,
for the word *carmen* is identical with the Sanskrit *karma*, which
must be understood here in its special sense of "ritual action."[8]
The poet himself, the interpreter of the "sacred language,"
which is like a transparent veil over the divine word, was *vates*,
a word that implies a certain degree of the prophetic inspiration. Later, by a further degeneration,[9] the *vates* became no
more than a common "diviner,"[10] and *carmen* (whence the word
"charm") no more than a "spell," that is, something brought
about by low magic. We have here yet another illustration of

[6] One can say, in a general way, that art and science have become
profane by a similar degeneration which has stripped them of their
traditional character and consequently of everything that has a higher
meaning. This subject has been discussed at length in *L'Esotérisme de
Dante*, Chap. 2; *The Crisis of the Modern World*, Chap. 4; and *The Reign
of Quantity and the Signs of the Times*, Chap. VIII.
[7] The Sanskrit *deva* and the Latin *deus* are one and the same word.
[8] The word "poetry" is derived from the Greek word *poiein* which has
the same meaning as the Sanskrit root *kri* from which *karma* stems and
which is to be found in the Latin verb *creare* understood according to
its primal significance. The idea in question was thus originally quite
different from the mere production of artistic or literary works in the
profane sense that Aristotle seems to have had exclusively in mind
when speaking of what he called "poetic sciences."
[9] The first degeneration was the isolation of the *vates* from the general-
ity, that is, his becoming an exception rather than a norm (translator's
note).
[10] The word "diviner" itself has deviated just as much in meaning, for
etymologically it is no less than *divinus*, that is, "the interpreter of the
Gods." The "auspices" (from *aves spicere*, meaning to "observe the
birds"), omens drawn from the flight and song of birds, are more
particularly related to the "language of the birds" understood here in
the literal sense but nonetheless identified with the "language of the
Gods," since the Gods were held to make known their will through
these omens. The birds thus played the part of messengers analogous
(but on a very much lower plane) to the part that is generally attributed
to the angels (hence their name, since "messenger" is precisely the
meaning of the Greek *angelos*).

the fact that magic—we might even say sorcery—is the last thing to be left behind when traditions disappear.

These few indications should be enough to show how inept it is to make fun of stories that speak of the "language of the birds." It is all too easy and too simple to disdain as "superstitions" everything one cannot understand; but the ancients themselves knew very well what they meant when they used symbolic language. The true superstition in the strictly etymological sense *(quod superstat)* is what outlives itself, that is, the "dead letter"; but this very survival, however lacking in interest it may seem, is nonetheless not so totally insignificant, for the Spirit that "bloweth where it listeth" (and when it listeth) can always come to breathe fresh life into the symbols and the rites and give them back their lost meaning and the fullness of their original virtue.

Perennial Values in Islamic Art

BY TITUS BURCKHARDT

MUCH HAS BEEN written about the formation of Islamic art from preexisting elements, of Byzantine, Persian, Hindu, and Mongolian origin. But very little has been said about the nature of the power that wrought all those various elements into a unique synthesis. Nobody will deny the unity of Islamic art, either in time or in space; it is far too evident. Whether one contemplates the mosque of Córdoba or the great madrasah of Samarkand, whether it be the tomb of a saint in the Maghrib or one in Chinese Turkestan, it is as if one and the same light shone forth from all these works of art. What then is the nature of this unity? The religious law of Islam does not prescribe any particular forms of art; it merely restricts the field of their expression, and restrictions are not creative in themselves. On the other hand, it is misleading, to say the least, if one simply attributes this unity to "religious feeling," as one often does. However intense an emotion may be, it will never be able to shape a whole world of forms into a harmony that is at the same time rich and sober, overwhelming and precise. It is not by chance that the unity and regularity of Islamic art reminds us of the law working in crystals. There is something that evidently surpasses the mere power of emotion, which is necessarily vague and always fluctuating. We shall call it the "intellectual vision" inherent in Islamic art, taking "intellect" in its original meaning as a faculty far more comprehensive than reason or thought, a faculty involving the intuition of timeless realities. This is also the meaning of al-'aql in Islamic tradition. Faith is not complete unless it be illuminated by al-'aql which alone grasps the implications of at-tawḥīd, the doctrine of divine unity. In a similar way, Islamic art derives its beauty from wisdom.

The history of art, being a modern science, inevitably approaches Islamic art in the purely analytical way of all modern sciences, by dissection and reduction to historical circumstances. Whatever is timeless in an art—and sacred art like that of Islam always contains a timeless element—will be left out by such a method. One may object that all art is composed of forms and since form is limited, that it is necessarily subject to time; like all historical phenomena, forms rise, develop, become corrupted, and die; therefore, the science of art is of necessity a historical science. But this is only one half of the truth: A form, though limited and consequently subject to time, may convey something timeless and in this respect escape historical conditions, not only in its genesis—which partly belongs to a spiritual dimension—but also in its preservation, to a certain extent at least, for it is with regard to their timeless meaning that certain forms have been preserved in spite of and against all material and psychic revolutions of an epoch; tradition means just that.

On the other hand, the modern history of art has derived most of its aesthetic criteria from classical Greek or from postmedieval art. Whatever its more recent evolution has been, it has always considered the individual as the real creator of art. In this view, a work is "artistic" insofar as it shows the stamp of an individuality. Now, from an Islamic point of view, beauty is essentially an expression of universal truth.

Thus it is not astonishing that modern science, in studying Islamic art, often stops short at a negative judgment. We find such negative judgments in many if not in most of the learned works on Islamic art; they are more or less the same, though different in degree. One often reads that Islamic art was creative only at its first stage, while integrating and transforming earlier legacies, and that later on it congealed more and more into sterile formulas. These formulas, we further learn, have not quite canceled the ethnic differences of the peoples of Islam, but they have unfortunately suffocated the individual initiative of the artist. This happened all the more easily—so it seems—as Islamic art was deprived of a most vital and profound dimension through the religious interdiction of images. We have quoted all these judgments in their most acute form, well knowing that few European scholars would subscribe to all of them. Yet it is good to look these judgments in the face, for they will help us by their very limitation to point out the view that really corresponds to the nature of Islamic art.

Let us first consider the last of the aforementioned reproaches, that which concerns the religious interdiction of images. This interdiction is twofold. On the one hand, there is the Koranic condemnation of idolatry which from the general Muslim point of view involves all visual representation of God in any form, the nature of God being beyond all description, even in words. On the other hand, there are the sayings of the Prophet according to which wanting to imitate the Creator's work by imitating the form of living beings and particularly the form of man is irreverent and even blasphemous. This last injunction has not always and everywhere been strictly observed, since it concerns more the intention than the deed. In the Persian and Indian world especially, it was argued that an image that does not claim to imitate the real being but is no more than an allusion to it, is allowed. This is one of the reasons for the nonillusive style of Persian miniatures, the absence of shadows and perspective in them. However, no mosque has ever been decorated with anthropomorphic images.

If we consider things superficially, we may be tempted to liken the Islamic point of view to that of Puritanism which ignores symbolism and therefore rejects all sacred art as a lie. Symbolism is based on the analogy between the different degrees of being. As Being is one *(al-wujūdu wāḥid)*, everything that *is* or exists must in some way reflect its eternal source. Islam by no means ignores this law, which the Koran proclaims in a thousand metaphors: *Wa in min shay'in illa yusabbiḥu biḥamdiḥ* (There is nothing that does not exalt His praise; Koran 17:44). It is not by disregard for the sacred character of creation that Islam proscribes human images; on the contrary, it is because man is the vicegerent *(khalīfah)* of God on earth, as the Koran teaches. The Prophet explained that God created Adam "in His form" *('alā ṣuratiḥ)*, "form," in this case, meaning qualitative likeness, for man is gifted with faculties that reflect the seven "personal" qualities of God, namely, life, knowledge, will, power, hearing, seeing, and speech.

A comparison between the Islamic and the Christian attitudes toward the image of man will aid us to outline things more exactly. In response to the Byzantine iconoclasm, more or less influenced by the Islamic example, the seventh ecumenical council justified the use of icons in liturgy with the following argument: God is indescribable in Himself, but since the divine Logos assumed human nature, he reintegrated it into its original form and penetrated it with divine beauty. In representing the human form of Christ, art reminds us of the mystery of incarnation. No doubt there is a sharp distinction between this point of view and that of Islam, but nevertheless both refer to a common basis, namely the theomorphic character of man.

Here it is worth mentioning that one of the deepest explanations of the Christian attitude toward sacred art has been given by the famous sufi Muhyi-d-din ibn-Arabi, *ash-shaikh al-akbar*, who writes in his *Al-futūḥāt al-makkiyyah*: "The Byzantines developed the art of painting to perfection, because for them the unique nature *[fardāniyyah]* of Sayyidnā ʿIsā as expressed in his image, is the foremost support of concentration on Divine Unity." As this witness proves, the symbolic role of an image is not in itself unintelligible to contemplative Muslims, although, in obedience to the Koranic law, they will always reject the use of sacred images, thus giving precedence to *tanzīh* (incomparability) over *tashbīh* (analogy). In a way, the first of the two "aspects"—that of divine incomparability or transcendence—even absorbs the theomorphic character of man. In fact, the seven universal qualities that constitute the divine "form" of Adam—life, knowledge, will, power, hearing, seeing, and speech—all escape visual representation. An image has neither life nor knowledge nor power nor any of these qualities; it reduces man to his corporeal limits. Although limited in man, the seven qualities are potential bearers of a divine presence, according to the *ḥadīth qudsī*: ". . . I shall be the ear by which he hears, the eye by which he sees," and so on. There is something in man that no natural means of expression may render. The Koran says (33:72): "We offered the trust *[amānah]* unto the heavens and the earth and the hills, but they shrank from bearing it and were afraid of it. And man assumed it." This trust is merely potential in ordinary man; it is actual in perfect man, in messengers *(rusul)*, prophets *(anbiyā)*, and saints *(awliyā);* in them, it even overflows from the interior to the exterior, shining forth in their whole corporeal appearance. Fearing to offend this divine trust in man, Islamic art always shrinks from depicting the messengers, prophets, and saints.

Instead of "Islamic iconoclasm," we prefer to say "Islamic aniconism," for the absence of icons in Islam has not merely a negative but a positive role. In excluding all anthropomorphic images, at least within religious precincts, Islamic art aids man to be entirely himself; instead of projecting his soul outside of himself, he will rest in his ontological center where he is at once the vicegerent *(khalifah)* and the slave *('abd)* of God. Islamic art as a whole aims at creating an ambience that helps man to realize his primordial dignity; it therefore avoids everything that could be an "idol," even in quite a relative and provisional degree. Nothing shall stand between man and the invisible presence of God.

Thus Islamic art creates a void; in fact, it eliminates all the turmoil and passionate suggestions of the world and builds in their stead an order expressing equilibrium, serenity, and peace. From this, one will immediately understand how central the position of architecture is in Islam. Although the Prophet said that God favored his community by giving it the whole surface of the earth as a place of prayer, it is architecture that, in populated regions, has to reestablish the conditions of purity and calm elsewhere granted by nature. As for the beauty of virgin nature, which is like the imprint of the Creator's hand, it is realized by architecture on another level, nearer to human intelligence and therefore more limited, in a way, but nonetheless free from the arbitrary rule of individual passions.

In a mosque the believer is never a mere visitor; he is, so to say, at home, though not in the ordinary sense of the word. When he has purified himself by ritual ablution, being thereby freed from accidental alterations, and then recites the revealed words of the Koran, he symbolically returns to the "station" of Adam, which is in the center of the world. According to this, all Muslim architects endeavored to create a space entirely resting in itself and showing everywhere, in each of its "stations," the plenitude of spatial qualities. They reached this aim by means as different as the horizontal hall with pillars, like the ancient mosque of Medina or the concentric domes of Turkey. In none of these interiors do we feel drawn in any particular direction, either forward or upward; nor are we oppressed by their spatial limits. It has rightly been remarked that the architecture of a mosque excludes all tension between heaven and earth.

A Christian basilica is essentially a way leading from the outside world to the main altar. A Christian dome ascends to heaven or descends to the altar. The whole architecture of a church reminds the believer that the divine presence emanates from the Eucharist on the altar as a light shining in the darkness. The mosque has no liturgical center; its mihrab merely indicates the direction of Mecca, while its whole order of space is made to suggest a presence that encompasses the believer on all sides.

It is most revealing to see how the great Turkish architect Sinan, adopting the constructive scheme of Hagia Sophia, developed it according to Islamic vision until he reached the perfect order of the Selimiye Mosque in Edirne; the huge cupola of Hagia Sophia is supported by two half cupolas and extended by several small apses. The whole interior space is elongated in the sense of the liturgical axis, its different parts melting into each other in a kind of indefinite immensity. Sinan built the main cupola at Edirne on an octagon supported by straight walls on the cardinal sides and by vaulted apses on the four diagonal sides, creating a kind of clearly cut jewel, the contours of which are neither fluctuating nor narrow.

When Muslim architects took over and enlarged some Christian basilicas, they often changed the interior plan so that what had been its length became its width. Frequently—and even besides such transformations—the arcades in a mosque run across the main space. They do not "progress" in a certain direction like the arcades framing the nave of a cathedral; they rather stem the movement of the space without interrupting it, thus inviting one to rest.

Muslim architects spent much attention and love on the form of arcades. No wonder that the Arab name for arcades—*rawq* or *riwāq*—is almost synonymous with beautiful, graceful, and pure. European art knows mainly two forms of the arch: the Roman arch, which is plain, rational, and static, and the so-called Gothic arch—indirectly derived from Islamic art—with its ascending movement. Islamic art developed a great variety of arch forms, of which two are most typical: the Persian arch in the shape of a ship's keel and the Moorish arch in the shape of a horseshoe with a more or less accentuated point. Both arches combine the two qualities mentioned above, namely static calm and lightness. The Persian arch is generous and gracious at the same time; it ascends without effort like the calm flame of an oil lamp protected from the wind. As for the Moorish arch, its extreme width is balanced by the rectangular frame: a synthesis of stability and amplitude. There is in it a breathing without movement; it is the image of a space expanding inwardly by an overabundance of beatitude. In the words of the Koran (94:1): *"A lam nashraḥ laka ṣadrak"* ("Did we not widen your breast?").

A simple arcade, built according to right measure, has the virtue of transforming space from a purely quantitative reality into one that is qualitative. Qualitative space is no longer mere extension; it is experienced as a state of being *(wajd)*. Thus traditional architecture favors contemplation.

Between the architecture of a mosque and that of a private Muslim house, there is a difference in plan but not in style, for each Muslim dwelling is a place of prayer: The same rites are celebrated here as there. In general, Islamic life is not separated into a sacred and profane domain, just as the community is not divided into consecrated clergy and laymen: Each Muslim with a sound mind and morality can act as imam. This unity of life manifests itself by the homogeneousness of its frame; whether it be the interior of a mosque or that of a private house, its law is equilibrium, calm, and purity. Its decoration must never contradict the idea of poverty. In fact, ornament in Islamic architecture, in its rhythm and regularity, helps to create a void by dissolving the raw body of wall and pillars and thus enhancing the effect of the great white surfaces so characteristic of Muslim interiors.

The floor of a traditional Muslim dwelling, like the floor of a mosque, is never trodden on with shoes, nor are the rooms filled with furniture.

Much of the unity of Islamic life is lost when the clothes worn in everyday life are no longer adapted to the prescribed rites. Costume, indeed, is part of the frame that Islamic art created for Islam, and the art of dressing is not the least of Islamic arts; as the Koran commands explicitly (7:31): "O sons of Adam, take your ornament whenever you approach a mosque." The traditional masculine costume shows many variations, but it always expresses the role that Islam endows man with—that is, to be the vicegerent and the slave of God. Therefore, it is at the same time dignified and sober; we might even say majestic and poor. It veils the animal nature of man, enhances his features, dignifies his gestures, and makes easy the different postures of ritual prayer. Modern European costume, on the contrary, although it claims to free man from his servitude (*'ubūdiyyah*), in fact denies his primordial dignity.

We have seen that the exclusion of images from Islamic art— more severe in Sunnite than in Shi'ite countries—has a positive meaning, even on the level of art, as it restores to man the dignity that elsewhere is, so to speak, usurped by his image. The immobility with which Islamic art is reproached is in a certain sense connected with the absence of images, for it is by making images of himself that man changes. He projects his soul into the ideal he shaped, thus influencing himself until he is driven to change the image he made of himself, which in its turn will awaken his reaction, and so on, in a chain without end, as we can observe in European art since the so-called Renaissance, that is, since the purely symbolical role of the image was forgotten. Sacred art is normally protected by its traditional rules from falling into that torrent of change. However, the use of anthropomorphic images is always fragile, for man is inclined to transfer his own psychic limitations to the image he shapes, in spite of all canonical prescriptions, and then sooner or later he rebels against it, not only against the image but also against what it stands for. Those epidemic outbursts of blasphemy that marked certain epochs of European history are not conceivable without the existence and actual decay of anthropomorphic religious art. Islam cuts this whole problem at its root. In this respect as well as in others it manifests itself as the last of religions, one that takes heed of the weakness of present-day man and reveals itself as a return to primordial religion. The criticized "immobility" of Islamic art is simply the absence in it of all subjective motives; it is an art that is unconcerned with psychological problems and retains only those elements that are valuable at all times.

This is the reason for the extraordinary development of geometrical ornament in Islamic art. Attempts have been made to explain this development by the fact that the prohibition of images created a void to be filled by another kind of art. But this is not conclusive. The arabesque is no compensation for images; it is rather their opposite and the very negation of figurative art. By transforming a surface into a tissue of colors or into a vibration of light and shadows, the ornament hinders the mind from fixing itself on any particular form saying "I," as an image says "I." The center of an arabesque is everywhere and nowhere; each "affirmation" is followed by its "negation" and vice versa.

There are two typical forms of the arabesque. One of them is geometrical interlacing made up of a multitude of geometrical stars, the rays of which join into an intricate and endless pattern. It is a most striking symbol of that contemplative state of mind that conceives "unity in multiplicity and multiplicity in unity" *(al-waḥdatu fil-kathrati wa-l-kathratu fil-waḥdah)*.

The arabesque commonly so called is made up of vegetable motives, stylized to the point of losing all resemblance with nature and obeying only the laws of rhythm. It is a real graphic of rhythms, each line undulating in complementary phases and each surface having its inverse counterpart. The arabesque is at the same time logical and rhythmic, mathematical and melodious, and this is most significant for the spirit of Islam in its equilibrium of love and intellectual sobriety.

In such an art the individuality of the artist necessarily disappears, without his creative joy being abated; it is simply less passionate and more contemplative. Suppression of all creative joy is the privilege of modern industry alone. As for traditional art, be it even at the level of mere handicraft, its beauty proves the profound pleasure involved in it.

Moreover, the universal character of geometrical ornament—the fundamental elements of which are essentially the same, whether they appear in a bedouin rug or in a refined urban decoration—corresponds perfectly to the universal nature of Islam, uniting the nomads of the desert to the scholars of the city and this late epoch of ours to the times of Abraham.

By what we have said up to this point, we have implicitly answered the critics of Islamic art mentioned at the outset. We have still to say what the notion of art means in Islamic thought. From this point of view, art can never be dissociated either from a craft *(ṣan'ah)*, as its material foundation, or from a science *('ilm)* regularly transmitted. Art *(fann)* in its specific meaning partakes of both craft and science. The latter moreover has to be not only a rational instruction but also the expression of a wisdom *(ḥikmah)* that links things to their universal principles.

The Prophet said: "God prescribed that everything should be accomplished to perfection" (we might also translate, "in beauty"; *inna-Llāha kataba-l-iḥsāna 'alā kulli shay*). The perfection or the beauty of a thing lies in its praising God; in other words, it is perfect or beautiful insofar as it reflects a divine quality. Now, we cannot realize perfection in anything unless we know how that thing can be a mirror of God.

Taking architecture as an example, we see that its material foundation is the mason's craft while the science involved in it is geometry. In traditional architecture, geometry is not limited to its more or less quantitative aspects, as in modern engineering, for instance; it has also a qualitative aspect, which manifests itself in the laws of proportion by which a building acquires its almost inimitable unity. The laws of proportion are traditionally based on the division of the circle by inscribed regular figures. Thus all measures of a building are ultimately derived from the circle, which is an evident symbol of the unity of being containing in itself all possibilities of existence. How many cupolas there are with polygonal bases and how many vaults composed of alveolar squinches that remind us of this symbolism!

Considering the internal hierarchy of art, built on craft, science, and contemplative wisdom, it is easy to understand that a traditional art may be destroyed either from the top or from the bottom. Christian art has been corrupted by the loss of its spiritual principles; Islamic art gradually disappears because of the destruction of the traditional crafts.

We have mainly spoken about architecture, with regard to its central role in the Islamic world. Ibn Khaldun, indeed, relates to it most of the minor arts, such as carpentry, joinery, sculpture in wood or stucco, mosaic in earthenware, decorative painting, and even carpet-making, so characteristic of the Islamic world. Even calligraphy can be related to architecture in the form of decorative inscriptions. In itself, however, Arabic calligraphy is not a minor art; since it is used for the writing of the Koran, it occupies the highest rank among all Islamic arts.

It would lead us too far to display the whole fan of Islamic arts. Let it suffice to consider two extreme poles of visual art: architecture and calligraphy. The first of these is the art that is the most conditioned by material circumstances, whereas the second is the freest of all arts in this respect. It is nonetheless dominated by severe rules with regard to the distinctive forms of the letters, proportions, continuity of rhythm, and choice of style. On the other hand, possible combinations of letters are nearly unlimited, and styles vary from the rectilinear Kufic to the most fluid Neskhi. The synthesis of utmost regularity and utmost liberty lends Arabic calligraphy its royal character. In no other visual art does the spirit of Islam breathe more openly.

The frequency of Koranic inscriptions on the walls of

mosques and other buildings reminds us of the fact that the whole of Islamic life is interwoven with quotations from the Koran and spiritually supported by its recitation as well as by prayers, litanies, and invocations drawn from it. If we are allowed to call the influence emanating from the Koran a spiritual vibration—and we find no better word for it, since that influence is at the same time of a spiritual and of an auditive nature—we may well say that all Islamic art must bear the imprint of that vibration. Thus visual Islamic art is but the visual reflection of the Koranic word; it cannot be otherwise. However, there is a paradox, for if we look for Koranic models of art, we cannot find them, either in the contents of the Koran or in its form. On the one hand, except in certain Persian miniatures, Islamic art does not reflect the stories and parables contained in the Koran, as Christian art, for instance, depicts the episodes of both testaments, nor is there any cosmology in the Koran, which could be translated into architectural schemes, as Vedic cosmology finds its expression in Hindu architecture. On the other hand, it is in vain to search in the Koran for something like a principle of composition that might be transposed into any art. The Koran is of a startling discontinuity; it shows no logical order nor any interior architecture. Even its rhythm, powerful as it is, obeys no constant rule, whereas Islamic art is all made of order, clarity, hierarchy, crystalline form. In fact, the vital link between the Koranic word and visual Islamic art must not be sought for on the level of formal expression. The Koran is no work of art but something entirely different, notwithstanding the overwhelming beauty of many of its passages, nor does Islamic art derive from its literal meaning or its form, but from its *ḥaqīqah*, its nonformal essence.

At its beginning Islam had no need for art, no religion cares for art when it first enters the world. The need for a protective frame made up of visual and auditive forms comes later, just like the need for extensive commentaries of the revealed book, although every genuine expression of a religion is already included as a latent possibility in its original manifestation.

Islamic art is fundamentally derived from *tawḥīd*—that is, from an assent to or contemplation of divine unity. The essence of *at-tawḥīd* is beyond words; it reveals itself in the Koran by sudden and discontinuous flashes. Striking the plane of visual imagination, these flashes congeal into crystalline forms, and it is these forms in their turn that constitute the essence of Islamic art.

Arab or Islamic Art?

The Impact of the Arabic Language on the Visual Arts

BY TITUS BURCKHARDT

THE EXPRESSION "Arab art" is commonly employed to designate Islamic art; however, the legitimacy of this term has often been contested with the aid of arguments that are seemingly plausible but that in reality are vitiated by a superficial or even prejudiced view of things. The question to be asked first of all is the following: What is it that characterizes the Arab genius, and how may this be discerned in art? The only arts possessed by the pre-Islamic Arabs, who were mostly nomads living at the crossroads of several civilizations, were a rectilinear architecture and the various kinds of crafts—which, incidentally, it would be wrong to underestimate, and whose influence was later to become very great. Be that as it may, the predominant and most striking expression of the Arab genius is the language, including its script. The Arabs bequeathed their language to the whole civilization of Islam, and it not only was the means of preserving the Arabs' heritage outside Arabia but even caused this to bloom at a far remove from its own racial source. By the intermediary of this language, every essential of the Arab genius was effectively communicated to the whole of Islamic civilization.

The extraordinary normative power of the Arab language derives both from its role as a sacred language and from its archaic character, these two things, moreoever, being connected. It was its archaism that predestined Arabic to the role of a sacred language, and it was the Koranic revelation that in a sense actualized its primordial substance. In the linguistic realm, archaism is by no means synonymous with structural simplicity; quite the reverse. Languages are generally impoverished with time; they lose both the hierarchical differentiation of meanings and the logical concision of forms, while becoming complicated on the plane of rhetoric, in order to compensate this impoverishment. What surprises historians of language is that Arabic has been able to preserve a morphology already exemplified by Hammurabi's code in the nineteenth or eighteenth century B.C.[1] and a phonetic system that perpetuates, apart from one single sound, the very rich sound range borne witness to by the most ancient Semitic alphabets discovered,[2] and that it has done so despite the absence of any "literary tradition" that might have acted as a bridge between this remote age of the patriarchs and the time when the Koranic revelation was to fix the language forever. The explanation of this perenniality of Arabic resides precisely in the conservative role of nomadism. It is in the towns that language decays, by the very fact that it becomes attached to things and institutions and undergoes their fate. The well-nigh timeless life of the nomad, on the contrary, protects the language and permits it to bloom in all its fullness. The portion of primordial symbolism that fell to the lot of the nomads was the art of speech, which is not bound to place and whose dynamic character corresponds to that of nomadic life itself, whereas the sedentary peoples developed the plastic arts, which require stability and which in their symbolism are connected, quite naturally, to the idea of a center in space.[3] It can thus be stated, in general terms, that the Arabic language guarantees the survival, on the mental plane, of a primitive Semitism, nomadic in character.

To explain in a few words, and without the need of any special linguistic knowledge, what is the specific nature of this

---

[1] *Cf.* Edouard Dhorme, "L'arabe Littéral et la Langue de Hammourabi," in *Mélanges Louis Massignon* (Damascus, 1957).

[2] The most ancient Semitic alphabets comprise twenty-nine sounds or letters, of which Arabic has preserved twenty-eight, the "lost" sound being a variant of *s.* It may be that the reduction of the alphabet to twenty-eight letters reflects a symbolic intention, since some Arab authors consider that the sounds correspond to the twenty-eight lunar mansions; the phonetic cycle ranging from the gutturals to the palatals, dentals, and labials retraces the "lunar" phases of the primordial sound emanating from the sun.

[3] As René Guénon has pointed out. See Chapter XXI, "Cain and Abel," in *The Reign of Quantity and the Signs of the Times* (Baltimore, Md.: Penguin Books Inc, 1972).

language, it should be recalled firstly that every language comprises two roots or poles, one or the other of which will predominate, and which may be designated by the terms "auditive intuition" and "imaginative intuition." The first is normally manifested by the fact that a given word is derived from a simple combination of sounds that, as such, expresses a typical event or more exactly, a fundamental action. It does this in a more or less immediate manner, not by means of onomatopoeia, but because the sound itself is an event that unfolds in time, so that it corresponds a priori, and independently of all semantic conventions, to action. Speech is essentially act, and according to this logic, the language fundamentally conceives everything that it names as an action or an object of action. Imaginative intuition, on the other hand, is manifested in language by means of the semantic association of analogous images. Every word pronounced inwardly evokes a corresponding image, which calls forth others, general images dominating more particular images, according to a hierarchy that in turn is inherent in the structure of the language. The Latin languages belong mainly to this latter type, whereas Arabic displays an almost pure auditive intuition or phonetic logic, the identity of sound and act, as well as the primacy of action, being affirmed throughout the rich tissue of this language. In principle, every Arabic word is derived from a verb whose root, consisting of three invariable sounds, is like the sonorous ideogram of a fundamental act such as "gathering together," "dividing," "including," "penetrating," with the full physical, psychical, and spiritual polyvalence of the idea in question. From one single root, up to twelve different verbal modes are developed—simple, causative, intensive, reciprocal, and so on—and each of these modes produces, by the polarization of the active and the passive, of the subject and the object, a whole pleiad of substantives and adjectives, whose meaning is always connected, in a more or less direct manner, with the fundamental act represented by the triliteral[4] root of the whole verbal "tree."

[4] There are in fact verbs composed of four or five root sounds, but in these cases groups of consonants such as *ts* or *br* play the role of simple sounds.

It is obvious that this semantic transparency of the language, the fact that, in its symbolism, it derives entirely from the phonetic nature of the verb, is a proof of its relative primordiality. In the origin, and in the very depth of our consciousness, things are spontaneously conceived as determinations of the primordial sound that resounds in the heart, this sound being none other than the first and nonindividualized act of consciousness. At this level or in this state, "to name" a thing is to identify oneself with the act or the sound that produces it.[5] The symbolism inherent in language—more or less veiled or deformed by acquired habits—grasps the nature of a thing not in a static manner, as one grasps an image, but, so to speak, *in statu nascendi*, in the act of becoming. This aspect of language in general and of the Arabic language in particular is, moreover, in the Muslim world, the object of a whole group of sciences, some philosophical, others esoteric. It may be said that Muslim scholars not only have preserved this structure of Arabic but have even contributed to rendering it explicit.

In order to understand how Arabic, which is of bedouin origin, could become, with almost no borrowings, the language of a civilization that was intellectually very rich and differentiated, it is necessary to know that its verbal roots are capable of expressing, in an "active" manner, determinations that the Indo-European languages generally express by an adjective associated with the verb "to be." The root *bṭn*, for example, comprises the meaning of "being inside," and the root *zhr* that of "being outside"; the verbal root *rḥm* summarizes all the modes of "being merciful" or "having compassion," etc. The fundamental act that is at the root of a "tree" of expressions is thus not necessarily an action in the ordinary sense of the term; it may be an existential act, like that of light that radiates, or even a purely logical act, such as "being big" or "being small," and it is in this possibility of gathering every manner of being of a thing into a principial act that the great power of abstraction of the Arabic language resides. What we must grasp here, so far as art is concerned, is the implicitly auditive character of

[5] According to the Koran, it was Adam who knew how to "name" all beings, whereas the angels could not do so.

this abstraction. The passage from the particular to the general or principial is a priori indicated by the presence, in a given expression, of root sounds that recall a given prototypal act.

The relationship between prototypal acts and their verbal derivations is, however, not always easy to grasp, because of the sometimes very particular and conventionally fixed meaning of such and such a derived term, and also, above all, because the fundamental ideas expressed by the roots are of an eminently complex nature. An Orientalist went so far as to say that "the structure of the Arabic language would be of an incomparable transparency if the meaning of the verbal roots was not arbitrary"; it is, however, scarcely possible that the basis of a language should be arbitrary. In fact, the verbal roots mark the threshold between discursive thought and a kind of synthetic perception that has its models both in the spirit and in the body; the Arabic language is as though suspended from auditive intuition.[6]

If these data are transposed into the realm of art, with all the reservations that generalizations of this nature presuppose, it can be said that the Arab is a priori an auditive rather than a visual type—that is to say, that he is the former before he is

[6] The phonetic symbolism that underlies the Arabic language shows itself more particularly in the permutation of the root sounds. In fact, according to *al-Jafr*, the science of letters, the words that are formed from the same letters arranged in different orders all spring from the same "Pythagorean number" and therefore from the same idea. This is not easy to grasp, however, owing to the often too particularized use of the words, but it can be sensed in certain cases. The root *rḥm*, for example, means "being merciful," "having pity," whereas its permutation *ḥrm* has the meaning of "forbidding," "making inaccessible," *sacrum facere*. The underlying complementarism is to be seen more clearly in the most simple nouns derived from these two roots: *RaaḤM* means "womb" and by extension "bond of relationship," whereas *ḤaRaM* means "sacred place"; we can divine here the idea of maternity in both its inclusive and its exclusive character. Another example is offered us by the root *rfq*, which has the meaning of "accompanying," "binding," and its permutation *frq*, which means "separating," "dividing" (the Latin *furca* seems to be derived from an analogous root), whereas the group *fqr* means "being poor, needy" (whence the expression *al-faqīru ila-Llah*, "the needy unto God," "the poor in Spirit"); these give us three variants of the theme "polarity": joining (*rfq*), separation (*frq*), and dependence (*fqr*).

the latter.[7] In fact, his need for artistic exteriorization is largely absorbed by the culture of his language, with its fascinating phonetism and its almost unlimited faculty of producing new verbal derivations. Nor is the Arab a contemplative in the ordinary sense of the word, if one means by this the type of man who looks or contemplates rather than acts and who spontaneously reduces perceived forms to prototypal forms that are in principle immutable. The Arab loves to analyze things in view of their intrinsic functions and of the activities reflected in them; this is to say that his mentality is not static, but essentially dynamic. However, since he is nevertheless a contemplative—Islam proves it, and the Arabic language includes this possibility—he finds access to unity by means of rhythm, which is like the refraction of the eternal present in the current of time.

The plastic examples that illustrate these tendencies spring to mind. The arabesque, in particular, with its deployment at once regular and indefinite, is indeed the most direct expression of rhythm in the visual order. It is true that its most perfect forms are not conceivable without the artistic contribution of the nomads of central Asia; nevertheless, it was in an Arab milieu that it had its fullest development. Another typical element of Muslim art, and one whose development goes hand in hand with Arab domination, is the interlacing motif; it appears in all its perfection from the time of the Omayyads, in the form of sculpted lattices in the windows of mosques and palaces (in the Omayyad mosque at Damascus, for example, or in the palace of Khirbet al-Mafjar). To enjoy the geometrical interplay that constitutes the interlacing motif, it is not enough to look at it directly; it is necessary to "read" it by following the course of the forces that cross one another and compensate one another. Interlacing already exists in the pavement mosaics of later antiquity, but in a rudimentary state and deriving from a naturalistic conception devoid of the complexity and the rhythmic precision of the Arab-Muslim interlacing. These examples belong to abstract, not figurative, art, and this likewise

[7] Which obviously does not exclude the existence of pure visual types in the Arab race.

characterizes the Arab genius; contrarily to what is usually believed, the average Arab scarcely possesses a "luxuriant imagination." Insofar as this appears in Arab literature, for example in the stories from *The Thousand and One Nights*, it is non-Arab in origin, being in this case Persian and Indian; only the art of storytelling is Arab. The creative spirit of the Arabs is a priori logical and rhetorical, the rhythmical and incantatory; the richness is in the mental arabesque and not in the profusion of images evoked.

The more or less categorical rejection of images in the art of Islam obviously has its explanation in reasons of a theological order. But it is a fact that the Semitic nomads did not possess a figurative tradition—the pre-Islamic Arabs imported most of their idols—and that for the Arabs images never became a transparent and spontaneous means of expression,[8] as it is for Iranians and Mongols who are Muslim by religion. The reality of the verb eclipsed that of static vision; compared with the word, which is always in act and whose root plunges into the primordiality of sound, a painted or sculpted image appears as a troubling congelation of the spirit. For the pagan Arabs, it pertained to magic.

But the Arabic language is not entirely dominated by the idea of the verb-act; it also comprises a static, or more exactly, a timeless pole, which shows itself in particular in what is called the "nominal sentence," in which the "noun" (subject) and the "predicates" are juxtaposed without a copula. This permits the formulation of a thought in a lapidary fashion and outside any consideration of time. A sentence of this sort is like an equation, but the use of certain prepositions can impress on it an internal logical movement. The most striking example of this kind is the formula constituting the fundamental "testimony" of Islam, *lā ihāha illa 'Llāh* ("There is no divinity apart from God"), a phrase that would be translated literally as "No divinity if not the Divinity"; in Arabic, the symmetry of the

[8] It is not absolutely certain that the miniatures of the "Baghdad school" are attributable to the Arabs; in any case, their style is crude and owes its few positive elements to Byzantine and Asiatic influences.

negations—*lā* and *illā*, "not" and "if not"—is even more apparent. In this formula the static character of the nominal phrase disappears in favor of a purely intellectual action, which corresponds to an integration: "There is no autonomous being apart from the only Being." It is the distinction between the relative and the absolute and the reduction of the first to the second. The Arabic language thus comprises the possibility of condensing a whole doctrine in a brief and concise formula, which will appear like a diamond with sharp edges and reverberating facets. It is true that this possibility of expression is only fully actualized by revelation—it belongs above all to the Koran—but it is nonetheless inherent in the genius of Arabic and is reflected in its fashion in Arabo-Islamic art, for this is not only rhythmical, it is also crystalline.

The concision of the Arabic sentence, while it obviously does not limit the profundity of the meaning, nevertheless does not favor a synthesis at the level of description. Arabic rarely accumulates several conditions or circumstances in a single sentence; it prefers to link together a whole series of short sentences. In this connection, an agglutinating language like Turkish, which is related to the Mongol languages, is less dry and more supple than Arabic; it is clearly superior when it comes to describing a situation or a landscape, which is true also of Persian, which is an Indo-European language close to Gothic. Nevertheless, both of these languages have borrowed not only their theological terminology but also almost all their philosophical and scientific terminology from Arabic.

The extreme opposite of Arabic is a language like Chinese, which is dominated by a static vision of things and which groups the elements of a thought around typical "pictures," as the ideographic character of Chinese script itself indicates.

The Turks are of nomadic origin like the Arabs, but their language connects them to a very different mental type. The Arab is incisive and dynamic in his way of thinking; the Turk, on the other hand, is enveloping and prudent. Within the general framework of Islamic art, the Turkish genius is revealed in a powerful capacity for synthesis, one might almost say by its totalitarian spirit. The Turk possesses a plastic or sculptural gift which the Arab does not have. His works always derive from an inclusive conception; they are as though chiseled out of a single block. The interior of the most ancient Turkish mosques with a cupola recalls the closed space of the yurt, and Turco-Arabic calligraphy reveals a Mongol influence.

As for Persian art, it is distinguished by its sense of hierarchical differentiations. Persian architecture is perfectly articulated, without ever being "functional" in the modern sense of the term. For the Persian, unity is manifested above all by harmony. The Persians, moreover, are "visuals" by nature and by culture, but lyrical visuals, so to speak, their artistic activity being animated by an inward melody. It is commonly said in the East that "Arabic is the language of God, and Persian the language of Paradise," which sums up very well the difference that exists, for example, between a typically Arab architecture, like that of the Maghrib, where the crystalline geometry of the forms proclaims the unitary principle, and Persian architecture with its blue cupolas and floral ornaments.

The Arab architect is not afraid of monotony; he will add pillar after pillar and arcade after arcade and will dominate this repetition only by rhythmical alternation and by the qualitative perfection of each element.

The language of the Koran is everywhere present in the world of Islam. The whole life of the Muslim is constellated with Koranic formulas, as well as prayers, litanies, and invocations in Arabic, whose elements are derived from the sacred Book; innumerable inscriptions bear witness to this. One might say that this ubiquity of the Koran acts as a spiritual vibration—there is no better term to designate an influence that is both spiritual and sonorous in nature—and that this vibration necessarily determines the modes and measures of Muslim art; the plastic art of Islam is thus in a certain manner the reflection of the Koranic word. It is nonetheless very difficult to grasp the principle that unites this art to the Koranic text, not on the narrative plane, which plays no part in the normal plastic art of Islam, but on the plane of formal structures, for the Koran obeys no law of composition, either in the internal relationships of its contents, which are strangely discontinuous, or in its verbal style, which eludes all metrical rules. Its rhythm, although so powerful and so penetrating, follows no fixed measure; it is composed entirely of the unforeseen, sometimes employing a striking rhyme, then suddenly changing its breadth and pace and upsetting cadences in a manner that is as unexpected as it is remarkable. To assert that the Koran is Arabic poetry because it comprises passages in monotonous rhyme, similar to the bedouin *rajaz*, would be an error; but to allege that its monotonies and abrupt discontinuities do not correspond profoundly to the Arab soul would be an error likewise. In reality, the state of inward harmony that the Koran engenders and to which both its consonances and dissonances, both its beauty and its harshness, contribute, is situated on a completely different plane from that reached by art. Perfect poetry—like every perfect work of art—plunges the soul in a certain state of plenitude; the Koran, on the other hand, engenders in whoever hears its words and experiences its sonorous magic both plenitude and poverty at one and the same time. It gives and it takes; it enlarges the soul by lending it wings, then lays it low and strips it bare; it is comforting and purifying at one and the same time, like a storm. Human art can scarcely be said to have this virtue. This amounts to saying that there is no Koranic "style" that can without more ado be transposed into art; but there exists a state of soul that the recitation of the Koran supports and that predisposes to certain formal manifestations while excluding others. The diapason of the Koran always unites intoxicating nostalgia with the greatest sobriety; it is a radiation of the divine sun on the human desert. To a certain extent, the fluid and the flamboyant rhythm of the arabesque and the abstract and crystalline character of architecture correspond to these two poles; they are two elements that constantly recur.

The most profound link, however, between Islamic art and the Koran is of a completely different kind. It resides not in the form of the Koran, but in its *haqīqah*, its supraformal essence, and more particularly in the idea of *tawḥīd* (unity or union), with its contemplative implications. Islamic art—in the sense of all the plastic arts of Islam—is essentially the projection, in the visual order of certain aspects or dimensions of the divine unity.

Let us not forget, nevertheless, that sacred calligraphy reflects in its fashion the majestic style of the Koranic *sūrahs*, without it being possible to define the nature of this analogy in detail. By the very fact that writing serves to fix the word of God, it is the noblest art of Islam,[9] and it is likewise, almost by definition, the most typically Arab art.

In this latter connection, it is significant that the abstract nature of the signs—the Arabic script being purely phonetic—gives rise to an extraordinary development of graphic rhythms, without the essential forms of the letters being thereby diminished. The general and to some extent natural development of Arabic writing tends toward a fluidity of forms, but in parallel with this tendency there is also a hieratic stylization of these same forms; very different styles not only follow one another, but exist side by side, especially in monumental epigraphy. Arabic calligraphy is at the antipodes of Far Eastern calligraphy, which should be mentioned here because it too represents a peak in the art of writing. The Chinese or Japanese calligrapher isolates the signs, each of which corresponds to a distinct idea; using the paintbrush, he invokes in a few more or less broad strokes a key picture or a visual nucleus of related ideas. The Arab, on the other hand, traces with the pen precise and often interlacing lines. As far as possible he joins the letters to each other, while stressing their contrasts. The writing runs from right to left, and it is in this horizontal direction that the forms interlink and marry with one another, whereas in the vertical direction the uprights of the letters stand out in isolation and in a sense punctuate the continuous melody of the lines. From the point of view of the symbolism of the spatial axes, which is appropriate here, and which moreover is also inherent in the art of weaving, the vertical elements of the letters, which "transcend" the flow of the writing, correspond

---

[9] In a certain sense its role is analogous to that of the icon in Christianity, since it represents, like the icon, the visible form of the divine word.

to their essences, while the horizontal movement represents the "material" continuity of their forms. The upright is like a ray of the one essence, which distinguishes by its very unity, just as the present instant distinguishes between the past and the future. The horizontal movement, on the other hand, which proceeds in continuous waves, is the image of becoming or of life. In certain calligraphic styles such as thuluth, for example, this polarity is carried to its limit; in the direction of the horizontal current, the melody of the ample and varied curves corresponds to the rhythm of the incisive uprights, formed especially by the vertical lines of the *alif* and the *lam.* It is like a tireless attestation *(shahādah)* of unity accompanied by a joyous and serene expansion of the soul.

The classical poetry of the Muslim Arabs is linked by its form—its monotonous rhyme and its complex meter—to the pre-Islamic bedouin poetry. It thus shows the influences of the Koran only through the ideas that it may vehicle. But there exists a semipoetic literature whose very forms reflect the Koran, namely that of the prayers, litanies, and incantations composed by the holy masters. One example of this sort is the *Dalāil al-khairat* of Shaikh al-Jazūlī, a collection of praises of the Prophet or more exactly of "prayers upon the Prophet." The Muslim addresses his prayers only to God Himself, in conformity with his unitary perspective, but by asking God to bless the Prophet, he communicates in fact with the latter. These prayers evoke one after the other the human and cosmic perfections present in the nature of Mohammed, the synthesis of all the divine reverberations within creation. Sometimes the form of the prayers or incantations remains the same, while their terms of comparison vary, going from the virtues to the beauties of the visible and invisible universe, and sometimes the subject of the prayers is constant, and their forms change; and this alternating repetition describes a spiral movement, whose aim is the integration of all the positive aspects of the world in the spirit, in the inward prophet, who is "nearer to men than their own souls," according to a verse of the Koran.

The inversion of perspective in relation to Christianity will be noted: Whereas the latter views God from the starting point of man, Islam views man from the starting point of God, which excludes any fixation of an anthropomorphic image. The image of the divine man is as it were dissolved in its elements; it disappears in the universal theophanies, whence its absence from plastic art, which becomes an impersonal incantation like the waves of the sea or the twinkling of the stars.

The predominance of the auditive over the visual in the Arab soul has to show itself even in plastic art; and it is the same for a certain form of spiritual intuition or ecstasy, which finds its support more especially in rhythm and sound. It is like a sudden cessation of time, an immobilization of all movement in the lightning flash of the pure present. The world may henceforth be compared to a waterfall, which flows without changing form, or to a flame that, although being consumed, appears motionless. Arabo-Muslim ornamentation essentially expresses this suspension of becoming in the instant.

The Influence of Sufism
on Traditional Persian Music

BY SEYYED HOSSEIN NASR

(*Translated from the Persian by William C. Chittick. The present
article was originally a speech delivered in November, 1970, in Tehran.
Although the English version has been slightly revised by the author,
it should be borne in mind that the speech was meant for a Persian-
speaking audience and that therefore certain references may seem unfamiliar or strange in English. The Persian text was published in
Tehran in the magazine* Talash, *No. 26, and the journal* Ma' arif-i-
islāmi [Islamic Studies], *No. 12.*)

TRADITIONAL Persian music, like all art of a spiritual nature,
arises from silence. Its peace and calm manifest the eternal
truth in the framework of sounds belonging to the world of
forms and appearances, although that truth itself transcends
every kind of form, determination, and particularization. The
quiet and serenity of this music is the seal of the world of the
spirit impressed upon the countenance of the world of form.
The root of every melodious sound takes shape within the
depths of this vast world of silence, a world that transcends
every kind of sound, although all sounds draw their existence
from its life-giving power.

Man himself is situated between two worlds of silence, which
in a certain respect are ambiguous and unknown for him. The
first is the period before birth and the second that after death.
Between them human life is an instant that like a sudden cry
shatters the infinite silence for a brief moment, only to become
united with it. But a deeper study shows that what appears to
man as nothingness, that is, the stage beyond the life of this
world, is pure being, and what is apparently being—that is, the

fleeting instants of life in this material universe—is only the reflection and shadow of that transcendent being. Man's life also is no more than noise and clamor in the face of that eternal silence that in fact is the most profound of all music; and the life of this world comes to possess meaning only when it joins that silence and transforms the noise and uproar of the external world into the enchanting song of the world of man's inner dimension.

Sufism is a way that gives access to that silence that is hidden at the center of all men's beings, that silence that is the most beautiful form of music and the source of all meaningful activities and actions and that itself is the origin of life and of man's existence. Sufism is a divine trust originating in the mercy of God and placed within Islam, a religion revealed by heaven. It is a key given to man with which he can unlock the secret of his own existence and come to possess the forgotten and neglected treasure hidden within his being. Sufism gives to man the means to know himself and thus to know God. With the help of the doctrines and methods of the spiritual path man is enabled to understand who he is and to die to what he "is" in an illusory manner in order to come alive to what he is in reality. Sufism is able to lead man to that quiet and peace that is hidden at the center of his being and whose attainment is possible at all times and all places. It can deliver him from the crushing storm of events in this life and the uproar of the external world, without it being necessary that he abandon that world. Rather, in Sufism man is delivered by means of an inner transformation that takes place here and now, within the framework of his normal life. As a result he is enabled to hear the inward music of all beings and, above the noise of everyday life, to listen to the music of the silence of eternity.

In order to express its truths Sufism can make use and has made use of every legitimate means, from weaving to archery, from architecture to music, and from logic to traditional theosophy *(ḥikmat-i ilāhī)*. The goal of Sufism is to lead man from the world of form to the world of the spirit; but since man lives in the world of form and at the beginning of the spiritual path is not detached from it, by means of this very world of form Sufism turns his attention toward the spiritual world.

Form is the veil of the spiritual world, but at the same time it is its symbol and the ladder by means of which union with it can be attained. As the poet Awhadī Kirmānī has said:

زان سی نگرم بــه چشم سر در صــورت

زیرا کــه ز معنــی است اثر درصورت

این عالم صــورت است و ما در صرریــم

معنی نتــوان دید مگــــر در صورت

I gaze upon form [sūrat] with my physical eye
　　because there is in form the trace of the Spirit [ma'nā].
This is the world of form and we live in forms; the
　　Spirit cannot be seen save by means of form.

A limited few can reach the stage of complete detachment from the material world (tajarrud) without need of material and formal support, but most people who possess the qualifications for the spiritual life can reach the world of the spirit only through form, but a form that has become so polished and refined by traditional art that the darkness and opacity of multiplicity has been lifted from it so that, like a mirror, it reflects the beauty of the spiritual world. This form can be a geometrical figure in architecture, a design in painting or calligraphy, or a melody in music. For this very reason Sufism has made use of all these possibilities and has left a profound effect upon nearly all aspects of Islamic art.

But among the traditional arts music has a special place, for it deals with material forms and shapes less than do all the other arts and is connected more directly to the world of spiritual essences (mujarradāt). It is not without reason that the Hindus consider the first art sent from heaven for men to have been music, and that the Muslim gnostics ('urafā') consider music to be the best means to express the subtlest of divine mysteries. In the words of Jalal-ud-din Rumi:

مطـرب آغـازید نـزد تـرك مست
در حجاب نغمـه اسرار السـت

> The musician began to play before the drunken Turk
> within the veil of melody the mysteries of the eternal
> convenant between God and man *[asrār-i alast]*.

Although its origin is the transcendent world, man's spirit
became joined to the earthly body through a talisman, whose
secret is known only to God, and thus his life in the lower
world came into being. But the spirit always retains a memory
of its original dwelling and first homeland, and all of man's
efforts to reach perfection, even if limited to the material world,
have their root in this remembrance. In the transcendent world
the spirit of man listened perpetually to a never-ending concert, whose harmony and beauty it benefited from and par-
ticipated in. By means of traditional music the spirit in its
bodily prison once again remembers its original homeland. The
talisman through which it has been joined to the body may even
be broken, thus allowing the bird of the spirit, even if only for
a few moments, to spread its wings and fly in the unlimited
expanse of the spiritual world and to participate in the joy and
ecstasy that is an essential aspect of this world. In the words
of Sa'd al-Dīn Hamūyah:

دل وقتِ، سمــاع بـسوی دلـدار بــرد
جان را به سرا پردهٔ اسرار بـــــرد
این زمزمه مرکبی است مــر روح تــرا
بر دارد و خوش بـه عالـم یاربــرد

> When the heart attends the spiritual concert *[sama']* it perceives
>   the Beloved and lifts the soul to the abode of the divine
>   Mysteries.
> The melody is the steed of thy soul; it raises it up and takes
>   it joyful to the world of the Friend.

The man who has reached the state of spiritual perfection has of course no need for any kind of steed or vehicle, for he himself possesses the power of flight. But until this stage is reached, music of a spiritual nature, such as the traditional music of Persia, can be one of the most powerful means for awakening the qualified person from the sleep of forgetfulness *(ghaflah)*. It is a sure and dependable steed, one that is able to take man from the abyss of the material world with all its hardship and pain to the zenith of the limitless world of the spirit, within which all pain and suffering is transformed into happiness and joy. Sufism took the music of ancient Persia and like so many other forms polished and perfected it until it became the required vehicle. That is why, from the point of view of the effect this music leaves on the soul of man, it matters little what its origin might have been, whether it is of the Bārbadi school or reaches back to the Achaemenean period. What is important is that it was able to come under the influence of Sufism and to be transformed by it in such a way that within it an inward and spiritual dimension came into being which is able to bring the spirit of the person qualified for spiritual ascent into union with the Beloved, to free man for a moment from limitation and from the material world that encompasses him.

The relationship of traditional Persian music with Sufism is not accidental, nor is it merely historical. Rather, it is a profound reality that has left a considerable influence upon the way this music affects the soul of the listener. In order for this point to be fully understood it is necessary to take into consideration the stages of the spiritual path *(sayr wa sulūk)*. Although there are various ways of describing and explaining the way toward union with God in Sufism, these can be summarized in three main stages: The first is that of contraction *(qabd)*. In it a certain aspect of the human soul must die; this stage is connected with asceticism and piety and with the manifestation or theophany *(tajallī)* of the divine justice and majesty. The second stage is expansion *(bast)*, in which an aspect of the human soul is expanded so that man's existence passes beyond its own limits until it embraces the whole universe, and man can say with Sa'dī,

به جهـــان خـــرم از آنــم

که جهان خـــرم از اوســت

I am joyful in the world because the world is joyful in Him.

This stage is joined to happiness and ecstasy and is the manifestation of the divine beauty and mercy. The third stage is union with the truth *(wisāl bi'l-haqq)* by means of reaching the stations of extinction *(fanā)* and permanence *(baqā')*. At this level the gnostic has passed beyond all other states *(ahwāl)* and stations *(maqāmāt)* and has attained to contemplation of the face of the beloved. He sees with manifest clarity that, in the words of Hātif of Isfahan:

کــه یکی هست و هیــچ نیست جــزاو

وحـــــــده لا الــه الا هـــــو

He is one and there is naught but He:
There is no God save Him alone.[1]

Music is concerned with the second and third stages and not with the first. That is why in Islam, while the divine law, or *Sharī'ah*, forbids listening to music unless it be that highest and purest form of musical melody, the recitation of the verses of the Holy Koran—for the injunctions of the *Sharī'ah* are concerned only with religious commands and prohibitions and with the divine justice—in Sufism, which is concerned with the spiritual path, music has been permitted and in some orders like the Mawlawiyyah and the Chishtiyyah has even possessed considerable importance.

[1] This verse is the "refrain" of Hātif's celebrated *Tarjī' band*, one of the most famous poems in Sufism, which was translated by E. G. Browne in his *Literary History of Persia*, Vol. IV (Cambridge, 1924), pp. 292–297.

The spiritual profundity of present-day traditional Persian music is not, as certain short-sighted people have imagined, in spite of the religion of Islam. Rather, its origin is the Islamic teachings themselves, which cut music off from the external aspects of life and turned it toward the world of the spirit. For the same reason, while Western music during the past two centuries has been for the most part an attempt to reach the second of the above three stages without passing initially through the first, that is, the stage of asceticism, piety, and detachment from the world—and thus it causes the soul to undergo an expansion that is not always connected with a spiritual influence—the traditional music of Persia and of the other Islamic countries has been based on the first stage. This is especially true of the music of North India, which has been composed and performed to a large extent by Sufis and many of whose greatest masters down to the present day, such as Ridā Qulī Khān, 'Alā'uddin Khān, and Bismillāh-Khān, have been Muslims. The profundity of traditional Islamic music, which pulls man away from the material world and plunges the roots of the tree of his existence into the world of the Spirit, is due to the fact that the men who have composed and performed this music have themselves reached the stage of detachment and possess spiritual states *(ḥāl)* in the truly gnostic *('irfānī)* meaning of the term.

The Sufis have been completely aware of the above facts and have considered listening to music and "spiritual concerts" *(samā')* as permissible only for those who have gone beyond the first stage in the development and perfection of the soul, which is none other than the subjugation of the animal passions. Ghazzali in his book *Alchemy of Happiness (Kimiyā-yi sa'ādat)* has written the following in the chapter called "On Discussions of Listening to Music *[samā']* and the Explanation of What Is Permitted of It and What Is Forbidden":

Know that God, the Exalted, possesses a secret in the heart of man which is hidden like fire in iron. Just as the secret of fire becomes manifest and apparent when iron is struck with a stone, so listening to pleasing and harmonious music brings man's essence into movement and causes something to come into being within man without his having a choice in the matter. The reason for this is the relationship that exists between the essence of man's heart and the transcendent world, which is called the world of Spirits *[arwāh]*. The transcendent world is the world of loveliness and beauty, and the source of loveliness and beauty is harmony *[tanāsub]*. All that is harmonious manifests the beauty of that world, for all loveliness, beauty and harmony that is observable in this world is the result of the loveliness and beauty of that world.

Therefore the pleasing and harmonious song has a certain resemblance to the wonders of that world, and hence an awareness appears in the heart, as well as a movement *[harakat]* and a desire, and it may be that man himself does not know what it is. Now this is true of a heart that is simple, that is free of the various loves and desires which can affect it. But if it is not free of them, and if it is occupied with something, that thing comes into movement and becomes influenced like a fire which is blown upon. Listening to music *[samā']* is important for him whose heart is dominated by the love of God, for the fire is made stronger, but for him in whose heart is love for vanity, listening to music is a deadly poison, and it is forbidden to him.[2]

The Sufis have allowed participation in the spiritual concert only to those individuals who are qualified—that is, those who have escaped from the abyss of the material world and its attractions. Thus, in the words of Sa'di:

نگویم سماع ای بـرادر کـه چیسـت   مگر مستمع را بدانـــم که کیست

گـر از برج معنـی پرد طیـــــر او   فرشته فرو مانـــد از سیـر او

وگـر مرد سهواست و بـــازی و لاغ

---

[2] Ghazzali, *Kimiyā-yi sa'ādat*, edited by Ahmad Aram (Tehran), p. 370.

قویتر شود دیوش انـــدر دمـــاغ

بریشان شود گل بــــــــه بـاد سحر

لـــه هیزم کــه نشکافدش جـــزتبر

جهان بــر سماع است و مستــــی و شور

ولیکن چه بیند در آئینـــــه کــور

I will not say, O brother, what the spiritual concert is,
    until I know who is listening to it.
If he begins his flight from the tower of the Spirit,
    the angels will not keep up with his soaring.
But if he be a man of error, vanity and play,
    the devil in his brain will grow more powerful.
The rose is torn apart by the morning breeze, but not
    the log; for it can only be split by an ax.
The world subsists on music, intoxication
    and ardor, but what does the blind man see in a mirror?

The influence of Sufism on traditional Persian music derives
more than all else from the fact that Sufism has made of music
a vehicle for the ascent of the spirit to the transcendent world,
but only for those who have taken upon themselves the difficulties of asceticism and spiritual discipline, the first stage of
which is piety and fear of God. For the same reason those who
enjoy this music without having passed through the first stage
of the spiritual path will never attain to the unlimited expanse
of the transcendent world, and if their soul takes to flight in
that world for a few moments with the help of this celestial
music, it will immediately fall back when the music ends, and
they will not be able to maintain their spiritual state and ecstasy. Moreover, how many are there for whom instead of
being a means to mount to the world of the spirit, this music
is like an intoxicant that frees them for a few moments from
the hardships and afflictions of the world?

    Then again, the musician who plays this music, precisely
because it was composed by men who themselves possessed

spiritual stations, who were empty of themselves and who played this music in a state of spiritual ecstasy, can only perform it well if he first forgets himself. Traditional Persian music is more profound than that a person could be continually in its intimacy and play it well without there first being some kind of spiritual transformation and forgetfulness of his ordinary, profane state. Many people ask why a group of those who perform traditional Persian music are addicted to narcotics. The probable reason is that many of them do not benefit from the grace that derives from Sufism and gnosis nor possess the means to reach spiritual states and stations through genuine Sufi and gnostic ways, and therefore they resort to the only way that they have to forget themselves for a few moments. In any case, what is certain from the point of view of Sufism is that spiritual profit from music is possible only through the polishing of the soul and the slaying of the dragon within ourselves. This alone can deliver the bird of the spirit and prepare it for the ascent that music of a spiritual nature can make possible.

The spiritual ascent that is accomplished by means of traditional Persian music is of several kinds. One kind is reached through the melody, which takes man step by step from one station to the next—that is, from one spiritual state to another and finally to the state of spiritual joy and ecstasy. Another is attained through the rhythm and meter of the music, which changes the relationship of man with ordinary time—the most important characteristic of the life of this world. Persian music possesses extemely fast and regular rhythms and moments in which there are no beats or any form of temporal determination. In the first instance man is united with the pulsation of cosmic life, which in the human individual is always present in the form of the beating of the heart. Man's life and the life of the cosmos become one, the microcosm is united to the macrocosm, and thus man's spirit undergoes expansion and participates in the joy and ecstasy that encompass the world and that man fails to perceive only because of his state of forgetfulness of God (*ghaflah*). In the second case, which transcends all rhythm and temporal distinction, man is suddenly cut off from the world of time; he feels himself situated face to face with eternity and for a moment benefits from the joy of extinction *(fanā')* and permanence *(baqā')*.

The perfect gnostic has no need of music or any other traditional art, for he and his life are themselves forms of art. Nevertheless, since his inward senses have been awakened, it can be said that he is constantly in the state of listening to the spiritual concert. The whole world is for him an eternal song. He sees existence forever accompanied by harmony and beauty. In the same way that through his vision he sees this beauty in the form of the colors and shapes of the world of nature and creation, through his hearing he hears it in the form of music. His life is never separated from music and its happiness and joy. If he listens to and enjoys what is usually called a musical composition, it is only because this music confirms his own inward states—if indeed it has originated in the silence of the spirit already alluded to. And if he seeks to keep away from what some people today call music, but which is no more than noise and cacophony devoid of any meaning or spiritual value, it is because listening to it disturbs his inner spiritual state; its lack of harmony disrupts and dissipates the song at the center of his being. At the same time, if this individual is talented in the composition and performance of music, as many of the Sufis have been—and the majority of the great masters of traditional Persian music have been connected with Sufism—what he composes and performs will be a reflection of his spiritual states covered by a veil of sounds, the combination of which will result in a melody that can guide the listener toward those states.

It can also be said that the Sufi is himself an instrument in the hands of the Creator, and what he produces is a song played by the celestial musician and heard within his being. The world itself is like a song composed of harmonious sounds, and since the gnostic has torn apart the veils of separative existence and become united with his original state and primordial nature, he also, like the world, is only an instrument on which God plays what He wills. In the words of Rumi:

ما چو چنگیم و تو ناخن میزنی

We are like a lyre and Thou pluckest.

What joy could be greater than that a man not only listen to the divine concert, but also be himself the means for playing its music; that man through submitting his own volition to the divine Will place himself completely in God's hands and become the source of melodies that spread joy and felicity and guide man toward his primordial home and ultimate abode?

In today's world when access to genuine spirituality becomes every day more difficult, and when that beauty that at one time was everywhere has come to be considered a luxury, traditional music possesses an extraordinary value, for it is like a refuge amid a terrifying storm and a fresh and luxuriant oasis in the midst of a burning desert. Today many are interested in this music without themselves knowing the profound reason. In reality these people are searching for the spiritual life and that quiet and peace that is hidden in the substance of music of a spiritual nature. They are seeking "the mysteries of the eternal covenant between man and God, within the veil of melody," the beauty of which attracts them to itself; its apparent sorrowful exterior is but the preface to the indescribable joy hidden within it.

The traditional music of Persia with its gnostic and Sufi character must be preserved in all of its authenticity, and quantitative expansion must not be confused at any cost with qualitative well-being. Obviously, the best way to preserve this music is to protect and maintain the Sufi tradition that has brought it into existence, and in the domain of the music itself to avoid all groundless innovation and imitation. This holds especially true as regards imitation of the music of contemporary Western civilization, for that civilization, because of its materialistic outlook, possesses values that are diametrically opposed to the goals of traditional music. Only those can add a new chapter to this music of the spirit who have themselves attained to union with the spiritual world and who at the same time are completely acquainted with the principles of the traditional music of Persia. Otherwise any alteration will mean transforming a ladder toward heaven into a purely earthly and worldly means of communication lacking any transcendent dimension. Today, for Persians as well as other Muslims and traditionally oriented people in general, traditional Persian music can be a spring full of grace for satisfying lost and thirsty souls, a place of refuge from the negative influences of the times, and, for some at least, a guide from its own wondrous beauty to the beauty of the Absolute. Since this music is the song of the eternal world in the world of time and place, it undergoes no degeneration or corruption. Like the sun at dawn, its message is always fresh and alive. It is for us to open our eyes and ears so that with the help of its melodies and of course with divine succor we can be delivered from that death that is falsely called life and attain that true life that knows no eclipse. It is for us to realize the worth of this valuable heritage, which, like the other aspects of the extremely rich culture of Islam, we are in need of now more than any other time in history. In the lyrics of Hafiz:

ساقـــی به نور باده بر افروز جـــام ـما

مطرب بگو که کار جهان شد به‌کام‌ما

مادر پیالــه عکس رخ یــار دیده‌ایم

ای بیخبر ز لذت شرب مدام ـــــما

هرگز نمیرد آنکه دنش زنده شد به عشق

ثبت است در جریدهٔ عالم دوام ـــما

O cup-bearer, brighten our goblet with the light of wine!
   O minstrel, tell how the world has succumbed to our
     desires!
We have seen in the cup the reflection of the face of the Friend,
   O you who know nothing of the joy of our eternal wine-
     drinking!
He whose heart has been made living by love never dies;
   our permanence is recorded within the pages of the cosmic
     text.

On the Margin of Liturgical
Improvisations

BY FRITHJOF SCHUON

THE LITURGY can be regarded in two very different ways: One may either take the view that the primitive simplicity of the rites has to be preserved from all sorts of cumbersome accretions or adopt the attitude that liturgical embellishment, if not contributing to the efficacy of the rites, at least enhances their radiance and consequently is a gift from God.

The point of view of simplicity can derive a certain justification from the fact that rabbinism had added an enormous number of practices and prayers to the religion of Moses and that Christ, the enunciator of inwardness, suppressed all these observances and rejected the long and complicated vocal prayers; for it was his wish that man should make his way to God "in spirit and in truth." The Apostles continued in this way, as did also the Desert Fathers, but gradually Christians lost sight of their worship "in spirit and in truth" and replaced it with vocal prayers and increasingly numerous observances; thus it is that the liturgy was born. In early times it took a rather simple form and was performed only in cathedrals around the bishop and only on the eve of the great festivals, when it was necessary to occupy the faithful who came to spend long hours in the church, but had grown weak in prayer. It was then taken up by the monks who, out of zeal, performed it daily. The liturgy of Saint Benedict was still quite simple, but it grew more complicated and heavier with time through continual additions.

This point of view unquestionably corresponds to a real aspect of things, but to a single aspect only; one would lay oneself open to serious error if one relied on it exclusively. For it is essential to take account in equal degree of the following data: Liturgical development stems not only from the negative factor of the spiritual deterioration of an increasingly numerous collectivity but also from the positive factor of a rigorously indispensable adaptation to new conditions; and this adaptation—or this flowering of a tangible symbolism—is in itself something wholly positive and in no wise opposed to the purest contemplativity. Nevertheless, there are two elements here to be distinguished: the symbolism of forms and acts on the one hand and verbal amplifications on the other. Doubtless both are useful, but formal symbolism by its very nature manifests the presence of the Holy Spirit in a more direct and incontestable fashion, given that what a pure symbol teaches is not subject to the limitations of verbal expression in general or to pious prolixity in this mode of expression in particular, where it happens to occur.

The first Christians called themselves saints and with good reason. In the primitive church there was an atmosphere of sanctity that doubtless could not prevent certain disorders but that at all events was dominant among the majority; the sense of the sacred was, so to speak, in the air. This well-nigh collective sanctity disappeared fairly rapidly and—men of the "dark age" being what they are—naturally enough, due chiefly to the rapid increase in the number of the faithful. It then became necessary to make the presence of the sacred more tangible so that on the one hand men whose outlook was growing increasingly profane might not lose sight of the majesty of the rites, and on the other, so that access to them should not be too abstract, if one may put it so.

Let it be noted here that one finds nothing of this kind in Islam, where the element of mystery does not penetrate in a quasi-material fashion into the exoteric realm.[1] On the other hand Mahayana Buddhism shows a liturgical development analogous to that of Christianity, but in neither case is the liturgy entirely reducible to a simple concession to human

---

[1] That is to say, the liturgical element, an extremely restrained one, is not superadded but is comprised in the Sunna itself; its principal content is the chanting of the Koran. In Judaism the Torah provides an example of a liturgy that is both very rich and integrally revealed.

weakness, since at the same time, and by the very nature of things, it possesses the intrinsic value of a tangible crystallization of the supernatural.

The first of the two points of view we have been comparing, that of original simplicity, is legitimate in the sense that the purely contemplative person, while not necessarily desiring it, is quite well able to do without any liturgical framework at all, and obviously he would prefer to see the sanctity of men rather than that of ritual forms, insofar as such an alternative presents itself.

There is no question here of ignoring the fact that the elaboration of the liturgy in the Catholic Church has been at certain times rather too facile. A simplification of the liturgy therefore is something that could be considered, especially since there have been precedents from the Middle Ages onward, and it could be justified by two reasons: the one intrinsic, aimed at expressions of a piety that had become at one and the same time too demanding and too contingent, and also at an overmeticulous legalism; the other extrinsic, namely the need to reckon, but in a dignified manner free from abject hastiness, with the rhythm, in itself abnormal, of our time.

The major error of the modernists is to believe that a liturgy can be invented and that the ancient liturgies were inventions or that elements added in a spirit of piety amount to such; this is to confuse inspiration with invention and the sacred with the profane.[2] Another no less pernicious error is to believe it possible to jump over one or two thousand years and retrace one's steps to the simplicity—and the sanctity!—of the primitive church; there is a principle of growth or of structure to be observed here, for a branch cannot again become the root. One must tend toward primitive simplicity by recognizing its incomparability and without imagining that it can be recaptured by external measures and superficial attitudes; one must

---

[2] One theologian has even had the temerity to write that Saint Paul, in order to apply the divine message, "had to invent," which is the most flagrant as well as the most ruinous error imaginable in this realm.

seek to realize primordial purity on the basis of the providentially elaborated forms and not on the basis of an impious iconoclasm.

We have recognized that it is not impossible, in a case like that of the Catholic liturgy, to return to greater simplicity by eliminating accretions stemming from later times; not, however, because they are not good enough for "our time" (allegedly so incomparable and so irreversible), but because they reflect a kind of piety that is not fundamental and because they run the risk of stifling or hiding from the sight of men more ancient and more substantial symbolisms. But if accretions, baroque or otherwise, are to be suppressed, let this be done prudently and respectfully, and let a stop be put to the introduction of a pedantic and vulgar sort of intelligibility into the rites, which is an insult to the intelligence of the faithful.

As to the replacement of the liturgical languages—whose quality is objective and not a mere matter of habit—by modern vernacular languages, it must be said that the least that can be expected of believers is the minimum of interest and respect required for learning the current liturgical formulas and for tolerating those they do not understand; a religious adherence that lays down vulgarization, extreme facility, and platitude as a prime condition is in every respect totally valueless.[3] To say that the quality of the liturgical languages is objective means that there exist languages that are sacred in character and that they possess this character either by nature or by adoption. The first case is that of the languages in which heaven has spoken

[3] In many cases the vernacular languages run the risk of becoming the instruments of alienation and cultural tyranny. Oppressed populations must henceforth have the Mass in the language of the oppressor, which is supposed to be theirs, and tribes speaking archaic languages—languages that thus are capable in principle of liturgical use though they are not widely prevalent—will find Latin replaced by another foreign language, linguistically inferior to their own and moreover charged for them with associations of ideas far removed from the sacred; the Sioux will have Mass, not in their noble Lakota, but in the English of the Far West. Doubtless it is impossible to translate the Mass into all the American Indian and African languages, but this is not the point, since the Mass in Latin does in fact exist.

and of the scripts—alphabets or ideograms—that heaven has inspired or confirmed; the second is that of the still noble languages that have been consecrated to the service of God.

All ancient languages are noble or aristocratic from the nature of things. They could not possess any element of triviality,[4] since this defect is a direct result of individualism and an indirect one of humanism. Being individualistic, modern languages are too loquacious, too tinged with sentimentalism, and at the same time too narrowly logical[5] to be suited for sacred usage. Ritual formulas uttered in French or English have something painfully individual about them, whereas formulas in Latin or Greek are invested with a majestic impersonality that permits the soul to find rest and to escape from its own pettiness.[6]

Low Latin, although not the language of Caesar, is nevertheless not a vulgar language like the various idioms derived from it. All things considered, it is a language that, if not transformed by the mold of Christianity, was at least adapted to it and stabilized by it and perhaps also influenced by the Germanic soul, more imaginative and less cold than the Roman soul. Moreover, the classical Latin of Cicero is not free from arbitrary restrictions as compared with the archaic language, certain values of which persisted in popular speech, so that

[4] In early ages the "people" possessed in a large measure the naturally aristocratic character that flows from religion; as for the "plebs" —made up of men who do not seek to rise above themselves—it could not determine the nature of the language in general. It is only democracy that seeks, on the one hand, to assimilate the "plebs" to the "people" and, on the other hand, to reduce the latter to the former; it ennobles whatever is base and debases whatever is noble.

[5] That is to say, they are overgiven to dotting the *i*'s, as the present author also is compelled to do—but then he is not writing for medieval readers, nor does he necessarily think in quite the same way as he writes.

[6] It should be noted that these fine shades of meaning seem to escape many of the Orthodox also, who appear to reason thus: Since Slavonic, which is not Greek, is worthy of liturgical use, modern French, which is not any more or any less Greek, is also worthy of such use. When one is alive to spiritual undertones and to the mystical vibrations of forms, one cannot but regret these false concessions, which moreover are not limited to the realm of language and which impoverish and disfigure the expressive splendor of the sacerdotal genius of Orthodoxy.

Low Latin, derived from the fusion of the two languages, is not a merely privative phenomenon.

In the Middle Ages, European intellectuality flourished within the framework of Latin.[7] With the abandonment of Latin, intellectual activity progressively made its imprint on the dialects in such a way that the modern languages that derive from them are on the one hand more supple and more intellectualist and on the other hand more blunted and profaned than the medieval ways of speaking. Now, from the point of view of sacred usage the decisive quality is neither philosophical suppleness nor psychological complexity—very relative factors in any case—but that character of simplicity and sobriety that is proper to all nonmodern languages. It takes the whole of twentieth-century insensitivity and narcissism to conclude that the present languages of the West, or any one of them, can be substantially and spiritually superior to the more ancient languages or that a liturgical text amounts practically to the same thing as a dissertation or a novel.

This is not to say that it is only the modern languages of Europe that are unsuited to sacred use. The general degeneration of humanity, which has been accelerating for several centuries, has had the particular effect, outside the West, of bringing about a deterioration in certain tongues existing on the margin of the sacred languages that they accompany. The cause here is not a lapsing into triviality, ideological and literary in its basis as is the case in Western countries, but a naïve de facto materialism, not philosophical but nonetheless favoring dullness and flatness, vulgarity even. Doubtless this phenomenon is not universal, but it exists, and it was necessary to note it in the present context. As for spoken languages that have not

---

[7] Latin nevertheless did not possess every kind of superiority. The Italian of Dante has many more musical and imaginative qualities; the German of a Walther von der Vogelweide or a Meister Eckhart has more plasticity, more intuitive and evocative power, and is of a more symbolic nature than Latin. But Latin enjoys obvious pre-eminence in relation to its derivatives and to the later Germanic dialects; it is furthermore the language of the Roman empire and imposes itself for this very reason, given moreover that there is no occasion for envisaging a plurality of liturgical languages in this linguistically and culturally overdivided sector.

been subject to this kind of deterioration, they too have lost at least much of their ancient richness, but without necessarily becoming unsuitable for a possible liturgical purpose.

Liturgical elaboration depends on the one hand on the genius of a religion and on the other on the ethnic receptacles concerned. It is providential, like the disposition and shape of the branches of a tree; moreover it is inappropriate, to put it mildly, to criticize it in terms of short-sighted retrospective logic[8] and to wish to correct it as if it amounted merely to an accidental succession of events. Assuming the Latin church has a right to exist, the Latin language is an immovable aspect of its nature and of its genius.

The innovators never tire of parading the abstract and ideological argument of "the times." This taboo phrase means for them that things that in fact are situated in what today appears to us as a "past" are ipso facto "antiquated" and "out of date," and, conversely, things situated in what seems to us subjectively as "the present," or, more precisely speaking, those things which they select arbitrarily for identifying with "our time" (as if other contemporary phenomena did not exist or belonged in a different period)—the whole of this arbitrarily delimited actuality is presented as a "categorical imperative" endowed with an "irreversible" motion. In reality, what gives time its significance here is the following factors: first, the progressive decadence of the human species in conformity with cyclic law; second, the progressive adaptation of religion to the collectivity as such; third, adaptation to the different ethnic groups concerned; fourth, the qualitative oscillations of the traditional collectivity in the grip of the temporal flux. It is to one of these factors, or to their various combinations, that everything can be referred that brings in "the times" by way of explanation.

[8] It goes without saying that logic is only valid provided it possesses sufficient data and draws real conclusions from them. But there is also the question of imagination, and not of logic only. An imagination which is completely at ease in a world of din and vulgarity, to the point of finding everything not belonging to it abnormal and ludicrous, divests itself of all right to pronounce on sacred matters.

As regards the adaptation of a religion in its first youth to a total society, this concerns the transition from the "catacomb" stage to that of a state religion; it is entirely false to assert that only the first is normal and that the second, or if one so prefers, the "Constantinian" stage, represents merely an illegitimate, hypocritical, and faithless state of petrification. A religion cannot remain forever in the cradle; it is by definition destined to become a state religion and in consequence to undergo the adaptations—in no wise hypocritical, but simply realistic—that this new situation demands. It cannot but ally itself with the ruling power, on condition, of course, that the ruling power submits to its guidance. On this account one has to distinguish thenceforth between two churches: the institutional church, immutable because of its divine institution, and the human church, necessarily political through being linked to a total collectivity, failing which it would have no earthly existence as a great religion. Granting that this state church is bad—and it is necessarily so to the extent that men are bad—the holy church has need of it in order to survive in space and time; it is from this human and imperial church that there springs that qualitative prolongation of the primitive church that is the Church of the Saints. Moreover to this transition from the "Church of the Catacombs" to the "Constantinian Church" there necessarily corresponds a liturgical and theological readaptation, for it is impossible to speak to an integral society as one would speak to a handful of mystics.

Mention has also been made of adaptation to providential ethnic groups, who in the case of Christianity are, broadly speaking—after the Jews—the Greeks, the Romans, the Germanic and Slav peoples, and a minority of Near Easterners. Here again it is wrong to speak of "a time" when we are dealing with factors that depend, not on a period as such, but on a natural unfolding that could take place in a variety of periods. Theological and liturgical forms clearly bear a relationship to ethnic mentalities, at least to the extent that the question of a diversity can arise in this domain.

There remains the paradoxical problem of what amounts in a certain sense to a progressive manifestation of the religious genius. On the one hand, religion displays its maximum sanctity at its origin; on the other hand, it requires time to implant itself solidly in the human soil, where it needs to create a humanity in its own image in order to bring about a maximal flowering of intellectual and artistic values coinciding with a new flowering of sanctity, which might make one think of an evolution. This unquestionably takes place, but only in a specified human respect and not in terms of intrinsic spirituality. In every religious cycle there are four periods to be distinguished: the "apostolic" period, then the period of full development, after which comes the period of decadence, and then the final period of corruption. Catholicism, however, exhibits an anomaly inasmuch as its period of development was brutally cut short by an influence wholly foreign to the Christian genius, namely the Renaissance, so that in this case the period of decadence was placed in a completely new dimension.

For the innovators, the expression "our time" is obviously not entirely devoid of meaning. In practice it is identified with the relativistic idea of evolution, and everything belonging to the past is viewed according to this false perspective, which ultimately reduces all phenomena to evolutionist or temporal fatalities, whereas the essential lies entirely in the eternal present and in the quality of absoluteness whenever values of the spirit are in question.

Starting from the idea that the liturgy is the outward clothing of the spiritual order and that in a religious, and hence normal, civilization nothing is wholly independent of the sacred, it will be admitted that the liturgy in the most ample sense of the term embraces all artistic and artisanal forms insofar as they are referable to the sacred realm, and that, for this very reason, these forms cannot be just anything;[9] this notwithstand-

[9] Anyone wishing to see a strictly liturgical and even truly celestial art should visit the Sainte Chapelle or, in Venice, the Basilica of Saint Mark (the later mosaics apart). People attribute some sort of "mystique of joy" to Baroque art. In reality its character of dreamlike inflation and dissolution partakes of satanism, be it said without exaggeration; it is the paradise of a nightmare. Greco-Roman classicism could never be harmonized definitively with the Christian mentality, even adulterated as this had become by the Renaissance; but instead of returning to the Romanesque and Gothic styles an attempt was made to satisfy the need for imaginativeness and musicality from below, whence the

ing the fact that in practice, one is obliged to understand by
"liturgy" only those forms that are directly sacred or pertaining to worship. The essential point here is that in Europe the
liturgy taken in its widest sense has been radically false for
several centuries, as if the visible and the invisible no longer
had any connection with one another; it would be absurd to
maintain that this state of affairs is devoid of influence on the
spiritual order, so far as the general conditions governing environment and development are concerned. A particular saint
may have no need of imaginative and aesthetic symbolism, but
the collectivity needs it and the collectivity should be able to
produce saints; whether one likes it or not, the big things in
this world are bound up with the small ones, at least extrinsically, and it would be unnatural to view the outward expressions of a tradition merely as an affair of decoration.

But let us return to the liturgy properly so called, or more
exactly to the problem of its possible readaptation. There is no
sort of charity that permits or demands degradation. To place
oneself at the level of childhood or of naïvety is one thing; to
sink to the level of vulgarity or pride is another. The faithful
have had imposed upon them the idea of the "people of God,"
or of the "holy people" even, and a sacerdotal function that
they have never even dreamed of has been suggested to them,
and this in an age when the people are as far removed as could
be from sanctity, so much so indeed that it is felt to be necessary
to lower the level of the liturgy, and even of the whole of
religion, for their use. This is all the more absurd from the fact
that the people still deserve something much better than the
leveling down that is wished on them in the name of a perfectly
unrealistic ideology; under the pretense of introducing a liturgy on a level with the people, it is the people who are forced
to lower themselves to the level of this substitute liturgy.[10]

Baroque style—already rendered alluring by Michelangelo—and its
indescribable prolongation in the eighteenth century.

[10] A most questionable Council wished to "open a window," but the
window should have been opened heavenward! That window was already open: It was the ancient liturgy. It is true that there are other
possible openings, also toward heaven, but these would never be so
much as mentioned.

From every point of view one would do well to remind oneself of this saying of Saint Irenaeus: "There can be no triumph over error through the sacrifice of any of the rights of truth."

Man dies alone; he is judged alone. He alone is responsible for his actions; he stands alone before God. No prayer in common can replace personal prayer; the intimate dialogue between the soul and God is incommunicable and irreplaceable. All the communal settings in the world can never alter this. What man seeks in the sanctuary is solitude with his Creator; so much the better if the sanctuary shelters more than one man's solitude.

To pretend that the ancient and normal, or sacerdotal and hence aristocratic, liturgy simply expresses "an age" is radically false for two reasons: first because an "age" amounts to nothing and explains nothing, at least in the order of values in question here, and second because the message of the liturgy, or its justification, lies in fact outside and beyond temporal contingencies. If one enters a sanctuary, it is with the object of escaping from time; it is to find an atmosphere of the "Heavenly Jerusalem" which delivers us from our earthly moment in time. The merit of the ancient liturgies is not that they expressed their historical moment but that they expressed something that went beyond it; and if this something gave its imprint to an age, this means that that age enjoyed the quality of possessing a nontemporal side, so much so that we have every reason for loving it to the extent that it possessed this quality. If "nostalgia for the past" happens to coincide with nostalgia for the sacred, this is a virtue, not because it is directed toward the past in itself, which would be quite devoid of meaning, but because it is directed toward the sacred, which transforms all duration into an eternal present and which cannot be situated elsewhere than in the liberating "now" of God.

Keys to the Bible

BY FRITHJOF SCHUON

In order to understand the nature of the Bible and its meaning, it is essential to have recourse to the ideas of both symbolism and revelation. Without an exact and, in the measure necessary, sufficiently profound understanding of these key ideas, the approach to the Bible remains hazardous and risks engendering grave doctrinal, psychological, and historical errors. Here it is above all the idea of revelation that is indispensable, for the literal meaning of the Bible, particularly in the Psalms and in the words of Jesus, affords sufficient food for piety apart from any question of symbolism; but this nourishment would lose all its vitality and all its liberating power without an adequate idea of revelation or of suprahuman origin.

Other passages, particularly in Genesis though also in texts such as the Song of Songs, remain an enigma in the absence of traditional commentaries. When approaching Scripture, one should always pay the greatest attention to rabbinical and kabbalistic commentaries and in Christianity to the patristic and mystical commentaries; then will it be seen how the word-for-word meaning practically never suffices by itself and how apparent naïveties, inconsistencies, and contradictions resolve themselves in a dimension of profundity for which one must possess the key. The literal meaning is frequently a cryptic language that more often veils than reveals and that is only meant to furnish clues to truths of a cosmological, metaphysical, and mystical order; the Oriental traditions are unanimous concerning this complex and multidimensional interpretation of sacred texts. According to Meister Eckhart, the Holy Ghost teaches all truth. Admittedly, there is a literal meaning that the author had in mind, but as God is the author of Holy Scripture, every true meaning is at the same time a literal meaning; for all that is true comes from the truth itself, is contained in it,

springs from it, and is willed by it. And so with Dante in his
Convivio (Trattato Secondo, I):

> The Scriptures can be understood, and ought to be ex-
> plained, principally in four senses. One is called *literal.* . . .
> The second is called *allegorical.* . . . The third sense is
> called *moral.* . . . The fourth sense is called *anagogical,* that
> is, beyond sense *[sovrasenso];* and this is when a Scripture
> is spiritually expounded, which, while true in its literal
> sense, refers beyond it to the higher things of the eternal
> Glory, as we may see in that Psalm of the Prophet, where
> he says that when Israel went out of Egypt Judaea became
> holy and free. Which, although manifestly true according
> to the letter, is none the less true in its spiritual meaning—
> viz., that the soul, in forsaking its sins, is made holy and
> free in its powers.

As regards biblical style—setting aside certain variations that
are of no importance here—it has to be understood that the
sacred or suprahuman character of the text could never be
manifested in an absolute way through language, which perforce is human; the divine quality referred to appears rather
through the wealth of superposed meanings and in the theurgic
power of the text when it is thought and pronounced and
written.

Equally important is the fact that the Scriptures are sacred,
not because of their subject matter and the way in which it is
dealt with, but because of their degree of inspiration, or what
amounts to the same, their divine origin; it is this that determines the contents of the book, and not the inverse. The Bible
can speak of a multitude of things other than God without
being the less sacred for it, whereas other books can deal with
God and exalted matters and still not be the divine word.

The apparent incoherency in certain sacred texts results ultimately from the disproportion between divine truth and human language. It is as if this language under the pressure of
the Infinite were shattered into a thousand pieces or as if God
had at His disposal no more than a few words to express a

thousand truths, thus obliging Him to use all sorts of ellipses and paraphrases. According to the Rabbis, "God speaks succinctly"; this also explains the syntheses in sacred language that are incomprehensible a priori, as well as the superposition of meanings already mentioned. The role of the orthodox and inspired commentators is to intercalate in sentences, when too elliptic, the implied and unexpressed clauses, or to indicate in what way or in what sense a certain statement should be taken, besides explaining the different symbolisms, and so forth. It is the orthodox commentary and not the word-for-word meaning of the Torah that acts as law. The Torah is said to be "closed," and the sages "open" it; and it is precisely this "closed" nature of the Torah that renders necessary from the start the Mishnah or commentary that was given in the tabernacle, when Joshua transmitted it to the Sanhedrin. It is also said that God gave the Torah during the day and the Mishnah during the night and that the Torah is infinite in itself, whereas the Mishnah is inexhaustible as it flows forth in duration. It should also be noted that there are two principal degrees of inspiration, or even three if the orthodox commentaries are included; Judaism expresses the difference between the first two degrees by comparing the inspiration of Moses to a bright mirror and that of the other prophets to a dark mirror.

The two keys to the Bible are, as already stated, the ideas of symbolism and revelation. Too often has revelation been approached in a psychological, hence purely naturalistic and relativistic, sense. In reality revelation is the fulgurant irruption of a knowledge that comes, not from an individual or collective subconscious, but on the contrary from a supraconsciousness, which though latent in all beings nonetheless immensely surpasses its individual and psychological crystallizations. In saying that "the kingdom of God is within you," Jesus Christ means, not that heaven, or God, is of a psychological order, but simply that the access to spiritual and divine realities is to be found at the center of our being, and it is from this center precisely that revelation springs forth, when the human ambience offers a sufficient reason for it to do so and when therefore a predestined human vehicle presents itself, namely, one capable of conveying this outflow.

But clearly the most important basis for what we have just spoken of is the admission that a world of intelligible light exists, both subjacent and transcendent to our consciousness. The knowledge of this world, or sphere, entails as a consequence the negation of all psychologism and likewise all evolutionism. In other words, psychologism and evolutionism are nothing but makeshift hypotheses to compensate for the absence of this knowledge.

To affirm that the Bible is both symbolistic and revealed means, then, on the one hand that it expresses complex truths in a language that is indirect and full of imagery and on the other that its source is neither the sensorial world nor the psychological or rational plane, but rather a sphere of reality that transcends these planes and immensely envelops them, while yet in principle being accessible to man through the intellective and mystical center of his being, or through the "heart," if one prefers, or pure "intellect." It is the intellect that comprises in its very substance the evidence for the sphere of reality that we are speaking of and that thus contains the proof of it, if this word can have a meaning in the domain of direct and participative perception. Indeed the "classical" prejudice of scientism, or the fault in its method if one wishes, is to deny any mode of knowledge that is suprasensorial and suprarational, and in consequence to deny the planes of reality to which these modes refer and that precisely constitute the sources both of revelation and of intellection.

Intellection in principle is for man what revelation is for the collectivity; in principle, we say, for in fact man cannot have access to direct intellection—or gnosis—except by virtue of the preexistent scriptural revelation. What the Bible describes as the fall of man or the loss of paradise coincides with our separation from total intelligence; this is why it is said that "the kingdom of God is within you," and again: "Knock, and it shall be opened unto you." The Bible itself is the multiple and mysterious objectivation of this intellect or Logos. It is thus by way of images and enigmas the projection of what we carry in a quasi-inaccessible depth at the bottom of our heart; and the facts of sacred history—where nothing is left to chance—are themselves cosmic projections of the unfathomable divine truth.

The Meaning of the Temple

BY LEO SCHAYA

IN ORDER to obtain a comprehensive understanding of Jewish doctrine concerning the Temple of Jerusalem, it is necessary to refer not only to the descriptions given in the Bible but also to the oral tradition; this includes both the Talmudic and rabbinical writings, which proceed from the outward to the inward meaning of the revealed word, and the Kabbala, the purely inward doctrine. It is obviously impossible here to consider all the scriptural texts referring to the temple and the numerous commentaries dealing with them; it will be sufficient for our present purpose to touch on only a few essential aspects and to observe how these proceed from the purely spiritual doctrine and lead to an "inward vision" of the sanctuary.

The temple in Jerusalem has the same fundamental meaning as the tabernacle, its movable prototype. It is God's "dwelling" *(mishkan)* or the holy place of His "indwelling" *(shekhinah)* in the midst of Israel. "And I will dwell among the children of Israel, and will be their God. And they shall know that I am YHWH,[1] their God, that brought them forth out of the land of Egypt, that I may dwell among them: I am YHWH their God" (Ex. 29:45–46). God wished to live in the "sanctuary" *(miqdash)* in order to be known; in it His presence was to appear, speak, command: "There I will appear to thee, and I will commune with thee from above the mercy seat, from between the two cherubims which are upon the Ark of the Covenant, of all things which I will give thee in commandment unto the children of Israel" (Ex. 25:22). These words were addressed to Moses and applied not only to the Holy of Holies within the

---

[1] In accordance with Jewish custom, the Tetragram is not vocalized. Its pronunciation is no longer known, and it has been forbidden to the Jews, for spiritual reasons, for about two thousand years.

tabernacle, but also to that of the temple, which Solomon called an oracle *(d'bir)*, for it was here that was revealed God's "word" or "command" *(dibrah)* and thus also the "prophetic message" *(dibber)*.

Moses erected the tabernacle for God's "indwelling" *(shek-hinah)*, and Solomon erected the temple for God's "name" *(shem)*. Thus their two works were essentially one, just as God is truly present in His name, this being precisely His "indwelling" or "habitation." The most sacred duty of the high priest consisted in the invocation of the name of God. He called upon Him, and the *shekhinah* was revealed. God Himself spoke of the indwelling of His name in the Temple of Jerusalem: "Since the day that I brought forth My people out of the land of Egypt I chose no city among all the tribes of Israel to build an house in, that My name might be there; neither chose I any man to be a ruler over My people Israel. But I have chosen Jerusalem, that My Name might be there; and have chosen David to be over My people Israel" (II Chron. 6:5-6). And Solomon, who handed down these words of God, added: "YHWH said to David my father: Forasmuch as it was in thine heart to build an house for My Name, thou didst well in that it was in thine heart: notwithstanding thou shalt not build the house; but thy son which shall come forth out of thy loins, he shall build the house for My Name" (II Chron. 6:8-9). That God Himself dwelt therein is evident from, among other things, the following passage which refers to the temple: "I will perform My word with thee, which I spake unto David thy father: and I will dwell among the children of Israel, and will not forsake My people Israel" (I Kings 6:12-13).

The tabernacle had provided the presence of God with no permanent habitation, for it was set up after the model of His heavenly "vehicle" *(merkabah)*, in which He would lead His people through the wilderness to the fixed "center of the world," Jerusalem. The oral tradition tells us that in the wilderness the bearers of the Ark of the Covenant were miraculously carried by it as by a vehicle. Not only did they feel no weight, but they soared with it like angels, penetrated by the light of the holy Ark and raised to prophetic vision. When God's vehi-

cle came to rest, it was His throne; but the true earthly image
of His throne, the fixed habitation of God here below, was not
the tabernacle, but the temple. For this reason the latter alone
is called God's "house" *(beth)* or His "Lower Throne." In themselves His vehicle and His throne are one and the same universal center, but here below it is the temple alone that "solidifies"
the latter. In it is found—according to the Talmud (Yoma 54*b*)
—the "foundation stone" *(eben shetiyah)*, around which the earth
was created and on which the whole world rests. Thus the
Kabbala (Zohar: Terumah 157*a*) also says that the Holy Land
is the center of the world, Jerusalem is the center of the Holy
Land, and the Holy of Holies is the center of Jerusalem. Onto
this central point all good and all nourishment descended for
distribution to the entire world.

The presence of God itself descended into His earthly dwelling, and in it appeared, spoke, listened, forgave, and blessed,
so that Israel and all mankind might be raised up to Him.
"Moreover concerning the stranger, which is not of Thy people
Israel, but is come from a far country for the sake of Thy great
Name, and Thy mighty hand, and Thine outstretched arm; if
he comes and prays in this house: then hear Thou from the
heavens, even from Thy dwelling place, and do according to
all that the stranger calleth to Thee for; that all the peoples of
the earth may know Thy Name, and fear Thee, as doth Thy
people Israel, and may know that Thy Name was invoked upon
this house which I have built." Thus Solomon prayed at the
consecration of the Temple (II Chron. 6:32–33). The Chosen
People were the intermediary between all peoples and the Lord
of the worlds, just as the high priest was the intermediary
between Him and His people. All Israel was a "kingdom of
priests." Its mission consisted in "being holy" in the likeness
of Holy God and thereby sanctifying the whole world, in following the commandments, in inner purification and spiritual
realization, and in the total surrendering of the heart. Of these
inward operations the sacrifices and prayers of the temple were
but the outward and visible expression. Without inward conversion the offering made in the sanctuary was not accepted
by the *shekhinah*. The oral tradition describes the clear signs of

God's hearkening or anger in the temple. From the center—the Holy of Holies—proceeded not only blessings and the light of grace but also lightning and punishment.

Israel was "chosen" in order to espouse the indwelling (habitation) of God and thus to unite what is above with what is below, "the *shekhinah* with the Holy One, may He be blessed." This union of the presence of God—and, in it, of all existence—with His infinite majesty constituted the exalted mystery of the "center of the world." This mystery, also called the "union of the name"—the name that contains both the hidden essence and the universal manifestation of God—was first performed in the tabernacle through the mediation of Moses and Aaron and then through the successors of the high priest in the first and second temples. After their destruction "the *shekhinah* accompanied Israel into exile." God destroyed both temples, just as He had destroyed the first two Tables of the Law by the hand of Moses, because of Israel's sins. He punished His people very harshly but did not forsake them, and everywhere that they went glorifying His name the "scattered sparks of the *shekhinah*" shone forth brightly and led back those illumined to the original sun. Yet Israel would never again possess a third temple until the messianic rebuilding of the sanctuary foretold by the prophets.

Although the temple represented the fixed house of God or the fixed center of the world, it was itself only a "pattern" and not yet the definitive descent of the heavenly throne, sanctuary, or Jerusalem on earth. This "will not be built by human hands, but by God Himself" as the indestructible center of the messianic kingdom. Solomon's prototype—or rather, his anticipated image—of this divine center was as such destructible, yet not completely so, for in it an invisible spiritual "river" was crystallized and flowed forth toward all the directions of space, its vibration continuing until the final achievement of its goal. This is "the river Jobel flowing from highest Eden," the universal messianic redemption.

The spiritual stones, crystallized out of the river Jobel, were never destroyed. They are indestructible and await their final use. Thus it is said in the Kabbala (Zohar: P'qudé 240*b*), that it must not for a moment be imagined that the stones serving as a foundation for Zion and Jerusalem had fallen into the hands of alien peoples. In reality they had all been hidden and preserved by the Holy One, blessed be He, so that no single one is wanting; and when He will again raise up Jerusalem, these foundation stones will return to their original places "set round with sapphires." These are the stones of the Higher Throne, which in the Heavenly Jerusalem reflect the uncreated light streaming out from God. For the "pattern" of the earthly sanctuary is to be found in heaven, and the eternal prototype of the heavenly pattern is in God Himself. "Let them make Me a sanctuary, that I may dwell among them. According to all that I show thee, after the pattern of the Tabernacle, and the pattern of all the instruments thereof, even so shall ye make it" (Ex. 25:8–9). This pattern or prototype of the earthly sanctuary has, as has been said—following the Kabbala (Zohar: Terumah, 159*a*)—two overlapping aspects: one heavenly and one divine. God revealed to Moses, in the vision of the heavenly tabernacle and its objects, the supraformal, eternal prototypes of His earthly dwelling place, which are based on the ten *Sephiroth*, the synthetic "enumerations" of His infinite qualities. He allowed Moses to be present at the "service" of *Metatron*, the Heavenly Man and Prince of the Angels. *Metatron* is the lord of the heavenly Tabernacle, in which the sacrificial mystery is performed by the Archangel Michael as "high priest." But beyond that, hidden in God's reality itself, there is yet another "tabernacle," whose "high priest" is the "divine light."

These three hierarchic aspects of the universal dwelling place of God have their image here below in the tripartite division of the sanctuary: the "divine" Holy of Holies, the "heavenly" Holy, and the "earthly" outer court. Here the vestibule of the temple symbolizes the "earthly paradise." Here below God dwells in the darkness of the Holy of Holies, for "above" also His absolute essence rests in eternal invisibility, from out of which His shining being and its indwelling reveal themselves. The light of His indwelling radiates from the Holy of Holies to the Holy and shines upon the seven-branched candlestick, just as above God descends from His infinity in

order to sit in state above the seven heavens as Lord of the
worlds, in the radiant crown of the seven all-determining, all-
illumining aspects of His countenance. Finally, the outer court,
like the whole earth, serves as a permanent point of departure
for the return of man to God: It is the "footstool for His feet"
before which man must prostrate himself in awe, and before
which the altar, on which all bodily things are offered, is set
up, as is the water basin in which all souls are purified in order
to appear before Him. "Woe unto the soul that does not purify
itself: it shall be purified in the 'river of fire' *[nahar dinur]!*"

"Thus saith YHWH, the heaven is My throne, and the earth
is My footstool: where is the house that ye build unto Me? and
where is the place of My rest?" (Isa. 66:1). God dwells in the
immeasurable, He is omnipresent, and because of this He is to
be found in the smallest space, as He Himself has said, according to oral tradition: "If I will, I can dwell in a space of the
extent of twenty boards to the North, twenty to the South and
eight to the West. More than that, I can descend and enclose
my *shekhinah* in one square cubit" (Ex. R. 34:1). His infinite
presence rests in the Holy of Holies, His immense heavenly
world in the Holy, and the whole inward reality of the physical
universe in the outer court of His earthly dwelling.

Thus here, in the outer court, the earthly is sacrificed on the
brazen altar, and the fleshly soul *(nephesh)* is purified in the
water of the sacerdotal basin. Only thus purified may the soul
enter the Holy, and, once penetrated and filled with the spirit,
it assumes the nature of the spiritual soul *(ruah)*. Then is revealed to it the seven-armed candlestick, the sacred face of God
in His seven universal properties, with which the soul is
clothed. Now the soul itself shines in the sevenfold light of God
and becomes shewbread for all creatures. Man is completely
purified, illumined, spiritualized, and sanctified and transmits
the light of life and of salvation thus received to all those who
earnestly seek it. One with God's entire creation, man's sanctified soul *(neshamah)* rises like incense from the golden altar of
his heart and presses through the most inward curtain of his
being to the Holy of Holies within it. Here, over the sacred Ark
of its intimacy with God, the soul finds the redeeming cover

of the reconciliation of all duality. The two cherubim are united in the presence of the One, in Whom the soul recognizes its eternal life and its own union with Him. Henceforth the soul is called the eternally "living" (*ḥayah*), the "one and only" (*yeḥidah*). The faith of Israel is realized: *Eḥad,* "One."

The temple has been destroyed, but not the path of purification, illumination, and union that lay concealed in it. Nor was His name destroyed, "Who is near to all who call upon Him in truth." The path begins with "conversion"; it is a permanent "conversion," a turning back to God. The entire work of the spirit has to do with conversion or return, and this is why the masters of Israel teach as follows (Lev. R. 7:2): "Why is it that when someone is converted, it is accounted of him as if he had been lifted up to Jerusalem, had re-built the Temple, erected an altar and carried out all the sacrifices prescribed by the Law? Because, according to the following passage (Ps. 51:19), 'the sacrifice which most pleases God is an extinguished spirit. . . .' "

That which must be extinguished in the human soul is the vain, the false, the ungodly, that which is not really man's own, but which clings to him like a darksome "shell" (*q'lipah*). When this is extinguished, the spirit rises once again to its own original being, which is completely filled with God. The whole man arises anew as a temple of God, a source of blessing for the world.

Rites and Symbols

BY RENÉ GUÉNON

ALL THE constituent elements of a rite have necessarily a symbolic sense, while on the other hand a symbol itself in its commonest acceptation, as a support for meditation, is destined essentially to give results that are exactly comparable to the results of rites. Let us add that when it is a matter of truly traditional rites and symbols (and ones that are not so do not deserve the name at all, but are really only counterfeits or even parodies), their origins in either case are equally "nonhuman"; thus the general impossibility of assigning them any definite author or inventor is not due to ignorance as profane historians may suppose,[1] but it is a natural consequence of these origins, which can be questioned only by people who are wholly unaware of the true nature of tradition and of everything that is integrally bound up with it, as both rites and symbols clearly are.

If the fundamental identity of rites and symbols is more closely examined, it may be noted in the first place that a symbol, understood as a graphic figuration, as it is most commonly, is only as it were the fixation of a ritual gesture.[2] In fact it often happens that the actual tracing of a symbol to be regular must be made under conditions that give it all the characteristics of a true rite; a very clear example of this in a low domain, that of magic (which is nonetheless a traditional science), is provided in the preparation of talismanic figures; and on the plane

---

[1] If for want of a better solution they are not driven to look on them as the product of a sort of "collective consciousness," which if it even existed would in any case be quite incapable of producing things of a transcendent order such as these.

[2] These considerations relate directly to what we have called the "theory of gestures" which we have several times had occasion to allude to, but without its having been possible to treat of it up to the present.

that more immediately concerns us the tracing of yantras in the Hindu tradition is no less striking an example.[3]

But this is not all, for the above-mentioned conception of the symbol is really much too narrow. There are not only figurative or visual symbols but also auditory symbols, a division into two fundamental categories that in the Hindu doctrine are those of the yantra and the mantra. Their respective predominance is characteristic of the two kinds of rites, which relate in the beginning to the traditions of sedentary peoples in the case of visual symbols and to those of nomadic peoples in the case of auditory ones; of course it will be understood that between the two no absolute separation can be made (hence the word "predominance"), every combination being possible as a result of the multiple adaptations that have come about with the passage of time and given rise to the various traditional forms that are known to us today. These considerations clearly show the bond that exists in a perfectly general way between rites and symbols, but we may add that in the case of mantras this bond is to be more immediately seen. In fact while the visual symbol, once traced, remains or may remain in a permanent state (which is why we have spoken of a fixed gesture), the auditory symbol on the other hand becomes manifest only in the actual performance of the rite. This difference, however, is attenuated when a correspondence is established between visual and auditory symbols, as in writing, which represents a true fixation on sound (not of sound itself as such of course, but of a permanent possibility of reproducing it); and it need hardly be recalled in this connection that every writing, at least in origin, is essentially a symbolic figuration. The same is true of speech itself whose symbolic character is no less inherent in its very nature; it is quite clear that a word, whatever it may be, can never be anything but a symbol of the idea that it is intended to express. Thus every language, be it spoken or written, is

[3] The "tracing board" of the lodge in ancient Masonry, which indeed formed a true yantra, may be likened to it. The rites concerned with the construction of monuments for traditional ends might also be cited as examples here, for monuments of this sort in themselves have necessarily a symbolical character.

truly a body of symbols, and it is precisely for this reason that
in spite of all the "naturalistic" theories invented to explain it,
language can never be either a more or less artificial human
creation or a mere product of man's individual faculties.[4]

Among visual symbols themselves there is also an example
of "instantaneity" which is fairly comparable to that of sound
symbols. This is the case of symbols that are not traced permanently but only employed as signs in initiatory rites (notably
the "signs of recognition")[5] and in more general religious rites
(the "sign of the cross" is a typical example known to all); here
the symbol is truly one with the ritual gesture itself.[6] In any
case a "graphic" symbol is, we repeat, itself the fixation of a
gesture or a movement (the actual movement or series of movements that has to be made to trace it), and in the case of sound
symbols one also may say that the movement of the vocal organs that is necessary to produce them (whether it be a matter
of uttering ordinary words or musical sounds) is as much a
gesture as are all the other kinds of bodily movements, from
which it can never be entirely isolated.[7]

Thus the notion of the gesture, in its widest acceptation

[4] It goes without saying that the distinction of "sacred tongues" and
"profane tongues" only arises secondarily; with languages, as with the
arts and sciences, their profanity is only the result of a degeneration,
which may arise earlier and more easily in the case of languages on
account of their more current and more general use. (See "La Science
des Lettres" in *Symboles Fondamentaux de la Science Sacrée*, Chap. 6.)
[5] Utterances that serve a similar purpose, passwords for example, fall
naturally into the category of sound symbols.
[6] A sort of intermediary case is that of the symbolical figures that are
traced at the beginning of a rite or preparatory to it, and effaced as soon
as it is ended; such is the case of many yantras, and used once to be
the same with the "tracing board" of the lodge in Masonry. The practice does not represent a mere precaution against profane curiosity,
which as an explanation is always much too simple; it should be looked
on first and foremost as an immediate consequence of the intimate bond
uniting symbols and rites, in such a way that the former have no cause
for visible subsistence apart from the latter.
[7] Note especially in this connection the part played in rites by the
gestures called in the Hindu tradition mudras, which form a veritable
language of movements and attitudes; the "handclasps" used as "means
of recognition" in initiatory organizations in the West as well as in the
East are really only a particular case of mudras.

(which indeed is better in accord with the real meaning of the word than the more restricted acceptation allowed by current usage), brings back all these various cases to unity and allows us to discern in it their common principle, and this fact has a deep significance in the metaphysical domain which we cannot enlarge upon at present.

It will now be easily understood that every rite is literally made up of a body of symbols; and these include not only the objects used or the figures represented but also the gestures effected and the words pronounced (the latter according to what we have said being really only a particular case of the former)—in short, all the elements of the rite without exception —and these elements thus have the value of symbols by their very nature and not in virtue of any superadded meaning which might have become attached to them from outward circumstances without being really inherent in them. Again, it might be said that rites are symbols "put into action," that every ritual gesture is a symbol "acted"; this is only another way of saying the same thing, but putting rather more specially in evidence the characteristic of a rite that like every action it is something that is necessarily performed in time,[8] while the symbol as such may be considered from a timeless standpoint. In this sense it is possible to speak of a certain preeminence of symbols over rites; but rites and symbols fundamentally are only two aspects of a single reality, and this is none other than the "correspondence" that binds together all the degrees of universal existence in such a way that by its means our human state can enter into communication with the higher states of being.

[8] In Sanskrit the word *karma*, whose first meaning is that of "action" in general, is also used in a "technical" sense to mean "ritual action" in particular; what it then directly expresses is this same characteristic of the rite that we are noting here.

Hermes

by René Guénon

THE HERMETIC tradition is, strictly speaking, concerned with knowledge that is not metaphysical but only cosmological, in the double sense of "macrocosmic" and "microcosmic." This statement must not be taken in any sense as a depreciation of the traditional sciences that come under the heading of Hermetism or of those that correspond to them in other doctrinal forms of East and West; but if everything is to be put in its rightful place, then it must be admitted that these sciences, like all specialized knowledge, are merely secondary and derivative with regard to the principles. In fact they are no more than a particular application of the principles at a lower level of reality. To maintain the contrary would mean giving precedence to "Royal Art"[1] over "Sacerdotal Art."

It cannot be contested that it is from Hermes that Hermetism takes its name. The Greek Hermes has in fact characteristics that correspond exactly to the sciences in question and that are strikingly expressed, for example, by his chief attribute, the Caduceus. No doubt there will be a further opportunity to examine its symbolism more fully; suffice it to say for the moment that this symbolism is essentially and directly related to what might be called "human alchemy" and is concerned with the possibilities of the subtle state, even if these are to be taken merely as the preparatory means to a higher realization, as are, in Hinduism, the equivalent hatha-yoga practices. This can moreover be transferred to the cosmic order, since everything

[1] With regard to the expression "Royal Art," which Freemasonry still uses, we may note here the curious resemblance between the names Hermes and Hiram; this does not mean, needless to say, that these two names have the same linguistic origin, but their constitution is nonetheless identical, and the combination HRM from which both are essentially formed suggests other comparisons also.

in man has its correspondence in the outer world, and vice versa.[2] Here again, and by reason of this very correspondence, the domain in question is the "intermediary world," where are brought into play forces whose dual nature is very clearly figured by the two serpents of the Caduceus. It may be remembered also, in this connection, that Hermes is represented as the messenger of the gods and as their interpreter *(hermeneutes)*, that is, precisely, an intermediary between the celestial and terrestrial worlds, and that he has in addition the function of "guide of the souls of the dead" which, in a lower order, is clearly related also to the domain of the subtle possibilities.[3]

It might be objected that insofar as concerns Hermetism, Hermes takes the place of the Egyptian Thoth with whom he has been identified, and that Thoth represents wisdom, which is related to the priesthood as guardian and transmitter of the tradition. That is true, but since this identification cannot have been made without some reason, it must be admitted that it concerns more especially a certain aspect of Thoth which corresponds to a certain part of the tradition, the part that comprises those branches of knowledge that are related to the "intermediary world"; and the remains that the ancient Egyptian civilization has left behind do in fact show that the sciences of this order were much more developed there and had taken on an importance far more considerable than anywhere else. There is moreover another comparison, we might even say another equivalence, which shows clearly that this objection would have no real bearing: In India the planet Mercury (or Hermes) is called Budha, a name of which the root letters mean

---

[2] As is said in *Rasā'il ikhwān as-safā*, "The world is a great man and man is a little world" *(al-ālam insān kabir wa 'l-insān ālam saghir)*. It is moreover in virtue of this correspondence that a certain realization in the "microcosmic" order can cause, accidentally as regards the being who has achieved it, an outward realization relating to the "macrocosmic" order without any special effort having been exerted in that direction, as has been known to happen, for example, in certain cases of metallic transmutations.

[3] The functions of divine messenger and "guide of souls" could, astrologically, be related respectively to a diurnal and a nocturnal aspect; they may also be said to correspond to the descending and ascending currents symbolized by the two serpents of the Caduceus.

wisdom; here again, it is enough to specify the domain in which this wisdom (in its essence the inspiring principle of all knowledge) is to find its more particular application when it is related to this specialized function.[4]

Strange though it may seem, the name Budha is in fact identical with that of the Scandinavian Odin, Woden, or Wotan;[5] there was thus nothing arbitrary in the Roman assimilation of Odin to Mercury, and in some Germanic languages the day of Mercury (in French *mercredi*) is still called the day of Odin, which is precisely what the word "Wednesday" means.

Still more remarkable, perhaps, is the fact that this same name is to be found exactly in the Votan of the ancient traditions of Central America who has moreover the attributes of Hermes, for he is Quetzalcohuatl, the "bird-serpent," and the union of these two symbolic animals (corresponding respectively to the two elements air and fire) is also figured by the wings and the serpents of the Caduceus.[6] One must indeed be

---

[4] Budha is not to be confused with Buddha, the title of Shākya-Muni, although both appellations have clearly the same radical meaning, and although certain attributes of the planetary Budha were eventually transferred to the historic Buddha, who is represented as having been "illuminated" by the irradiation of this planet, whose essence he was said to have absorbed into himself. It may be noted in this connection that the mother of the Buddha is called Māyā-Dēvī and that, for the Greeks and Romans, Maia was also the mother of Hermes or Mercury.
[5] The change of *b* to *v* or *w* is an extremely frequent linguistic phenomenon.
[6] See in this connection "La Langue des Oiseaux" (*Symboles Fondamentaux de la Science Sacrée*, Chap. 7). The serpent is opposed or allied to the bird according to whether it is being considered in its malefic or benefic aspect. Moreover, a figure such as that of an eagle holding a serpent in its claws (which is to be found, precisely, in Mexico) does not evoke exclusively the idea of that antagonism that is represented, in the Hindu tradition, by Garuda's fight against Nāga. On occasion, especially in heraldic symbolism, the serpent is replaced by the sword, and this substitution is all the more striking when the weapon in question has the form of a flaming sword, which is moreover closely akin to the lightning in the grasp of Jupiter's eagle; and the sword, in its highest sense, is a figure of wisdom and the power of the Word (see, for example, Revelation 1:16). It may be noted that one of the chief symbols of the Egyptian Thoth was the ibis, destroyer of reptiles and hence a symbol of Christ; but in the Caduceus of Hermes we have the serpent in its two contrary aspects as in the medieval figure of the "amphisbaena."

blind not to see, in such facts, a sign of the fundamental unity of all traditional doctrines.

Another equally interesting point is that in the Islamic tradition the Prophet Idris is identified both with Hermes and with Enoch; this double assimilation seems to indicate a continuity of tradition going back beyond the Egyptian priesthood which, as far as Enoch is concerned, could only have been heir to the heritage of what he represents, for he himself clearly belongs to an earlier age.[7] At the same time, the sciences attributed to Idris and placed under his special influence are not the purely spiritual sciences, which belong to Christ, but alchemy and astrology and other "intermediary" sciences; these are, in fact, the sciences that can, strictly speaking, be called Hermetic. But this brings us to another consideration, which might seem, at any rate at first glance, to be a rather strange reversal of the usual correspondences. For each of the planetary spheres there is a major prophet who presides over it and is its "pole" *(qutb)*. Now, it is not Idris who presides over the Heaven of Mercury, but Christ, whereas Idris presides over the Heaven of the Sun; and, naturally, this involves the same transposition in the astrological correspondences of the sciences that are attributed respectively to these two "poles." This raises a very complex question, the full treatment of which would be quite beyond the scope of the present article; we may have occasion to come back to it, but for the moment the following few remarks will perhaps afford a glimpse of the solution and will in any case show that far from being a mere confusion, the reversal that might seem erratic in the eyes of a superficial and "outward" observer has in fact a deep-rooted cause.

First, it is not a single isolated case in traditional doctrine,

[7] Should it not be concluded from this same assimilation that the Book of Enoch, or at any rate what is known by this name, must be considered as an integral part of the whole corpus of the "Hermetic books"? On the other hand, some say also that the Prophet Idris is the same as the Buddha. What has already been said shows well enough how we are to take this assertion which refers in fact to Budha, the Hindu equivalent of Hermes. It could not refer to the historic Buddha, whose death is known to have taken place, whereas Idris is expressly said to have been borne up to heaven alive, just as is Enoch in the Bible.

for it has something like a counterpart in Hebrew angelology. Generally speaking, Michael is the angel of the Sun and Raphael is the angel of Mercury, but sometimes the relationship is reversed. On the other hand, if Michael, as the representative of the solar Metatron, is assimilated esoterically to Christ, Raphael, according to the meaning of his name, is the "divine healer," and Christ appears also as "spiritual healer" and as "repairer"; one could find also other connections between Christ and the principle represented by Mercury among the planetary spheres.[8] It is true that, for the Greeks, medicine was attributed to Apollo, that is, to the solar principle, and to his son Asklēpios (in Latin Aesculapius); but in the "Hermetic books" Asklēpios becomes the son of Hermes, and it is also to be noted that the staff that is his attribute is closely related, symbolically, to the Caduceus.[9] The example of medicine shows us how one and the same science can have aspects that relate to different orders and that therefore have different corre-

---

[8] If Hindu doctrine considers the Buddha as being the ninth avatar of Vishnu, that is the *Mleccha* (foreign) avatar, this does not necessarily exclude other divine interventions that have taken place on behalf of "foreign" (non-Hindu) peoples during this same period. In particular, Christ might even be said to share with the Buddha the ninth avataric function, since his first coming was, for the West, what the advent of the Buddha was for the Far East (and what the Koranic "descent" was for the "middle" region). Now, as we have seen in connection with the Buddha, the ninth avatar is a "Mercurial" manifestation. It would seem then that the two comings of Christ may be related to his "Mercurial" and "Solar" aspects, the Solar Christ being Christ Glorious, that is, the tenth or Kalki avatar, who is to come at the end of the cycle, the "white horse" of this final descent being a solar symbol par excellence. As to the first coming of Christ, it may be mentioned that the month of May takes its name from Mercury's mother, Maia, who is said to be one of the Pleiads and to whom that month was consecrated in ancient times; and in Christianity it has become "the month of Mary," by an assimilation, which is doubtless not merely phonetic, between Maria and Maia.

(This note has been somewhat modified by the translator in the light of conversations that he had with the author many years after the article had been written.)

[9] Around the staff of Aesculapius is coiled a single serpent, which represents the benefic force, the malefic force being bound to disappear inasmuch as the attribute in question belongs to the genius of medicine. The relationship may also be noted between this same staff of Aesculapius, as an emblem of healing, and the biblical symbol of the "brazen serpent" (see *Symboles Fondamentaux de la Science Sacrée*, Chap. 20).

spondences, even if the outward effects obtained seem to be alike, for there is purely spiritual or "theurgic" medicine, and there is also Hermetic or "spagyric" medicine; this is directly related to the question we are considering and helps to explain why medicine, from the traditional point of view, was considered essentially as a sacerdotal science.

On the other hand, there is nearly always a close connection made between Enoch (Idris) and Elijah (Ilyās), both of whom were taken up to heaven without passing through bodily death,[10] and the Islamic tradition places both in the sphere of the sun. Similarly, according to the Rosicrucian tradition, Elias Artista, who presides over the Hermetic "Great Work,"[11] has his dwelling place in the "Solar Citadel," which is moreover the abode of the "Immortals" (in the sense of the Chirajīvīs of Hinduism, that is, beings "endowed with longevity," whose life lasts throughout the whole cycle[12]) and which represents one of the aspects of the "Center of the World." All this is certainly worth reflecting on, and if one adds also the traditions, from almost all parts of the world, that liken symbolically the sun itself to the fruit of "the Tree of Life," one will perhaps understand the special relationship between the solar influence and Hermetism, inasmuch as the essential aim and end of Hermetism, as of the "Lesser Mysteries" of antiquity, is the restoration of the human "primordial state." Is this not the "Solar Citadel" that, according to the Rosicrucian doctrine, is to "descend from Heaven to earth at the end of the cycle, in the form of the Heavenly Jerusalem," realizing the "squaring of the circle" according to the perfect measure of the "golden reed"?

[10] It is said that they are to appear on earth again at the end of the cycle; they are the two "witnesses" mentioned in Revelation, Chap. 11.

[11] He incarnates as it were the nature of the "philosopher's fire," and according to the Bible narrative, the Prophet Elijah was taken up to heaven on a "chariot of fire"; this is related to the "fiery vehicle" (*taijasa* in the Hindu doctrine) which in the human being corresponds to the subtle state.

[12] Let us recall also, from the alchemical point of view, the correspondence between the sun and gold, which Hinduism denotes as "mineral light"; the *aurum potabile* (drinkable gold) of the Hermetists is moreover the same as the "draft of immortality," which is also called "liquor of gold" in Taoism.

The Sword of the Spirit

The Making of an Orthodox Rosary

BY D. M. DEED

WHEN A MONK or nun is professed in the Orthodox Church, he or she is given, as part of the investiture, a knotted cord. The Greeks call this κομβοσχοινιον, from κομβος, a knot, and σχοινιον, a cord. The Russians call it *Tchotki*, a word derived from the verb meaning "to count," but the old Slavonic name was *Vervitsa*, meaning a cord, or *Lestovka*, a ladder. The words of investiture used in the Slavonic rite are "Take, brother, the sword of the spirit, which is the word of God, for continual prayer to Jesus; for thou must always have the Name of the Lord Jesus in mind, in heart and on thy lips." This cord is also used by priests who are not professed monks and by lay people. It is associated with the recitation of the Jesus Prayer. The cord traditionally given is made of black wool, and the most usual formula of the prayer is "Lord Jesus Christ, Son of God, have mercy on me." Sometimes the word "sinner" is added, but whether it is explicitly included or not it is always implied. Variants of this formula are also used; some change the "me" to "us," and others shorten or lengthen the formula. Essentially and always the Jesus Prayer consists of the recitation of a formula in which the name of Jesus is invoked, and whether the word "sinner" is expressly included or not, it is always implied.

It is not generally known or appreciated that the knots are made in a very complex and peculiar way, which is described in this article. The making of the cord seems to the writer to be of great symbolical interest, and for this reason the process is described in detail.

The wool required is first measured, and the number of strands needed, which varies with the thickness of the wool and the size of the knots desired, are cut into the required lengths. The length necessary is eight arm lengths and another half length for the cross which completes the rosary. The number of strands will be twelve or more if the wool is of the thickness usually required for making socks. The wool is divided into two strands, which I will subsequently refer to as Strands A and B. These are knotted loosely together. This first knot does not subsequently form part of the rosary. It is later untied and is only made for convenience in order to keep A and B together at their source while the first permanent knot is made. It should not therefore be considered as playing any part in the symbolism of the rosary, though for convenience and clarity it is referred to in the text and shown in the illustrations as though it remained throughout the making of the cord and as if A and B preceded as well as followed its making. This of course is not the case, since before we began there was only the undivided stream of wool from which all the knots are made. There is one God and Creator of all "by Whom all things were made," and therefore there is one source from which the whole rosary derives. We start from unity, but duality is inherent in creation. God made light and dark, heaven and earth, male and female, soul and body, and so we make our two strands A and B in imitation of the divine pattern. From now on we work with these two threads, which we shall weave into a complicated pattern, always ordered, though it may seem at times to be disordered. We use now one thread, now the other, but each is always related to the other and to the knot itself.

The process of making each knot may be divided into twelve distinct "movements," each of which is described in what follows.

1. See Figure 1. Place the knot behind the first finger and take strand A across the palm and between the third and fourth fingers of the left hand; take strand B behind the three fingers and back onto the palm of the hand between the third and fourth fingers. The two equal parts into which the wool has been divided may be regarded as the two opposing or complementary elements in the created world, the active and passive principles, black and white, good and evil, expansion and con-

FIG. 1

traction, etc. Throughout the making of each knot the palm of the hand may be considered as the field of creation, or the more limited field of work of each one of us, that area of space and time within which we are permitted to "live and move and have our being." It is circumscribed and limited, yet, on it and by means of it, the whole knot is formed. The back of the hand is equally important, although we cannot see it, and we do not consciously work with it. It may be thought of as symbolizing those hidden influences that are continually at work in the whole of creation and in our individual lives, though we are unaware of them until their results become apparent, and then we realize their immense significance. In the same way that the wool that has passed behind the fingers is integrated into the knot when it emerges onto the palm of the hand, forming an essential part of each knot, so these hidden forces are an essential part of the whole creation, and so also they influence and are integrated into the life of each one of us. Without the "work" that goes on behind the backs of the fingers the knot would never be tied; and without the work that goes on in the hidden part of the soul nothing would be achieved. Let us therefore consider that strand A represents the light or the active principle while strand B represents the darkness or the passive principle. It is to be noted that A is in full view in front of the fingers while B is hidden behind them and comes to light again only when A and B cross between the fingers.

FIG. 2

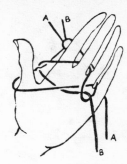

FIG. 3

2. See Figure 2. The second movement is made entirely with B, which is taken around the thumb and crossed over itself at the center of the palm, thus making a first, though rudimentary, cross. At this stage it is made entirely of B, a hidden, dark cross at the center of our being; perhaps a cross in embryo only, a foretaste of what is to come. A does not participate in the making of this cross.

3. See Figure 3. The third movement is a very complicated interweaving of the two strands by which they become inextricably entangled in each other. It may be described as follows: Pick up strand B at a point near the thumb and place it over the second finger; pick up strand A, through the loop of B, and slip it over the thumb, then slip B off the thumb. A square has been formed in the palm, and this has been firmly secured by two loops, namely A around the thumb and B around the second finger. These are at opposite corners of the square, which now surrounds the palm. We may think of it as a symbol of form and hence of matter, which is bounded, as the square is bounded by four sides, by four elements and four cardinal directions. There is, thus, a clearly defined circumscribed form in the palm of the hand made by the two opposite (or complementary) strands. The "earth" is no longer "without form and void." A form is there, and out of this will come the perfect knot.

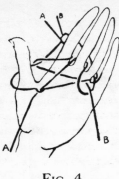

FIG. 4　　　　　　　　FIG. 5

4. See Figure 4. Take A behind the two middle fingers and over B, threading it under the strand of itself which comes from the thumb. By this process a very important step is taken. A cross is made by the two strands in the center of the palm. The square of the world and of ourself has been filled by the cross. There is no need to enlarge on the meaning of this, since it is clear.

5. See Figure 5. *Take up the cross.* This is of course a very significant action. There is no hope of reaching the perfection of the end unless the cross is taken up unhesitatingly. It is placed over the thumb leaving the palm empty and thus ready and able to receive. By this action the self has been emptied of itself, self-naughted and denied. The world holds nothing for one who has taken up his cross and denied himself, and therefore his hand is empty. Bordering the empty palm, the two strands A and B hang down freely, parallel to each other. They still appear as two opposite forces, but they are now firmly interwoven with each other and emerge in orderly fashion to surround and limit the field of work.

6. See Figure 6 & 7. Take B behind the two middle fingers and underneath the three strands between the thumb and the original knot and let it hang down over the palm.

7. See Figure 6 & 7. Take A (under B) behind the same two fingers and under the three strands between the thumb and the

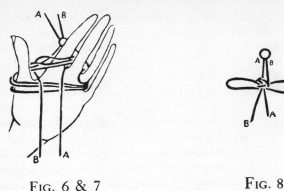

FIG. 6 & 7   FIG. 8

second finger, letting it also fall freely down over the palm. The picture is now that of a still smaller and more circumscribed square. The field of our work has narrowed down to a smaller space; it is more clearly bounded, more tightly and firmly held, and the interweaving threads are more closely bound together. A and B still hang down on each side of this space, but they have changed places—B is now on the left and A on the right. Is there much difference between darkness and light? Do they not both come from the same source? We are beginning to see as we make our knot that these apparent opposites are the very warp and woof of life. Both are necessary, and both are closely interwoven in the whole created world of which we ourselves are a part. It is to be noted that the palm of the hand is still empty. There is no central point visible, and the two strands are joined together at their source, the original knot, which is still there at the beginning of all this complicated business of interweaving.

8. Here is the turning point. The direction given is to search for and find the original strand A behind the thumb as it comes from the first knot, hang on to it, and throw all the other strands that are behind the thumb into the palm of the hand. Now search for B in the same manner. It is the loop safely secured around the third finger. Place this on the second finger and throw all the rest into the palm of the hand. This direction

tells us quite plainly to go back and look for the source, to find the threads that lead to it, and to hold on to them, securing them firmly one on each side of the palm. Duality is still there, A and B still exist, but we are quite clear now that there is unity behind this duality, that there is one God and Father of all, one Creator from Whom and also in Whom all things exist and have their being. We have firm hold of the two threads that lead us to Him. However curiously interwoven these two have become, we know that they link us to God Himself and that, were it not so, there would be no knot, no field in which to work, and nothing but a fruitless and disordered end to our labors. It is this link that keeps us steady and that will ultimately prove to be the end as well as the beginning. We still hold the first knot. It has been there behind the first finger all the time, even if we have forgotten it.

9. See Figure 8. We are now faced with what looks like an inextricable tangle in the palm of the hand. Everything, except the original knot and the two strands leading to it, has been thrown into the palm, which we can still consider to be our field of work. There the wool lies in what looks like a complete muddle. The direction given is *arrangez joliment au centre*. In other words, there is order in this apparent chaos, and we must find it and arrange it around a central point to form the knot. This is achieved by holding tight to the three secure points and pulling gently on the two threads that hang down. If this is done carefully, and with little pulls of adjustment here and there, the result is a cross that can be slipped off the hand altogether. The two horizontal arms are formed by the loops A and B, which we held around the thumb and second finger respectively; the stem consists of the two strands A and B, which we left hanging down, and at the top is the original knot. At the center, if all has been done correctly, is the virtual knot, not yet in its final form but nevertheless containing in itself all that is needed to make the perfect knot itself.

We have trusted and we have believed that out of the tangle order would come; we have held on to the thread which has never broken and which has always linked us to Him to Whom we owe our whole existence as well as the conditions within which we can work and which we have accepted with all their apparent limitations and difficulties: Now the end is in sight.

10. The next direction is to run the knot up the stem toward its source by pulling the top threads of the right and left loops. If we have made the least mistake, the knot will not run up the stem. If this should happen, there is nothing we can do except start again. If we pray harder and concentrate better, our next attempt may succeed. But if we have made each move correctly, then our embryo knot will move smoothly up the stem until it reaches the first knot, or if others have been previously made, the one immediately before it. This immediately preceding knot will be our link with the first source of all the knots. There is still more work to do, but we are free now of the earlier limitations; we are in direct touch with the chain that leads us back to the beginning. Nothing can stop us except some foolish last mistake, and we begin to experience the joy of good work accomplished. Is this not natural? We are nearer both to the beginning and the ending, to God the Father of all, and to Him Who brings all things to fulfillment.

By this movement the very center of the cross is drawn back toward the source from which it came. It is significant that the center itself moves vertically up the stem. This word calls to mind the symbolism of the Tree of Life, of *l'axe du monde*, and reminds us of the importance of the central point where this axis meets each plane of existence. We are also reminded, as the knot moves upward, of that which came after the cross, the resurrection.

At this point we can associate the two strands with the two natures of Christ, and we may also remind ourselves of the interweaving of the divine and human in all that happens in this world. There is a wealth of meaning that pours out upon us. Sometimes we may see one aspect more clearly and sometimes another.

11. Hold the right loop B against the stem and work first with the loop A, pulling it three times through the knot. Then hold the left-hand loop A against the stem and work with B. Pull B through the knot once, then allow it to fall naturally through the loop A, and finally pull it once more through the knot.

These threefold moves probably have many meanings, as indeed have all the previous moves. For a Christian they are likely to be associated especially with the mystery of the Trinity, first as it is in the Godhead and second (during the moves with strand B) in relation to the world and ourselves. The interlocking of the two loops, one falling through the other, can then be considered as symbolizing the incarnation, the descent of God into flesh and the union of the two natures, and finally the deification of man.

We can also think of these triple moves as symbolizing the "three worlds" of body, soul, and spirit; or the three parts of ourselves occupied in the Jesus Prayer: the discursive intelligence, which repeats the name of Jesus, the intellect, which is wholly concentrated on the name, and the spirit, which creates in us compunction and love. (*Cf.* Saint Theolepte as referred to in "La Prière de Jesus" by a monk of the Eastern Church.) Or, again, we may think of the three stages of purification, illumination, and union; or the three margas of the Hindu tradition, the way of action, the way of love, and the way of knowledge by which the prayer itself may lead us.

There is a sense of rhythm in the triple moves by which first A and then B is pulled through the knot and made firm. It suggests the association of the Jesus Prayer with the rhythm of respiration and the beating of the heart. It may be connected in our thought with the indrawing and outflowing not only of our own breath but of the breath of God Himself. The Jesus Prayer is also associated with the beating of the heart, when the lips may be stilled and there is left to us only a listening, since the prayer says itself in the depth of the heart. We may find all this, and more, symbolized in the later stages of tying the knot. Whatever we may learn is integrated into a whole, but we see it as such only when the knot is finished.

12. The knot is now finished. All that remains is to pull the two ends down evenly so that the two loops are absorbed into the knot and A and B disappear in what seems a strange and quite surprising manner. There are no longer two separate strands; they have been integrated into the completed knot. But this knot is not an isolated creation; it is part of a whole chain

of knots, making a complete circle which is finally finished by untying our original loose knot and making a final knot which unites the beginning of the rosary to its end, and the whole is completed by making a small cross from the woolen ends that remain.

The making of such a rosary or cord is a whole day's work, and, throughout, the Jesus Prayer should be repeated continuously. It is said that if each knot is not correctly made, it is because the maker has not prayed continuously and with due attention, for without prayer nothing can be right, since God alone can perfect the work.

No mention has been made in this article of the symbolic significance of the numbers involved. There are two of particular note. The turning point comes after seven movements, and the whole knot is completed in twelve. These numbers are obviously important, though the writer prefers to leave others to draw their own conclusions, merely drawing attention to the seven days of creation of the Book of Genesis and the seven Churches of the Book of Revelations and to the twelve tribes of Israel, the twelve apostles, and the twelve gates of the heavenly city, the New Jerusalem. It is not a mere accident that these numbers have an important place in the making of each knot.

It may well be asked who invented such a complicated knot and who was the first to make it. The answer given to the writer's inquiry was "the blessed Mother of God, Herself; who else could have thought of it."

Old Lithuanian Songs

BY MARTIN LINGS

LITHUANIAN is the oldest, that is, the most archaic in form, of all living Indo-European languages. It still retains a complexity comparable to that of Sanskrit[1] and classical Greek. Various historical and geographical reasons are given by scholars for this "lack of development"—so called out of deference to progressism and evolutionism—but there can be little doubt that the direct reason why the language has been so remarkably preserved from decay is the presence, until very recent times, of a deep-rooted oral tradition powerful and vital enough to fulfill many of the functions of literature. We are accustomed to distinguishing between living and dead languages, but in the domain of living languages a further distinction could be made between those that possess a written literature and those that rely entirely on oral tradition, for there is no doubt that "the letter kills" and that among peoples who are almost wholly illiterate, language can possess a vitality—and in consequence a relative immunity from degeneration—that for us is almost unimaginable. This question has been treated elsewhere;[2] the question now to be considered is not one of language in itself, but it is not altogether unconnected, for the songs that are our theme were handed down from a remote past by that oral tradition that has helped to keep the Lithuanian language so intact.

Since these songs form part of what is often called Lithua-

[1] It is also the *nearest* of the European languages to Sanskrit, not only in virtue of its undegeneracy but also by reason of its "orientality." Lettish, the language of Latvia, is the only other surviving member of the Baltic group of languages to which Lithuanian belongs, but it is less archaic than Lithuanian.
[2] A. L. Coomaraswamy, *The Bugbear of Literacy*, and Martin Lings, *Ancient Beliefs and Modern Superstitions*, pp. 8–15.

nian folklore, let us quote what Guénon says about folklore in general:

The very conception of *folklore*, in the generally accepted sense of the term, is based on an idea that is radically false, the idea that there are "popular creations" spontaneously produced by the mass of the people; and one sees at once the close connection between this way of thinking and "democratic" prejudices. As has been very rightly said, "the profound interest of all so-called popular traditions lies in the fact that they are not popular in origin";[3] and we will add that where, as is nearly always the case, ther is a question of elements that are traditional in the true sense of the word, however deformed, diminished, and fragmentary they may be sometimes, and of things that have a real symbolic value, their origin is not even human, let alone popular. What may be popular is solely the fact of "survival," when these elements belong to vanished traditional forms, and in this respect "folklore" takes on a meaning rather close to that of "paganism," if we consider only the etymology of the word "pagan" and not its "polemical" use as a term of reproach. The people preserve, without understanding them, the relics of former traditions which even go back sometimes to a past too remote to be dated, so that it has to be relegated to the obscure domain of the "prehistoric"; they thereby fulfill the function of a more or less subconscious collective memory, the contents of which have clearly come from elsewhere.[4] What may seem most surprising is that on the closest scrutiny the things so preserved are found to contain above all, under a more or less veiled form, abundant information of an esoteric order, which is, in its essence, precisely what is least popular, and this fact suggests in

[3] Luc Benoist, *La Cuisine des Anges, une Esthétique de la Pensée*, p. 74.
[4] "This is an essentially 'lunar' function, and it is in fact to the Moon that the mass of the people corresponds astrologically, which is a clear indication also of the purely passive character of that mass, incapable as it is of initiative or of spontaneity."

itself an explanation, which may be summed up as follows:
When a traditional form is on the point of becoming extinct, its last representatives may very well deliberately
entrust to this aforesaid collective memory the things that
would otherwise be lost beyond recall; that is in point of
fact the sole means of saving what can in a certain measure
be saved. At the same time, that lack of understanding that
is one of the natural characteristics of the masses is a sure
enough guarantee that what was esoteric will be nonetheless undivulged, remaining merely as a sort of witness of
the past for such as, in later times, shall be capable of
understanding it.[5]

The four songs that follow illustrate every point that is made
in the above quotation. As far as one knows, they were handed
down entirely by word of mouth until the eighteenth century,
and in more recent times[6] children used to learn them by heart
at school. As to their deeper meaning, the veil is in many places
a thin one, and many if not all the comments made in this
article will seem superfluous to the reader who has a knowledge
of symbolism. In any case, it is preferable not to break up the
text with comments, but to let each song be read uninterrupted
as a poem, for they certainly have their rights in this respect.
Would it be an exaggeration to say that the fourth and last of

[5] René Guénon, "Le Saint Graal" in *Symboles Fondamentaux de la Science
Sacrée*, pp. 50–51.
[6] That is, between the two world wars. In 1940 the Soviet army occupied Lithuania, whereupon such members of the government as
could not escape were sent to Siberia, and a carefully chosen Communist government was set up, whose first act was to request the incorpo-
ration of Lithuania into the Soviet Union. The request was granted.
Except for the scarcely less terrible period of German occupation during the war, Lithuania has been swallowed up in Russia ever since,
with no apparent hope of liberation except that the Western powers
have never formally recognized the annulment of her independence.
After the war, until about 1953 when they were finally rounded up,
hundreds of thousands of young Lithuanian men and women took
refuge in the forests of their country, preferring to live there in great
hardship rather than be victims of the mass deportations to Siberia and
elsewhere which were part of the Soviet method of russification and
sovietization.

those given here is one of the greatest lyrics in the world? And through it, do we not breathe something of the fresh air of a remote antiquity?

The translations given here are taken from a little volume entitled *Old Lithuanian Songs*⁷ which is an anthology of forty-seven songs, selected and translated into English by Adrian Paterson. Let us quote what he says of them: "I have tried as far as possible to render the grace of cadence of the originals, and for this reason I have avoided regular rhymes, which would have given an effect too hard and glib; instead I have done my best to reproduce something of the Lithuanian assonance."

> Moon took to be his bride
> Sun in the first spring tide.
>
> When Sun woke up at dawn,
> Moon from her side was gone.
>
> Moon, as alone he roved,
> Morn's Star beheld and loved.
>
> Then Thunder, wroth, with His blade
> cleft him in two and said:
>
> Why didst abandon Sun?
> Why, Morn's Star's minion,
> by night didst rove alone?

The language of symbolism is universal, and the sun, whether it be feminine as here and in the Germanic tradition, or masculine as in the Hindu and Greek traditions, always has

⁷ This now very rare book was published in Lithuania only a few weeks before the war. One or two complimentary copies reached Western Europe, including one for me, since I had written the preface. I was intending to return, after the long vacation, to the University of Vitautas the Great in Kaunas (then the temporary capital of Lithuania) where I was lecturer, but the way back was blocked in the first days of the war, and I have never returned there since. Nor have I any reason to suppose that the entire edition, except for the few copies mentioned, was not destroyed during the terrible years that followed. The translator had left Lithuania several years previously, and at the time of publication he was in Egypt, where he died the following year.

a spiritual or celestial significance in relation to the moon which, in a positive sense, stands for earthly or human perfection. Thus in Christian iconography the cross is often represented with the sun on its right and the moon on its left because Christ, the second Adam, unites in himself two natures, heavenly and earthly; and with the same symbolism the creation of the first Adam, also possessed of two natures, is represented in this song by the marriage of the sun and the moon in the first spring.

The sun, as spirit, is the daughter of God *(Dievo dukrytè[8])*. God Hìmself is Perkūnas,[9] literally "Thunder"; and according to the discourse that Plato, in his *Symposium*, puts into the mouth of Aristophanes, primordial men were of a twofold nature until Zeus, who like Perkūnas has thunder for his chief attribute, cut them in two. But the doctrine of the song is more complete than that of the discourse, for it tells of a double scission: First and "vertically" there is the separation of sun and moon, that is, spirit and soul; then, as a result of man's loss of connection with his higher possibilities, there is a "horizontal" scission within the soul itself. Man is inwardly divided, since he now lacks contact with the transcendent principle that alone can resolve opposites into complements. In other words, he has become subject to the "Knowledge of Good and Evil." It is this division within the soul of man that is represented in the song by the cutting of the moon in two. The soul-dividedness of fallen man, as Titus Burckhardt remarks,[10] is as it were the starting point of alchemy; the "chemical marriage," that is, the "marriage of sulfur and quicksilver," would thus be, in Lithuanian terms, "the putting together again of the two halves of the moon," whereas the "mystical marriage" would be the "remarriage of the moon with the sun."[11]

[8] The Sanskrit equivalent, *Dēva-duktrī,* may be mentioned to show how close, on occasion, these two languages can be.
[9] In Sanskrit *Parjanya,* whom the Rig-Vēda mentions as having thunder for his attribute.
[10] *Alchemy* (Baltimore, Md.: Penguin Books Inc, 1971), Chap. 11.
[11] In alchemy the "chemical marriage" is sometimes also called "the marriage of the sun and the moon," but in the Lithuanian perspective the sun is always transcendent.

The Morning Star, Ausrine, is in some respects none other than Lucifer, whereas in other respects she is comparable to Eve. In the second song, which needs no comment, the correspondence is to Lucifer:

> Sun, 'tis time you went
> over the firmament,
> Sun, 'tis time to fare
> through the air.
> Sun, 'tis time you counted
> if all the stars are mounted.
>
> Whether I count or no,
> already one will not show,
> and that the star most bright
> which rose up with the light
> and retired late at night.

In the following song the Morning Star represents, like Eve, the fallen human race as a whole:

> Morn's Star held a wedding feast.
> Thunder galloped through the gate
> and struck down the green oak tree.
>
> The blood of the green oak tree trickled,
> and stained my apparel,
> and stained my garland.
>
> The Sun's daughter wept,
> and for three years gathered
> withered foliage.
>
> And where, O mother mine,
> shall I wash my apparel,
> where wash away the blood?
>
> O daughter mine so youthful,
> go to the lake there yonder
> where are poured the streams of nine rivers.

> And where, O mother mine,
> shall I dry my apparel
> where in the wind shall I dry it?

> O daughter mine so youthful,
> in yonder garden green
> where are flowering nine roses.

> And when, O mother mine,
> shall I put on my apparel,
> put it on in its whiteness?

> O daughter mine so youthful,
> on that same day of singing
> when there shall shine nine suns.

Owing to a difference of symbolism, this song appears on the surface very different from the first, except that the Morning Star's wedding feast clearly recalls the illicit union which, in the other song, likewise provoked the wrath of Perkūnas. But if we consider the relationship between certain symbols, in particular the sun and the tree, we shall find that the theme of the first song is altogether comprised within the song of the Morning Star and the oak, though this last song takes us further, tracing out not only the Fall but also the path of return to the primordial state.

The Tree of Life rises from the center of the earthly paradise connecting earth with heaven. Man's loss of connection with his higher possibilities is thus, in the language of Genesis, his loss of access to the Tree of Life, and we have also seen this same loss symbolized also by the moon's separation from the sun. In our third song the Tree of Life is the oak, which in the Lithuanian tradition is the most holy of trees,[12] being especially sacred to Perkūnas.[13] It might at first seem strange that the

---

[12] As also for the Celts and others. See René Guénon, *Le Roi du Monde*, p. 21, note 1.

[13] We see here yet another connection between Perkūnas and Zeus, who is not only the God of thunder but also the God of the oak. Moreover, most etymologists are agreed that *Perkūnas* and *quercus* (Latin for oak) were originally one and the same Aryan word. Its wide differentiation according to its Lithuanian and Latin "dialects" is analogous to that of the word for five, which became in Lithuanian *penki* and in Latin *quinque*.

Thunderer should strike his own tree, but history offers examples of great sanctuaries being destroyed by heaven in reprisal for human sacrilege, and here also it is in reality against man's connection with the sanctuary that Perkūnas aims his bolt. Ultimately, therefore, this symbolism comes close to that of Genesis, at least in the sense that in both cases man has lost his access to the Tree of Life. But in the song this scission is also represented by the separation of the leaves from the tree. The analogy between the leaves and the human soul (and therefore the "moon") is clear enough if we remember that when the cross symbolizes the two natures of Christ, the horizontal line denotes his human nature, which is likewise represented by the leaf-bearing branches of the Tree of Life, whose trunk, like the vertical of the cross, stands for his divine nature. The symbolism of the leaves becomes even clearer when we consider that the Tree of Life is sometimes also called the "Tree of the World" or the "Axis of the World,"[14] and as such it is occasionally represented with its roots in heaven[15] and its branches constituting this world or, microcosmically, the human soul.

If the separation of the foliage from the tree corresponds to the separation of the moon from the sun in the first song, the subsequent scattering of the foliage corresponds to the cleaving of the moon, that is, to the psychic disintegration consequent upon the Fall. The gathering together of this foliage is thus the first phase of the spiritual path, the reintegration of the psychic elements. When all the foliage has been gathered, fallen man turns again to the spirit. It is as if the moon, now on the way to regaining his primal fullness, were to turn once more to the sun; but the song we are now considering shows us another aspect of the sun. Instead of being man's Celestial Bride, she is here, as in most other Lithuanian songs, his Divine Mother.

[14] See René Guénon, *The Symbolism of the Cross*, Chap. 9, note 1.
[15] A symbol, being merely a reflection, can never show every aspect of the higher reality that it symbolizes. To have a fuller representation of the relationship between heaven and earth we have therefore to conceive of the Tree of Life as a tree that grows not only upward, in the direction of man's spiritual aspirations, but also downward, because it is in fact rooted in the spirit, that is, in the "sun." In the case of the "normal" tree the sun is, as we shall see, the fruit; but there is no contradiction here, for the fruit contains the seed which is itself virtually the root.

For if she is the daughter of Perkūnas, she is also, as the Hindus would say, his Shakti, and as such she is the personification of mercy and the other "feminine" attributes of the Divinity.

In the purification by the elements, that is, by water, wind, and sun, which now takes place under the direction of the spirit, the element earth is not mentioned, perhaps because man himself is in a sense earth.

Nine, which is, one might say, the very essence of this song, is a celestial number. There are nine celestial spheres, and nine degrees in the hierarchy of the angels. Moreover, nine corresponds, geometrically, to the circumference of the circle[16] and therefore to the movements of the heavenly bodies and to the visible form of the firmament which is itself the great symbol of heaven. Nine is therefore also—and here lies the key to this song—the symbol of the earthly paradise which, as the chief reflection of heaven upon earth, is always represented as circular, and although in the perspective of later and more "sedentary" religions the restoration of perfection is the "squaring of the circle"[17]—the Heavenly Jerusalem, for example, is square—in the earlier and more nomadic perspectives the inverse of the Fall is always a return to the earthly paradise. It is therefore not surprising that the number nine should be so much stressed in this song whose theme is, precisely, the recovery of the primordial state.

In particular, as regards the "nine suns," there may be here an implicit reference to the restoration of the Tree of Life, for in various traditions there is mention of the shining of a plurality of suns at the end of the cycle, and as Guénon remarks: "The

---

[16] As Guénon remarks, 10 is the number of the circle, being the number of cyclic perfection, and he adds: "1 corresponds to the center and 9 to the circumference. . . . It is because 9, and not 10, is the number of the circumference that it is normally measured in multiples of 9 (90 degrees for the quadrant, and then 360 degrees for the whole circumference)." "La Tétraktys et le Carré de Quatre" in *Symboles Fondamentaux de la Science Sacrée*, p. 128.

[17] As regards the relationship between the square and the circle, see Titus Burkhardt, *Sacred Art in East and West*, p. 18, and as regards the roundness of nomadic and seminomadic sanctuaries, see *ibid.*, p. 22.

image of the sun is often connected with that of the tree, as if the sun were the fruit of the Tree of the World."[18] He mentions, as regards the Hindu doctrine of the end of the cycle, "the tree whose fruits are twelve suns."[19] He also draws our attention to the fact that even where there is no specific mention of suns in connection with the Tree of Life, it is often represented as bearing "solar" fruits: "The fruits of the Tree of Life are the golden apples of the Garden of the Hesperides; the golden fleece[20] of the Argonauts, which was also placed on a tree and guarded by a serpent or a dragon, is another symbol of the immortality which man has to reconquer."[21] Finally he mentions that in China one finds also, as a symbol of the completion of the cycle (which in the macrocosm means a new Golden Age and in the microcosm the return to the primordial state), the tree with ten suns; and this brings us back to our song, for as we have already seen, nine and ten are sometimes interchangeable in that both can represent the circle which is itself the figure of cyclic perfection. Analogously one can say of the Garden of Helicon, which, as Dante tells us, is none other than the earthly paradise, that it bears the seal of nine or of ten according to whether or not we count, with the nine Muses, Apollo himself, who is the center around which they form the circumference.

> Fly little hawk,
> near to the lake,
> near that same lake
> where a whirlpool seethes
>
> Near to that whirlpool
> there's a rue garden.
> In that same garden
> weeps a maiden.

[18] Guénon, *The Symbolism of the Cross*, p. 52.
[19] *Ibid.*
[20] A doubly solar symbol, in virtue of the solar animal as well as the solar metal.
[21] Guénon, *The Symbolism of the Cross*, p. 52.

I have no mother,
a dowry to gather,
I have no father
to apportion my share.

I have no brother
to saddle horses,
I have no sister
to plait a garland.

Sun, thou mother,
Sun, thou mother,
Sun, thou mother,
gather me a dowry

Moon, thou father,
Moon, thou father,
Moon, thou father,
apportion my share.

Star, thou sister,
Star, thou sister,
Star, thou sister,
oh plait my garland!

Greatwain, thou brother,
Greatwain, thou brother,
Greatwain, thou brother,
oh drive me through the meadows!

The hawk, with all the other members of its tribe, above all
the eagle, is a solar bird, and as such a symbol of the spirit. But
in particular it may be remembered that whereas the eagle is
the bird of Zeus, the hawk is one of the emblems of Apollo, God
of inspiration, and in this song the prayer of the maiden is
clearly uttered under the inspiration of the hawk, whereas
there can be no doubt that the initial imperative addressed to
the hawk is a divine command. In ancient Egypt the equivalent
of Apollo was Horus; and it is perhaps not irrelevant to recall

here, especially in view of the end of the song, the temple paintings that represent him as the hawk-headed usher of righteous souls into the presence of Osiris.

Rue has been used from time immemorial to ward off evil influences and to purify sanctuaries and habitations in cases of pollution, so that among plants it is one of the outstanding symbols of purity. As such it plays a particularly important part in Lithuanian tradition.[22] The "rue garden" or "Garden of Purity," which is difficult of access and "guarded" by the whirlpool as by a dragon, and which is, moreover, to be the starting point of the maiden's celestial journey, can be none other than the earthly paradise. This is also confirmed by the outstanding "simplicity," "childlikeness," and "spiritual poverty" of the maiden herself, these being among the terms in which readiness to enter "the Kingdom of Heaven" is universally described by religion.

The "garland" mentioned in this and in the previous song (there the "staining of the garland" means loss of innocence) is the garland of rue which in Lithuania was traditionally part of the insignia of maidenhood and especially of the virgin bride who wore it as a wreath on her wedding day.

The "dowry" that the "sun" is to "gather"[23] is contrasted with the "share" to be "apportioned" by the "moon." Together they represent the maiden's title to be married, that is, since the marriage is celestial, her "eligibility" in the eyes of heaven. As such, the solar treasure can be nothing other than spiritual riches, whereas the lunar "share" consists of the human virtues that are the "reflections" of those riches. Being of this world,

[22] Rue (Lithuanian *rūta*, Greek *rutē*) is also called in English "herb of grace," which suggests that its symbolism was originally the same here as there. But already by Shakespeare's time it had acquired a somewhat sorrowful significance (see for example the last lines of Act III in *Richard II*), no doubt because of frequent punning on it and the verb "rue," which, etymologically, is quite unconnected with the name of the plant.
[23] This is a somewhat free though adequate translation of *kloti*, which means literally "cover." The reference is no doubt to the bridal treasure which the mother would store up for her daughter and which would not be displayed, whereas the "share" is the marriage portion which would be assessed by the father.

which is the world of forms, the virtues can be analyzed,[24] differentiated, counted, and measured.[25] But the synthesis of the spiritual treasure itself is above form and beyond all reckoning; it is therefore to be "gathered" and "stored up" but not "apportioned."

This song begins where the previous song ended; its theme is not the Lesser Mysteries but the Greater Mysteries, for the starting point is the state of human perfection. The sun and the moon are once more in their primordial relationship, and the maiden is to set off on her journey wearing the Crown[26] of Purity.

[24] Since light is a symbol of knowledge, reflected light, of which moonlight is the outstanding example, is a symbol of indirect, "analytical" knowledge, that is, individual, human, mental knowledge. In other words, moonlight is a "mental" feature of the macrocosm just as the mind is a "lunar" feature of the microcosm; and it is to be noticed how persistently in the Indo-European languages this profound yet not immediately obvious connection between man (characterized by mind) and moon (Lithuanian *menuo*) is stressed by the recurrence of the root *mn* in connection with things or actions specifically mental and therefore reflective or analytical, such as *mind* (Sanskrit *manas*, Lithuanian *manymas*, Latin *mens*) and *memory* (the lost *n* is found in *reminiscence,* Lithuanian *mintis,* Greek *mnēma*). Let us cut short this list of examples, which could be a long one, with the name of the Roman goddess of learning, that is, of indirect knowledge, *Minerva,* whose bird is the owl, nocturnal and lunar, as opposed to the hawk, which is, as we have seen, the bird of Phoebus Apollo, the God of inspiration, that is, of direct knowledge.

[25] The lost *n* is found in such words as *incommensurable* which are closer to the Latin *mensura.*

[26] *Vainikas,* "garland," is also the ordinary word for "crown." The star is not named; but if she is Ausrine, the Morning Star, then it is at the very least a remarkable coincidence, as the translator once remarked to me, that according to the Jewish tradition Lucifer was, before the fall of the angels, Hekathriel, that is, the "Angel of the Crown."

The Human Margin

Understanding and Believing

BY FRITHJOF SCHUON

I T IS GENERALLY recognized that man is capable of believing without understanding; one is much less aware of the inverse possibility, that of understanding without believing, and it even appears as a contradiction, since faith does not seem to be incumbent except on those who do not understand. Yet hypocrisy is not only the dissimulation of a person who pretends to be better than he is; it also manifests itself in a disproportion between certainty and behavior, and in this respect most men are more or less hypocritical, since they claim to admit truths that they put no more than feebly into practice. On the plane of simple belief, to believe without acting in accordance with the dictates of one's belief corresponds, on the intellectual plane, to an understanding without faith and without life; for real belief means identifying oneself with the truth that one accepts, whatever may be the level of this adherence. Piety is to religious belief what operative faith is to doctrinal understanding, or, we may add, what sainthood is to truth.

If we take as a starting point the idea that spirituality has essentially two factors, namely discernment between the real and the illusory and permanent concentration on the real, the *conditio sine qua non* being the observance of traditional rules and the practice of the virtues that go with them, we shall see that there is a relationship between discernment and understanding on the one hand and between concentration and faith on the other. Faith, whatever its degree, always means a quasi-existential participation in being or in reality; it is—to take a basic hadith—"to worship God as if thou sawest Him, and if thou seest Him not, yet He seeth thee." In other terms, faith is the participation of the will in the intelligence; just as on the physical plane man adapts his action to the physical facts that

401

determine its nature, so also, on the spiritual plane, he should act in accordance with his convictions, by inward activity even more than by outward activity, for "before acting one must first be," and our being is nothing else but our inward activity. The soul must be to the intelligence what beauty is to truth, and this is what we have called the "moral qualification" that should accompany the "intellectual qualification."

There is a relationship between faith and the symbol; there is also one between faith and miracles. In the symbolic image as in the miraculous fact, it is the language of being, not of reasoning, that speaks; to a manifestation of being on the part of heaven, man must respond with his own being, and he does so through faith or through love—which are the two faces of one and the same reality—without thereby ceasing to be a creature endowed with thought. In plain terms, one might wonder what basis or justification there can be for an elementary faith that is disdainful, or almost so, of any attempt at comprehension; the answer has just been given, namely that such faith is based on the illuminating power that belongs in principle to the symbols, phenomena, and arguments of revelation.[1] The "obscure merit" of this faith consists in our not being closed to a grace for which our nature is made. There is room for differences, on the human side, as regards the modes or degrees of receptivity and also the intellectual needs. These needs do not in any sense mean that the thinking man lacks faith; they merely show that his receptivity is sensible to the most subtle and most implicit aspects of the divine message. Now, what is implicit is not the inexpressible but the esoteric, and this has the right to be expressed.[2] Attention has already been drawn to the relationship between faith and miracles;

[1] The "signs" *(āyāt)* of which the Koran speaks and which may even be natural phenomena envisaged in the light of the revealed doctrine. A remark that should be made in this context is that the insensibility of the believers of any intrinsically orthodox religion to the arguments of another religion does not in any sense come into question here, since the motive for refusal is in that case a positive factor, namely an already existing faith, which is in itself valid.

[2] It goes without saying that the implicit is to be found even on the plane of the literal meaning, but this mode of indication causes practically no problems and is not in question here.

perfect faith consists in being aware of the metaphysically miraculous character of natural phenomena and in seeing in them, by way of consequence, the trace of God.

The demerit of unbelief or lack of faith does not therefore lie in a natural lack of special aptitudes, nor is it due to the unintelligibility of the message—for then there would be no demerit. It lies in the passionate stiffening of the will and in the worldly tendencies that bring about this stiffening. The merit of faith is fidelity to the supernaturally natural receptivity of primordial man; it means remaining as God made us and remaining at His disposition with regard to a message from heaven which might be contrary to earthly experience, while being incontestible in view of subjective as well as objective criteria.[3]

It is related that Ibn Taimiyyah[4] once said, while coming down from the pulpit after a sermon: "God comes down from Heaven to earth as I am coming down now."[5] There is no reason to doubt that he meant this to be taken literally, with a literalism defying all interpretation, but his attitude has nonetheless a symbolic value that is independent of his personal opinions. The refusal to analyze a symbol by discursive and separative thought—in order to assimilate it directly and as it were existentially—does in fact correspond to a perspective that is possible and therefore valid in the appropriate circumstances. "Blind faith" may be seen to coincide here with an attitude that is its opposite while being at the same time

[3] To say that Abraham and Mary had the merit of great faith means that they were sensible to the divine criteria despite the apparent impossibility of the message; this means also that the men of old were by no means credulous, if we may be allowed to make this remark in a context that goes beyond the level of ordinary humanity, since we are speaking of prophets.
[4] Arab theologian of the thirteenth century, Hanbalite by origin and the protagonist of an extreme exoterism.
[5] With reference to the hadith of "the descent" *(an-Nuzūl):* "Our Lord—Blessed and Exalted be He—cometh down each night unto the nethermost heaven [*as-samā'ad-dunyā,* a Koranic term that signifies, not the lowest of the seven heavens, but the terrestrial firmament] while the last third of the night yet remaineth, and He saith Who calleth upon Me, that I may answer him? Who asketh of Me, that I may give unto him? Who seeketh My forgiveness, that I may forgive him?"

analogous, namely the assimilation of truth through the symbol and by means of the whole soul, the soul as such.

Faith as a quality of the soul is the stabilizing complement of the discerning and as it were explosive intelligence. Without this complement, intellectual activity lets itself be carried away by its own movement and is like a devouring fire; it loses its balance and ends either by devouring itself in a restlessness without issue or else simply by wearing itself out to the point of sclerosis. Faith implies all the static and gentle qualities such as patience, gratitude, confidence, generosity; it offers the mercurial intelligence a fixative element and thus realizes, together with discernment, an equilibrium that is like an anticipation of sainthood. It is to this polarity—at its highest level—that the complementary terms "blessing" (or "prayer," *salāh*) and "peace" (or "greeting," *salām*) are applied in Islam.

It must be stressed again that an intellectual qualification is not fully valid unless it be accompanied by an equivalent moral qualification; herein lies the explanation of all the fideist attitudes that seem bent on limiting the impetus of the intelligence. The upholders of tradition pure and simple *(naql)* in the first centuries of Islam were deeply conscious of this, and Ash'ari himself must have sensed it (although it took him in the opposite direction, since he ventured onto the plane of theological reasoning) when he attributed to God an unintelligibility that, in the last analysis, could only signify the precariousness of man's intellectual means in the face of the dimension of absoluteness.

One can meditate or speculate indefinitely on transcendent truths and their applications—that is moreover what the author of this paper does, but he has valid reasons for doing it, nor does he do it for himself—one can spend a whole lifetime speculating on the suprasensorial and the transcendent, but all that matters is the "leap into the void," which is the fixation of spirit and soul in an unthinkable dimension of the real. This leap, which cuts short and completes the in itself endless chain of formulations,[6] depends on a direct understanding and on a

---

[6] But for this completion there would be no such thing as doctrines, these being by definition forms, delimitations, mental coagulations.

grace, not on having reached a certain phase in the unfolding of the doctrine, for this unfolding, we repeat, has logically no end. This "leap into the void" we can call faith; it is the negation of this reality that is the source of all philosophy of the type that may be described as "art for art's sake" and of all thought that believes it can attain to an absolute contact with reality by means of analyses, syntheses, arrangements, filtrations, and polishings—thought that is mundane by the very fact of this ignorance and because it is a vicious circle that not merely provides no escape from illusion, but even reinforces it through the lure of a progressive knowledge that in fact is nonexistent.[7]

In view of the harm that the prejudices and tendencies of ordinary piety can sometimes do to metaphysical speculations, we might be tempted to conclude that piety should be abandoned on the threshold of pure knowledge, but this would be a false and highly pernicious conclusion. In reality, piety—or faith—must never be absent from the soul, but it is only too clear that it must be on a level with the truths that it accompanies, which implies that such an extension is perfectly in its nature, as is proved by the Vedantic hymns, to take just one particularly conclusive example.

The Hindus have been reproached for being inveterate idolators and for finding in the least phenomenon a pretext for idolatry; we are referred, for example, to an annual festival at which, so it seems, the artisan gathers his tools together in order to worship them. The truth is that the Hindu refuses to become rooted in outwardness: he readily looks to the divine substratum of things, whence his acute sense of the sacred and his devotional mentality; this is the last thing that modern man wants, monstrously "adult" as he has become in conforming to the worst illusion that has ever darkened the human outlook.

---

[7] A valid doctrine is a "description" that is based on direct, supramental knowledge, and the author is therefore under no illusion as to its inevitable formal limitations; on the other hand, a philosophy that claims to be a "research" is a mere nothing, and its apparent modesty is no more than a pretentious negation of true wisdom, which is absurdly called metaphysical dogmatism. There is clearly no humility in saying that one is ignorant because everyone is ignorant.

The reflection of the sun may not be the sun, but it is nonetheless "something of the sun," and in this sense it is not wrong to speak elliptically of a kind of identity, the light being always the one light and the cause being really present in the effect. Whoever does not respect the effect makes himself incapable of respecting fully the cause, apart from the fact that the cause withholds itself from whoever despises its reflections; whoever understands the cause perceives it also in its earthly traces. The sense of the sacred: This word felicitously expresses a dimension that should never be absent, either in metaphysical thought or in everyday life; it is this that gives birth to the liturgies, and without it there is no faith. The sense of the sacred, with its concomitances of dignity, incorruptibility, patience, and generosity, is the key to integral faith and to the supernatural virtues that are inherent in it.

If one adopts the distinction made by the alchemists between a "dry path" and a "moist path," the former corresponding to "knowledge" and the latter to "love," one should also be aware that the two poles "fire" and "water"—which these paths represent respectively—are both reflected in each path, so that "knowledge" has necessarily an aspect of "moisture," and "love" an aspect of "dryness." Within the framework of a path of love, this aspect of "dryness" or of "fire" is doctrinal orthodoxy, for it is well known that no spirituality is possible without the implacable and immutable bulwark of a divine expression of the saving truth; analogously and inversely, the aspect of "moisture" or of "water" that, being feminine, is derived from the divine substance (*Prakriti*, the Shakti), is indispensable to the path of "knowledge" for the evident and already mentioned reasons of equilibrium, stability, and effectiveness.

When comparing the quality of "knowledge" with fire, one is aware that this comparison cannot perfectly and exhaustively account for the metaphysical reaches of the intelligence and for its activity of realization. Fire in itself, besides its qualities of luminosity and ascension, has in fact an aspect of agitation and destructiveness, and it is this aspect—the very one that the fideist opponents of kalam have in mind—that proves that the "fiery" element in knowledge is not self-sufficient and that it has in consequence an imperative need of a "moist" element, which is none other than faith with all its fixative and peace-giving virtues.[8] Even the most penetrating intelligence, if it relies too much on its own strength, runs the risk of being abandoned by heaven; forgetting that the subject, the knower, is God, it closes itself to the divine influx. Profane thought is not confined to thought that is ignorant of metaphysical and mystical truths,[9] but also includes thought that, while knowing these truths well enough in theory, has nonetheless a dispro-portionate approach to them, an approach that is unaccom-panied by a sufficient adaptation of the soul; not that such thought is profane by definition as in the case of ignorant thought, but it is so secondarily or morally and lies in grave danger of error, for man is not merely a mirror, he is a cosmos that is both complex and fragile. The connection—often af-firmed by tradition—between knowledge and peace shows in its own way that in pure intellectuality the mathematical ele-ment is not everything and also that fire by itself could not be the symbol of intellectuality.[10]

The two principles "fire" and "water" come together in "wine," which is both "liquid fire" and "igneous water."[11] Libe-

---

[8] "There is no lustral water like unto knowledge," says the Bhagavad-gita; it is here water, not fire, that is related to jnana.

[9] "Metaphysical": concerning universal realities considered objec-tively. "Mystical": concerning the same realities considered subjec-tively, that is, in relation to the contemplative soul, insofar as they enter operatively into contact with it.

[10] Shankara, affirming his identity with "inward Wisdom," calls it: "That which is the stilling of mental agitation and the supreme ap-peasement . . . that which is the pool Manikarnika . . . that which is the Ganges"—images referring to water, not to fire. Islam, for its part, associates coolness, the color green, and streams with paradise.

[11] When the American Indians called alcohol firewater, they were ex-pressing, without knowing it, a profound truth: the alchemical and almost supernatural coincidence of liquidity and ignition. According to the Brihad Aranyaka Upanishad and the Shatapatha Brāhmana, the Divine Fire *(agni)* is engendered in the undifferentiated Self *(atmā)* by the tension between igneous Energy *(tejas)* and the Water of Life or the Elixir *(rasa); agni* is "churned" and "born of the Waters" or "born of the Lotus"; he is the Lightning hidden in the Celestial Waters.

rating intoxication proceeds precisely from this alchemical and as it were miraculous combination of opposite elements. It is thus wine, and not fire, that is the most perfect image of liberating gnosis, envisaged not only in its total amplitude but also in the equilibrium of its virtual modes, for the equilibrium between discernment and contemplation can be conceived at every level. Another image of this equilibrium or of this concordance is oil; it is moreover through oil that fire is stabilized and that it becomes the calm and contemplative flame of the lamps in sanctuaries. Like wine, oil is an igneous liquid, which "shineth even though the fire have not touched it," according to the famous Verse of Light *(āyat an-Nūr).*

From a certain elementary point of view, there is a connection between the emotional path of "warriors" and water, which is passive and "feminine," just as there is a connection between the intellectual path of "priests" and fire, which is active and "masculine"; but it remains abundantly clear that water has a sacerdotal aspect of peace and that fire has a warlike aspect of devouring activity and that each path has necessarily a "dry" pole and a "moist" pole. All these considerations converge on the problem of the relationships between speculative intelligence and faith: Faith is a pure and calm "water"; intelligence is an active and discriminating "fire." To say that water is pure amounts to saying that it has a virtual quality of luminosity, that it is thus predisposed to be a vehicle for fire and to be transmuted into wine, as at the marriage in Cana. When considered with regard to its possibilities, water is a virtual wine, since it already possesses luminosity by reason of its purity, and in this sense it is comparable to oil; like wine, oil is igneous by its very nature, but at the same time it does not correspond exactly to wine except when combined with the flame that it feeds, whereas wine has no need of any complement to manifest its nature.

It follows from all that has been said so far that faith and intelligence can each be conceived at two different levels. Faith as a quasi-ontological and premental certitude ranks higher than the discerning and speculative aspects of intelligence,[12] but intelligence as pure intellection ranks higher than that faith that is no more than an adherence of the sentiments; it is this ambivalence that is the source of numerous misunderstandings but that makes possible at the same time an exo-esoteric language that is both simple and complex. Faith in its higher aspect is what we might call *religio cordis;* it is the "inward religion" that is supernaturally natural to man and that coincides with *religio caeli*—or *perennis*—that is, with universal truth, which is beyond the contingencies of form and time. This faith can be satisfied with little. Unlike an intelligence that is all for exactness but never satisfied in its play of formulations and that passes from concept to concept, from symbol to symbol, without being able to make up its mind for this or for that, the faith of the heart is capable of being satisfied by the first symbol that providentially comes its way[13] and of living on it until the supreme meeting.

The faith in question, which we have called *religio cordis*—the subjective and immanent side of *religio caeli*—has two poles, in conformity with the distinction between the "dry" and the "moist" paths; they are represented in the Buddhism of the North by Zen and Jodo respectively. Both turn away from verbal comprehension, the one to plunge into our very being and the other to plunge into faith. For Zen, truth must coincide with reality, and this is our substratum that is both existential and intellectual, whereas for Jodo, truth-reality is attained in perfect faith, the giving up of oneself to the universal Substance

[12] This higher faith is something altogether different from the irresponsible and arrogant taking of liberties so characteristic of the profane improvisors of Zen or of jnana, who seek to "take a short cut" by stripping themselves of the essential human context of all realization, whereas in the East, and in the normal conditions of ethical and liturgical ambience, this context is largely supplied in advance. One does not enter the presence of a king by the back door.

[13] In the lives of the saints, the spiritual career is often inaugurated by an outward or inward incident which throws the soul into a particular and definitive attitude with regard to Heaven; the symbol here is not the incident itself, but the positive spiritual factor that the incident serves to bring out.

that is mercy and that is manifested in some sign or some key.[14]

The spiritual dimension symbolized by wine or intoxication is represented in the Mahayana by the union of the two poles *vajra* ("lightning" or "diamond") and *garbha* ("matrix") or *mani* ("jewel") and *padma* ("lotus") or by the conjunction of "expressed truth" *(upāya)* and "liberating gnosis" *(prajnā)*; the "great bliss" *(mahāsukha)* that results from the union of the two poles, evokes the beatitude *(ānanda)* of *atmā*, wherein is the meeting of "consciousness" *(chit)* and "being" *(sat)*. According to its most outward acceptation, this directly or indirectly sexual symbolism expresses the equilibrium between mental knowledge and virtue; on this basis, the equilibrium may be that between doctrinal investigation and spiritual practice or that between doctrine and method. All these modes can be brought back to a confrontation between a "knowing" and a "being" or between an intellectual objectivation and a volitive or quasi-existential participation, or, we might say, between a mathematical or architectural dimension and an ethico-aesthetic or musical dimension, in the vastest sense that these terms can have, bearing in mind that phenomena have their roots in the Divine. It is true that from a certain point of view, the element "being" is more than a complement, inasmuch as it combines the elements "knowing" and "willing"; and in this case it represents the synthesis of holiness that underlies the polarity "intelligence-beauty," which brings us back to the symbolism of love and wine and to the mystery of the coincidence of faith and gnosis.

The cult of a goddess, of a Shakti, of a *Tārā*—of a "Lady" one might simply say—may indicate the predominance of a perspective of love or of dogmatic and methodic bhakti, but it may equally well be the sign, even within a perspective of gnosis or of jnana, that emphasis is being placed on the element of

[14] In Amidism faith is ultimately based on intuition of the essential goodness of reality which is divinely "the Other" in relation to the existence-bound subject; in Zen, on the contrary, what we call faith is based on intuition of the essential reality of our "self," of our subjective essence in its nirvanic transpersonality.

"faith" in the higher sense of the term in which Zen and Jodo conceive it, the one according to the "dry path" and the other according to the "moist path." This is also what Ibn 'Arabī meant—and in his case there cannot be the slightest doubt that the perspective was that of gnosis—by the "religion of Love," which he identified with *al-Islām*, the essential conforming of the intelligence and the soul to the divine nature, which is beyond forms and oppositions.

The Human Margin

BY FRITHJOF SCHUON

CHRIST, IN rejecting certain rabbinical prescriptions as "human" and not "divine," shows that according to God's scale of measurement there is a sector that, while being orthodox and traditional, is nonetheless human in a certain sense; this means that the divine influence is only total for the Scriptures and for the essential consequences of the revelation and that it always leaves a "human margin" where it exerts no more than an indirect action, letting ethnic or cultural factors have the first say. It is to this sector or this margin that the speculations of exotericism largely belong; orthodoxy is on the one hand homogeneous and indivisible, while on the other hand it admits of degrees of absoluteness and relativity. We should not therefore be too scandalized at the anathemas that Dyophysites, Monophysites, Aphthartodocetae, Phartolotrae, Agnoetae, Aktistetae, and Ktistolotrae hurl at each other's heads over the question of knowing whether Christ is of an incorruptible substance or whether, on the contrary, he was like other bodies, or whether there was any human ignorance in the soul of Christ, or whether the body of Christ is uncreated while being at the same time visible, or whether it was created, and so on.[1]

What is surprising in most cases, though in differing degree, is the vehement desire to commit oneself and others on ques-

---

[1] The following divergence may be noted with regard to the Blessed Virgin: Was Mary a priori delivered from being capable of sin, or was she sinless through the superabundance of her virtue? In other words, was she impeccable because of the absolute holiness of her nature, or was she holy as a result of the absolute impeccability of her intelligence and of her will? Those who maintain the first thesis seek to avoid attributing to Mary any imperfection of substance; those of the second seek to avoid depriving her of the perfection of merit; but both parties seem to lose sight of the fact that at the degree of the Blessed Virgin such an alternative loses all its meaning. The "immaculate conception" —attributed to Mary also by the Islamic tradition—admits of every meritorious attitude by its very nature, rather as a substance contains in synthesis all its possible accidents; and inversely, perfect impeccability—out of the question for the ordinary man—is ipso facto equivalent to the absence of original sin.

tions that are not of crucial importance and the incapacity to allow a certain latitude as regards things that the revelation did not deem it indispensable to lay down in precise terms; yet all that was necessary, from the mystical as well as from the dogmatic point of view, was to admit that Christ as living form of God had for that reason to display in his humanity supernatural prerogatives that it would be vain to try to enumerate, but that inasmuch as he was incontestably man, he was bound to show certain limits, as is proved by the incident of the fig-tree whose sterility he did not discern from afar. The question of the *filioque* is a clear example of this tendency to pointless preciseness and to a dogmatization that has yielded a luxuriant crop of variances and anathemas.

One fact that forces itself upon us in this connection is that fallen or post-Edenic man is a kind of fragmentary being; we are therefore bound to open our eyes to the obvious truth that the sanctity of a man does not preclude the possibility of his being a poor logician or more sentimental than intellectual, and of his feeling, despite this, a call to fulfill some teaching function, not of course through pretension, but through "zeal for the house of the Lord." Inspiration by the Holy Ghost cannot mean that the Spirit puts itself in the place of the human intelligence, liberating it from all its natural limitations, for that would be revelation; inspiration means simply and solely that the Spirit guides man in accordance with the divine intention and on the basis of the capacities of the human receptacle. If this were not so, there would be no theological elaboration, nor would there be any divergences in orthodoxy, and the first Father of the Church would have written one single theological treatise that would have been exhaustive and definitive; there would never have been a Thomas Aquinas or a Gregory Palamas. Things being so, there are men who are inspired by the Holy Ghost because they are saints and in proportion to their sanctity, whereas there are others who are saints because they are inspired by the Holy Ghost and in proportion to their inspiration.

The most ordinary examples of the human margin that heaven concedes to traditions are to be found in the splits within the intrinsically orthodox religions; and this is altogether unrelated to the question of heterodoxy, for intrinsic heresies lie beyond the margin in question. There is no denying that collective human thought is not good at conceiving fluctuations between different points of view on the one hand and aspects to which they correspond on the other, or between different modes of the subjective and the objective; consequently there are polarizations and scissions that, however inevitable and providential they may be, are nonetheless dangerous imperfections. Heaven allows man to be what he is, but this condescension or this patience has not the meaning of a full approval on the part of God.

Insofar as ecclesiology is concerned, the most ancient Christian texts sometimes uphold the Latin thesis and sometimes the Greek; from this it follows that the ideal, or rather the normal, situation would be an Orthodox Church recognizing a pope who was not totally autocratic but in spiritual communion with the whole body of bishops or patriarchs. There would then be a pope without *filioque*, but nevertheless having the right to certain theological, liturgical, and other particularities, opportune or even necessary in a Latin or Germanic setting. The disorders—of a gravity without precedent—with which the Roman Church is now rife prove that the Latin conception is theologically narrow and juridically excessive; if it were not so, these disorders would be inconceivable.[2] There seems moreover to be something tragically insoluble in the very structure of Christendom: Give the total supremacy to the Pontiff, and he will become a mundane, conquering Caesar; give the supremacy to the Emperor, and he will make the Pontiff his pawn and his tool.[3] However, it must be admitted that we have here

[2] The coming of Protestantism, in the Latin West, moreover affords the same proof. Psychologically—not doctrinally—Protestantism in fact reedits, though needless to say in a much more excessive form, the protest of Arianism which comprises, in spite of everything, a particle of truth and an element of equilibrium.

[3] Most paradoxically, the one does not prevent the other. That is what actually happened in the Latin West, where the Papacy finally became the prey, not of the Emperor needless to say, but of politics and consequently of democracy which determines them. Since the French Revo-

a vicious circle, the traces of which are found wherever there are men.

The "unfathomable mystery" of the theologians is sometimes merely the expression of a metaphysical insufficiency, or else it refers to the unquestionable fathomlessness of the divine subjectivity; the latter is mysterious for the objectivizing and separating faculty of thought as the optic nerve is for sight, but the impossibility of the eye's seeing the optic nerve is not in the least mysterious. Very often the thesis of "mystery" is either a gratuitous affirmation called in to cover up a theological contradiction or else a truism pure and simple, seeing that we know what thought is and what are its obvious limitations.

All the drama of the theologies lies in the incompatibility between their sublimism—prone as it is to simplification—and the idea of maya at the degree of Divinity, that is, the idea of divine relativity; the deadlocks caused by their deep-rooted voluntarism have thus to be overcome by means of philosophical expedients that are "providential" insofar as they are psychologically opportune with regard to this or that collectivity. One of the great difficulties of Sufism is that in it the highest metaphysics finds itself inextricably bound up with theology, which tarnishes it by its habitual confusions with regard to "omnipotence" unless we admit that in this case it is the metaphysical penetration that deepens the theology by

---

lution, the church has been as it were substantially at the mercy of the laicist republics—including the in fact republican pseudomonarchies—for it is their ideology that decides who is to be a bishop; and thanks to a particularly favorable conglomeration of historical circumstances, politics have succeeded in pumping into the mold of the church a human matter that is heterogeneous to the church. The last council was ideo-political, not theological: its irregularity springs from the fact that it was determined, not by concrete situations assessed on a theological basis, but by antitheological, ideo-political abstractions, or more precisely by the democratism of the world monstrously setting itself up as Holy Ghost. "Humility" and "charity," ready to take on any shape but henceforth limited to one direction only, are there to ensure the success of the enterprise.

eventually inculcating into it some liberating gleams of light.[4] The theologies, by taking upon themselves the contradiction of being sentimental metaphysics, are condemned to the squaring of the circle. They are ignorant of the differentiation of things into aspects and standpoints, and they work in consequence on the basis of arbitrarily rigid data, the antinomies of which can be solved only beyond this artificial rigidity; their working has moreover a sentimental slant, which is what is called "thinking piously."[5] In Christianity there is the will to admit a differentiation in the Divine Oneness and the equally imperious will not to admit, practically speaking, that there is any differentiation at all—the Hypostases being "merely relationships"—as if the three dimensions of space were to be willed into one dimension only. In Islam, an obstinate unitarism comes into collision with the existence of the world, whereas there would be no conflict if the unitarism were metaphysical and therefore transparent and supple as its nature demands. On the one side there is a certain dispersion in the object of worship: God, the Persons, Christ, the Eucharist, the Sacred Heart; on the other side there is on the contrary an excess of centralization, on a plane where it cannot possibly be imposed, namely a refusal to admit any cause except God or to be dependent on anything but on Him alone, thus flying in the face of immediate evidence, when in reality such evidence in no sense prevents everything from depending upon God and when one only needs to be conscious of this to be on the side of truth. There is a zeal that is ever ready to replace thought

[4] The deterioration in question is to be felt not only on the speculative plane but also on the operative plane where the volitive element too often confers on the method a somewhat violent aspect, as a substitute for a more intellectual alchemy; accidents of psychic rupture result from this cause, for the gates of heaven cannot be forced by unintelligent excesses, however great their attendant heroism may be. There must be a balance between the quantitative and the qualitative, the volitive and the intellective, but to this need a moralizing popularization turns a blind eye. It is moreover this popularization that involves the imagery of extravagant prodigies and, on the rebound, the equally unfortunate depreciation of true miracles.

[5] The councils would sometimes degenerate into free fights, which is not very metaphysical but is always preferable to flabby indulgence with regard to manifest error on the pretext of "charity" or "humility."

by virtue and truth by heroism; in saying this, one is very far from overlooking that a devotional attitude is normal to man and therefore normative, and that there is no balanced intellectuality without it; but everything must be put in its proper place, and this has become particularly difficult for the passional humanity of the Iron Age. What needs to be understood is that a soul filled with piety is capable of thinking with detachment, in perfect harmony with its own piety and not in spite of it, the more so since the depth of the instinct to worship increases in exact proportion to its impregnation with truth.[6]

From the standpoint of an extreme trinitarianism God is certainly One, but He is only so while being Three, and there is no One God except in and by the Trinity; the God who is One without Trinity, or independently of all hypostatic deployment, is not the true God, for without this deployment unity is meaningless. And it is here that the full gravity of trinitarianism comes to light; there are Christians who, in disagreement moreover with the opinions of most theologians, are incapable of seeing in Islam the least value; for them Islam and atheism are equivalent, and if they do not level the same reproach at Judaism, this is simply and solely because they project into it their own trinitarism as something that is taken as a matter of course to be implicit. On this showing the Muslim reproach of "tritheism" becomes justified; anyone who, because of his trinitarianism, is incapable of seeing that the Koran speaks of the God of Abraham—even supposing that it does so imperfectly—and that Muslims worship God, and nothing else, really deserves the reproach in question. Christ, in speaking of the supreme commandment or in teaching the Lord's Prayer, did not speak of the Trinity any more than did the God of Sinai, who deemed it sufficient to define Himself in these words: "Hear, O Israel: the Lord our God is One Lord."

As we have already mentioned on more than one occasion, trinitarism is a conception of God determined by the mystery of divine manifestation; if we seek in God the prefiguration of

[6] The Vedantine texts confirm this, and the "monotheistic" theologies themselves quite evidently comprise sectors that bear witness to the same quality.

this mystery, we discern the Trinity. When applied to every religion, monotheistic or not, the same idea calls for the following formulation: The essence has become form, in order that form may become essence; all revelation is a humanization of the Divine in view of a deification of the human.

Judaism and Islam make the following objections to trinitarism: You say that the Son is begotten and that He is God; but God is not begotten, He is Absolute. You say that the Holy Ghost emanates and that he is delegated and that he is God; but God does not emanate from anything, nor is He sent. And you say that the Father is God and that he begets; God creates, but He does not beget, otherwise there would be two Gods. Moreover, how can the Son and the Holy Ghost each be identical with God and not be identical with one another?

To these objections a Christian might reply that in Judaism and Islam the divine mercy is not identical with the divine vengeance but that both are identical with God; Jews and Muslims will reply that this is by no means the same thing, for while mercy and vengeance are incontestably divine, it would be false to affirm that God is reducible to one or the other.[7] The equation is only relative, and there lies the root of the problem: Judaism and Islam admit in a certain sense relativity *in divinis* —they distinguish between the essence and the attributes— whereas Christianity, at least at the theological level, seems to want to bring everything back to absoluteness, whence the problematic ellipses of trinitarian theology.

"I am in the Father, and the Father is in me": This is the identity of essence. But "my Father is greater than I": This is the difference of degree within the principial reality, that is, at a level that is still uncreated or metacosmic. The sense of an absolute equation has been conferred on the first utterance, while the second has been made relative; instead of the two

---

[7] Mercy is God, but God is not only mercy. Yet God is mercy much more directly—the verb "to be" indicating here an identity of essence and not an equation pure and simple—than He is vengeance, which is extrinsic and conditional, whereas mercy is intrinsic and therefore unconditional, without however being identical with absoluteness as such.

being taken together and explained each in the light of the other, the second utterance has been arbitrarily attributed to the human nature alone.

The previously mentioned argument that God creates but does not beget, otherwise there would be two Gods, needs to be qualified, for the sake of precision, by adding the words: unless we admit the notion of maya, which makes it clear that the hiatus between Creator and creature is necessarily prefigured *in divinis* by the differentiation between the absolute as such and the absolute relativized in view of one dimension of its infinitude, but this difference, precisely, is only real from the standpoint of relativity. For the Vedantines, the separation between the absolute *(paramatmā)* and the relative *(māyā-ishvara)* is as rigorous as is, for the Semites, the separation between Creator and creature; but, by compensation, there is an aspect that admits of union between the created and the uncreated, inasmuch as nothing that exists can be other than a manifestation of the principle or an objectivization of the self; "all is atman."[8]

In other terms: There is atman, and there is maya; but there is also atman as maya, and this is the manifesting and acting personal divinity; and inversely, there is also maya as atman, and this is the whole universe when seen as one polyvalent reality. The world will then be the divine aspect that is termed "universal man" *(vaishvānara)* or, in Sufism, "the outward" *(az-zāhir);* this is moreover the deepest meaning of the Far Eastern yin-yang. Also it is in the light of this doctrine that it has been possible to say that the avatara was "created before creation," which means that before creating the world, God has to "create Himself" *in divinis,* if such an expression be permissible, the word "create" having here a higher and transposed meaning, which is precisely that of maya.[9]

---

[8] If philosophical pantheism had this aspect of things in view—which it has not, being ignorant both of the degrees of reality and of transcendence—it would be legitimate as a synthetic or inclusive perspective. In the polemics of the theologians these two kinds of pantheism are readily confused.

[9] For Parmenides, pure being coincides with pure knowledge; all the rest is "opinion," *doxa,* which is not unrelated to the notion of maya, with the reservation however that, Vedantically speaking, being as

The distinction between the human and divine natures reflects or symbolizes the distinction, within the divine nature itself, between inequality in relation to the Father and equality, or between relativity and absoluteness; viewed from another angle, this principial distinction is also affirmed on the plane of the human nature itself, in which one dimension is marked by earthly contingence, whereas the other is as it were divine, whence the monophysite interpretation. It is not surprising that this combination of three polarities—man and God, earthly man and divine man, hypostatic God and essential God—should have given rise in its complexity to the diverse opinions already alluded to, orthodox or heretical as the case may be; it is the basic polarity atman-maya that repeats itself or reverberates in numberless modalities, of which the most important for man is the confrontation between God and the world. The first verse of John enunciates this polarity, applied to Christ, by placing side by side two affirmations: *Et Verbum erat apud Deum, et Deus erat Verbum:* the dimension of subordination, then the dimension of equality or identity.

The whole of Arianism can be explained by an unconscious urge to take into consideration the principle of relativity *in divinis* and therefore maya. If Arius teaches that the Son, without having been created "in time" as were all created things (time having begun only with the creation), was nonetheless "drawn from nothingness" but that the Son is divine inasmuch as he is the principle of cosmic creation, that is, of creation in the normal sense, he really means that the Word, while being divine, has nonetheless an aspect of relativity. It is true that Arius spoils his thesis by some erroneous speculations about the person of Christ; but it must be recognized that there is in his doctrine a true and profound intuition, although it is clum-

conceived by Parmenides does not escape absolutely from maya but is to be identified with its summit, *ishvara.* Correlatively with their cult of perfection, the Greeks always display a certain fear of the infinite, which is very visible even in their architecture; the Parthenon has real grandeur, but it expresses the religion of the finite and rational perfect which, because it confuses the unlimited with the chaotic, the infinite with the irrational, is opposed to virgin nature.

sily formulated in terms of Semitic and creationist anthropomorphism. Instead of rejecting Arianism altogether, it would have been better to have adopted its positive theological intention, that of the divine relativity as prototype of cosmic limitation. The Word is neither totally other than the Absolute, as Arius would have it, nor totally—or in every respect—identical with the Absolute, as the Homousiasts would have it; if ever there was a need for antinomy in metaphysical dialectic, it is here. The very expansion and tenacity of Arianism, at a time so close to the origins of Christianity, proves that there was more to it than a mere human error; the Nicene council thus marks, not exactly the victory of truth, but the victory of the most important truth to the detriment of essential metaphysical shades of meaning. It is true that dogmatic theology has to simplify, but a unilateral or fragmentary outlook is what it is, and cannot avoid giving rise to disequilibriums in the very measure that its own contents demand a pluridimensional expression.

In any case it must be admitted that the theological formulation of the Trinity constitutes, in a given environment, a providential form destined not only to be the protective vehicle of the mystery but also to serve, by its very paradox, as a landmark for the total and therefore necessarily pluridimensional doctrine.

A distinction has to be made between metaphysical knowledge and the ability to express it: The Greeks and above all the Hindus have long possessed the dialectical instrument, for it corresponds to their sense of objectivity,[10] whereas the primitive Semites—and therefore also Islam at its outset—were somewhat lacking in it, but it goes without saying that this casts

---

[10] As for the Far Easterners, they are contemplative, but symbolists not logicians; they are above all "visual." The purely Mongolian traditions are those of Fo-Hi with its Taoist and Confucianist branches, then Shinto, not to speak of the various Far Eastern and Siberian shamanisms; but the Mongol soul has also set its imprint on Buddhism which has thus become partially representative of the spiritual genius of the yellow race, particularly in the case of Zen and, more generally, in the whole field of sacred art.

no reflection on the degree of wisdom of the individuals in question, nor indeed could it, seeing that we find the profoundest metaphysics as it were condensed in certain biblical and Koranic formulas or in certain utterances of the saints who were inspired by these formulas at an early date and outside any possibility of Hellenistic influences. These remarks, and still more what was said earlier about the metaphysics underlying the various theologies, impel us to return to certain basic truths of the *sophia perennis* at the double risk of going outside the framework of our subject and of repeating things that have already been said. It is always a question of the notions of absoluteness and of relativity, so important or so fateful in the context of the "human margin."

The Islamic testification that there is no divinity but *the* Divinity has first of all, metaphysically speaking, the objective meaning of a discernment, therefore of a separation, between the real and the illusory or between the absolute and the relative; there is also the subjective meaning of a spiritual distinction between the worldly outward and the divine inward, and in this case the objective and transcendent Divinity appears as immanent and therefore subjective, but in a transpersonal sense, the subject being, not the human ego, but the pure intellect, with the purified ego as no more than the path of access. In order to be total, the doctrine has still need of a unitive dimension, expressed in Islam by the second testification: To say that "the Praised [Mohammed] is the Messenger of the [one and only] Divinity" means that the relative, inasmuch as it directly manifests the absolute, is not other than the absolute; and according to the subjective application, the outward, the world, is not other than the inward, the self.[11]

However, for the relative to be able to have this aspect of absoluteness that reintegrates it into the absolute—inasmuch as the universe could not exist on the basis of an ultimate

[11] The basic testification, or the first Shahādah, comprises a negative part, which rejects false divinities, and a positive part, which affirms the true God. The former is the "negation," the *Nafy*, and the latter is the affirmation, the *Ithbāt;* we have here the distinction between maya and atman. The second Shahādah, that of the Prophet, adds that maya is not other than atman, in its "not unreal" substance.

dualism—relativity must be prefigured in the absolute itself. Maya has its origin in atman; otherwise the subsequent difference between God and the world would be inconceivable. That is why Creation as a whole, while being on the one hand separate from the Creator, is on the other hand a prolongation of Him and a "divine aspect"; this is what the Divine name "the Apparent" *(az-Zāhir)* expresses, as opposed to "the Hidden" *(al-Bātin)*, and this is what enables certain Sufis to affirm that "all is God," in conformity with the Koranic verse: "Wheresoever ye turn, there is the Face of God." One particular apparition of the relative reintegrated into the absolute, or more precisely of the absolute manifested as relative, is the Logos, the Prophet; another is the heart, the place of inward and transmuting theophany.

Christianity, in its quintessence, expresses this relationship of identity as directly as possible: The Son is united with the Father; Christ is God. That man, who is relative, should be able to be identified with God presupposes that relativity has an aspect of absoluteness and that it is therefore prefigured *in divinis;* whence the doctrine of the Word. "God became man in order that man might become God." The absolute comprises relativity, and by this very fact relativity can be reintegrated into the absolute; the patristic formula that we have just paraphrased therefore means on the one hand that the human Logos directly manifests the absolute, and on the other, that man can be reintegrated into the absolute through being united with the human Logos, in and by which he is virtually identical with this absolute.

The objection that paradise is not the absolute and that in no religion is man literally supposed to become God does not in any sense invalidate what has just been stated; for it is in fact a question not of the individual as such being transmuted into the divine essence but, to begin with, of an "adoption" of man by God. Man is then directly beneath the divine axis, he is open in the innermost depth of his being to the infinite, he "wears a crown of uncreated light." There is no common measure between his spiritual secret, the mystery of identity or absoluteness, and the existence—or the subsistence—of the individual form, but the one does not prevent the other; man remains man despite the reality of absoluteness that penetrates him. Nirvana did not destroy the Buddha; it immortalized him; otherwise it would never be possible to speak of a human manifestation of the Logos. If God can "become man," this means that there can be no possible rivalry between the Divine and the human.

God and the world: Each of these terms admits of polarization into absoluteness and relativity, and the two terms themselves represent this polarization. In God there are the essence and the attributes and their life that they have in common; and in the world there are heaven and earth, heaven standing for the absolute and earth denoting the relative as such. Here, as *in divinis*, the Holy Spirit is the life that makes them one.

The theological equation between the uncreated and the absolute on the one hand and between the created and the relative on the other is altogether insufficient, for if it is true that the created pertains by definition to relativity, it is false to admit that the uncreated pertains in just the same way to absoluteness; only the essence is pure absolute, although the divine relativity clearly stands for the absolute in relation to the created. The manifested Logos also has this aspect or this function, but cannot be the "absolutely absolute"; if Christ addresses a prayer to his Father, it is not solely by reason of his human nature, it is also by reason of the relativity of the uncreated Logos. If the Son were merely an abstract "relationship of origin," he could not take on the adjunct of a human nature.

The dogma of the Trinity existed before trinitarian theology; the latter pertains to the human margin, whereas the dogma comes from revelation. It lays down metaphysical data; theology combines these data, and in so doing it Westernizes them.

A religion is not limited by what it includes but by what it excludes; this exclusion cannot impair the religion's deepest contents—every religion is intrinsically a totality—but it takes its revenge all the more surely on the intermediary plane that we call the human margin and that is the arena of theological speculations and of fervors both moral and mystical. It is certainly not pure metaphysics, nor is it esotericism which would lay us under the obligation of pretending that a flagrant contradiction is not a contradiction; all that wisdom allows us to do—or rather it obliges us—is to recognize that extrinsic contradictions can hide an intrinsic compatibility or identity, which amounts to saying that each of the contradictory theses contains a truth and thereby an aspect of the whole truth and a way of access to this totality.

When one religion places the human Logos of another religion in hell, or when one confession does the same with the saints of another confession, it cannot really be maintained, on the pretext that the essential truth is one, that there is no flagrant contradiction or that this contradiction is not by definition a serious infirmity on its own plane; all that can be put forward by way of attenuating circumstances is that this plane is not essential for the tradition that is mistaken, which means that its essential spirituality is not necessarily impaired by the error in question, inasmuch as contemplatives are not necessarily preoccupied by the extrinsic anathemas of their religion, and it could also be argued that in these anathemas the persons aimed at become negative symbols, so that there is merely an error of attribution and not of idea, an error of fact, not of principle.

As regards the ordinary theological ostracisms—be they of the West or of the East—there is a profound lesson to be learned from the fables of Aesop and of Bidpai; the story of the fox and the grapes that were too high for it to reach and that it therefore declared to be sour repeats itself in all sectors of human existence. In the name of wisdom, one vilifies one's neighbor's wisdom in order to console oneself—or by way of revenge—for not having discovered it oneself. Eminent theologians have not hesitated to say that the inner voice of Socrates was the devil and to declare diabolic all the wisdom of the Greeks—a pointless extravagance to say the least, seeing that Christianity, even in its Oriental branches, has not been able to dispense with the help of that wisdom altogether.

In the enclosed space of theology there are two openings: gnosis and the liturgy. It is immediately clear that gnosis consti-

tutes such an opening toward the unlimited; but it is necessary
to know that the formal language of the sacred, whether it be
the language of sanctuaries or of nature, is as the complement
or the prolongation of metaphysical wisdom. For beauty, like
pure truth, is calm and generous; it is disinterested and escapes
from stifling passions and disputes about words. One of the
reasons for the existence of sacred art—however much of a
paradox this may seem—is that it speaks to the intelligence of
the sage as well as to the imagination of the simple man, satisfying both sensibilities at one and the same time and nourishing
them according to their respective needs.

There are dialectical excesses that are not to be found in
divine language; but human language does not shrink from
these audacities, and it can only be concluded that in the judgment of man they serve some purpose or that his zeal finds
satisfaction in them. We have read in a Buddhist text: Follow
a master, even if he guides you to hell. An analogous expression
is to be found in Muslim texts: Be happy in the will of God,
even if it destines you for the eternal fire. Literally, such expressions are contradictory, for the whole point of a master is that
he should guide you to heaven, and happiness in God and
through Him coincides with salvation; but these expressions
have nonetheless a meaning, and it is indeed obvious that they
must have, since otherwise they would not exist in spiritual
contexts. The purpose in view is perfect detachment from the
ego; the absurdity of the image guarantees the efficacity of the
shock. We must act "as if the situation were such," although
it cannot be such, and we do so for the sole purpose of obtaining
a radical inward attitude not easily obtainable by any other
means from the point of view of sentimental voluntarism. This
last remark provides the key to the enigma: The mystic in
whom the will predominates often responds to biases, catapult
arguments, surgical violences, for the simple reason that at that
level the truth pure and simple seems to be no more than an
inoperative abstraction. For the "gnostic" or the "pneumatic"
it is the converse that takes place; while remaining insensible
to exaggerations and other means of putting pressure on the

soul, he has an immediate receptivity for the truth as such, because it is the truth and because the truth is what convinces and attracts him.

It is nonetheless a fact that there is no rigorous separation between the two languages. Gnosis also may use absurd formulations, but it does so by way of ellipsis or catalysis, while presupposing intellectual intuition. Thus, when it is said that the sage "is Brahma," a powerfully striking image is put forward by isolating, in order to make it stand out, a relationship that is metaphysically essential and humanly conclusive but not phenomenologically exhaustive, since other relationships also exist.

The dialectic of the Sufis tends to be a "dance of the seven veils." Starting from the idea that nothing must be divulged that would run the risk of being neglected, badly used, profaned, and then despised, and that it is essentially important to keep the balance between doctrinal knowledge and methodic realization, this dialectic is all for wrapping up spiritual truths in abstruse complications; to accept them, or to accept their existence, we need only to know the motive behind them.

A consideration that might not be out of place here is the following: It is necessary to react against the erroneous opinion that credits sainthood as such—not a particular kind of sainthood—with all imaginable qualities and therefore also with all possible wisdom; in this sense, the "wisdom of the saints"—of no matter what saints—has been set up against metaphysics in itself which is, so it would seem, merely a matter of "natural intelligence." Now, the phenomenon of sainthood consists of two things: on the one hand the exclusiveness, and on the other hand the intensity, of thought and of the will in view of the transcendent and of the beyond, or of "God" and of "Paradise." Sainthood in the most general sense is thus essentially a matter of exclusiveness and intensity on the basis of a religious creed; it is on these two qualities, supernaturally inspired, that the gift of miracles depends. In the case of wisdom, it is the depth and scope of the intellective knowledge that determine the exclusiveness and intensity of the spiritual deportment, but the two modes of perfection can touch or interpenetrate one another;

there is no incompatibility or rigorous separation between them, for if on the one hand "the Spirit bloweth where it listeth," on the other hand man always remains man.

The human margin is clearly not confined to the plane of doctrine or dialectic; this goes without saying and has already been alluded to when speaking of the rabbinical exaggerations stigmatized by Christ. Analogous to these are certain excessive practices, consecrated by tradition or tolerated by it, in Hinduism for instance, where certain opinions or attitudes, without being in general altogether unintelligible, are in any case disproportionate to the point of being truly superstitious. These things are to be explained partly by the constant care to preserve the tradition in its original purity—against one set of wrongs other wrongs are then brought to bear—and partly by a certain totalitarianism that is ingrained in human nature; the care for purity goes clearly together with the awareness that collectivities have need of formulations that are precise, and therefore incisive and in practice inordinate, failing which the teachings would be toned down to the point of vanishing altogether.

However, some of these excesses may perhaps harbor a realism that has the purpose of exhausting negative possibilities within the framework of the tradition itself, in much the same way that Holy Scriptures contain wisely providential imperfections or, as in sacred art, where monsters are to be seen side by side with divinities, and devils side by side with angels, in order to reduce to a minimum, by a kind of preventive and disciplined anticipation, the inevitable reactions of the powers of darkness.

If there are some variations, or even divergences, that are spiritually and traditionally legitimate or admissible, this is ultimately because there exist three basic human types together with their diverse combinations: the passional, the sentimental, the intellectual.[12] Every man is an "I" placed in the "world";

[12] The trivialization of certain terms makes it necessary to state here that the words "sentimental" and "intellectual" are to be understood in their intrinsic and neutral sense and without giving the word "senti-

that world comprises "forms," and the "I" comprises "desires." Now, the great question is to know how a man first feels or interprets, by his very nature, these four facts of human existence; for it is this spontaneous conception that is the mark of his spiritual type.

For the passional man the contingent facts of existence, the world and the "I" with their contents, men and things, good deeds and sins partake, practically speaking, of the absolute; God appears to him as a sort of abstraction, a background that does not a priori impose itself upon him. Passion dominates him and plunges him deeply into the world of appearances.[13] His path is thus first and foremost a penitential one, whether he redeems himself by a violent asceticism or whether he sacrifices himself in some holy war or in a servitude dedicated to God. The passional man is incapable of being intellectual in the full sense of the word; the doctrine, as far as he is concerned, is made up of threats and promises and of the metaphysical and eschatological minimum required by an intelligence that is mingled with passion.

For the man of intellectual type, on the contrary, the contingent facts of existence are immediately apparent as such; they are as it were transparent. Before asking "What do I want?" he will ask "What is the world?" and "What am I?" and this determines in advance a certain detachment with regard to forms and desires. It is true that he may have attachments in

---

mental" the pejorative overtone and "intellectual" the flat, profane overtone that common parlance endows them with. "Sentimental" means pertaining to sentiment, be it low or lofty, foolish or intelligent, worldly or centered on the sacred; "intellectual" means pertaining to the intellect, be it doctrinal or methodic, discriminative or contemplative. The term "intellectual" has not in fact the same ambivalence as the term "sentimental" for the simple reason that sentiment is a horizontal and ambiguous faculty, whereas the intellect—not just intelligence nor mere reason—is by definition a vertical and ascending faculty.

[13] It may be mentioned in passing that this is moreover the function of a great deal of "culture": to lure man down blind alleys of poisoned dreaming and mental passion, to draw him insidiously further and further away from "the one thing needful," to make him lose the taste of heaven. The great novels of the nineteenth century, for example, are there precisely for this purpose; we have in them the centrifugal modern substitute for the Golden Legend and the romances of chivalry.

virtue of heavenly realities that shine through their earthly reflections; a most contemplative child can be strongly attached to things that, in the human desert with which destiny may have surrounded it, seem like reminders of a paradise both lost and immanent. However that may be, it is the invisible that is the reality for the deeply contemplative man, whereas "life is a dream" *(la vida es sueño);* in him the Platonic sense of beauty takes the place of crude passion.

The third type is the emotional man, who might be called the musical type; he is intermediate, for he may tend toward the passional as well as toward the intellectual type, and he is moreover reflected in each.[14] It is love and hope that together constitute in him the dominant and operative element; he will be inclined to put special stress on devotional manifestations, with a predilection for musical liturgy. His is the spirituality of happiness, but it is also the spirituality of nostalgia.

All this amounts to saying that there are three fundamental ways of transcending terrestrial maya: first, the penitential crushing of the ego; second, the conversion of passional energy into celestial music; and third, intellectual penetration which reduces illusion to ashes or which brings it back to its quintessence.

It goes without saying that these three modes or these three human types necessarily give rise to diverse combinations, which are rendered still more complex by the intervention of ethnic, cultural, and other factors; one must also take into consideration not only the three types inasmuch as they characterize different individuals but also their presence in one and the same individual and even, to a certain extent, in every individual.[15] It is not however the complexity of the human being

[14] The purely profane mode here is individualistic lyric poetry; this is in principle less harmful than the novel—on condition that it be authentic and natural and not decadent and subversive—first because it is brief in expression and then because it may take its inspiration from a cosmic beauty that goes beyond the individuality of the poet. The case of music is analogous.

[15] The types in question, which refer to the ternary "fear-love-knowledge," scarcely coincide with the three types defined by gnosticism: the hylic, the psychic, and the pneumatic. The hylic is never a spiritual type; the passional is always a psychic, whereas the sentimental can be a pneumatic but more usually belongs to the psychic category.

that interests us here but the difference between men; it is the diversity of spiritual gifts, and above all the fragmentation of primordial man, that necessitates that interplay of veiling and unveiling of which traditional thought is made up.

It is rather tempting to attribute the apparent naïvety of the Holy Scriptures to the "human margin," stretching out as this does in the shadow of divine inspiration; it goes without saying, however, that there is no connection between the two, unless one takes this margin in a transposed and altogether different way, as will be done later, but it is clearly no such transposition that modern critics have in view when they bring up as an argument against the sacred books the apparent scientific errors they contain. Now the data—said to be naïve—of Genesis, for example, prove, not that the Bible is wrong, but that man ought not to be told any more, for the simple reason that he cannot cope with any more. Needless to say, no knowledge is harmful in itself, and there are necessarily always men who are capable of spiritually integrating all possible knowledge; nevertheless, the only kinds of knowledge that the average man is able to cope with are those that come to him through elementary, universal, age-old, and therefore normal experience, as the history of the last centuries clearly proves. It is a fact not only that scientific man—rough-cast by classical Greece and developed by the modern West—loses religion in proportion to his involvement with physical science, but also that the more he is thus involved, the more he closes himself to the infinite dimension of suprasensory knowledge—the very knowledge that gives life a meaning.

It is true that paradise is described in the Scriptures as being "up above," "in heaven," because the celestial vault is the only height that can be empirically or sensorially grasped; and for an analogous reason, hell is "down below," "under the earth," in darkness, heaviness, imprisonment. Similarly, for the Asiatics, samsaric rebirths, when they are neither celestial nor infernal, take place "on earth," that is, on the only plane that can be empirically grasped. What counts, for revelation, is the efficacy of the symbolism and not an indefinite knowledge of meaningless facts. It is true that no fact is totally meaningless in itself—otherwise it would be nonexistent—but the innumerable facts that escape man's normal experience and that scientism accumulates in our consciousness and also in our life are only spiritually intelligible for those who do not stand in any need of them.

Ancient man was extremely sensitive to the intentions inherent in symbolic expressions, as is proved on the one hand by the efficacy of these expressions throughout the centuries and on the other hand by the fact that ancient man was a perfectly intelligent being, as everything goes to show. When he was told the story of Adam and Eve, he grasped so well what it was all about—the truth of it is in fact dazzlingly clear—that he did not dream of wondering "why" or "how"; for we carry the story of paradise and the Fall in our soul and even in our flesh. The same applies to all eschatological symbolism: The "eternity" of the beyond denotes first of all a contrast in relation to what is here below, a dimension of absoluteness as opposed to our world of fleeting and therefore "vain" contingencies, and it is this and nothing else that matters here, and this is the divine intention that lies behind the imagery. In transmigrationist symbolisms, on the contrary, this "vanity" is extended also to the beyond, at least in a certain measure and by reason of a profound difference of perspective; here likewise there is no preoccupation with either "why" or "how," once the penetrating intention of the symbol has been grasped, as it were, in one's own flesh.

In the man who is marked by scientism, intuition of the underlying intentions has vanished, but that is not all; scientism, axiomatically closed to the suprasensory dimensions of the real, has endowed man with a crass ignorance and thereby warped his imagination. The modernist mentality is bent on reducing angels, devils, miracles, in short all nonmaterial phenomena that are inexplicable in material terms, to the domain of the "subjective" and the "psychological," whereas there is not the slightest connection between the two, except that psychism itself is also made—but objectively—of a substance that lies beyond matter; a contemporary theologian, speaking of the Ascension, has gone so far as to ask mockingly, "Where does this cosmic journey end?" a remark that serves to measure out the self-satisfied imbecility of a certain mentality that wants to be "in step with our own time." It would be easy to explain why Christ was "carried up" into the air and what is the meaning of the "cloud" that hid him from sight[16] and also why it was said that Christ "will come after the same fashion." Every detail corresponds to a precise reality that can easily be understood in the light of the traditional cosmologies. The key lies in the fact that the passage from one cosmic degree to another is heralded in the lower degree by "technically" necessary and symbolically meaningful circumstances that reflect after their fashion the higher state and that follow one another in the order required by the nature of things.

Howbeit, the deficiency of modern science is essentially bound up with universal causality; it will no doubt be objected that science is not concerned with philosophical causality but with phenomena, which is untrue, for evolutionism in its entirety is nothing else but a hypertrophy imagined in function of a denial of real causes, and this materialistic negation together with its evolutionist compensation belongs to philosophy and not to science.

From an altogether different point of view, it must be admitted that devotees of "progress" are not entirely wrong in thinking that there is something in religion that no longer works; in fact, the individualistic and sentimental argumentation with which traditional piety operates has lost almost all its power to move consciences, and the reason for this is not merely that modern man is irreligious but also that the usual religious arguments, through not probing sufficiently to the depths of things and moreover not having previously had any need to do so, are psychologically somewhat outworn and fail to satisfy certain requirements of causality. If human societies degenerate on the one hand with the passage of time, they accumulate

---

[16] Not a cloud made of oxygen and hydrogen but a supramaterial substance that had become visible in order to receive the body that was about to penetrate into the upper cosmos. Elijah's "chariot of fire" carries the same meaning, as also the "globe of light" seen at certain apparitions of the Virgin. All this has absolutely nothing to do with fairy stories, let alone "depth psychology."

on the other hand experiences in virtue of old age, however intermingled with errors these may be. This paradox is something that any pastoral teaching intended to be effective should take into account, not by drawing new directives from the general error, but on the contrary by using arguments of a higher order, intellectual rather than sentimental. By this means some at least would be saved—a greater number than one might be tempted to suppose—whereas by purveying a science-ridden and demagogic pastoral teaching one will not be saving anybody.

The notion of "human margin" can be understood in a higher sense which entirely transcends both the psychological and the terrestrial planes, and in that case we enter into an altogether new dimension which must on no account be confused with the vicissitudes of thought. What we have in mind here is the fact that this notion can also be applied to the divine order and at the level of the Logos, inasmuch as certain human divergences are providentially prefigured in the divine intelligence; this is then a case, not of a display of divergencies such as springs in the main from human weakness, but of adaptations willed by the divine mercy. Without there being any total difference of principle here, there is an eminent difference of dimension, analogous to the differences between the square and the cube or between whiteness and light.

When it is said that religious divergences are mere differences of formulation, this may be enough, provisionally, for those who are convinced in advance and in the abstract, but it is not enough when there is any question of entering concretely into details, since it also needs to be known why these formulations are manifested as so many mutually incompatible affirmations and not as simple differences of style. It is not enough simply to tell ourselves that the diverse traditional doctrines express "points of view" and therefore different "aspects" of the one truth; we need to know that it is necessarily so and that it could not possibly be otherwise, because no expression can possibly be exhaustive even while providing a key that is perfectly sufficient for the total truth. The same holds good for physical experience: It is impossible to describe a landscape so validly as to exclude all other descriptions, for no one can see the landscape in all its aspects at the same time, and no single view can prevent the existence and the validity of other equally possible views.

For man the historical facts on which his religion is based prove its exclusive truth precisely because they are facts and therefore realities; for God these same facts have merely the value of a symbolical and logical demonstration, and they can therefore be replaced by other facts just as one demonstration or one symbol can be replaced—always provided there is a good reason for the change—by another demonstration or another symbol. The essential content is always the same truth, on the one hand celestial and on the other hand salvational, but approached in diverse ways, since no angle of vision is the only possible one. This is what is indicated by the contradictions contained in the Holy Scriptures and also, no doubt to a lesser degree, by divergences in the visions of the saints.

Every religious belief is based on a point of view from which it, and it alone, appears sublime and irrefutable; not to share this opinion seems not only the worst of perversities, for it means standing in opposition to God, but also the worst of absurdities, for it means failing to see that two and two make four. Everyone in the West knows what grounds there are for the feeling that Christianity is obviously true, but it is much less known why other religions are refractory to this feeling. It cannot be denied that Christianity, in its immediate and literal expression—not in its necessarily universal and therefore polyvalent essence—addresses itself to sinners, to those who "have need of the physician"; its starting point is sin,[17] just as that of Buddhism is suffering. In Islam as in Hinduism—the oldest religion and the most recent religion paradoxically come

---

[17] Apart from the fact that the notion of sin itself admits of a transposition onto a higher plane—sin being then identified with that existential disequilibrium that is none other than the empirical ego or some aspect of it—the Gospel contains many sayings that reach beyond a moral alternative, sayings whose universal bearing can easily be grasped; but the Christian religion as such has nonetheless, practically speaking, its basis in the notion of sin in the ordinary sense.

together in certain features—the starting point is man in himself. By comparison the Christian perspective—still according to its literality which, outwardly speaking, is its "crowning proof"—will appear as limited to a single aspect of man and of the human state, an aspect that, for all its undoubted reality, is neither the only one nor exhaustive. It is not within the scope of prodigies, whatever they may amount to, to be able to shake this conviction, seeing that it relates to the nature of things and that nothing phenomenal can take precedence over the truth.

But it is unanimity that matters, not separate diversity, and there would be small profit in talking about the second without thinking of the first. If by "science" we mean a knowledge that is related to real things—whether or not they can be directly ascertained—and not exclusively a knowledge determined by some narrowly limited and philosophically defective program with a method to match, religion will be the science of the total hierarchy, of equilibrium and of the rhythms of the cosmic scale; it takes account, at one and the same time, of God's outwardly revealing manifestation and of his inwardly absorbing attraction, and it is only religion that does this and that can do it a priori and spontaneously.

There can be no doubt that the epistles of the New Testament are divinely inspired, but it is inspiration in the second degree; in other words they are not direct revelation like the words of Jesus and Mary or like the Psalms. It is this difference that accounts for a further difference of degree within this secondary inspiration, according to whether the spirit is speaking or allows man to be almost entirely himself the speaker. Man, in this context, is a saint, but he is not the Holy Ghost. The apostle recognizes this himself when, in giving certain counsels, he specifies that he does so of himself and not under inspiration of the Paraclete. "And unto the married I command, yet not I, but the Lord. . . ." Here it is clearly the spirit that is speaking. "Now concerning virgins I have no commandment of the Lord: yet I give my judgment, as one that hath obtained mercy of the Lord to be faithful. . . ." Here it is man who speaks. And likewise: "To the rest speak I, not the Lord. . . ." And again: "She is happier if she so abide, after my judgment: and I think also that I have the Spirit of God." (I Cor. 7:10, 12, 25, 40.)

We are here in the presence of the "human margin," but it comprises yet another degree. Following the apostle who gives his opinion, there come at a later date the Roman theologians who—not without unrealistic idealism and a confusing, when all is said and done, of asceticism with morals—deduce from it celibacy for all priests,[18] a measure that goes hand in hand with putting too extrinsic a motive on the sacrament of marriage and with forgetting, in consequence, the spiritual aspects of sexuality.[19] The result of this was, positively, the flowering of a sanctity of a particular type and, negatively, an accumulation of tensions responsible for all sorts of disequilibrium, culminating in the Renaissance and its consequences; not that the morally unrealistic and spiritually narrow pietism of a certain type of Christianity was the only cause of the subsequent naturalistic explosions, but it strongly contributed to this end, and it suffers to this day the consequences in its own flesh.

In a general manner, considering simply the nature of things without letting this lead one into underestimating theological intentions and mystical values, one has the impression that

[18] Whereas the Orthodox, who are equally Christian, did not draw this conclusion. Until the tenth century, the majority of Catholic priests were married. Gregory VII, renewing the anathemas of Nicolas II and Alexander II, finally imposed priestly celibacy, after violent resistance which went as far as riots and the ill treatment of bishops and pontifical legates.

[19] "So that they shall no longer be two, but of one flesh," declares the Gospel, putting the emphasis on the mystery of union—symbolized in a certain fashion by the miracle of Cana—and not on the two Pauline motivations, namely physical relief and procreation, reserved for those who are incapable of abstaining. If it is right to avoid the pitfall of a moral automatism that is both prudish and hypocritical, it is even more necessary to reject the opposite pitfall, namely that of a facile, naturistic, and vitalistic sexualism which by its profaning brashness runs contrary to the spiritual dignity of man. Sexuality is either sacred or subhuman.

Christianity, insofar as it is founded on the consciousness of sin and the sinful nature of man, has need of sin and even creates it, in a certain measure, by an appropriate moral theology, sin being, in this perspective, sexuality.[20] In other traditional perspectives, sexuality, in itself neutral, becomes intrinsically positive through a certain spiritual conditioning; obviously sin is always the harmful and prohibited act, whether sexual or otherwise, but it is also in a more fundamental sense profane distraction in itself, pleasure for the sake of pleasure, and as a result forgetfulness of God and worldly exteriorization.[21] Piety, whether it excludes nature-as-sin or includes nature-as-sacrament, does not go without a certain monotony; the guarantee of salvation lies essentially in the fixation of the heart in the consciousness of God, with all that this implies according to varying circumstances and vocations, whatever be the respective supports in the natural order.

It is no secret that Judaism, which accords to David and Solomon hundreds of wives, and Islam, which accords nine to its Prophet, are far from sharing the Pauline perspective. In general Christian theologians have no plausible explanation for Semitic polygamy, though inadmissible opinions are not lacking,[22] a fact that shows that there is a dimension here that escapes, not every Westerner needless to say, but the characteristic and therefore average perspective that has dominated the West for many centuries. Though highly efficacious on its own plane, it cannot be denied that this one-sided way of regarding natural things results in very regrettable misinterpretations as

---

[20] Quintessentially and not theologically speaking. The church is not Manichean; she does bless marriage, but this is considered both as a lesser good and as a lesser evil, which justifies—when one goes to the root of things—the association of ideas with the notion of "sin."

[21] Some religious authorities in whom a complex of complicity with regard to the Renaissance is combined with an inferiority complex with regard to the world of science exhibit an astonishing indulgence for profane distractions qualified by them as "innocent." Scientific progress, and the irreversible maelstrom that results from it, is all right provided one does not thereby lose one's faith; jumping into the water is all right, provided one does not get wet.

[22] It is, for instance, inadmissible to attribute to the author of the Psalms an insurmountable weakness of the flesh and to attribute the opposite virtue to any and every priest.

regards not only Islam—this is in no sense surprising—but also the ancient biblical world.

The Mosaic Law is given for all time, right up to the end of the world; nothing can be added to it, and nothing taken away. This is the thesis of Judaism, and it is irrefutable; Christianity has nonetheless, practically speaking, abolished the Law, since according to it "the spirit giveth life, the letter killeth," which amounts to saying—since Christianity is itself intrinsically orthodox—that the thesis of Judaism has an unconditional application only within the dimension that Judaism represents, namely religious legalism.[23] The negation, by Christians, of the esoteric dimension is strictly speaking an inconsequence, since without the esoteric point of view Christianity is inconceivable; if there is no esotericism, the Jewish argument has an absolute application, and Christianity is the transgression that it appears to be from the Jewish point of view. Moreover, if the spirit gives life and the letter kills, this cannot concern Judaism alone. If the "letter" of Judaism can become entirely relative from a certain spiritual point of view, then the "letter" of Christianity falls under the same law, especially since the "spirit which gives life" also "bloweth where it listeth," which opens the door not only to a Christian gnosis but also to the acceptance in principle of the non-Christian religions. Christianity was born of the distinction between form, which by definition is relative, and essence, which alone is absolute; if it does away with this distinction in favor of its own form, it robs itself, as it were, of the whole point of its existence.

Without these subtle truths of principle, the Christian contradiction with regard to Judaism remains unintelligible, at least if one is aware, as is but just, of the Judaic argument. At the same time these truths clearly do not take account of the

[23] We have been assured that there can be no question in Judaism of practicing the prescriptions mentally or of somehow compensating for them—in a word, of interiorizing prescriptions that have become impracticable. Nevertheless, it would seem that all the rules remain obligatory, regardless of circumstances. It would seem, however, that a religion cannot prescribe the impossible; the very fact that an observance is really impossible proves that it can be made up for, quite apart from any question of esotericism.

whole concrete reality of Christianity which, being a religion, cannot possibly put in question its "letter" or its form, on pain of annulling itself. What needs to be made clear is that the Christly message, as perspective of inwardness or essentialization, has the nature of an esotericism, but this message nonetheless comprises an exoteric outer form by reason of its voluntaristic and therefore de facto individualistic character, and of the dogmatizing tendency that results from its wish to expand, or from the necessity that it should expand.

If Christ is on the one hand the founder of a world religion, he is on the other hand a Jewish prophet sent to Israel and addressing himself to Israel. In this second respect—emphasized moreover in the Koran—Jesus has the function of a regenerator; he is the great prophet of inwardness, and in this respect he ought to have been accepted by Israel as Isaiah was.[24] All the same, this acceptance would have presupposed a spiritual suppleness that belongs more to India than to Judea. In theory, Judeo-Christianity ought to have perpetuated itself within the fold of Judaism—parallel to its function as a world religion—in the form of an esoteric community not unlike the Essenes; in practice various aspects of the "human margin" precluded this possibility.

Genesis relates how God "repented" when he saw the corruption of mankind: "And it repented the Lord that He had made man on the earth and it grieved Him at His heart."[25] In an analogous manner, there is something like a "divine repentance" from one revelation to another, in the sense that God manifests an aspect of the truth that corrects, not the aspect manifested previously, but human insistence on this aspect, or

---

[24] Christ, paraphrasing Isaiah, expresses himself thus: "This people honoureth me with their lips; but their heart is far from me. But in vain they do worship me, teaching for doctrines the commandments of men" (Matt. 15:7–9). And likewise: "Why do ye also transgress the commandment of God by your tradition?" (Matt. 15:3).

[25] "Perhaps they will listen and each one will turn from his perverse path: then I shall repent of the affliction which I am at present thinking against you" (Jer. 16:3). Likewise: "And God repented of the evil that he had said that he would do unto them" (Jon. 3:10), and other passages of a like kind.

the unilateral development given by the human receptacle to an aspect that in itself was much less limited.

The characteristic—and inevitable—misunderstanding of every exotericism is to attribute to God a human subjectivity and consequently to believe that every divine manifestation refers to the same divine "I" and therefore to the same limitation. This is to ignore the fact that that ego which, in the revelation, speaks and gives a law can only be a manifestation of the divine subject and not this subject itself; one must distinguish in God—always from the point of view of revelation—first the Word one and essential and then the manifestations or actualizations of this Word in view of particular human receptacles. The divine "I" that speaks to men—of necessity to "particular men"—could not possibly be the divine subject in a direct and absolute sense; it is the adaptation of that subject to a given human "container" and is consequently invested with something of the nature of this container, failing which all contact between man and God would be impossible, and failing which it would be absurd to allow that any revelation, Hebrew, Arabic, or other, could be word for word of divine origin.

Admittedly, God cannot contradict himself; but this axiomatic truth concerns the essential, unlimited, and formless truth, the only one that counts *in divinis*. Relative enunciations may perfectly well contradict themselves as between one revelation and another—exactly as human subjects and material forms mutually exclude and contradict one another—provided the essential truth is safeguarded and rendered as efficacious as possible. The particular divine "I" of a revelation is not situated in the divine principle itself; it is the projection, or emanation, of the absolute subject and is identified with the "Spirit of God," that is, with the cosmic center of which one might say that it is "neither divine nor nondivine." This revelation-giving "I" "is God" in virtue of the ray that attaches it directly to its source, but it is not God in an absolute fashion, because it is impossible for the absolute as such to speak a human language and utter human things. This is the meaning of the doctrine of the "descent" of the Koran by successive stages, and this also explains the discussions on the question whether the Koran is "created" or "uncreated" or in what manner and in what respect it is the one or the other; but this does not open the door to any naturalism or any humanism, for the earthly wording of a sacred scripture, although in a certain respect determined by human contingencies, remains divine in its celestial origin and also in its theurgic substance.

A particularly serious difficulty, in making an approach to Islam, is the accusation—leveled by Muslims against Jews and Christians—regarding their "falsification of the Scriptures." This accusation is aimed chiefly at what Islam considers to be a lack of due receptivity with regard to total revelation, which a priori is as if suspended between God and man and whereof the manifestation is determined by the human receptacle. Since the Jewish and Christian theologies comprise what are, from the Islamic point of view, restrictive crystallizations, Islam will present these restrictions of perspective as "falsifications," "Scripture" here being envisaged in its unmanifested and still celestial totality.

Islam would accept the concepts "Chosen People" and "Man-God" in a compensatory metaphysical context that reestablished the equilibrium of the total truths, but such a context, precisely, would appear to Jews and Christians as the abdication of their respective positions. Here it must be emphasized once again that every revealed and traditional symbolism is a key to the totality, but this does not nullify the distinction between spiritual forms which may open more particularly onto a way, either of works or of love or of gnosis, being fundamentally determined by one or other of these elements, without these determinations, however, having an exclusive character. In the economy of revelation, spiritual opportunity, in accordance with the respective human receptacles, requires limitations and consequently negations; to be exact, it is sometimes necessary to deny at the level of formal expression, without the essential truth ever being involved.[26]

---

[26] Interreligious ostracism is repeated within one and the same orthodoxy. When Saint Benedict condemns outright the Sarabaite and Gyrovague monks, he does so above all in the name of a methodological

"Falsification of the Scriptures"—Islam's reproach against the two monotheisms that preceded it—may also be reduced to a simple question of interpretation; thus Ibn Taimiyah, Hanbalite protagonist of an extreme literalism, reproaches Jews and Christians for having falsified the meaning of several passages in their Scriptures—the meaning, and not the text itself. A spiritual mentality may feel the need to fix dogmatically, and to develop theologically and liturgically, a given aspect of the truth to the detriment of another aspect possibly more important, but not absolutely indispensable; one has in mind here the Talmudic speculations and the vicissitudes of trinitarian theology, and also the factors that provoked the Christian schisms and the rupture between Sunnite and Shi'ite Islam.[27]

These somewhat remote interpretations do not claim to solve the whole problem of the divergences between the Bible and the Koran. Let us simply add that the Muslims consider it strange that the Bible should attribute the golden calf to Aaron without drawing all the consequences from this and that it should seriously accuse David and Solomon; or again, that it says that the hand of Moses became leprous when he withdrew it, as a sign, from his breast, whereas according to the Koran it became luminous "without any hurt."[28]

---

and disciplinary perspective, for it is impossible to accept that the situations of those monks—the ones living at home and the others wandering—did not correspond to real vocations, despite all the abuses which, more or less latterly, did in fact occur. Analogously, with regard to quietism—to quote one more example—the errors of certain seventeenth-century quietists cannot be said to invalidate the principle of quietude.

[27] The suppression of every form of gnosis, the condemnation of Origen, then the immense success of Arianism—not to speak of the excessive influence of that two-edged weapon Aristotelianism—all in a relatively very young Christianity, prove a difficulty of assimilation on the part of a human receptacle that was both too heterogeneous and too narrow.

[28] When one reads the predictions of Christ concerning the latter times, one is struck by the fact that they refer in part to the destruction of Jerusalem, but without the words distinguishing between different applications. As the ancient prophesies regarding Christ already indicate, it happens in fact that prophetic language cumulates two or more completely different, but obviously analogous orders; now, analogy is a certain mode of identity, metaphysically and "divinely" speak-'

Certain religious theses with a polemical flavor may seem inaccurate or crude, but it is precisely this veneer of excess that masks a divine "point of view" that goes beyond dogmatism as such. The reproach of "falsification of the Scriptures" may moreover be caused by the liberty that revelation sometimes takes with words. An example is the way in which certain passages of the Old Testament are reproduced in the New; there can be no doubt that in the eyes of the rabbis it is a question here of real falsifications,[29] whereas in reality, in cases of this kind, the same idea is divinely "rethought" in function of a new human receptacle.[30]

To return to the Muslim point of view, here it is basically a question of the following: If we take as our starting point the idea that "Scripture" is the "uncreated Koran," which, abiding with God, is none other than the divine word itself or the Logos, the recipient of every truth, then the revelations (which by definition are adapted in their expression to a given collective human receptacle—since "water takes on the color of its container," as Junayd said) are extrinsically restrictions with regard to the uncreated word and consequently "falsify" it, if we may here employ this term in order to indicate an analogy;

---

ing. There are coincidences or cumulations of the same kind in the prophesies of Isaiah concerning Cyrus, the liberator of Israel (44:28, 45:1–6, and 63:1–3), if we apply them to Islam as do the Muslims, basing themselves on the fact that the name of Cyrus—*Kōresh* in Hebrew—evokes the name of *Quraysh*, which is that of the tribe of Mohammed. It should be noted that in Persian the name Cyrus, *Kurush*, means "sun" while in the Elamite language *kurash* means "shepherd," a meaning taken up by Isaiah; the two meanings apply equally to the founder of Islam, who was originally a shepherd and later became a sun for a whole portion of the world.

[29] Nor is there any doubt that Christian theologians would be of the same opinion as the rabbis if it were a question of a non-Christian Scripture.

[30] The same can be said of the divergences between the Hebrew original and the Septuagint translation. According to Saint Augustine, the Septuagint translators were touched in their turn by the breath of revelation, and the divergences between their translation and the Hebrew text embodied in each case a meaning implicitly contained in the original text.

the "falsification" that the Muslim reproach has in view is above all a restriction of perspective and a limitation from the point of view of totality and universality.

In revelation one must distinguish three aspects, which are, first, the eternal word in God; second, its specification on the archangelic level, in view of a given human receptacle; third, its manifestation on earth and in time in order to meet circumstances that, while being no doubt providential, are nevertheless human and terrestrial.[31] The second or intermediate degree presents two aspects, the one essential and the other specific; thus the Koran having descended to the seventh heaven, on the one hand remains the absolute and undifferentiated divine word, while on the other it becomes the specific divine order or particular message. It is in the third degree that the Koran flows into human language and manifests its intentions of perspective, equilibrium, and salvation by means of human contingencies that determine a particular expression; the celestial Koran, and a fortiori the divine word in the absolute sense, does not speak of such and such a name or incident, but it contains the intention that, on earth, may be expressed by means of the most diverse human facts. To understand the nature of the Koran and the meaning of its discontinuities—not those that are due to simple contingencies of compilation—it is necessary always to keep in view these three degrees, intimately mingled in the verbal crystallization of the Book but nevertheless recognizable by sudden changes of level.

It results from what has just been said not only that the revealed Book essentially comprises three hypostatic degrees but also that at the terrestrial degree it could be other than it is. The events and the words do not in themselves have anything absolute about them; otherwise contingency would not be contingency. One might compare the Logos in God to a formless and uncolored substance, and the Logos when it has "descended" into the archangelic world to a religious perspective that is still superhumanly nonarticulated; terrestrial mani-

---

[31] Another example of this doctrine is to be found in the theory of the "three bodies of the Buddha": "terrestrial" (*nirmāna-kāya*), "celestial" (*sambhoga-kāya*), and "divine" (*dharma-kāya*).

festation would then be comparable to the dispersion of a heavenly substance into terrestrial coagulations, formed by the environment and by circumstances, but without affecting either
the celestial substance or its divine essence. Or again: If we
compare the eternal word of God to gold as such, and a given
celestial specification of this word to a particular mass of gold,
it can be seen without difficulty that all forms derivable from
this mass in no wise affect its weight or modify the nature of
the metal.

This doctrine of the three hypostatic degrees of the divine
word makes it possible to understand the principle of "abroga-
tion" *(naskh)*, which is manifested in every sacred Scripture at
the level of language, even if one draws no practical consequence from it; if there were no "human margin," no abroga-
tion would be possible.

Another principle connected with the same doctrine is that
of "personal revelation," which likewise is directly divine but
given to a saint without a strictly prophetic mandate. It is true
that every spiritual truth necessarily derives from the celestial
prototype of the Book, but it does so in a way completely
different from the descent of "personal revelation," in which
the literal wording is received, not by simple inspiration as in
the case of certain writings of saints and sages, but by revelation in the true sense, that is to say, by virtue of a direct divine
action. A celebrated case is that of Bhagavad-gita, which logically should be part of secondary inspiration *(smriti)*, since it
belongs to the Mahabhārata, but which in fact is considered as
an Upanishad, therefore as pertaining to directly celestial inspiration *(shruti)*; another case, in Islam this time, is that of his own
chapter on Adam which ibn-Arabi declared to be divine revelation—like the Koran—and which in fact is a masterpiece from
the double point of view of form and content. The sage, as soon
as he has become, by the effect of a very particular election, "his
own prophet" thereby likewise becomes "his own law"; this
election is at the same time a "celestial adoption," manifested
by objective signs, but of such a supereminent order that it
would be vain to hope that the spiritual degree in question
might be obtained through efforts and thanks to natural gifts.

Be that as it may, it will easily be understood that it was possible for the quality of "prophecy" *(nubuwwah)* to be attributed to certain Sufis; not a "law-giving" prophecy in that case, but nevertheless one that "radiated" in one way or another.[32] Objective and polyvalent revelation may repeat itself in some fashion in a given human microcosm, not in the sense of a general and obvious analogy—every intellection being a "revelation"—but in virtue of an entirely special possibility and of a participation, outside time, in the "descent," or rather in the "reception," of the uncreated Book.

[32] According to a hadith, no woman was ever a prophet, but here it is a question exclusively of law-giving prophecy; this would seem to be obvious. There is thus no reason for thinking, Islamically speaking, that the term "prophetess" *(nabiyyah)* does not fit the Virgin Mary and ought to be replaced by such a phrase as "of prophetic nature" *(naba-wiyyah)*, or that the eulogistic formula "on her be Peace" *('alayhā's-Salam)* should be replaced in her case by the formula, allotted to ordinary saints, "may God be satisfied with him or her" *(radiya Llāhu 'anhu or 'anhā)*; this is all the more obvious in that, from the point of view of cosmic manifestation, Mary eminently surpasses all the saints.